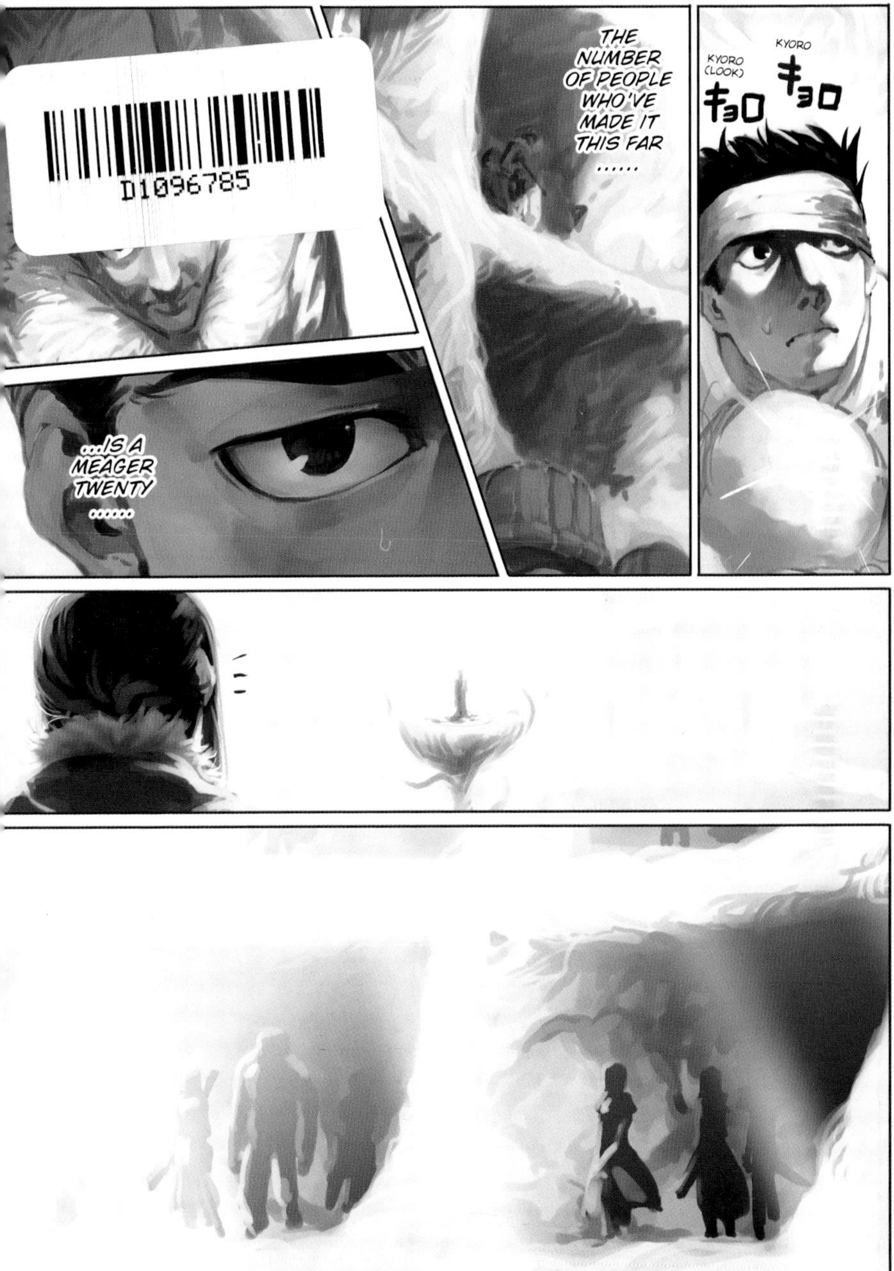
KYORO
キョロ
KYORO (LOOK)
キョロ
THE NUMBER OF PEOPLE WHO'VE MADE IT THIS FAR ......
...IS A MEAGER TWENTY ......

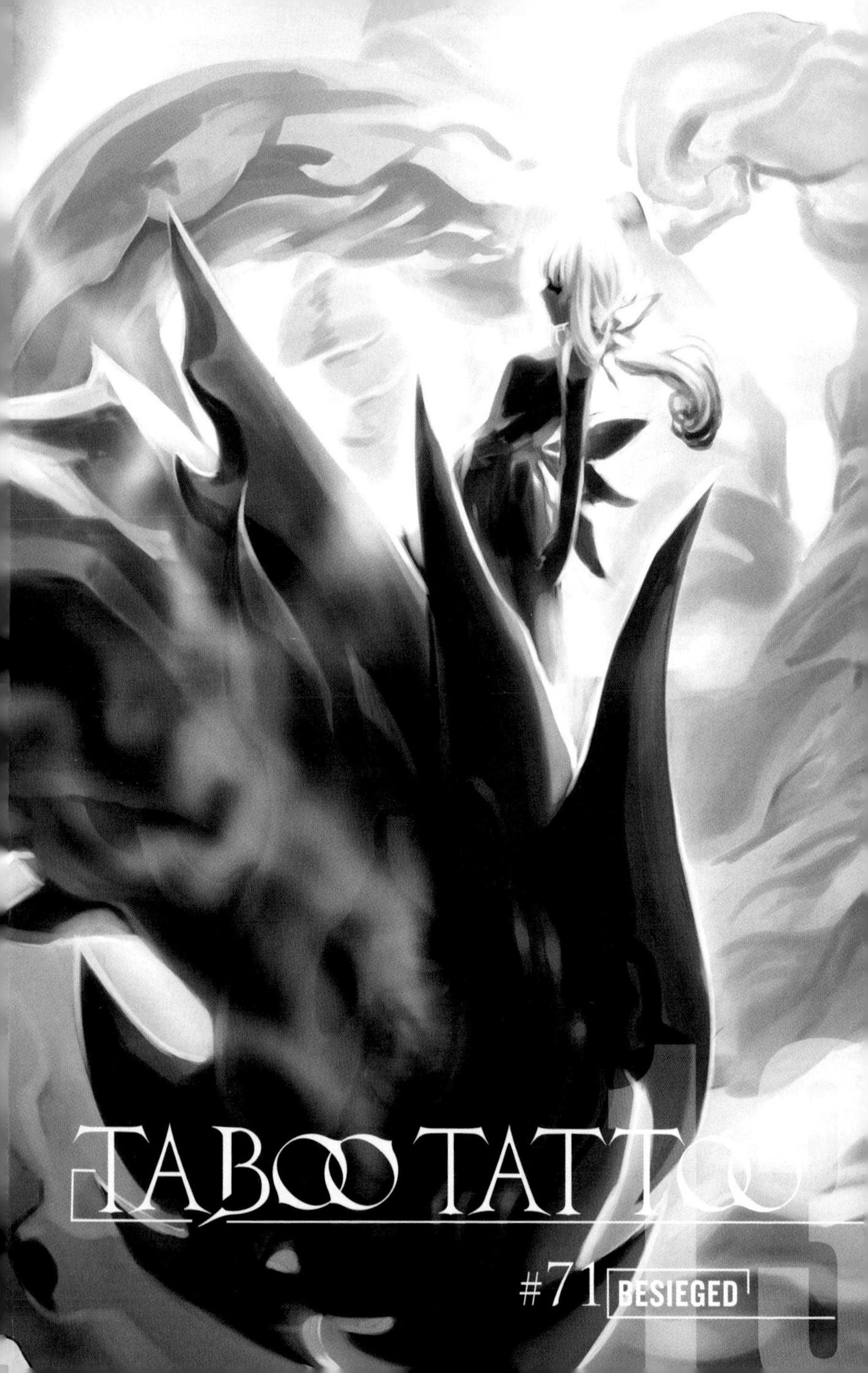
TABOO TATTOO
#71 BESIEGED

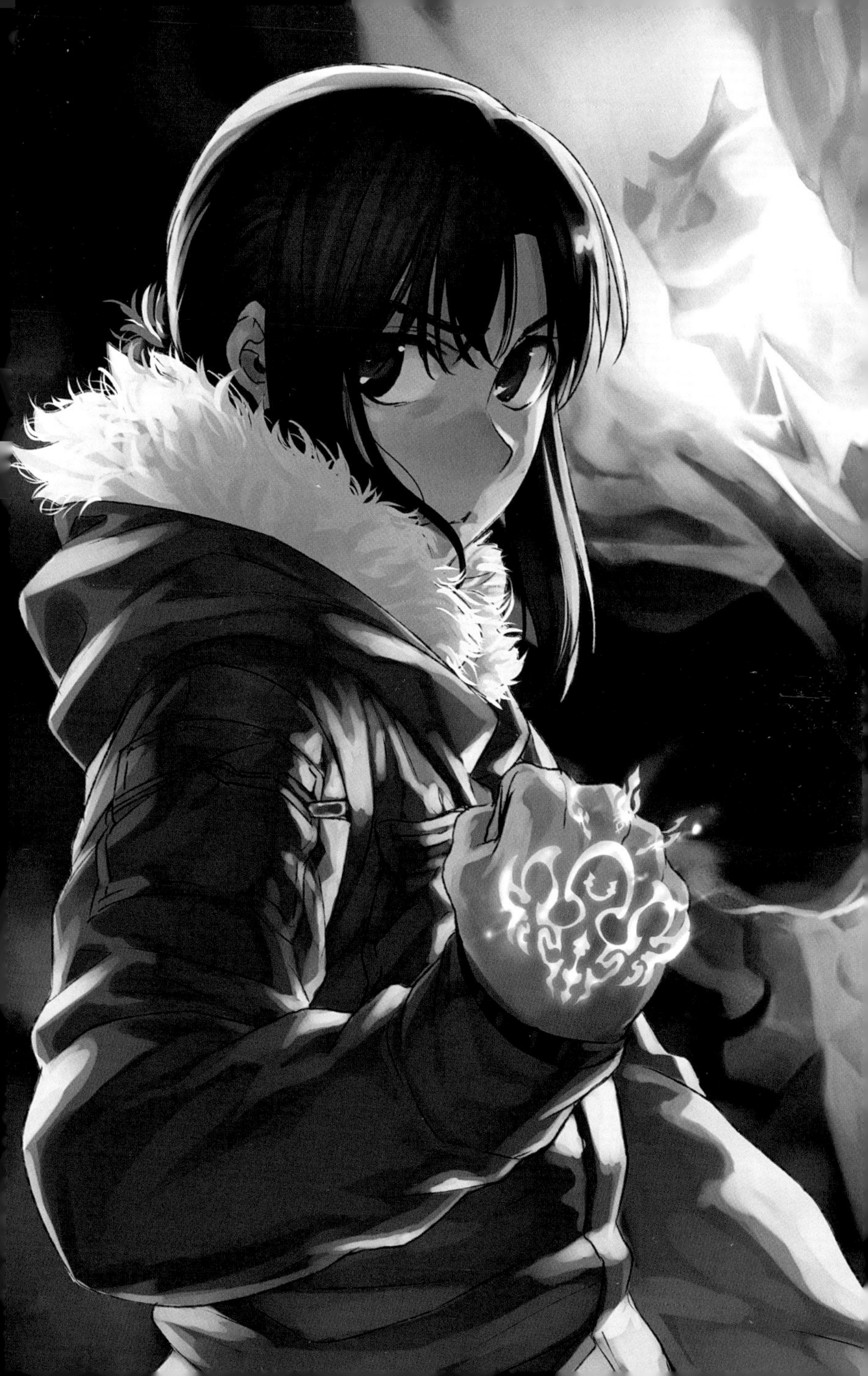

TABOO TATTOO

13

CONTENTS

#71 BESIEGED — 001

#72 SUICIDE — 029

#73 TRILATERAL — 055

#74 BORDER — 089

#75 OVERFLOW — 121

#76 LIFE — 143

#77 SPELL CREST — 165

#78 FUTURE — 201

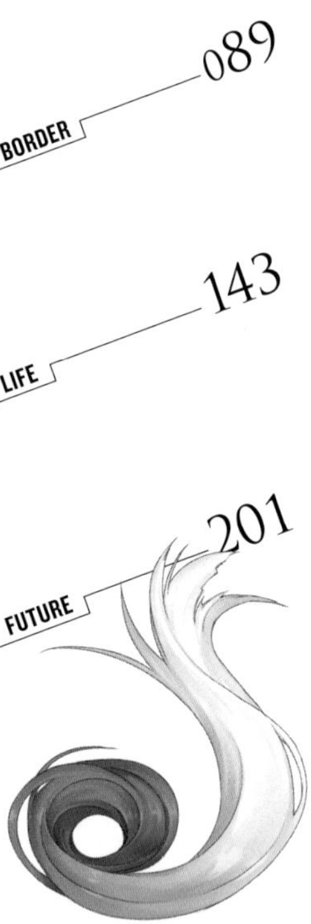

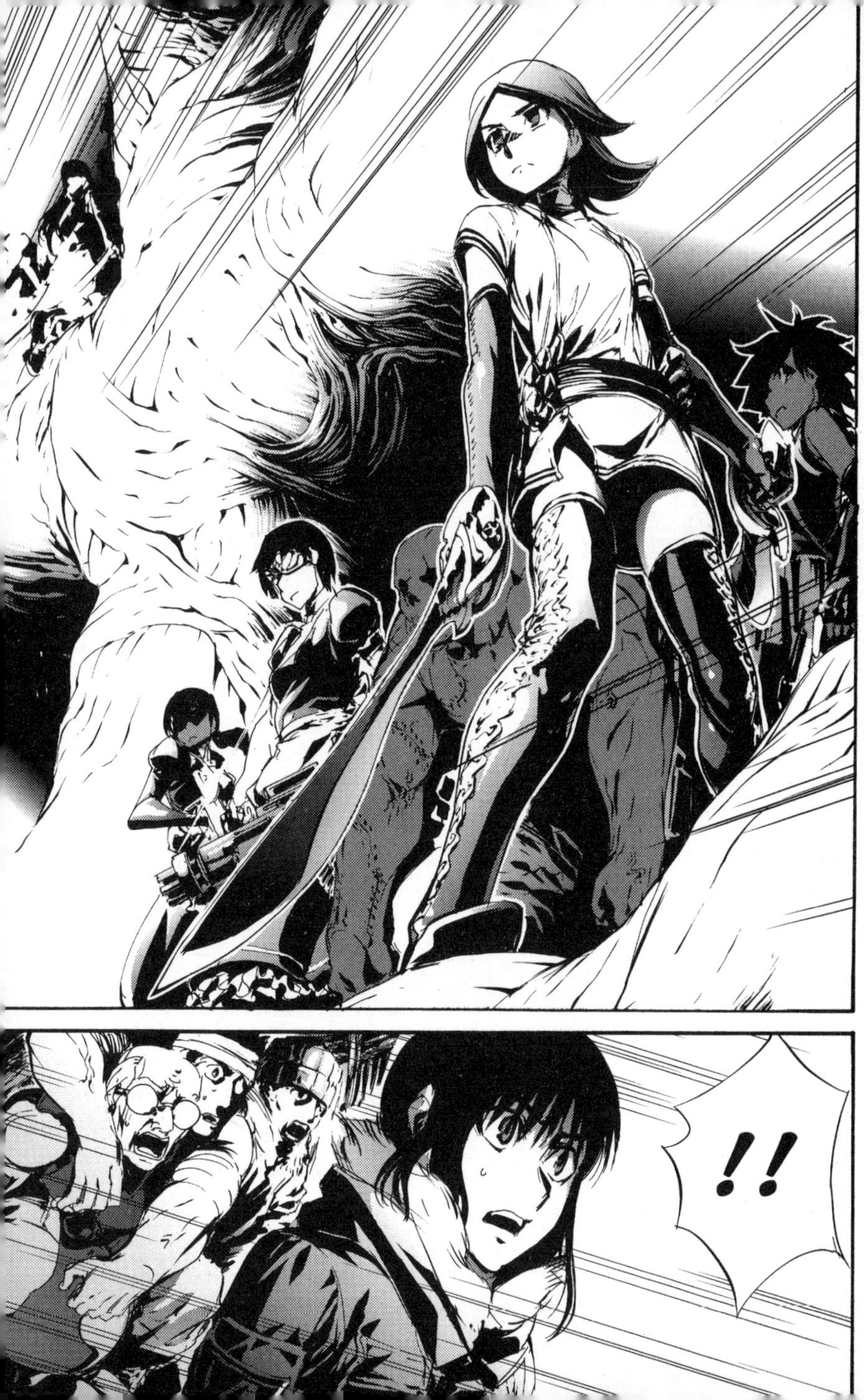
!!

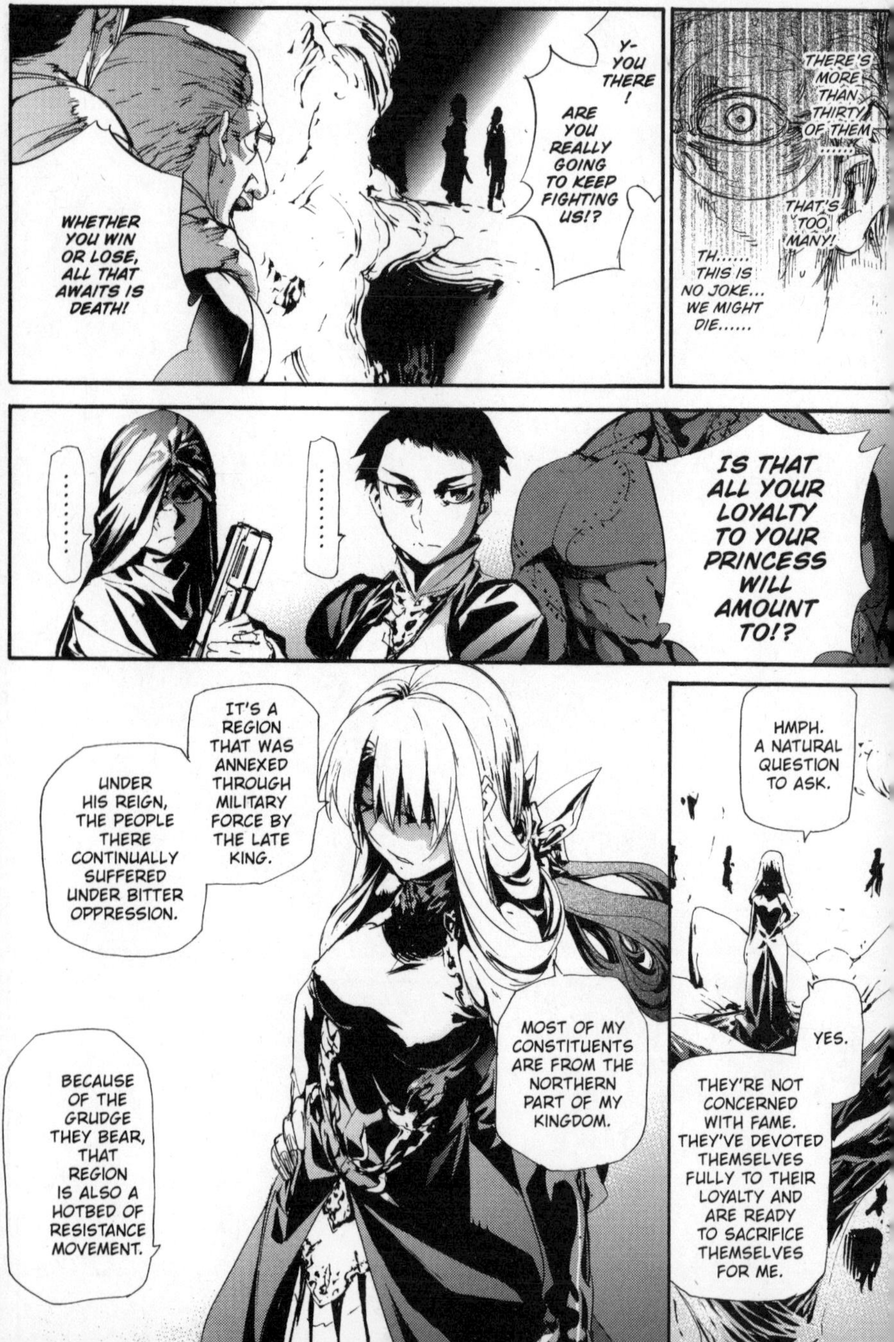
THERE'S MORE THAN THIRTY OF THEM......
THAT'S TOO MANY!
TH...... THIS IS NO JOKE... WE MIGHT DIE......
Y- YOU THERE!
ARE YOU REALLY GOING TO KEEP FIGHTING US!?
WHETHER YOU WIN OR LOSE, ALL THAT AWAITS IS DEATH!
IS THAT ALL YOUR LOYALTY TO YOUR PRINCESS WILL AMOUNT TO!?
......
......
HMPH. A NATURAL QUESTION TO ASK.
YES.
THEY'RE NOT CONCERNED WITH FAME. THEY'VE DEVOTED THEMSELVES FULLY TO THEIR LOYALTY AND ARE READY TO SACRIFICE THEMSELVES FOR ME.
MOST OF MY CONSTITUENTS ARE FROM THE NORTHERN PART OF MY KINGDOM.
IT'S A REGION THAT WAS ANNEXED THROUGH MILITARY FORCE BY THE LATE KING.
UNDER HIS REIGN, THE PEOPLE THERE CONTINUALLY SUFFERED UNDER BITTER OPPRESSION.
BECAUSE OF THE GRUDGE THEY BEAR, THAT REGION IS ALSO A HOTBED OF RESISTANCE MOVEMENT.

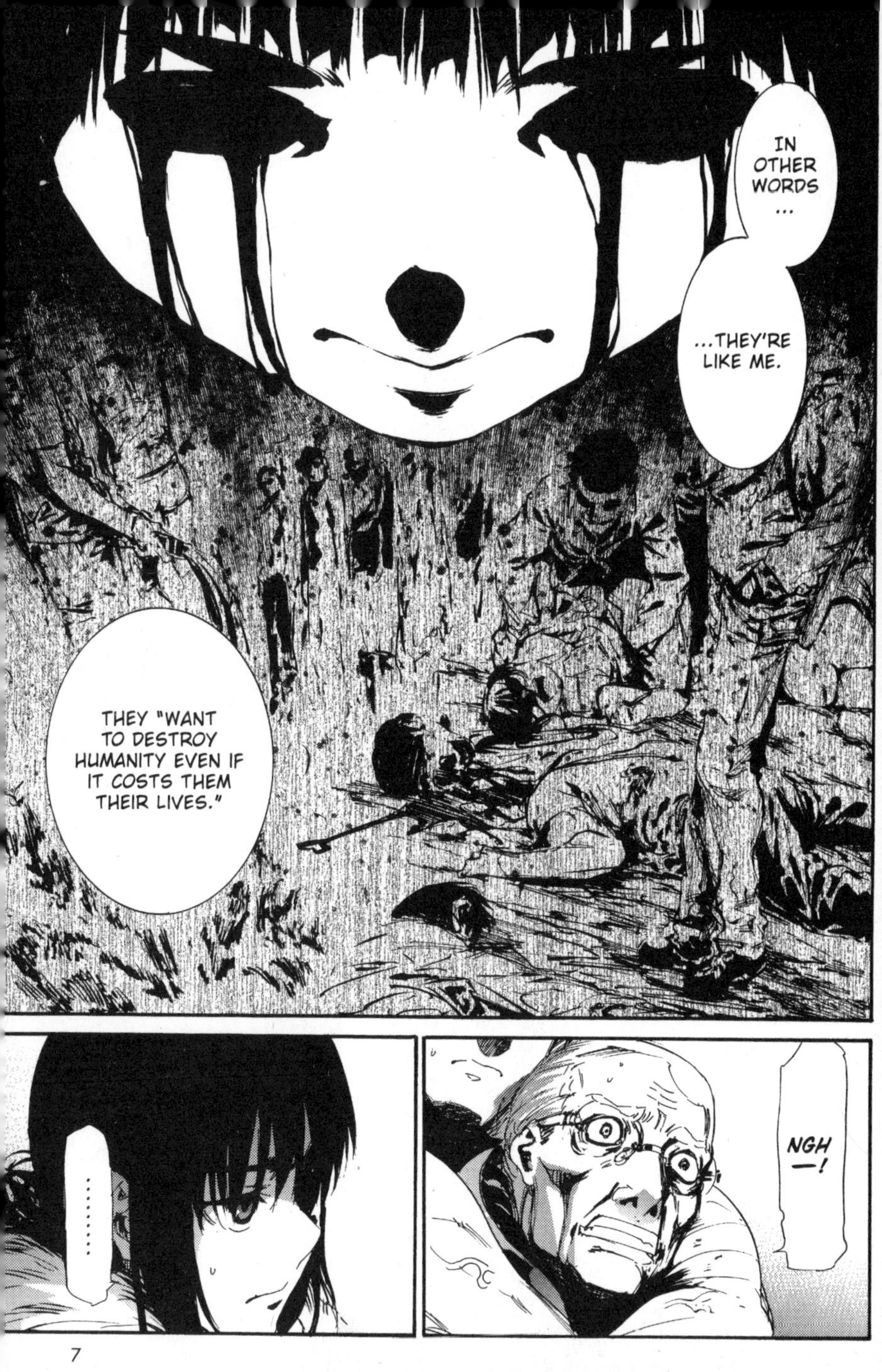
IN OTHER WORDS ...
...THEY'RE LIKE ME.
THEY "WANT TO DESTROY HUMANITY EVEN IF IT COSTS THEM THEIR LIVES."
NGH —!
....

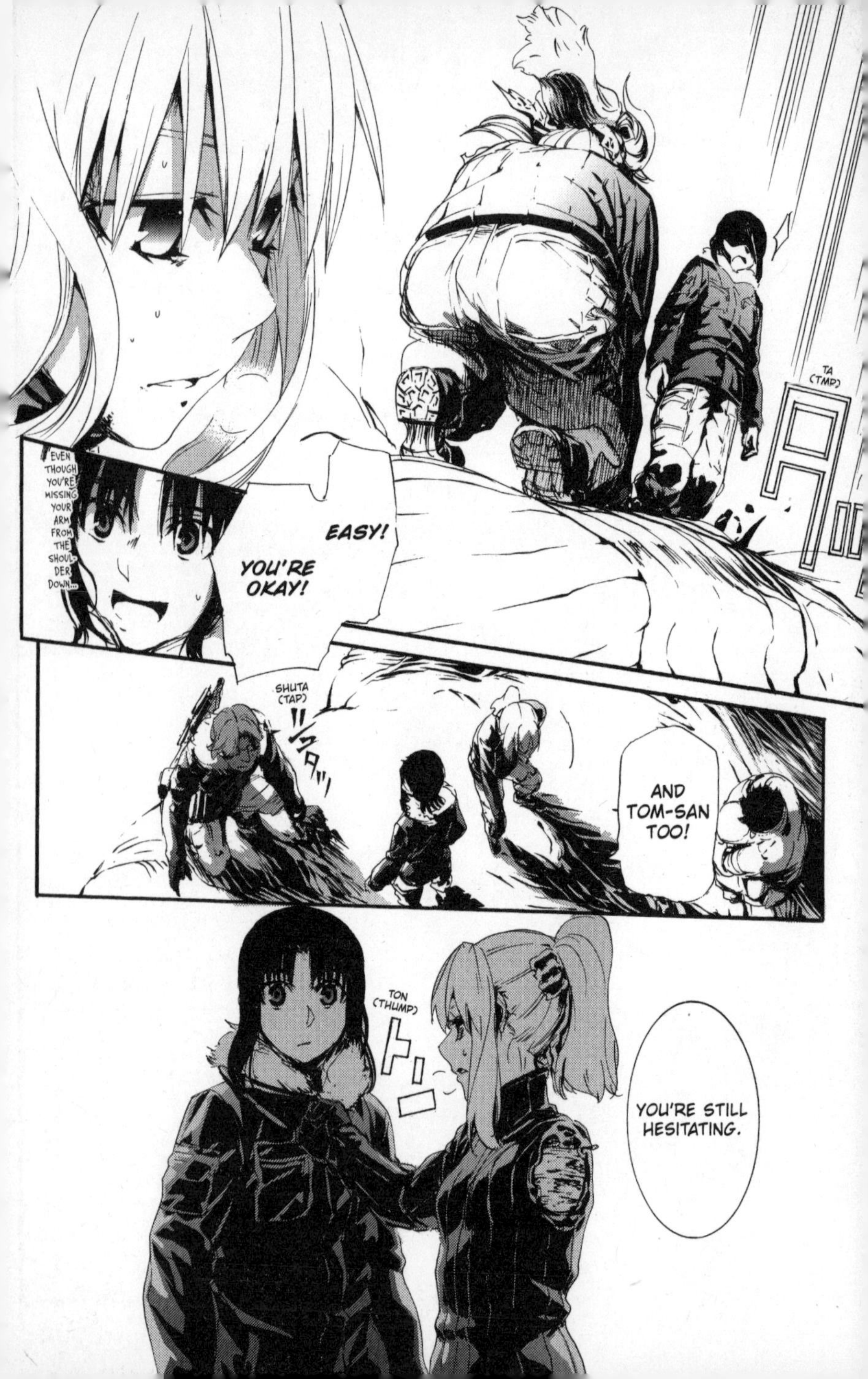

TA (TMP)
EASY!
YOU'RE OKAY!
EVEN THOUGH YOU'RE MISSING YOUR ARM FROM THE SHOULDER DOWN...
AND TOM-SAN TOO!
SHUTA (TAP)
YOU'RE STILL HESITATING.
TON (THUMP)

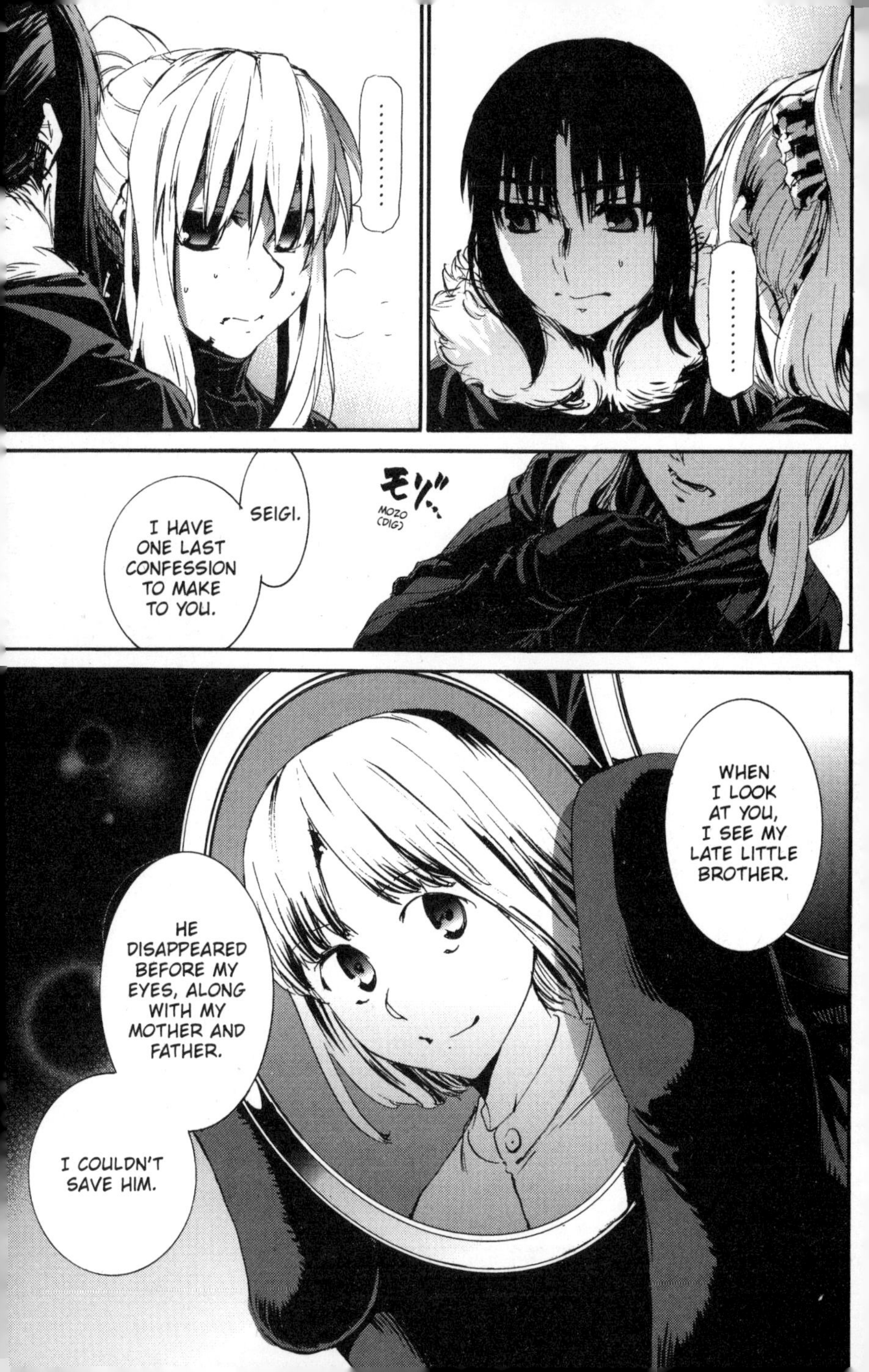
......
......
SEIGI.
I HAVE ONE LAST CONFESSION TO MAKE TO YOU.
モゾ
MOZO (DIG)
WHEN I LOOK AT YOU, I SEE MY LATE LITTLE BROTHER.
HE DISAPPEARED BEFORE MY EYES, ALONG WITH MY MOTHER AND FATHER.
I COULDN'T SAVE HIM.

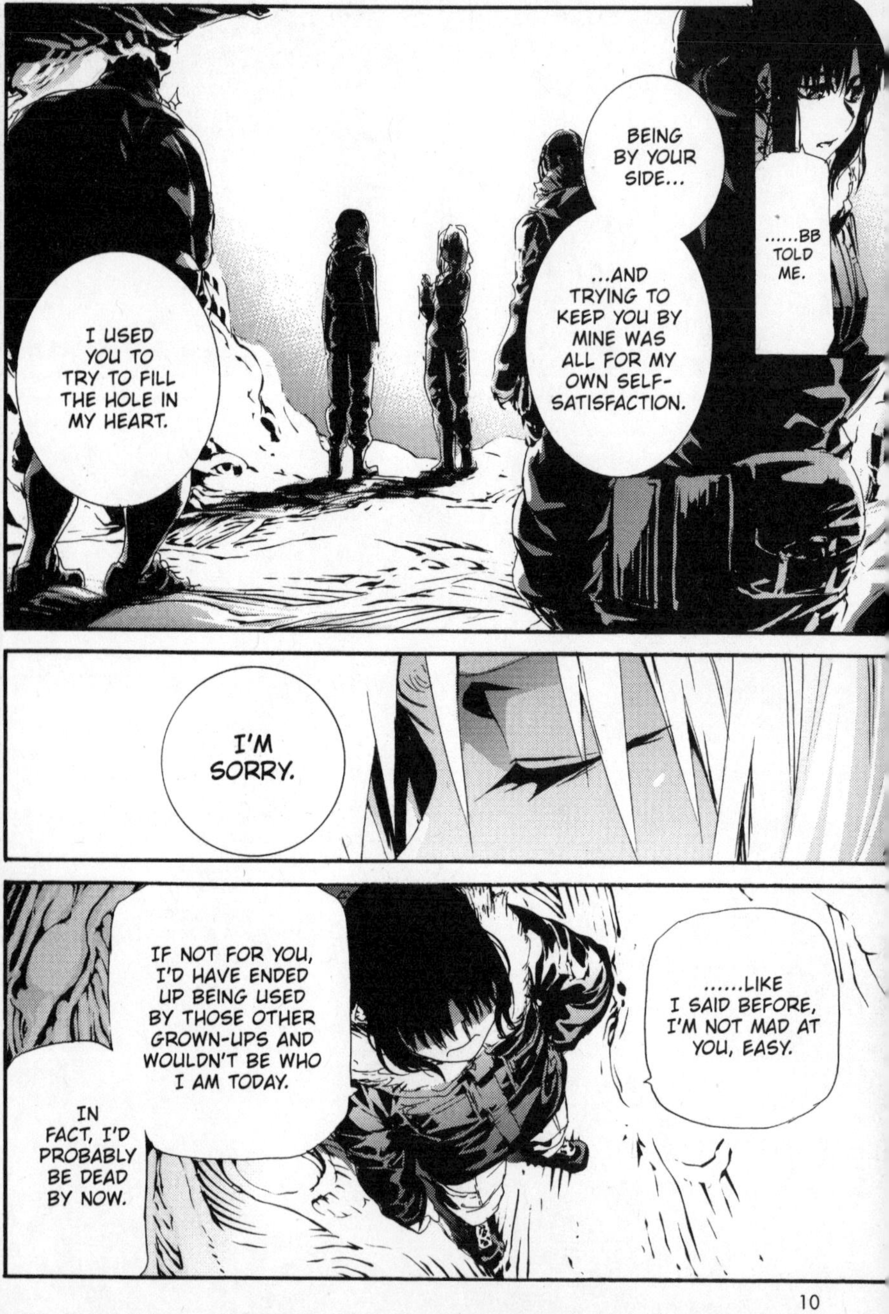
......BB TOLD ME.
BEING BY YOUR SIDE...
...AND TRYING TO KEEP YOU BY MINE WAS ALL FOR MY OWN SELF-SATISFACTION.
I USED YOU TO TRY TO FILL THE HOLE IN MY HEART.
I'M SORRY.
......LIKE I SAID BEFORE, I'M NOT MAD AT YOU, EASY.
IF NOT FOR YOU, I'D HAVE ENDED UP BEING USED BY THOSE OTHER GROWN-UPS AND WOULDN'T BE WHO I AM TODAY.
IN FACT, I'D PROBABLY BE DEAD BY NOW.

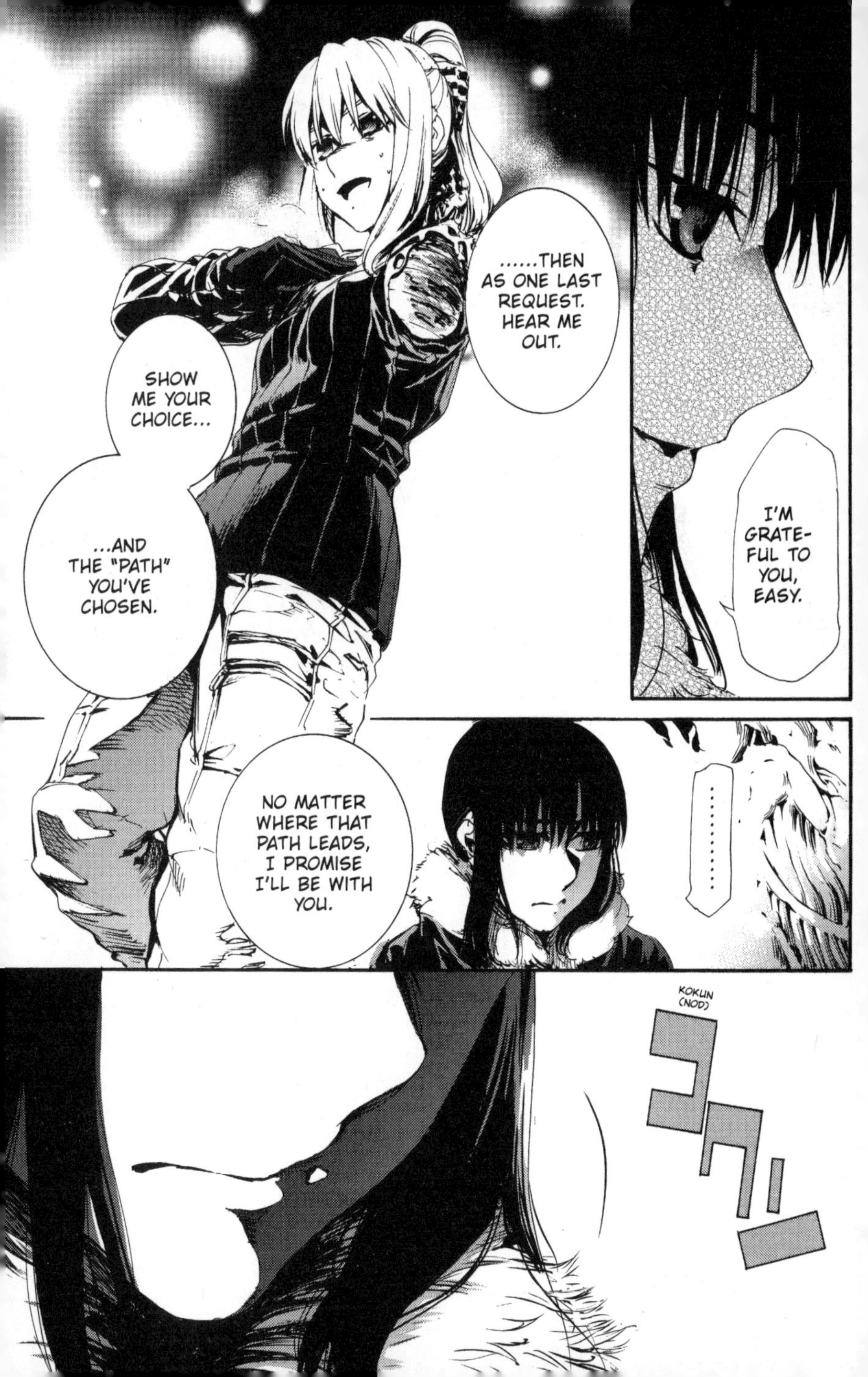
I'M GRATEFUL TO YOU, EASY.
......
......THEN AS ONE LAST REQUEST. HEAR ME OUT.
SHOW ME YOUR CHOICE...
...AND THE "PATH" YOU'VE CHOSEN.
NO MATTER WHERE THAT PATH LEADS, I PROMISE I'LL BE WITH YOU.
KOKUN (NOD)

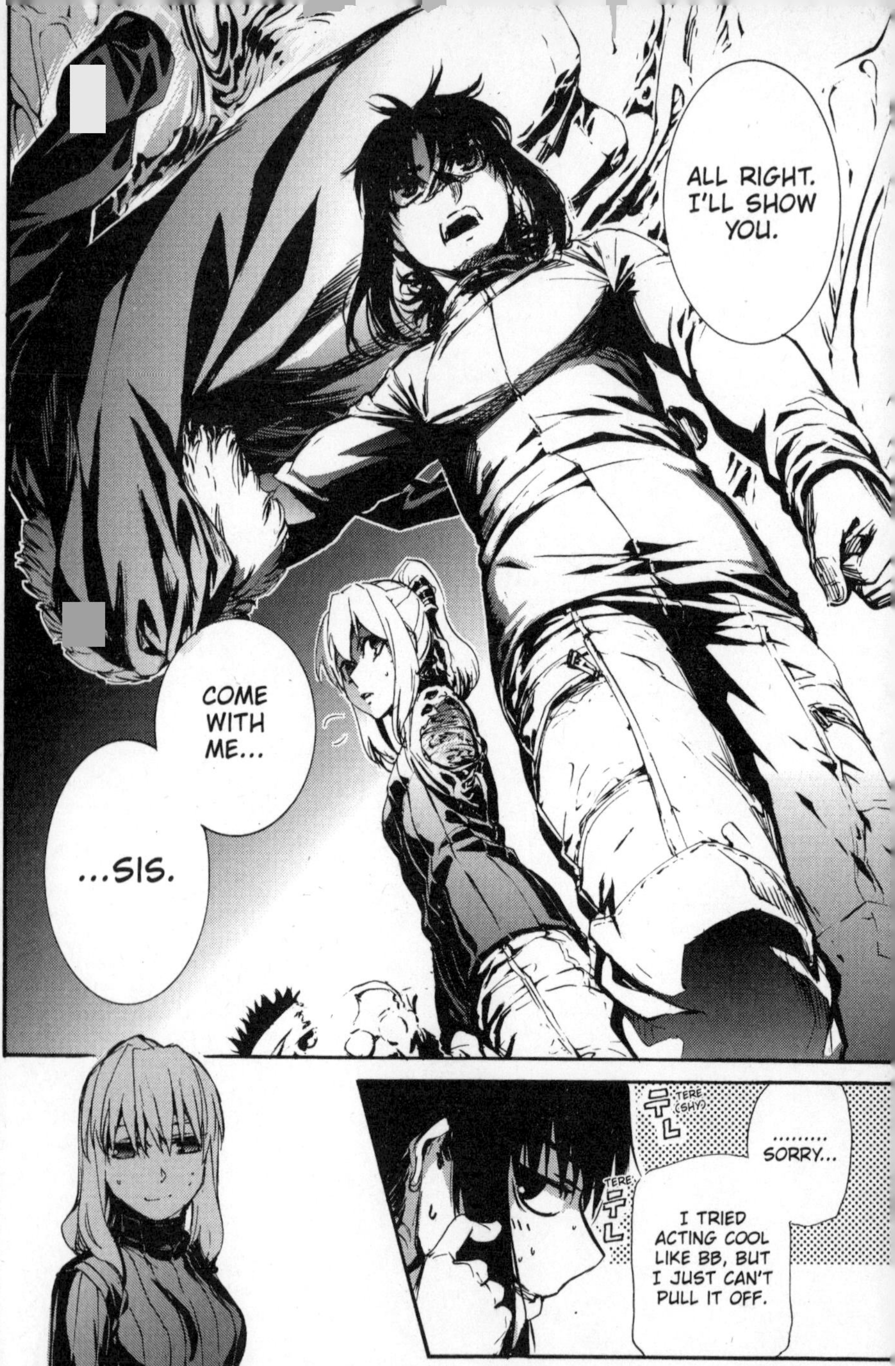
ALL RIGHT. I'LL SHOW YOU.
COME WITH ME...
...SIS.
TERE (SHY)
.... SORRY...
TERE
I TRIED ACTING COOL LIKE BB, BUT I JUST CAN'T PULL IT OFF.

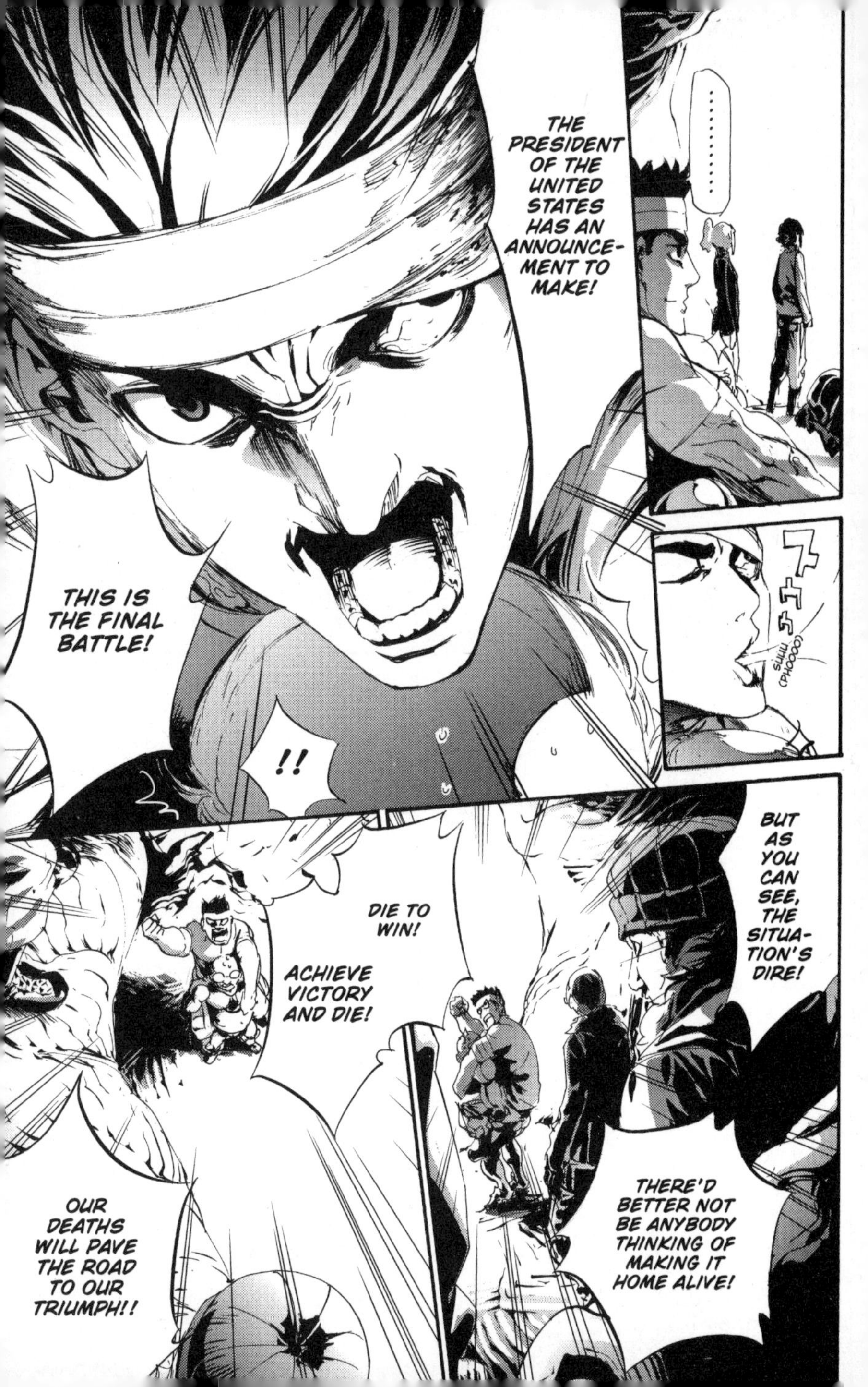
......
SUUU
(PHOOOO)
THE PRESIDENT OF THE UNITED STATES HAS AN ANNOUNCE-MENT TO MAKE!
THIS IS THE FINAL BATTLE!
!!
BUT AS YOU CAN SEE, THE SITUA-TION'S DIRE!
DIE TO WIN!
ACHIEVE VICTORY AND DIE!
THERE'D BETTER NOT BE ANYBODY THINKING OF MAKING IT HOME ALIVE!
OUR DEATHS WILL PAVE THE ROAD TO OUR TRIUMPH!!

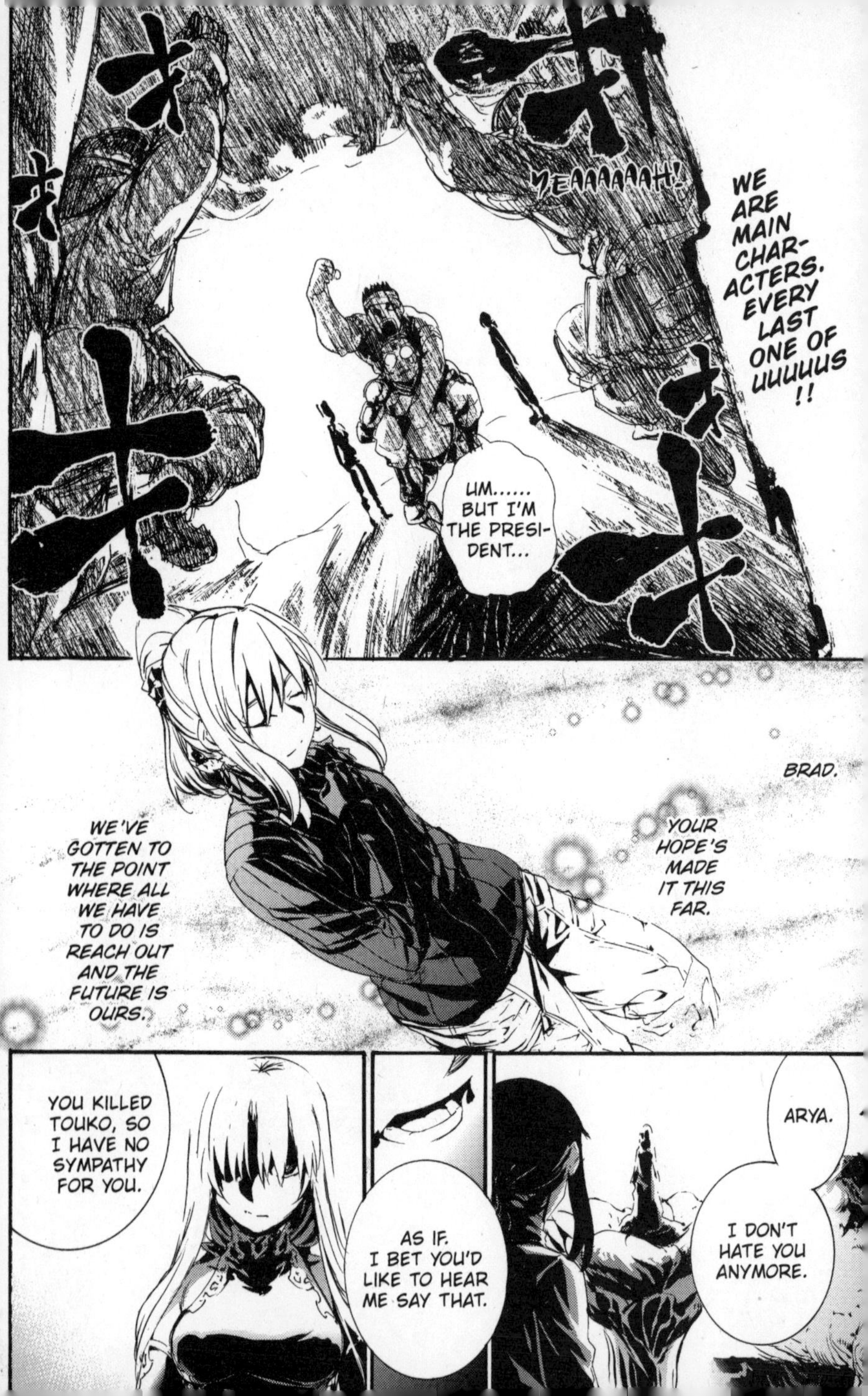
WE ARE MAIN CHAR-ACTERS. EVERY LAST ONE OF UUUUUS!!
YEAAAAAAH!
UM...... BUT I'M THE PRESI-DENT...
BRAD.
YOUR HOPE'S MADE IT THIS FAR.
WE'VE GOTTEN TO THE POINT WHERE ALL WE HAVE TO DO IS REACH OUT AND THE FUTURE IS OURS.
ARYA.
I DON'T HATE YOU ANYMORE.
AS IF. I BET YOU'D LIKE TO HEAR ME SAY THAT.
YOU KILLED TOUKO, SO I HAVE NO SYMPATHY FOR YOU.

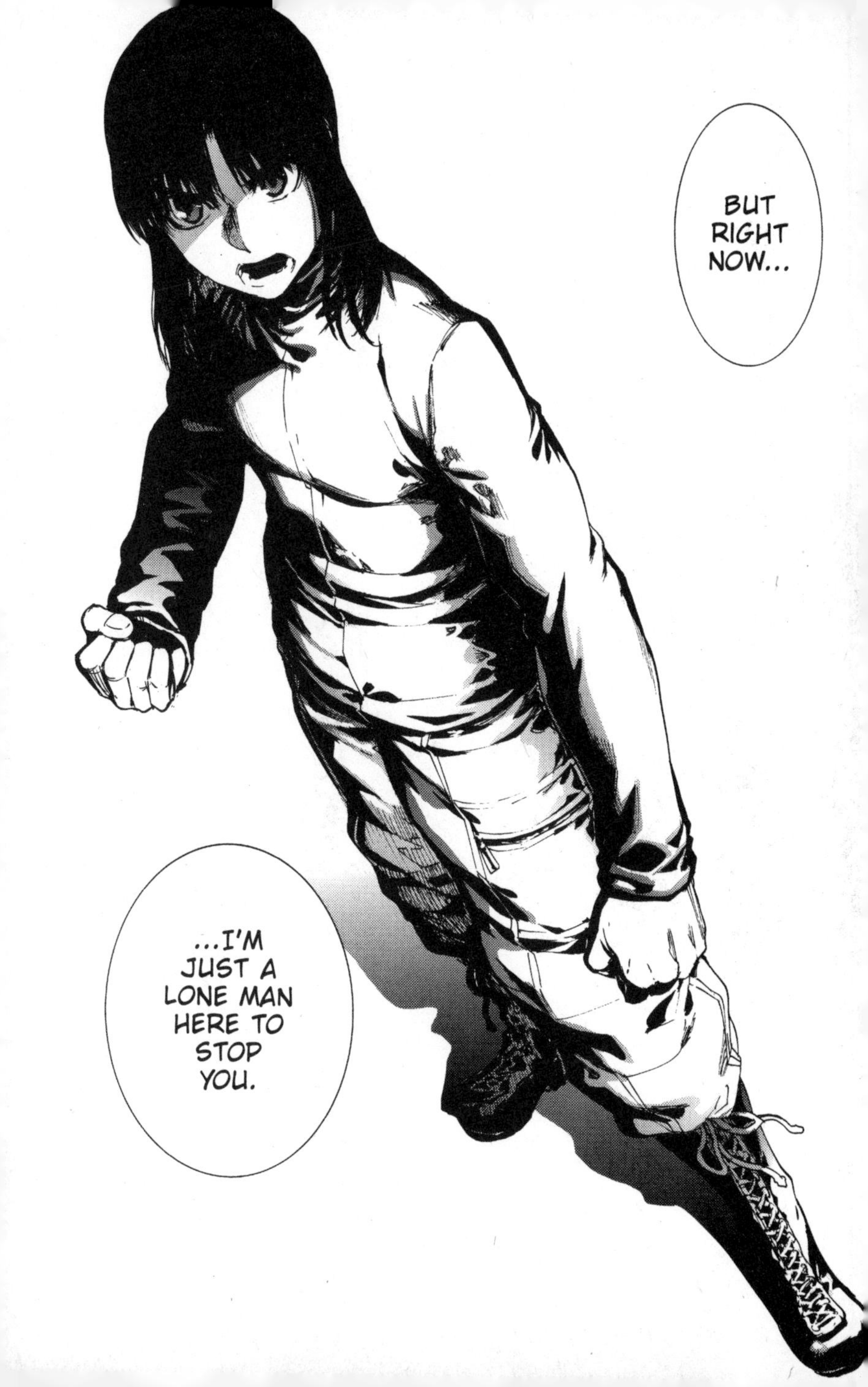
BUT RIGHT NOW...
...I'M JUST A LONE MAN HERE TO STOP YOU.

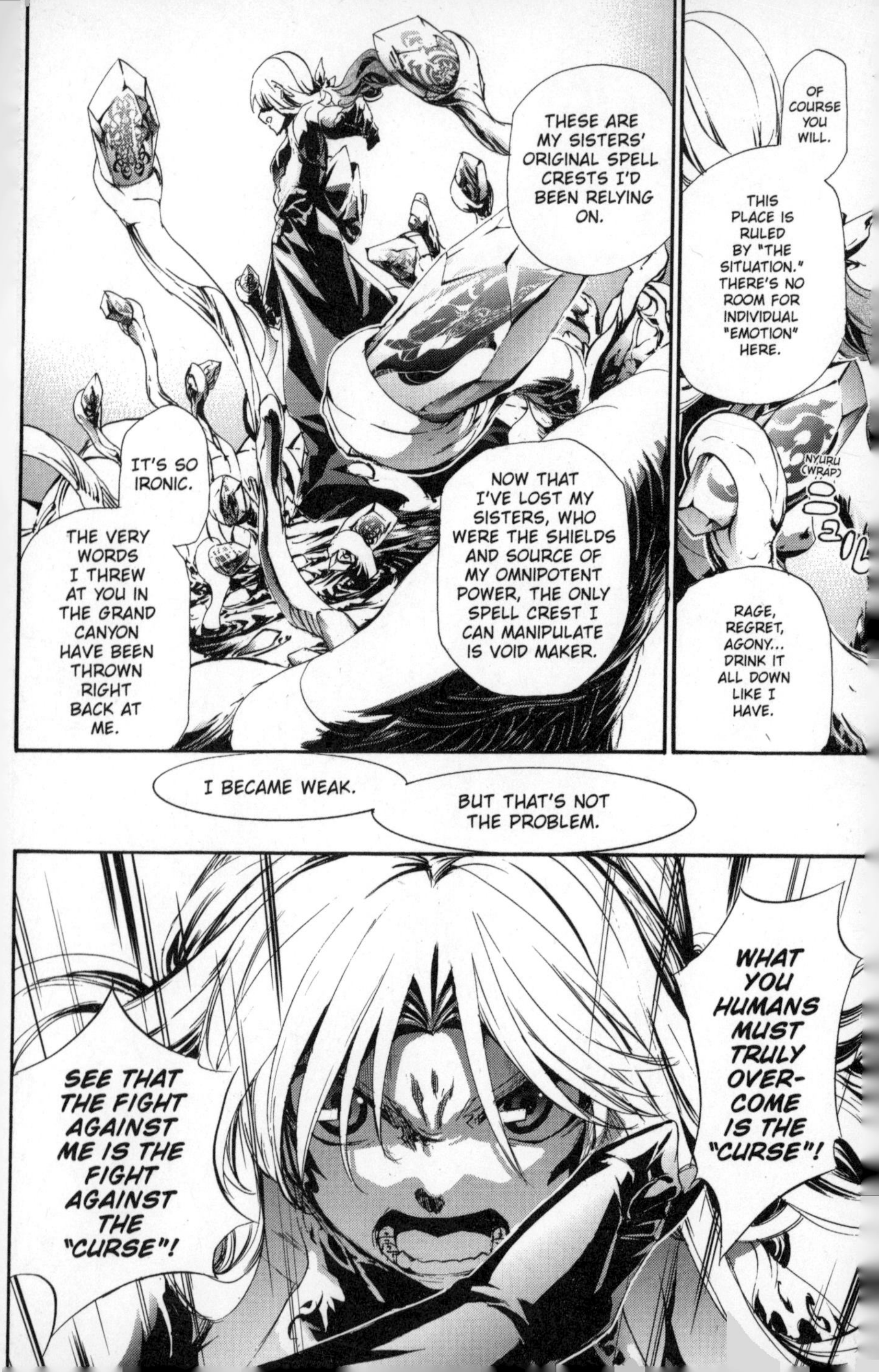
OF COURSE YOU WILL.
THIS PLACE IS RULED BY "THE SITUATION." THERE'S NO ROOM FOR INDIVIDUAL "EMOTION" HERE.
NYURU (WRAP)
RAGE, REGRET, AGONY... DRINK IT ALL DOWN LIKE I HAVE.
THESE ARE MY SISTERS' ORIGINAL SPELL CRESTS I'D BEEN RELYING ON.
NOW THAT I'VE LOST MY SISTERS, WHO WERE THE SHIELDS AND SOURCE OF MY OMNIPOTENT POWER, THE ONLY SPELL CREST I CAN MANIPULATE IS VOID MAKER.
IT'S SO IRONIC.
THE VERY WORDS I THREW AT YOU IN THE GRAND CANYON HAVE BEEN THROWN RIGHT BACK AT ME.
I BECAME WEAK.
BUT THAT'S NOT THE PROBLEM.
WHAT YOU HUMANS MUST TRULY OVER-COME IS THE "CURSE"!
SEE THAT THE FIGHT AGAINST ME IS THE FIGHT AGAINST THE "CURSE"!

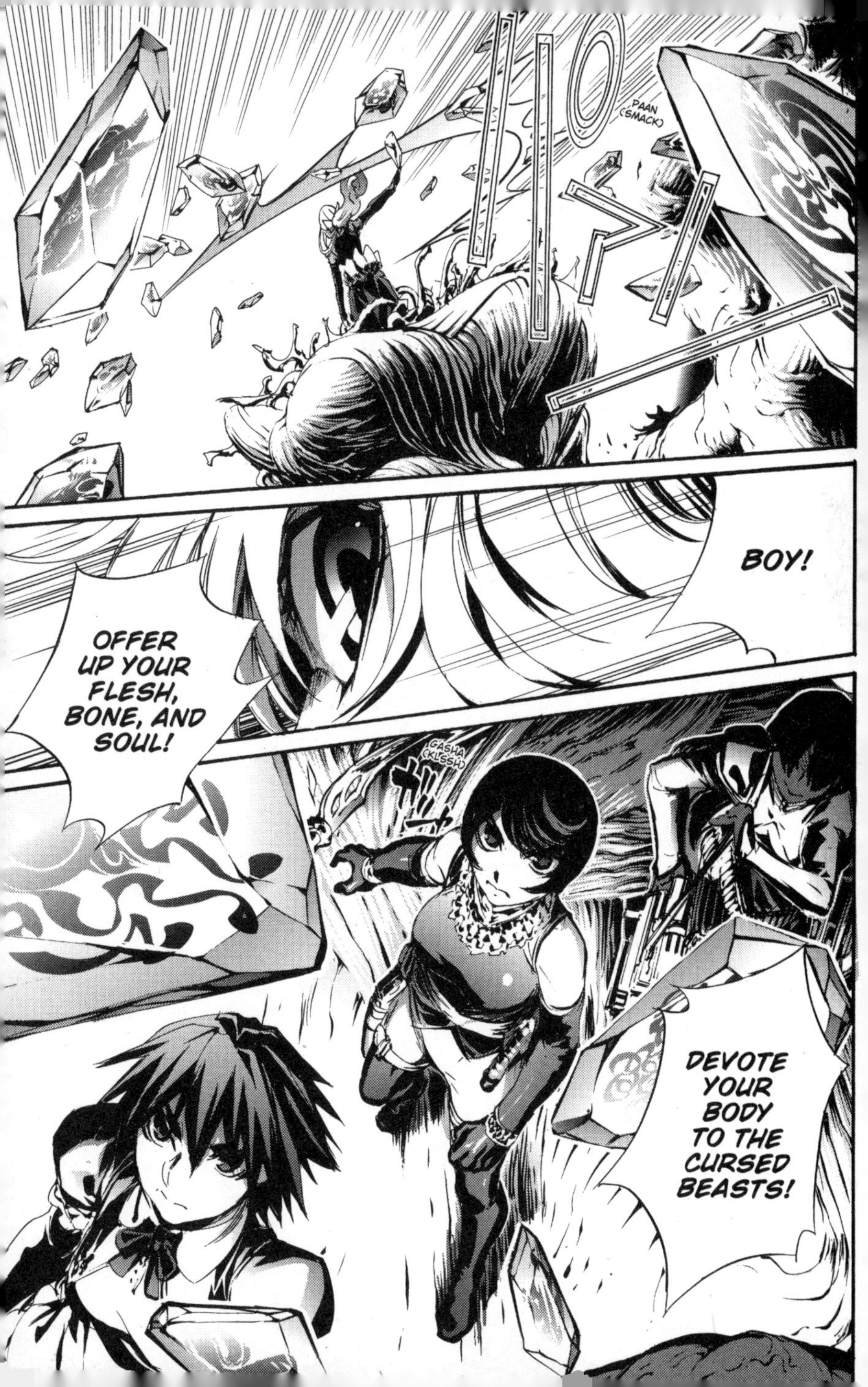
PAAN (SMACK)
BOY!
OFFER UP YOUR FLESH, BONE, AND SOUL!
GASHA (KLSSH)
DEVOTE YOUR BODY TO THE CURSED BEASTS!

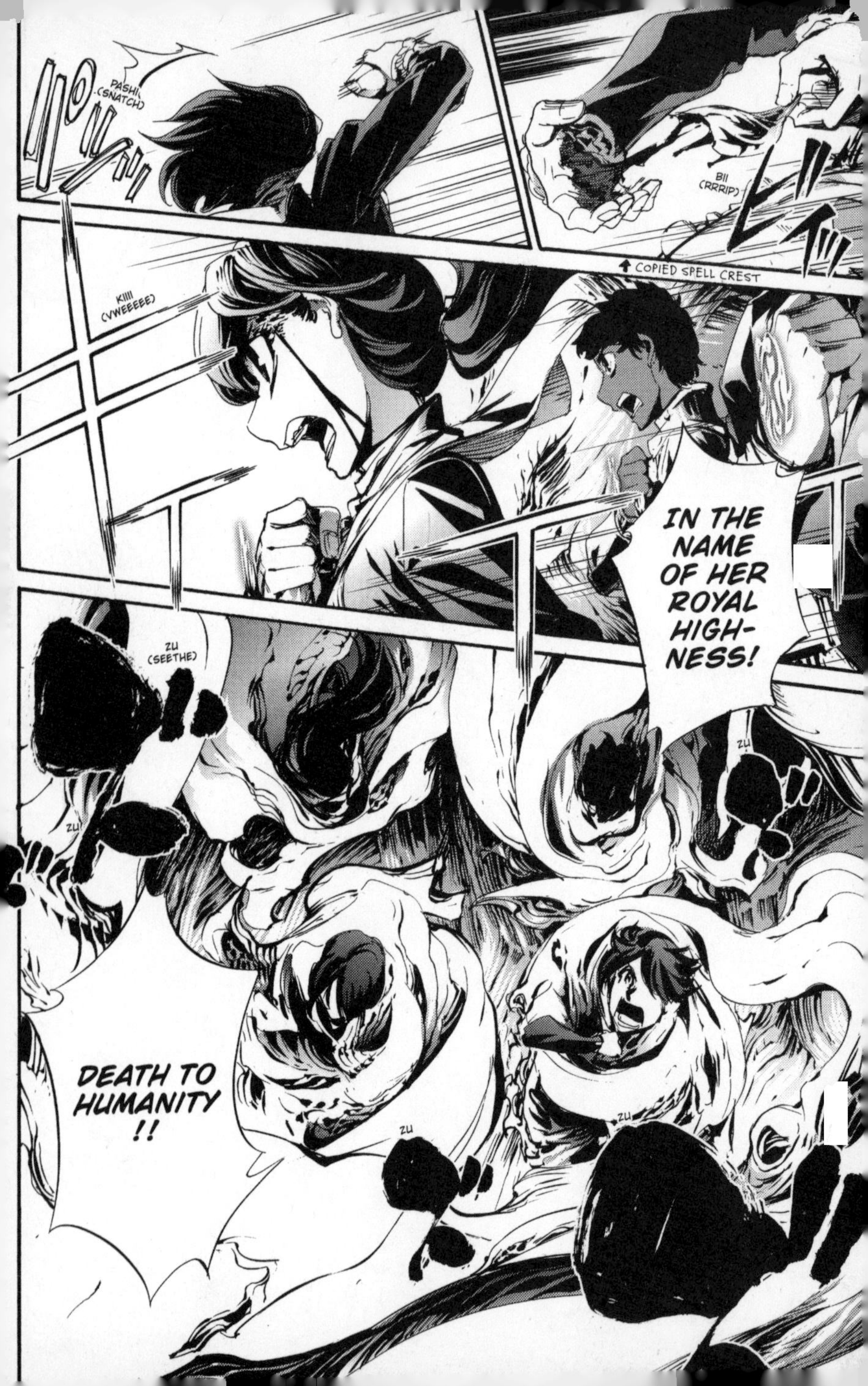
BII (RRRIP)
↑ COPIED SPELL CREST
PASHI (SNATCH)
IN THE NAME OF HER ROYAL HIGH-NESS!
KIIII (VWEEEEE)
ZU (SEETHE)
ZU
ZU
ZU
ZU
DEATH TO HUMANITY !!

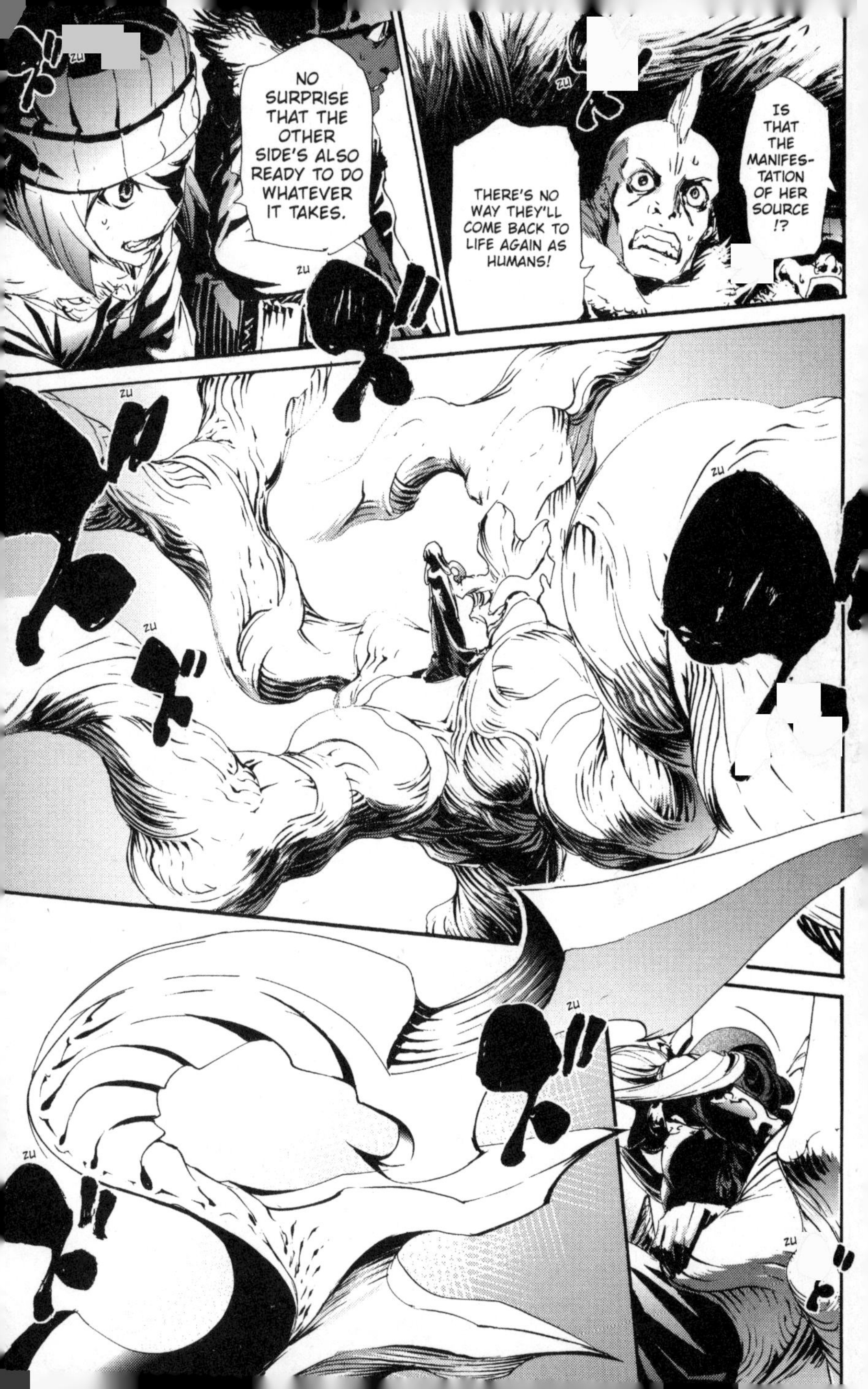
ZU
IS THAT THE MANIFESTATION OF HER SOURCE!?
THERE'S NO WAY THEY'LL COME BACK TO LIFE AGAIN AS HUMANS!
ZU
NO SURPRISE THAT THE OTHER SIDE'S ALSO READY TO DO WHATEVER IT TAKES.
ZU
ZU
ZU
ZU
ZU
ZU
ZU

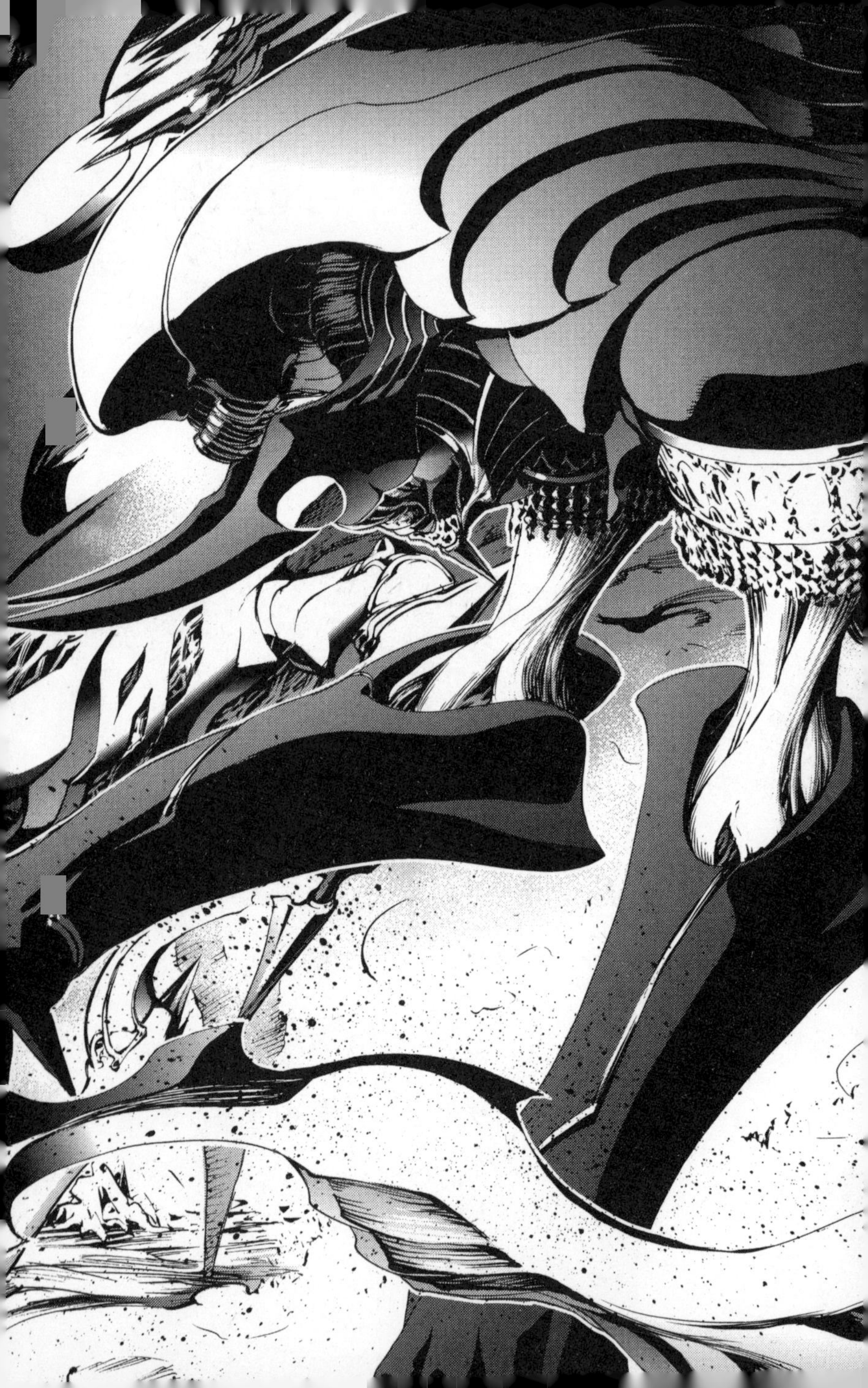

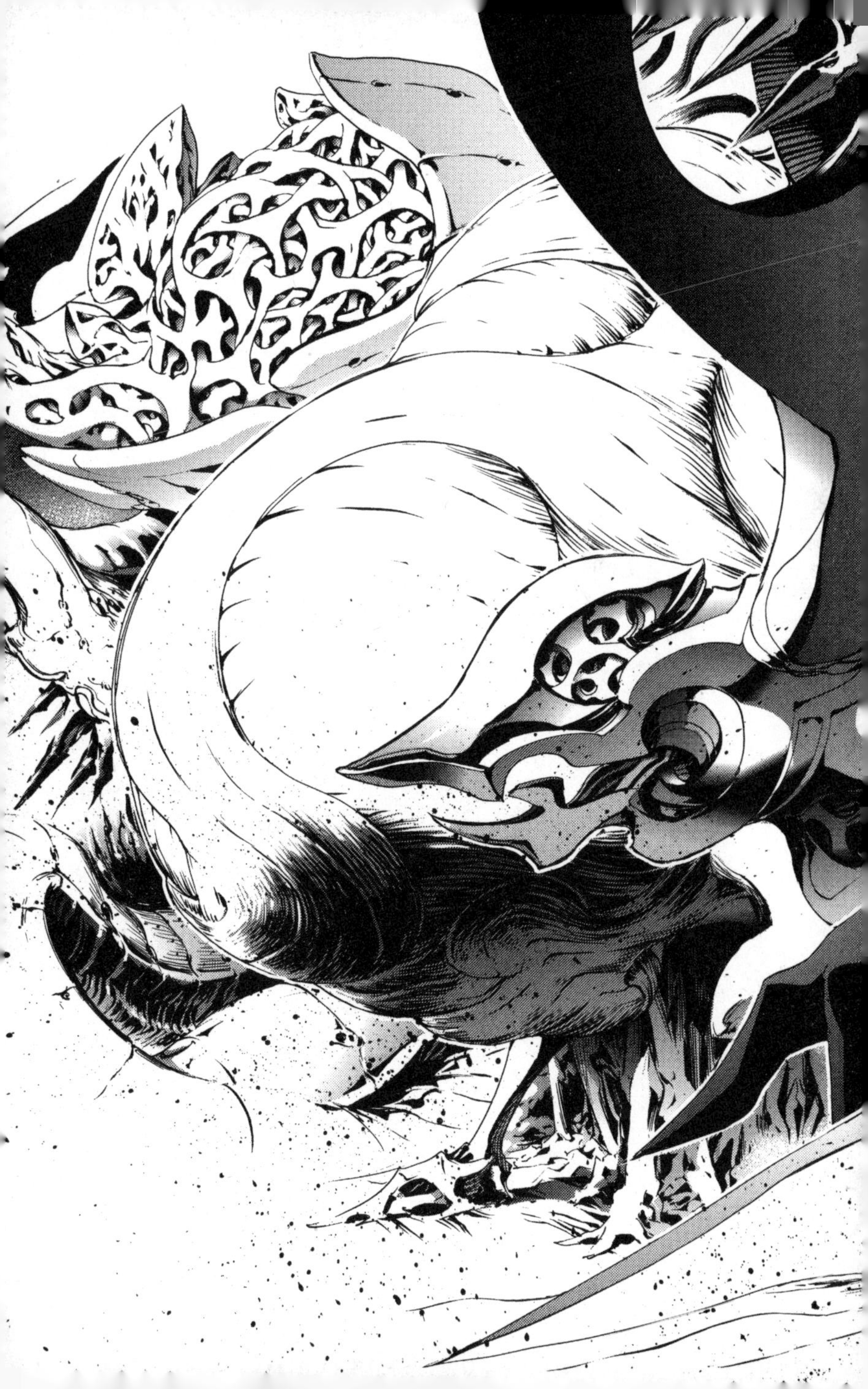

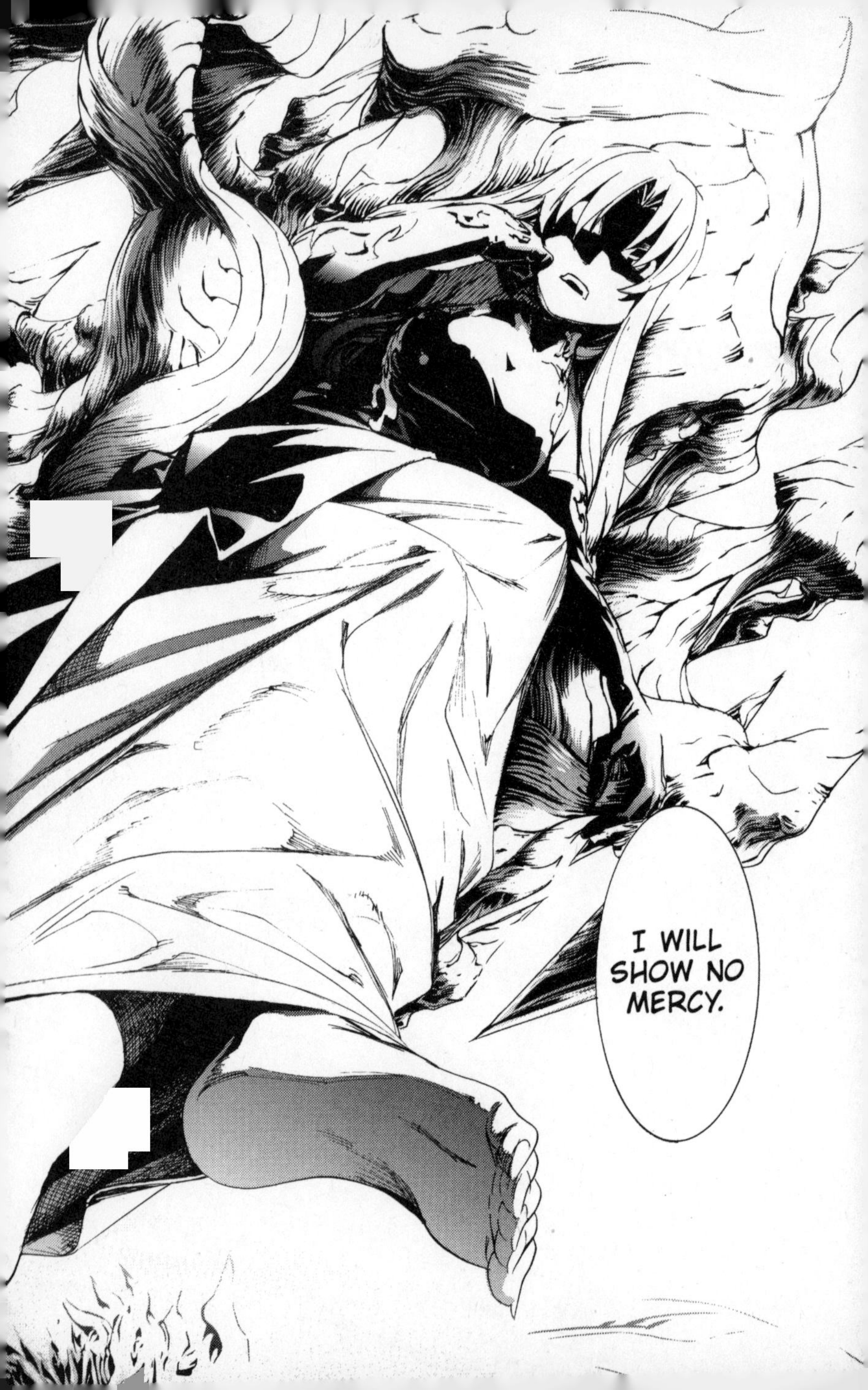
I WILL SHOW NO MERCY.

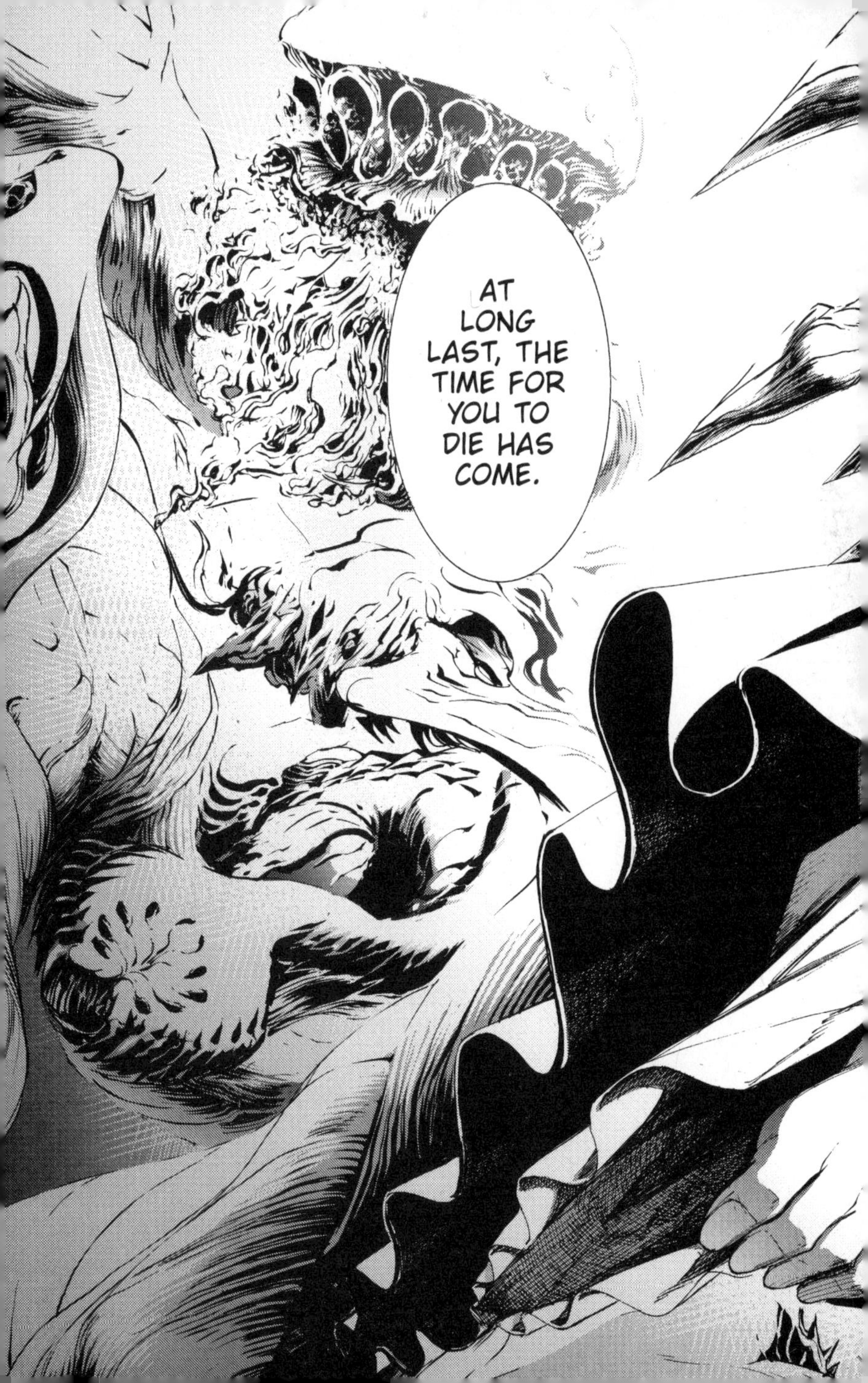
AT LONG LAST, THE TIME FOR YOU TO DIE HAS COME.

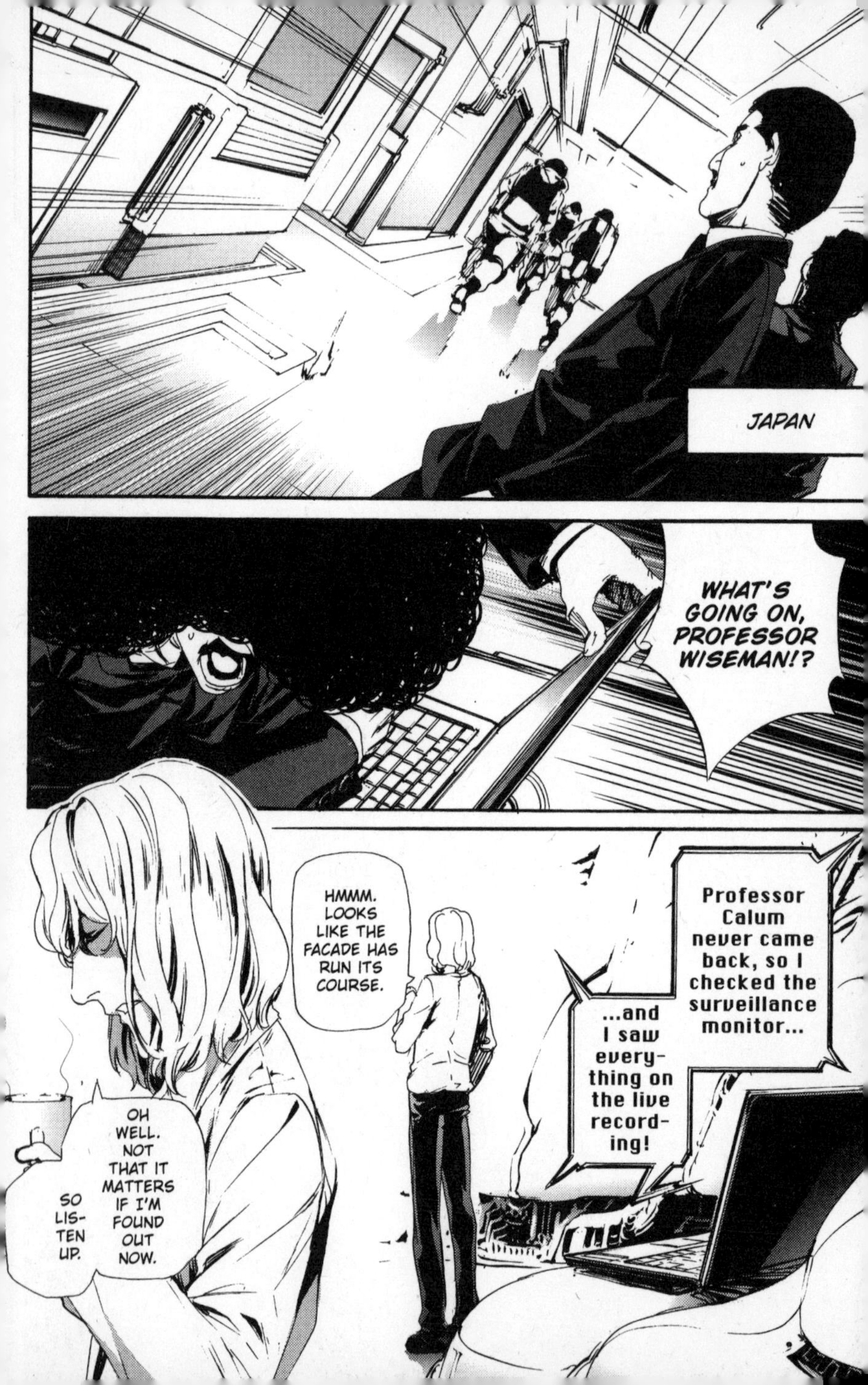
JAPAN
WHAT'S GOING ON, PROFESSOR WISEMAN!?
Professor Calum never came back, so I checked the surveillance monitor...
...and I saw every-thing on the live record-ing!
HMMM. LOOKS LIKE THE FACADE HAS RUN ITS COURSE.
OH WELL. NOT THAT IT MATTERS IF I'M FOUND OUT NOW.
SO LIS-TEN UP.

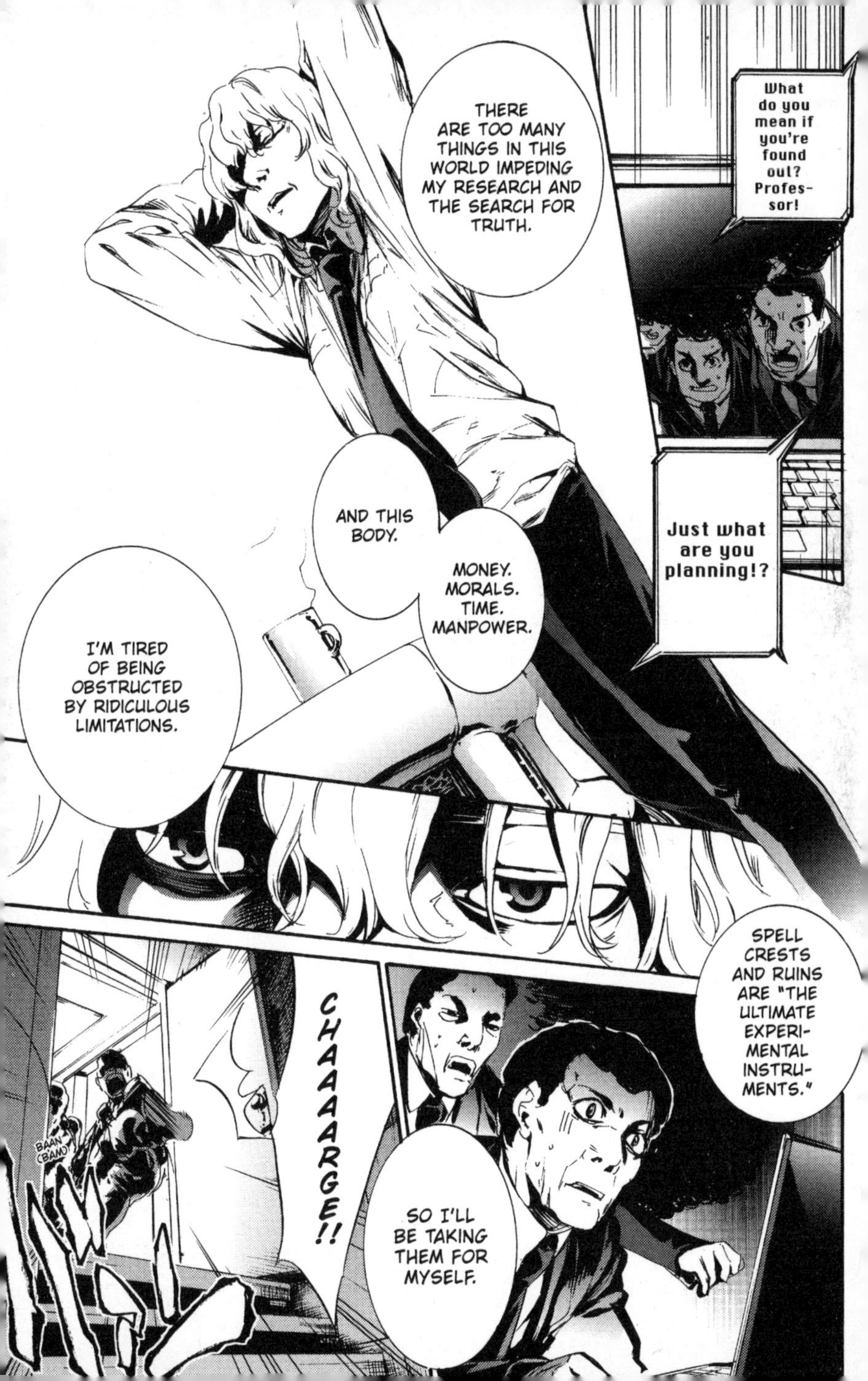
What do you mean if you're found out? Professor!
Just what are you planning!?
THERE ARE TOO MANY THINGS IN THIS WORLD IMPEDING MY RESEARCH AND THE SEARCH FOR TRUTH.
MONEY. MORALS. TIME. MANPOWER.
AND THIS BODY.
I'M TIRED OF BEING OBSTRUCTED BY RIDICULOUS LIMITATIONS.
SPELL CRESTS AND RUINS ARE "THE ULTIMATE EXPERIMENTAL INSTRUMENTS."
SO I'LL BE TAKING THEM FOR MYSELF.
CHAAAARGE!!
BAAN (BAM)

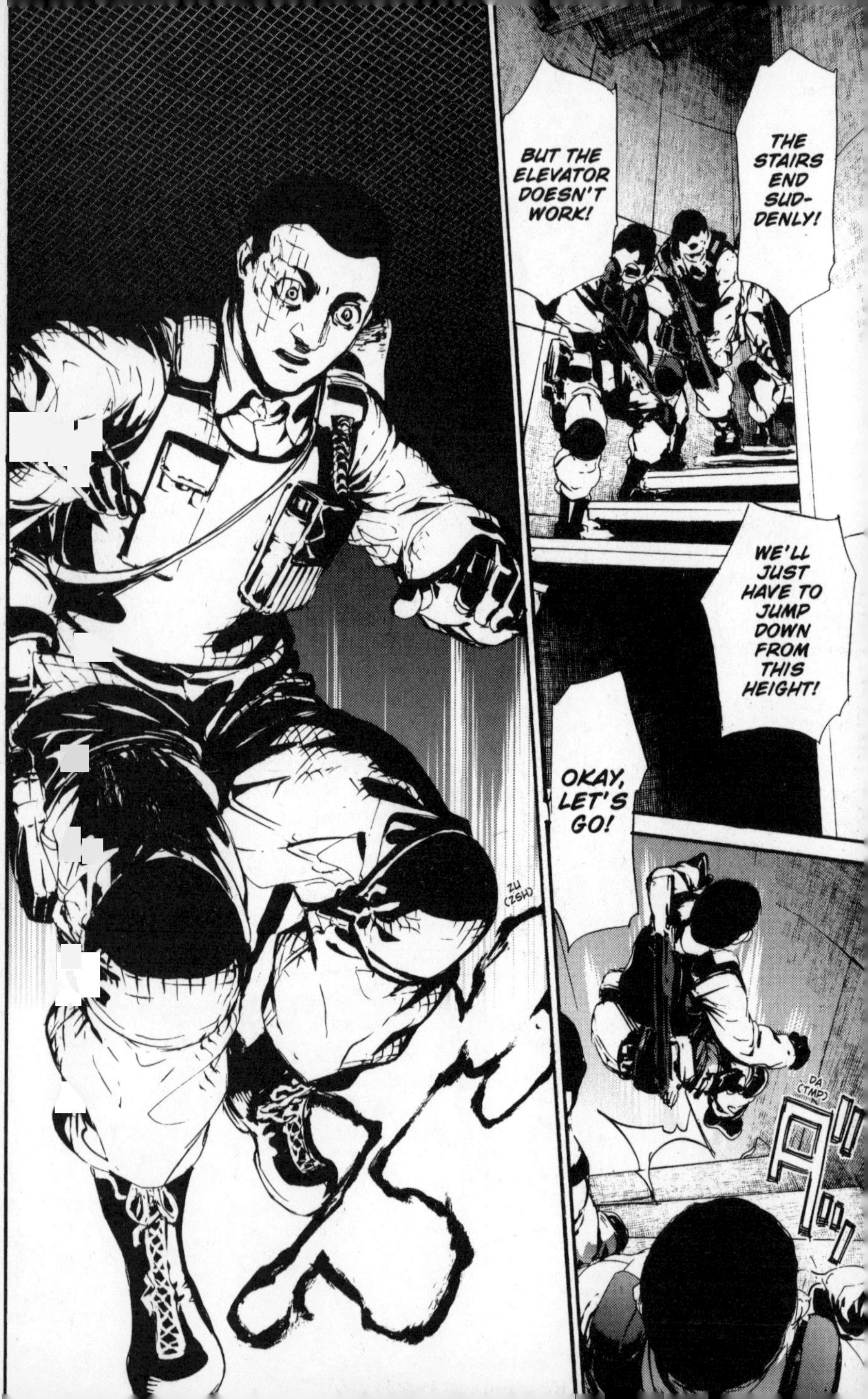
THE STAIRS END SUDDENLY!
BUT THE ELEVATOR DOESN'T WORK!
WE'LL JUST HAVE TO JUMP DOWN FROM THIS HEIGHT!
OKAY, LET'S GO!
DA (TMP)
ZU (ZSH)

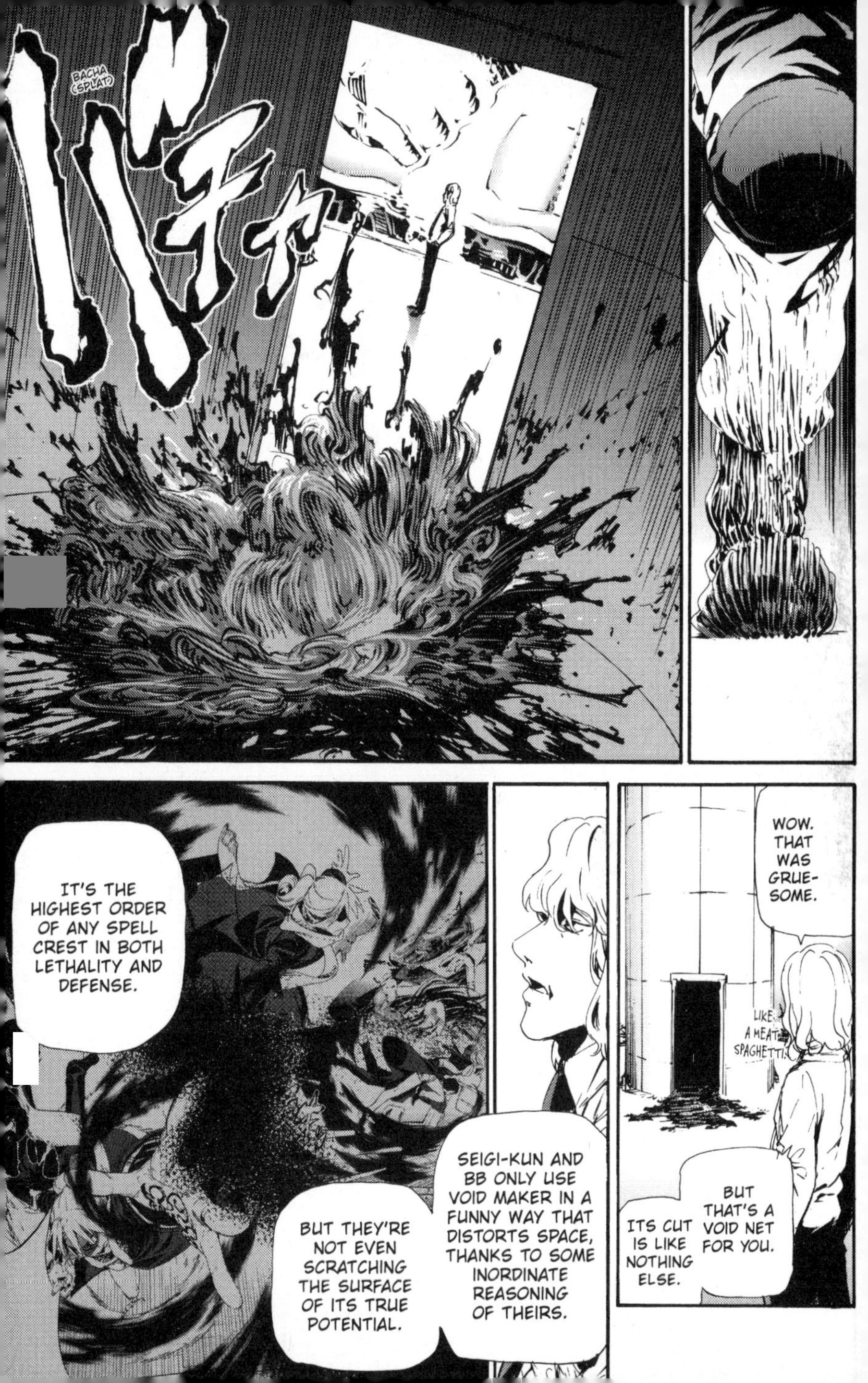
BACHA (SPLAT)
WOW. THAT WAS GRUE-SOME.
LIKE A MEAT SPAGHETTI.
BUT THAT'S A VOID NET FOR YOU.
ITS CUT IS LIKE NOTHING ELSE.
SEIGI-KUN AND BB ONLY USE VOID MAKER IN A FUNNY WAY THAT DISTORTS SPACE, THANKS TO SOME INORDINATE REASONING OF THEIRS.
BUT THEY'RE NOT EVEN SCRATCHING THE SURFACE OF ITS TRUE POTENTIAL.
IT'S THE HIGHEST ORDER OF ANY SPELL CREST IN BOTH LETHALITY AND DEFENSE.

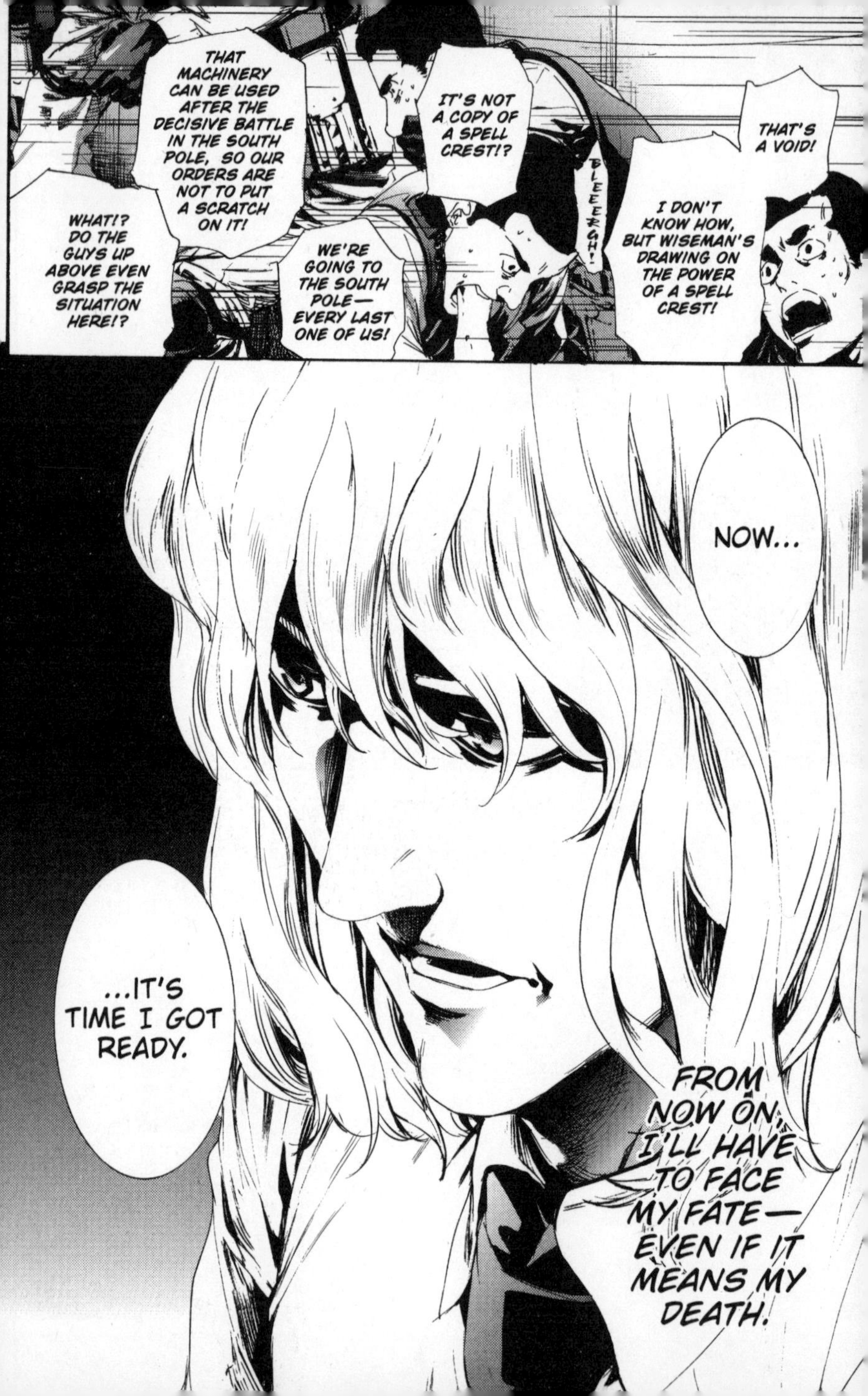
THAT'S A VOID!
I DON'T KNOW HOW, BUT WISEMAN'S DRAWING ON THE POWER OF A SPELL CREST!
BLEEERGH!
IT'S NOT A COPY OF A SPELL CREST!?
WE'RE GOING TO THE SOUTH POLE— EVERY LAST ONE OF US!
THAT MACHINERY CAN BE USED AFTER THE DECISIVE BATTLE IN THE SOUTH POLE, SO OUR ORDERS ARE NOT TO PUT A SCRATCH ON IT!
WHAT!? DO THE GUYS UP ABOVE EVEN GRASP THE SITUATION HERE!?
NOW...
...IT'S TIME I GOT READY.
FROM NOW ON, I'LL HAVE TO FACE MY FATE— EVEN IF IT MEANS MY DEATH.

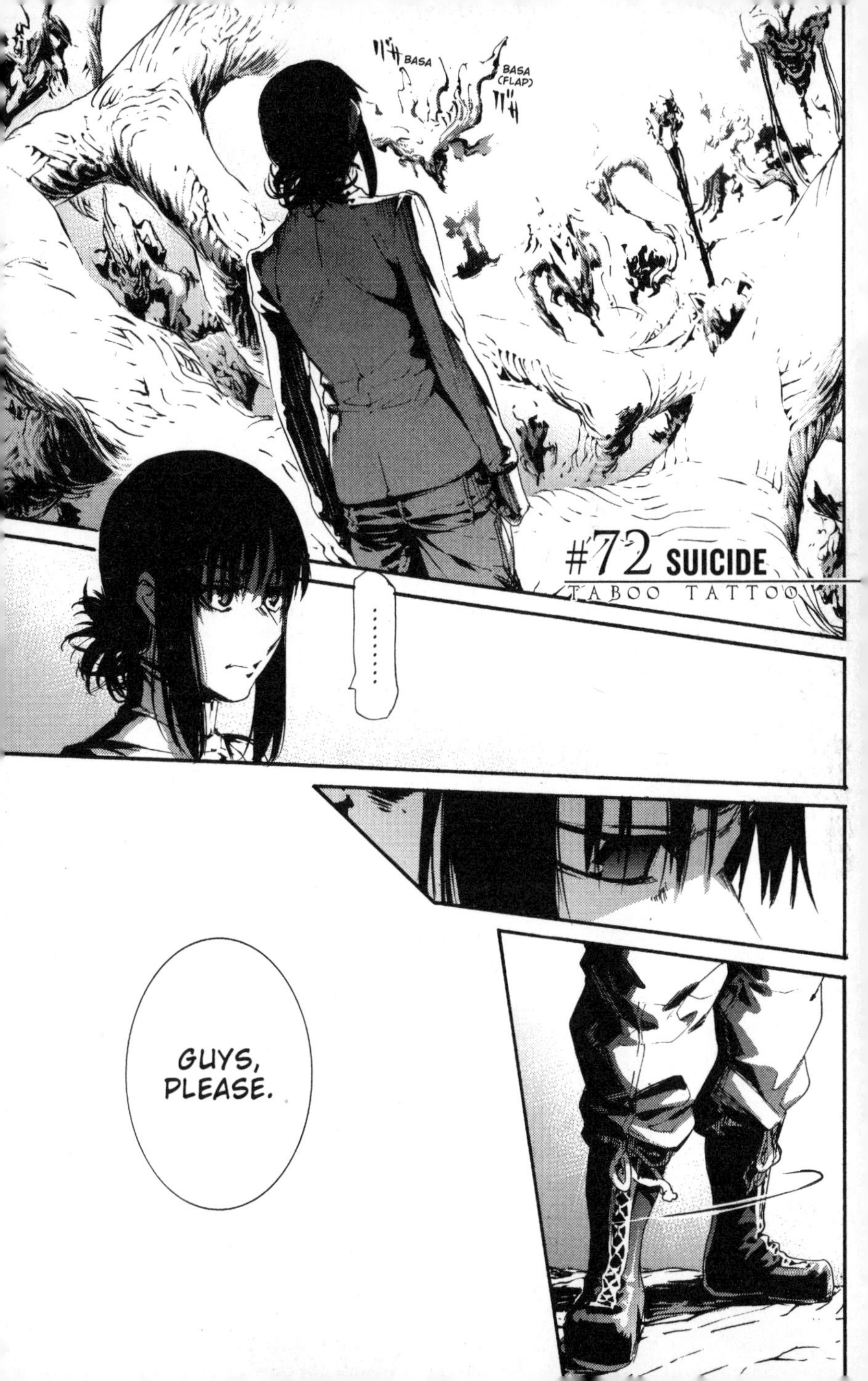
BASA
BASA (FLAP)
#72 SUICIDE
TABOO TATTOO
....
GUYS, PLEASE.

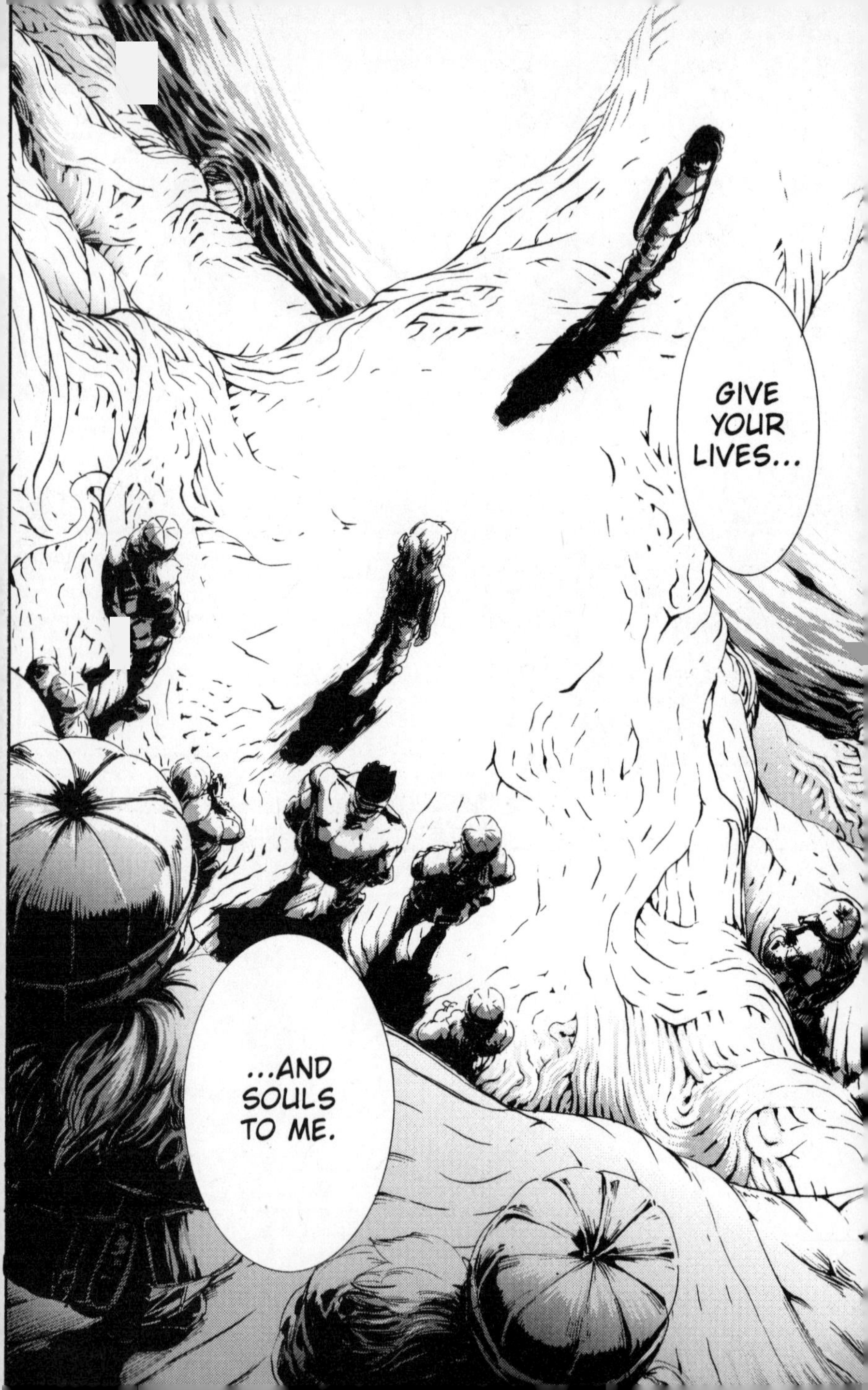
GIVE YOUR LIVES...
...AND SOULS TO ME.

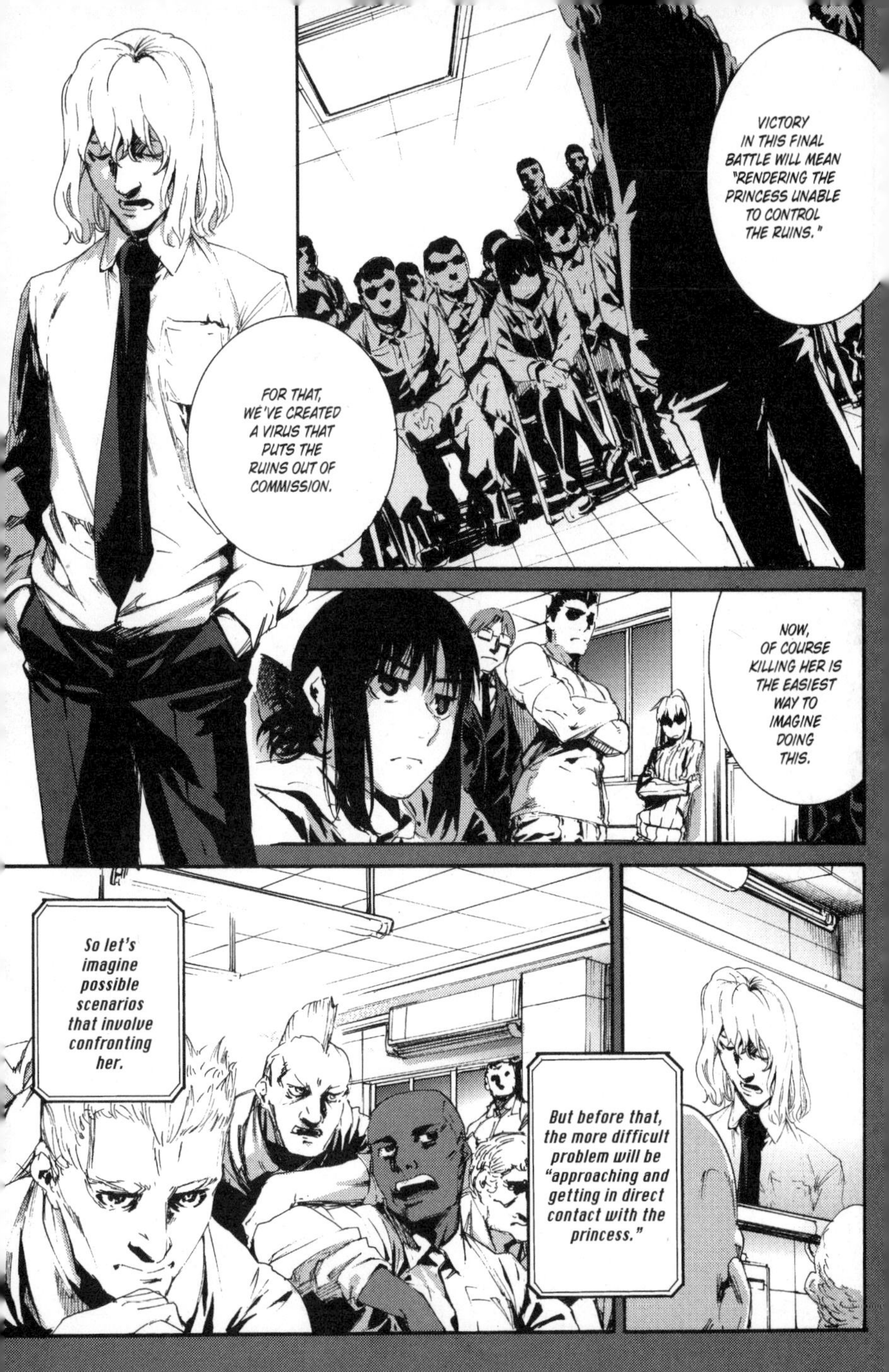
VICTORY IN THIS FINAL BATTLE WILL MEAN "RENDERING THE PRINCESS UNABLE TO CONTROL THE RUINS."
FOR THAT, WE'VE CREATED A VIRUS THAT PUTS THE RUINS OUT OF COMMISSION.
NOW, OF COURSE KILLING HER IS THE EASIEST WAY TO IMAGINE DOING THIS.
So let's imagine possible scenarios that involve confronting her.
But before that, the more difficult problem will be "approaching and getting in direct contact with the princess."

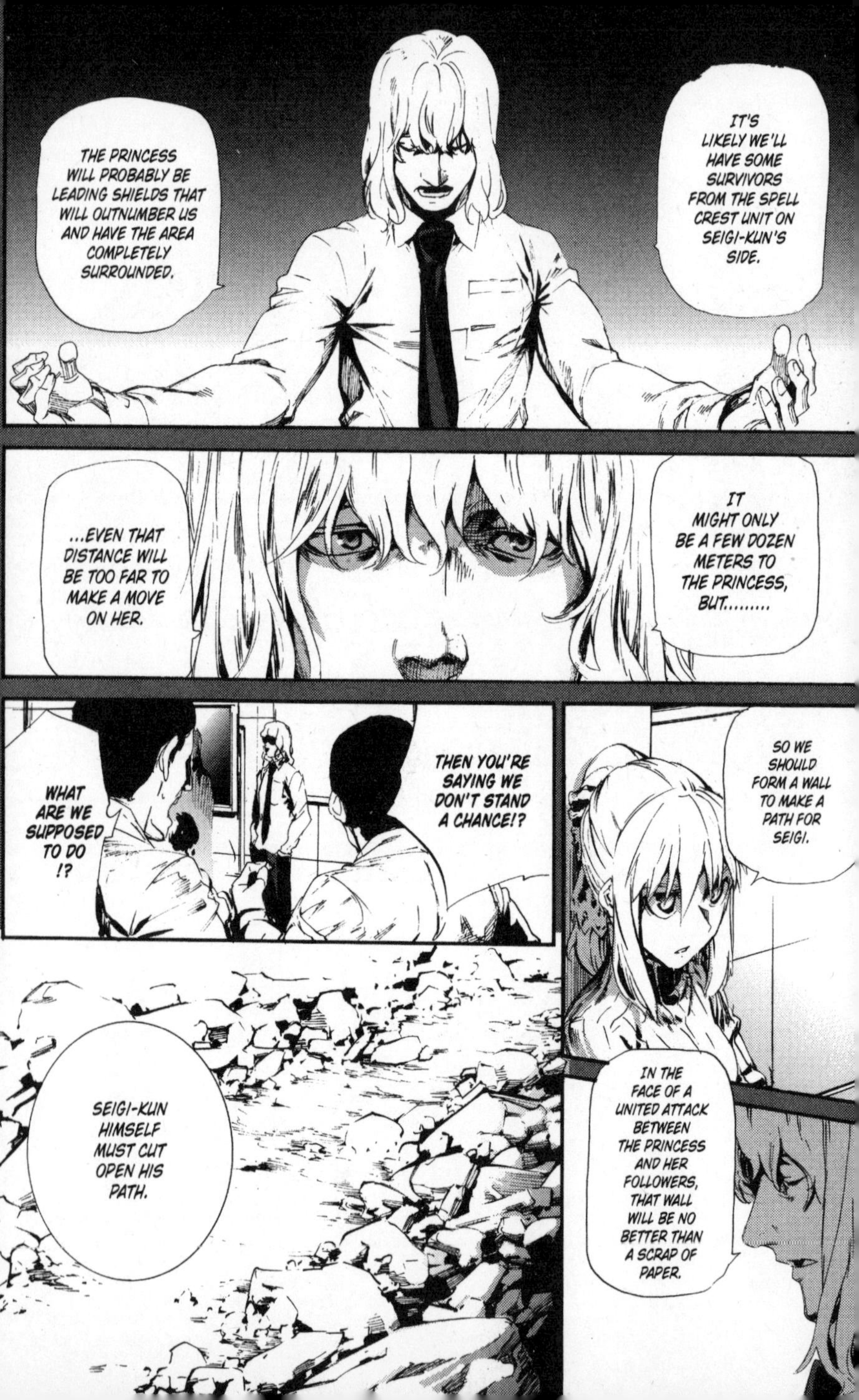
IT'S LIKELY WE'LL HAVE SOME SURVIVORS FROM THE SPELL CREST UNIT ON SEIGI-KUN'S SIDE.
THE PRINCESS WILL PROBABLY BE LEADING SHIELDS THAT WILL OUTNUMBER US AND HAVE THE AREA COMPLETELY SURROUNDED.
IT MIGHT ONLY BE A FEW DOZEN METERS TO THE PRINCESS, BUT........
...EVEN THAT DISTANCE WILL BE TOO FAR TO MAKE A MOVE ON HER.
SO WE SHOULD FORM A WALL TO MAKE A PATH FOR SEIGI.
IN THE FACE OF A UNITED ATTACK BETWEEN THE PRINCESS AND HER FOLLOWERS, THAT WALL WILL BE NO BETTER THAN A SCRAP OF PAPER.
THEN YOU'RE SAYING WE DON'T STAND A CHANCE!?
WHAT ARE WE SUPPOSED TO DO !?
SEIGI-KUN HIMSELF MUST CUT OPEN HIS PATH.

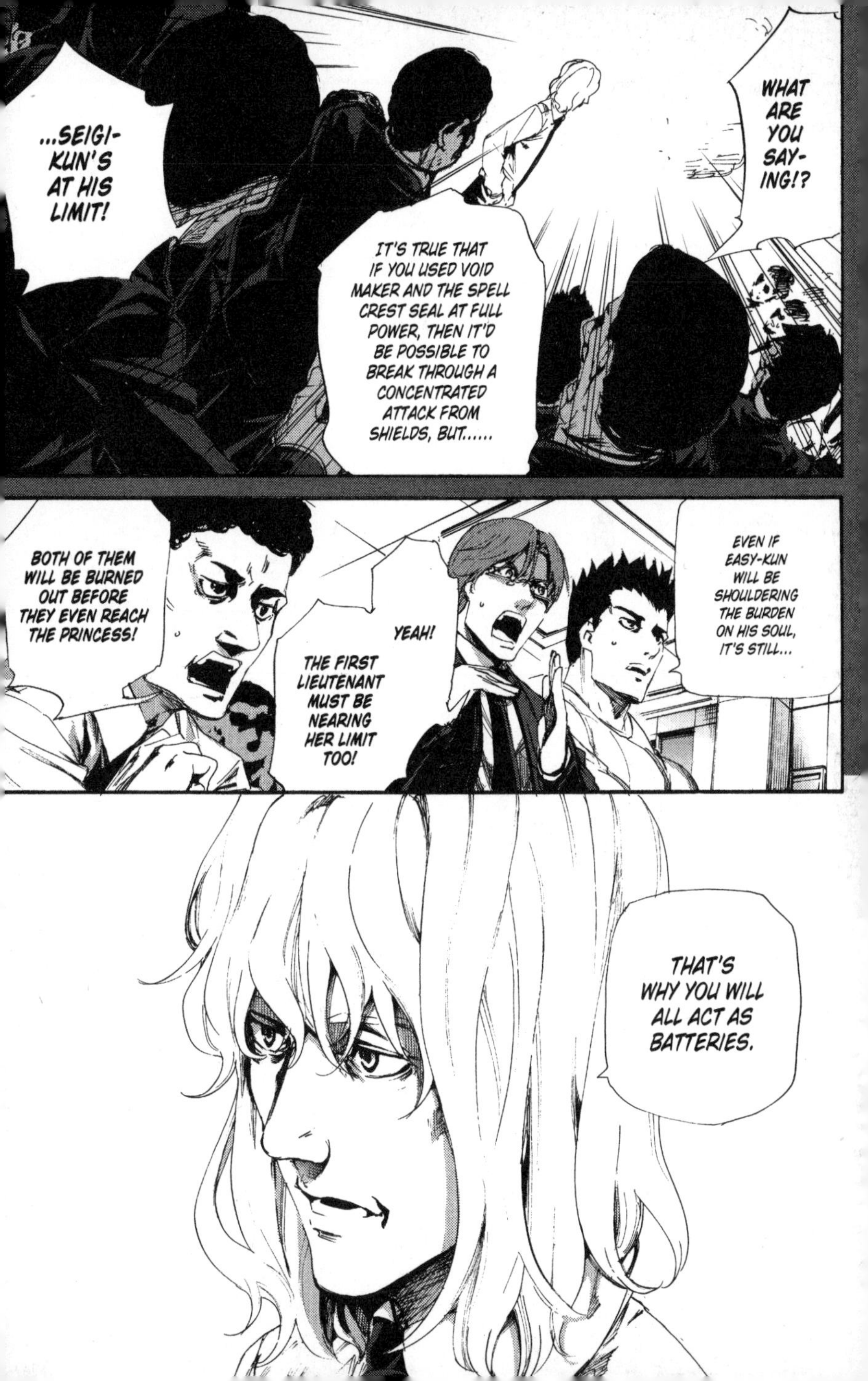
WHAT ARE YOU SAYING!?
...SEIGI-KUN'S AT HIS LIMIT!
IT'S TRUE THAT IF YOU USED VOID MAKER AND THE SPELL CREST SEAL AT FULL POWER, THEN IT'D BE POSSIBLE TO BREAK THROUGH A CONCENTRATED ATTACK FROM SHIELDS, BUT......
EVEN IF EASY-KUN WILL BE SHOULDERING THE BURDEN ON HIS SOUL, IT'S STILL...
YEAH!
THE FIRST LIEUTENANT MUST BE NEARING HER LIMIT TOO!
BOTH OF THEM WILL BE BURNED OUT BEFORE THEY EVEN REACH THE PRINCESS!
THAT'S WHY YOU WILL ALL ACT AS BATTERIES.

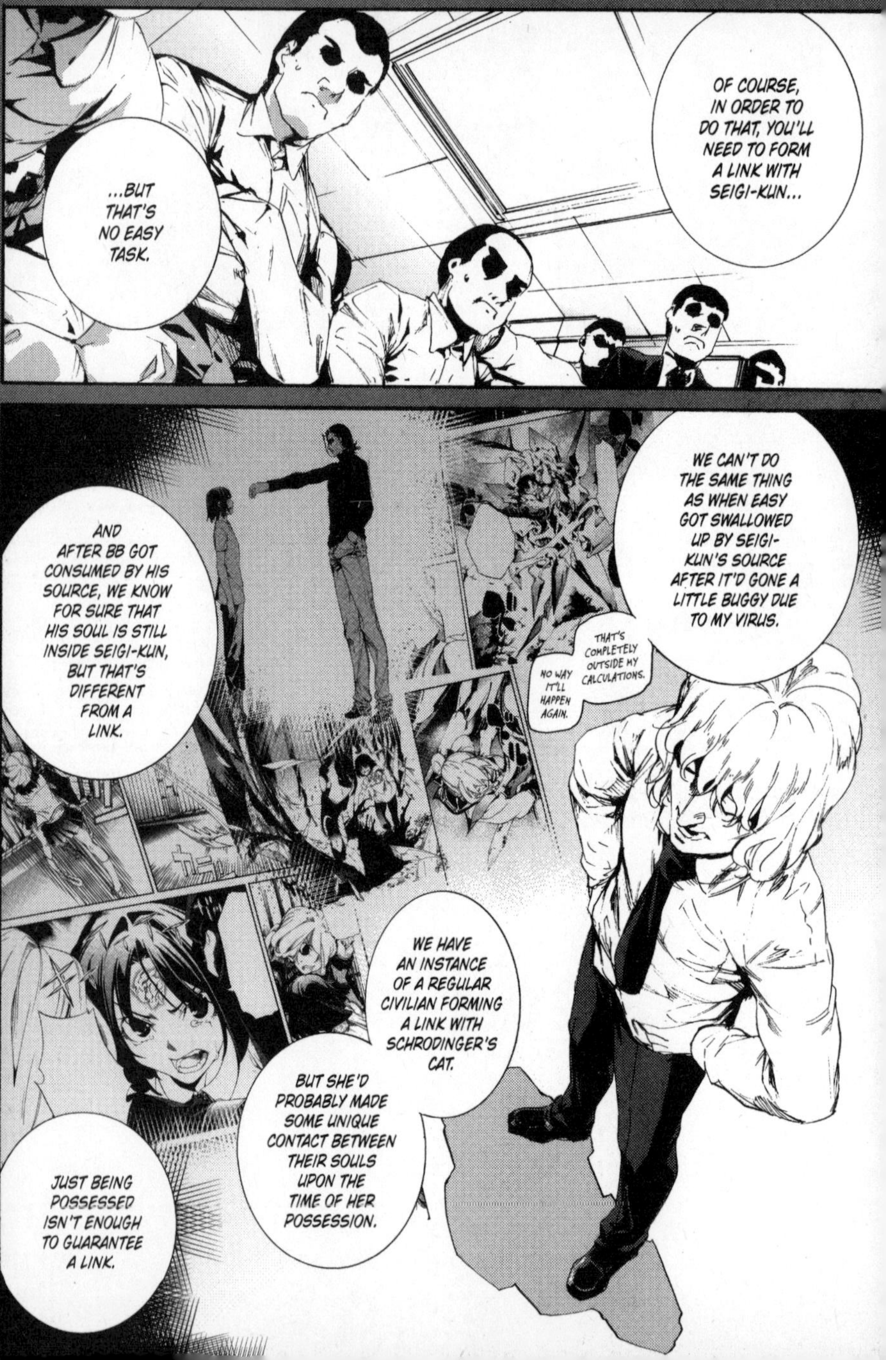
OF COURSE, IN ORDER TO DO THAT, YOU'LL NEED TO FORM A LINK WITH SEIGI-KUN...
...BUT THAT'S NO EASY TASK.
WE CAN'T DO THE SAME THING AS WHEN EASY GOT SWALLOWED UP BY SEIGI-KUN'S SOURCE AFTER IT'D GONE A LITTLE BUGGY DUE TO MY VIRUS.
THAT'S COMPLETELY OUTSIDE MY CALCULATIONS.
NO WAY IT'LL HAPPEN AGAIN.
AND AFTER BB GOT CONSUMED BY HIS SOURCE, WE KNOW FOR SURE THAT HIS SOUL IS STILL INSIDE SEIGI-KUN, BUT THAT'S DIFFERENT FROM A LINK.
WE HAVE AN INSTANCE OF A REGULAR CIVILIAN FORMING A LINK WITH SCHRODINGER'S CAT.
BUT SHE'D PROBABLY MADE SOME UNIQUE CONTACT BETWEEN THEIR SOULS UPON THE TIME OF HER POSSESSION.
JUST BEING POSSESSED ISN'T ENOUGH TO GUARANTEE A LINK.

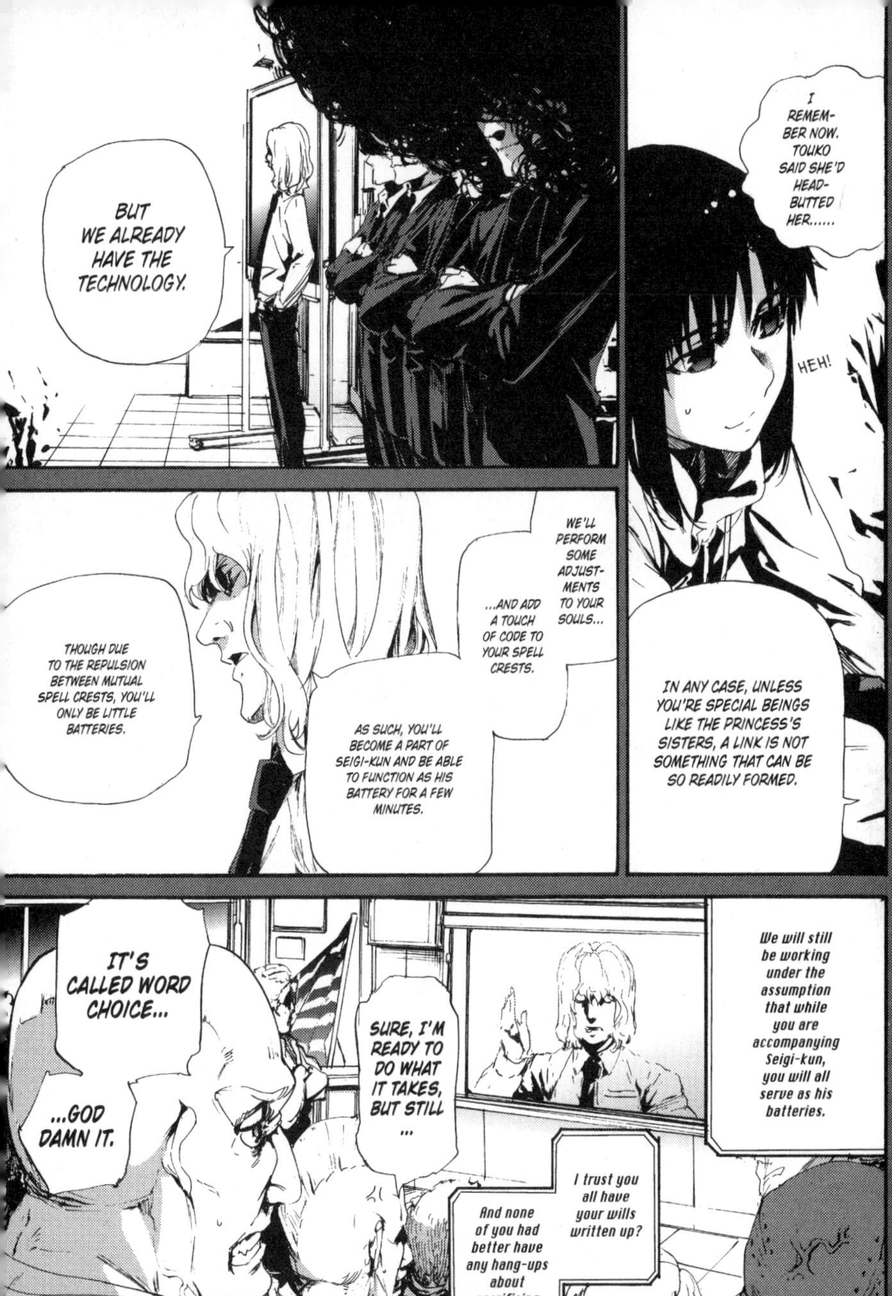
I REMEMBER NOW. TOUKO SAID SHE'D HEAD-BUTTED HER......
HEH!
IN ANY CASE, UNLESS YOU'RE SPECIAL BEINGS LIKE THE PRINCESS'S SISTERS, A LINK IS NOT SOMETHING THAT CAN BE SO READILY FORMED.
BUT WE ALREADY HAVE THE TECHNOLOGY.
WE'LL PERFORM SOME ADJUSTMENTS TO YOUR SOULS...
...AND ADD A TOUCH OF CODE TO YOUR SPELL CRESTS.
AS SUCH, YOU'LL BECOME A PART OF SEIGI-KUN AND BE ABLE TO FUNCTION AS HIS BATTERY FOR A FEW MINUTES.
THOUGH DUE TO THE REPULSION BETWEEN MUTUAL SPELL CRESTS, YOU'LL ONLY BE LITTLE BATTERIES.
We will still be working under the assumption that while you are accompanying Seigi-kun, you will all serve as his batteries.
I trust you all have your wills written up?
And none of you had better have any hang-ups about sacrificing your lives, you hear?
SURE, I'M READY TO DO WHAT IT TAKES, BUT STILL ...
IT'S CALLED WORD CHOICE...
...GOD DAMN IT.

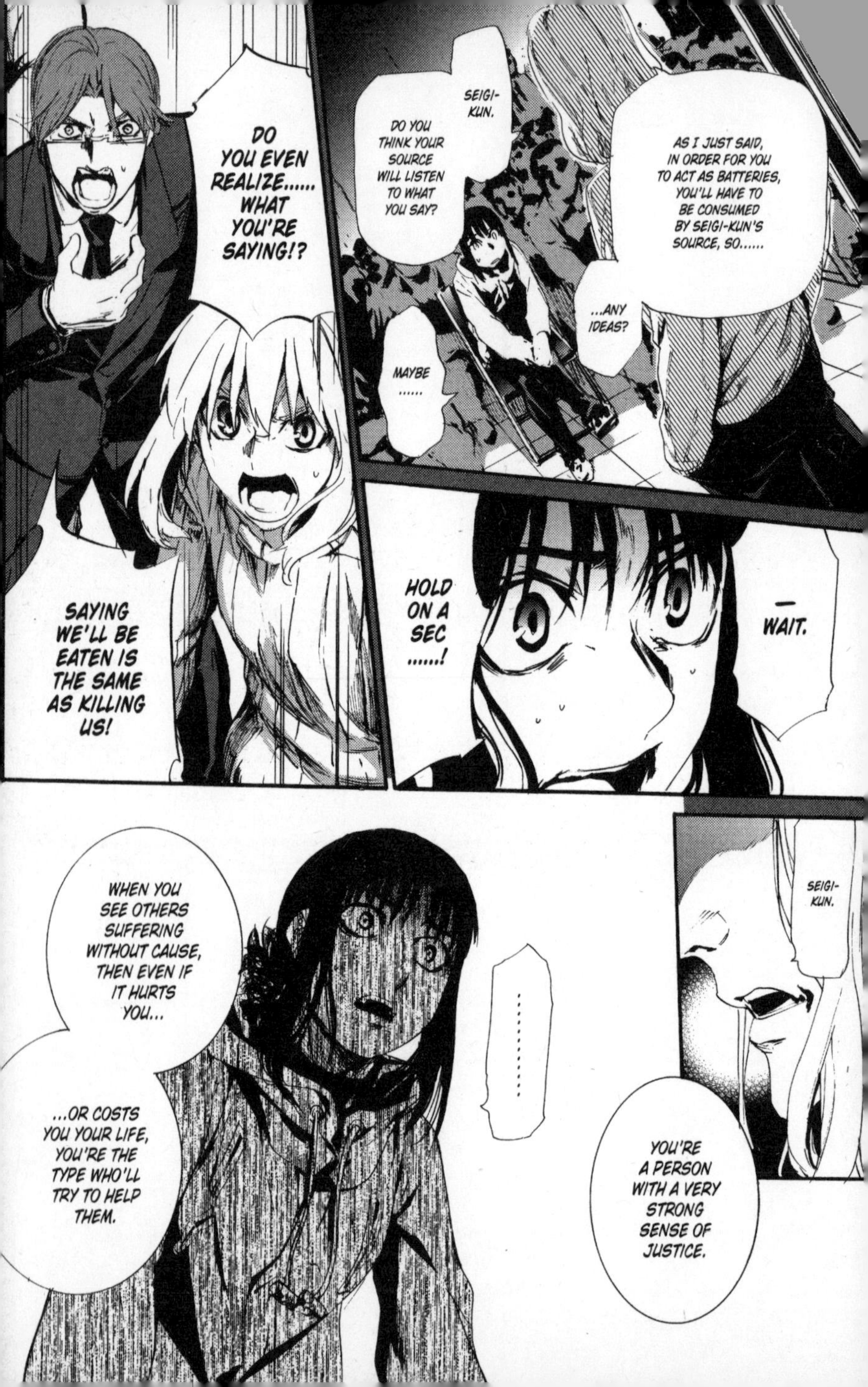
AS I JUST SAID, IN ORDER FOR YOU TO ACT AS BATTERIES, YOU'LL HAVE TO BE CONSUMED BY SEIGI-KUN'S SOURCE, SO......
...ANY IDEAS?
SEIGI-KUN.
DO YOU THINK YOUR SOURCE WILL LISTEN TO WHAT YOU SAY?
MAYBE ......
—WAIT.
HOLD ON A SEC ......!
DO YOU EVEN REALIZE...... WHAT YOU'RE SAYING!?
SAYING WE'LL BE EATEN IS THE SAME AS KILLING US!
SEIGI-KUN.
YOU'RE A PERSON WITH A VERY STRONG SENSE OF JUSTICE.
......
WHEN YOU SEE OTHERS SUFFERING WITHOUT CAUSE, THEN EVEN IF IT HURTS YOU...
...OR COSTS YOU YOUR LIFE, YOU'RE THE TYPE WHO'LL TRY TO HELP THEM.

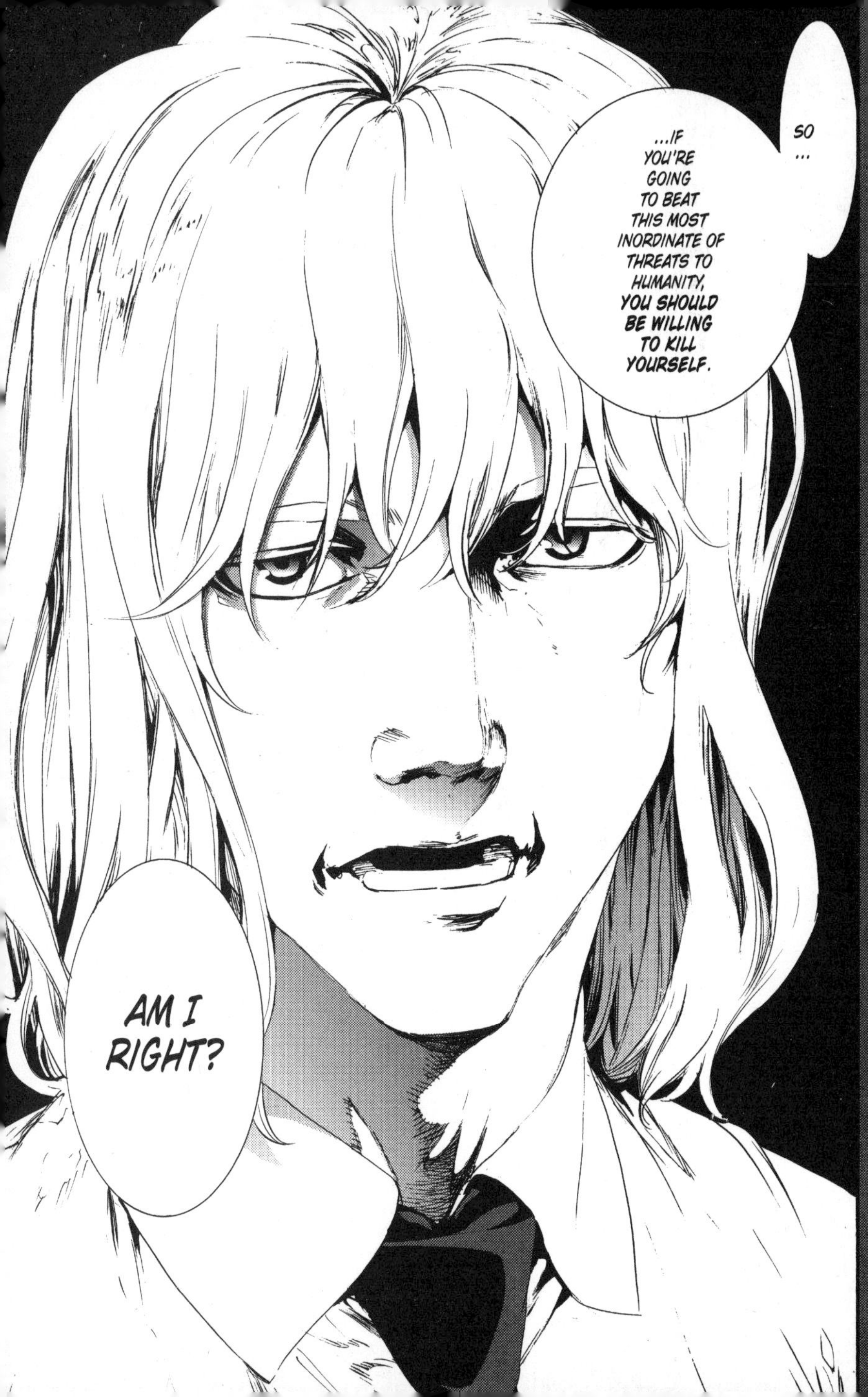
SO ...
...IF YOU'RE GOING TO BEAT THIS MOST INORDINATE OF THREATS TO HUMANITY, **YOU SHOULD BE WILLING TO KILL YOURSELF.**
AM I RIGHT?

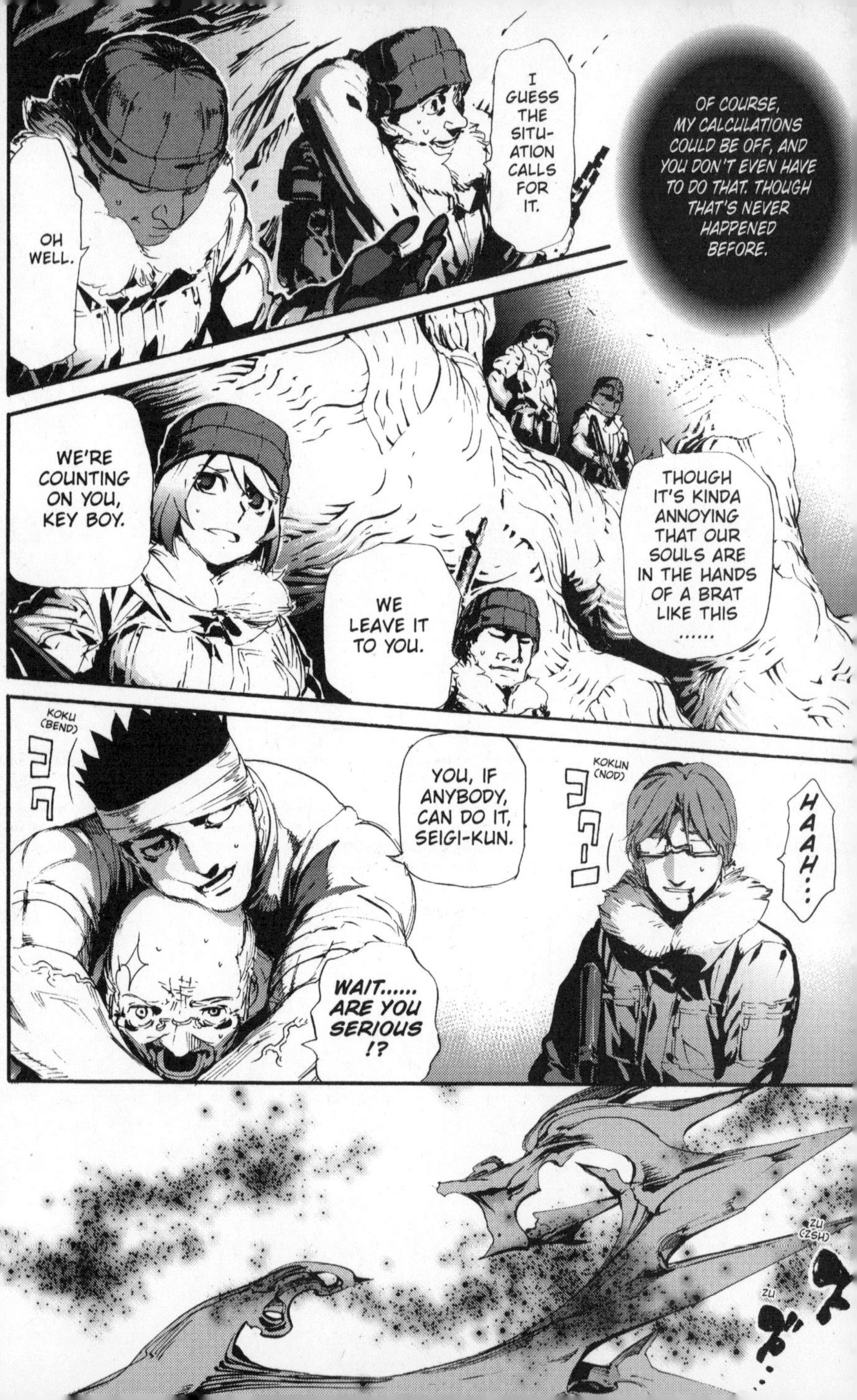
OF COURSE, MY CALCULATIONS COULD BE OFF, AND YOU DON'T EVEN HAVE TO DO THAT. THOUGH THAT'S NEVER HAPPENED BEFORE.
I GUESS THE SITU- ATION CALLS FOR IT.
OH WELL.
THOUGH IT'S KINDA ANNOYING THAT OUR SOULS ARE IN THE HANDS OF A BRAT LIKE THIS ......
WE LEAVE IT TO YOU.
WE'RE COUNTING ON YOU, KEY BOY.
HAAH...
KOKUN (NOD)
YOU, IF ANYBODY, CAN DO IT, SEIGI-KUN.
KOKU (BEND)
WAIT...... ARE YOU SERIOUS !?
ZU (ZSH)
ZU

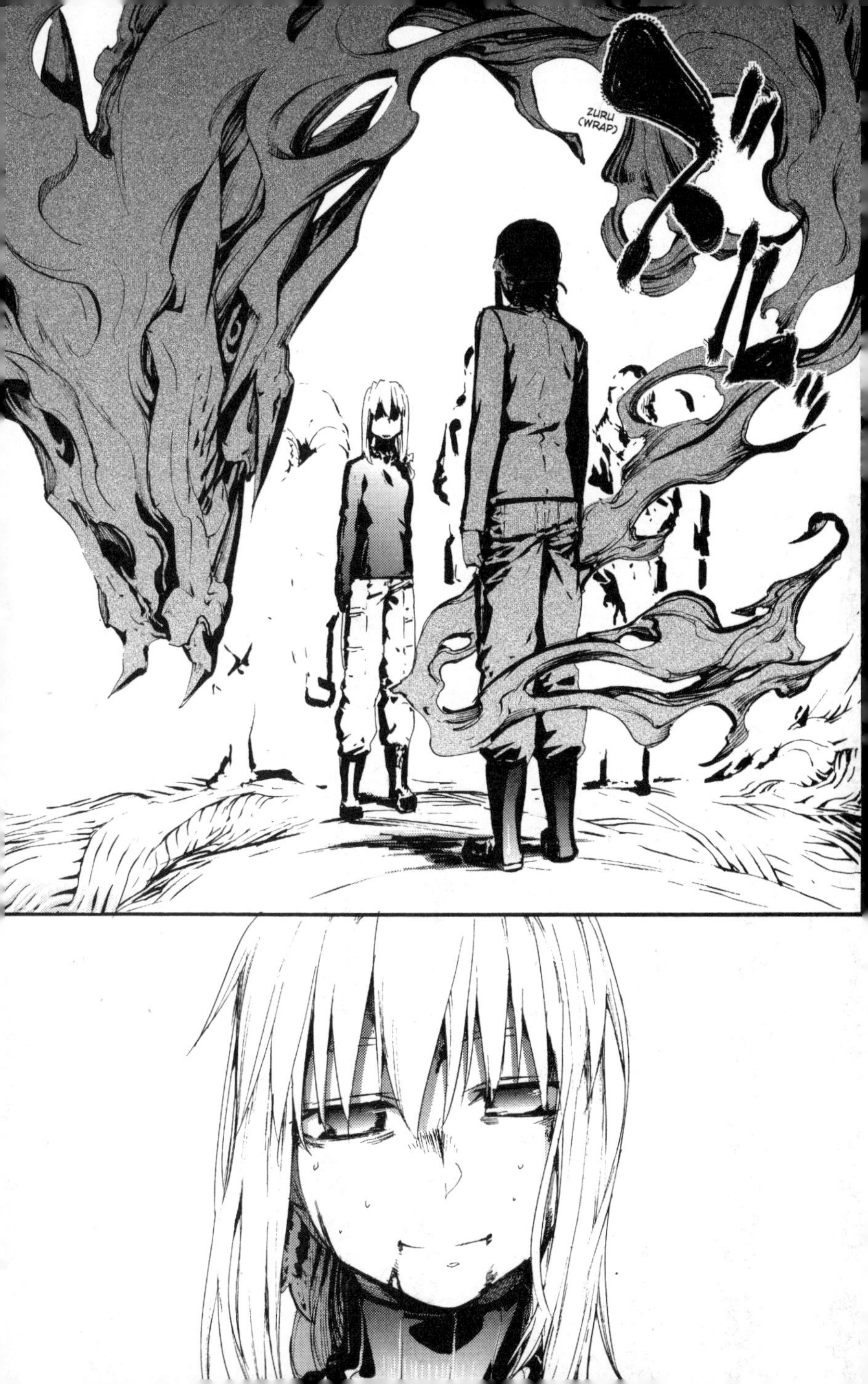
ZURU
(WRAP)

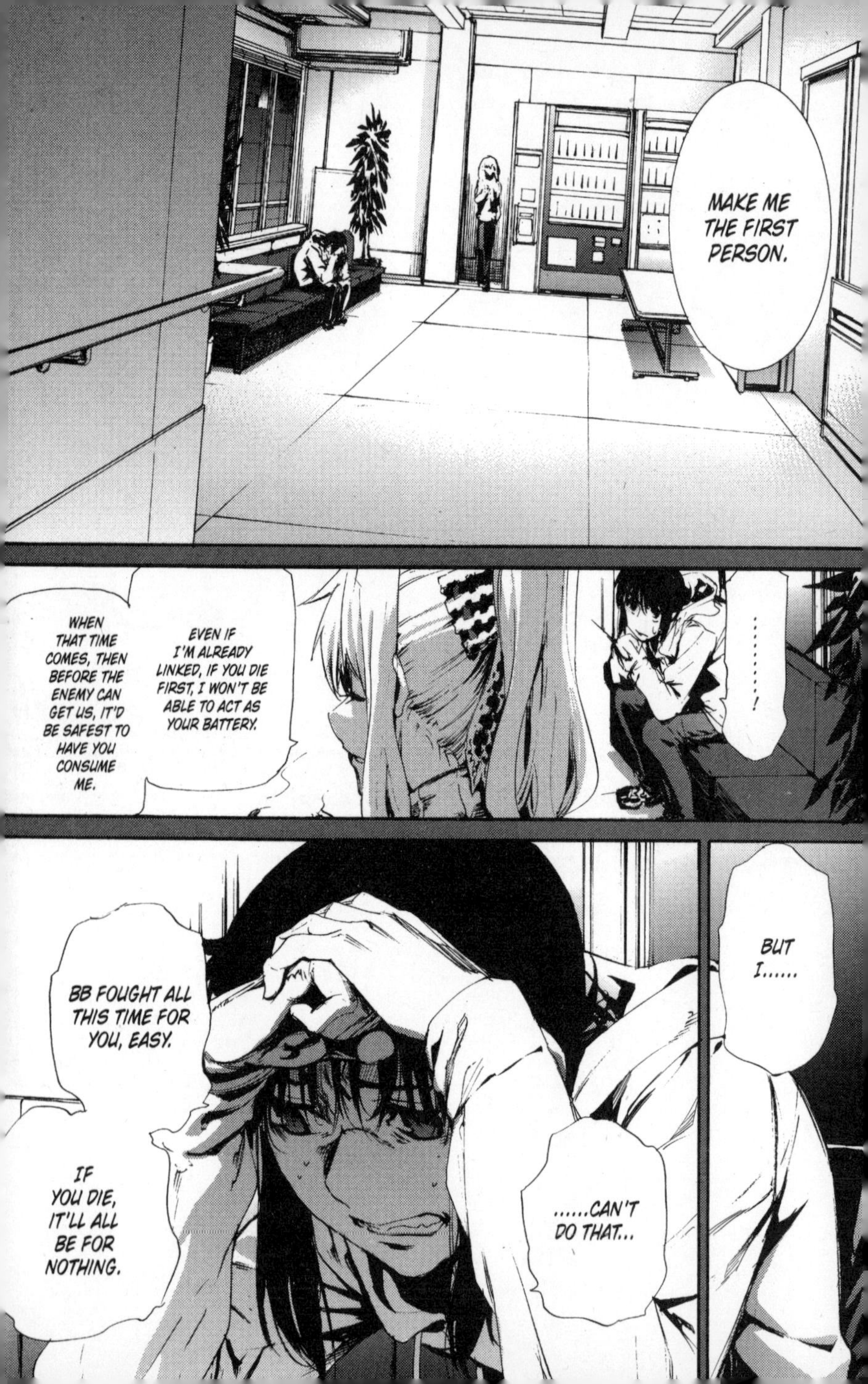
MAKE ME THE FIRST PERSON.
......!
EVEN IF I'M ALREADY LINKED, IF YOU DIE FIRST, I WON'T BE ABLE TO ACT AS YOUR BATTERY.
WHEN THAT TIME COMES, THEN BEFORE THE ENEMY CAN GET US, IT'D BE SAFEST TO HAVE YOU CONSUME ME.
BUT I......
......CAN'T DO THAT...
BB FOUGHT ALL THIS TIME FOR YOU, EASY.
IF YOU DIE, IT'LL ALL BE FOR NOTHING.

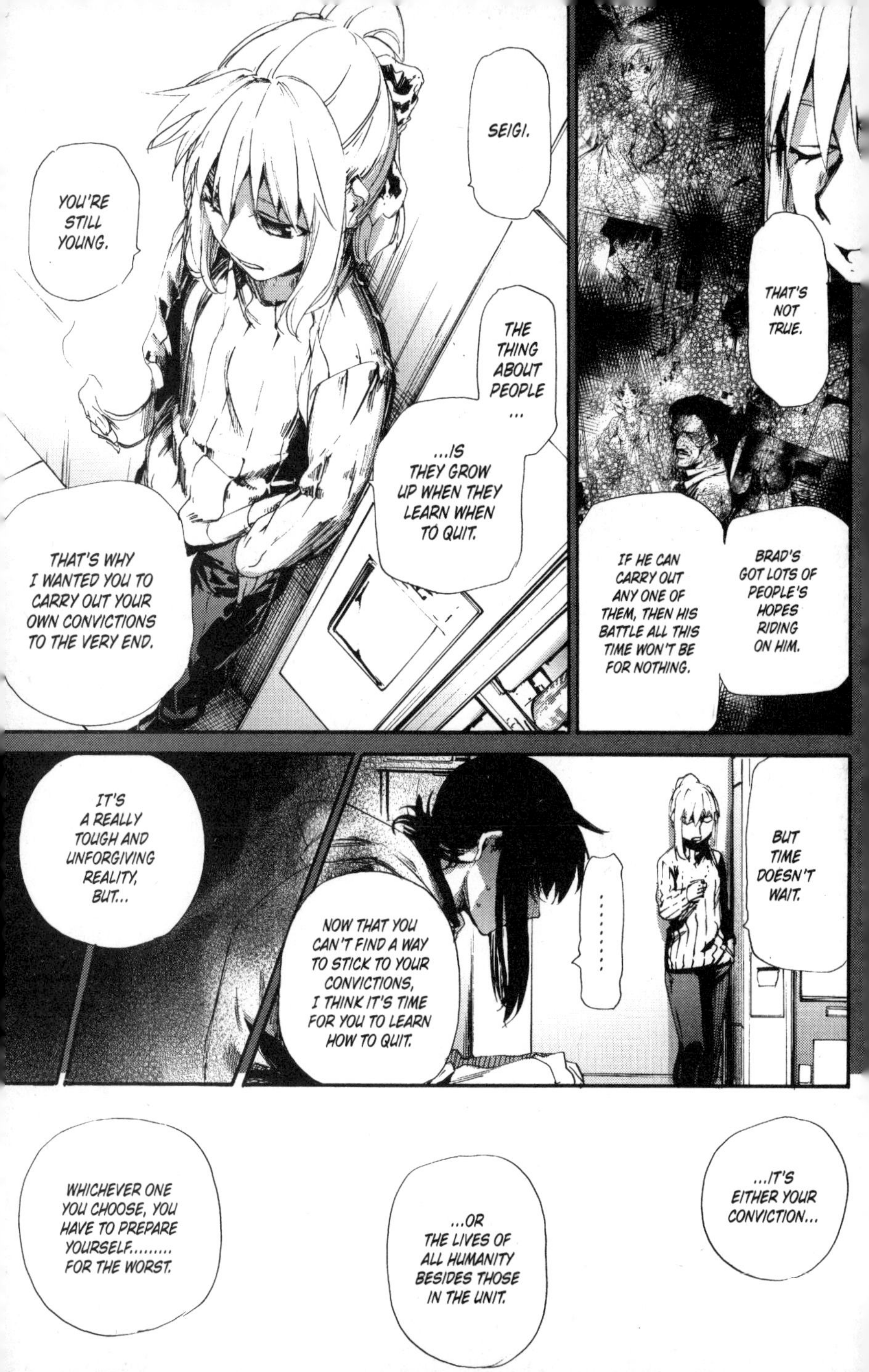
THAT'S NOT TRUE.
BRAD'S GOT LOTS OF PEOPLE'S HOPES RIDING ON HIM.
IF HE CAN CARRY OUT ANY ONE OF THEM, THEN HIS BATTLE ALL THIS TIME WON'T BE FOR NOTHING.
SEIGI.
YOU'RE STILL YOUNG.
THE THING ABOUT PEOPLE...
...IS THEY GROW UP WHEN THEY LEARN WHEN TO QUIT.
THAT'S WHY I WANTED YOU TO CARRY OUT YOUR OWN CONVICTIONS TO THE VERY END.
BUT TIME DOESN'T WAIT.
....
IT'S A REALLY TOUGH AND UNFORGIVING REALITY, BUT...
NOW THAT YOU CAN'T FIND A WAY TO STICK TO YOUR CONVICTIONS, I THINK IT'S TIME FOR YOU TO LEARN HOW TO QUIT.
...IT'S EITHER YOUR CONVICTION...
...OR THE LIVES OF ALL HUMANITY BESIDES THOSE IN THE UNIT.
WHICHEVER ONE YOU CHOOSE, YOU HAVE TO PREPARE YOURSELF........ FOR THE WORST.

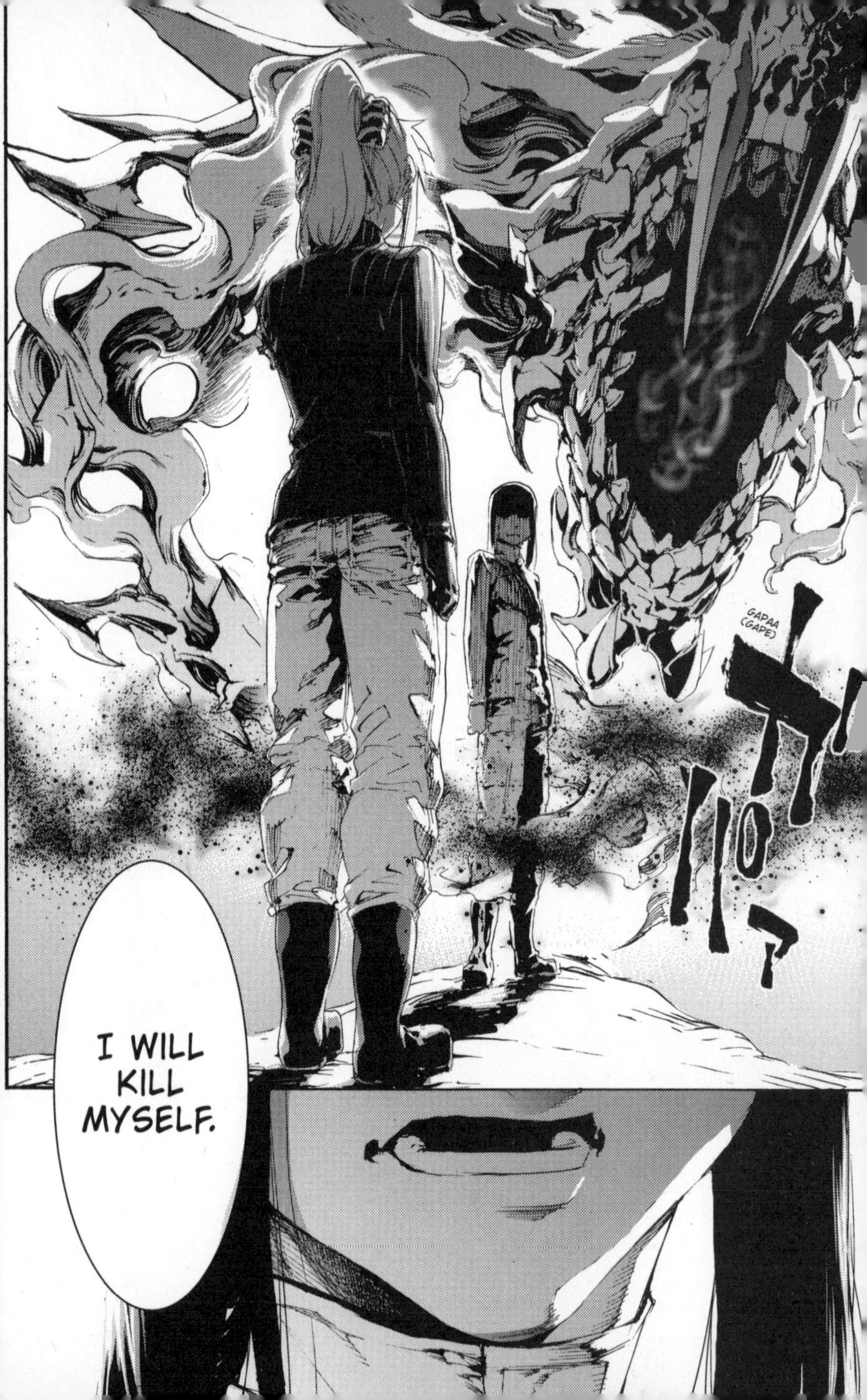
GAPAA (GAPE)
I WILL KILL MYSELF.

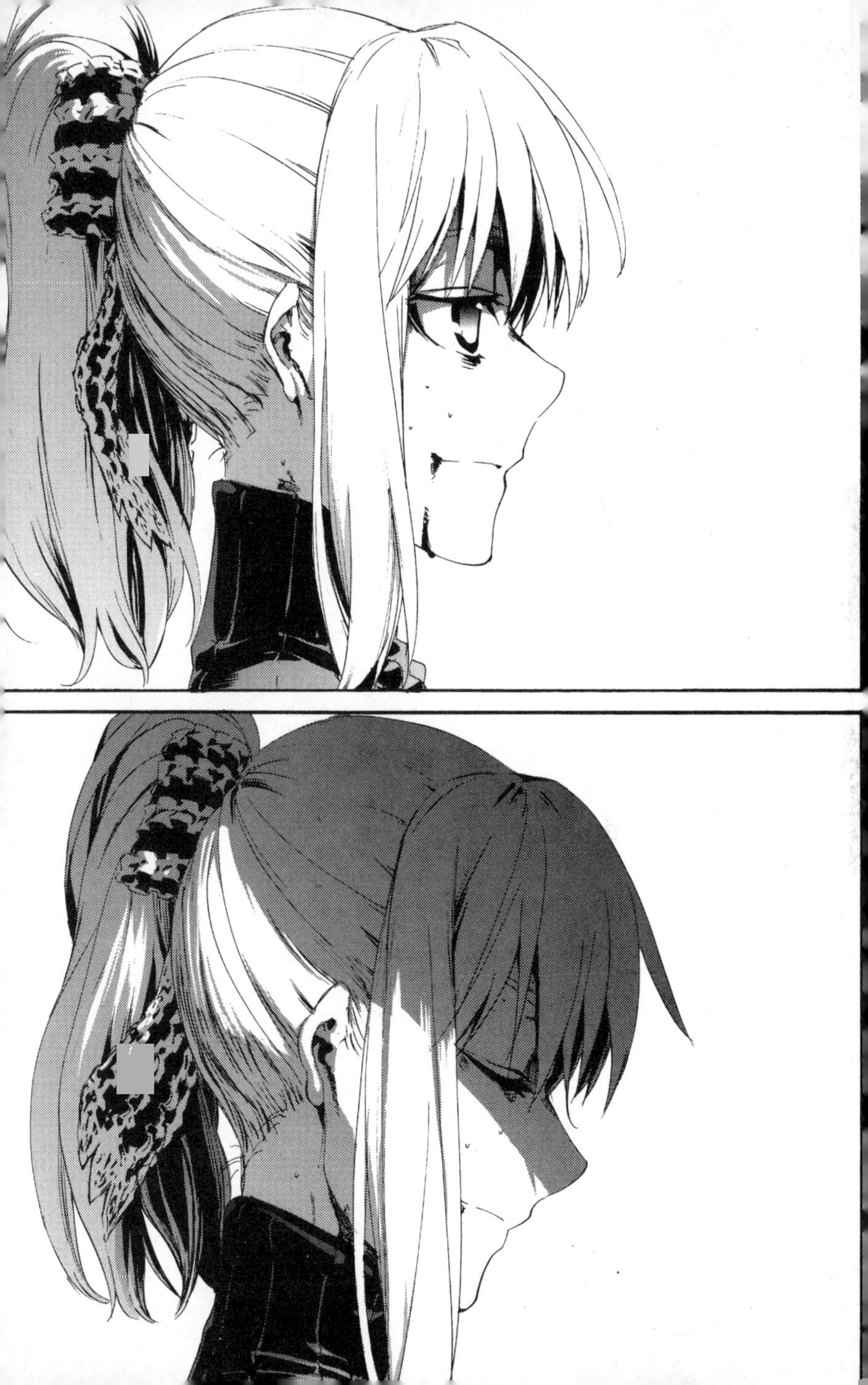

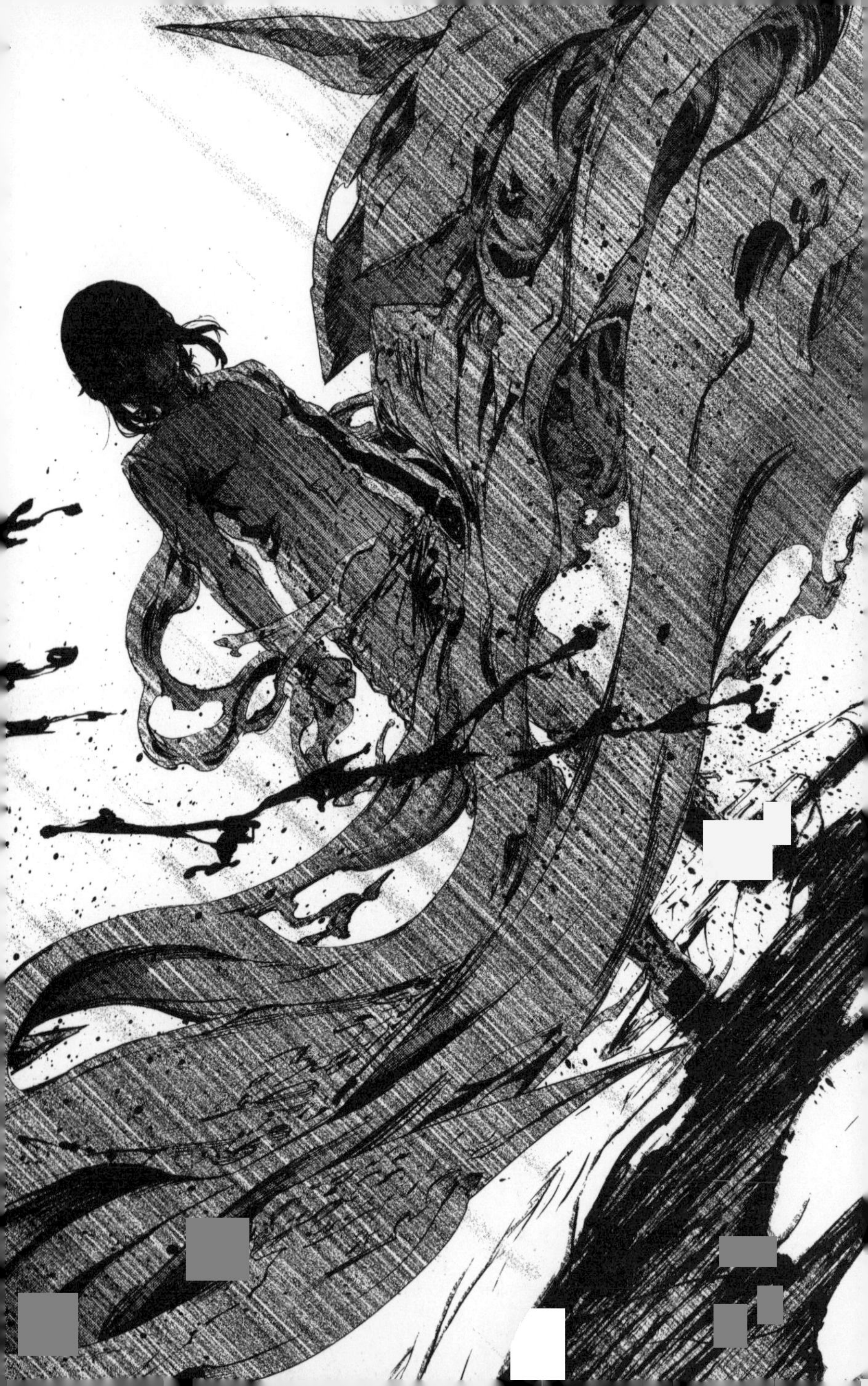

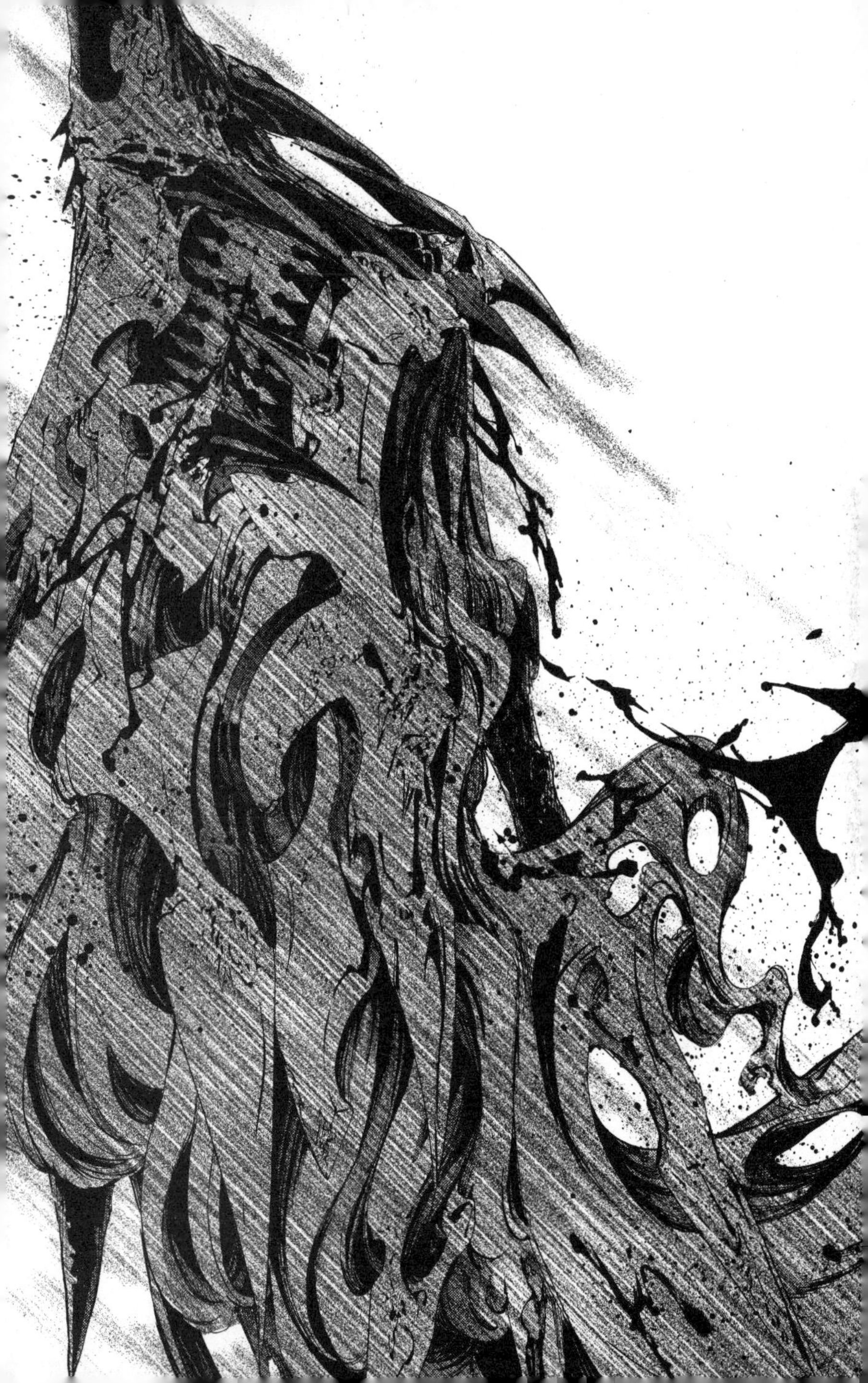

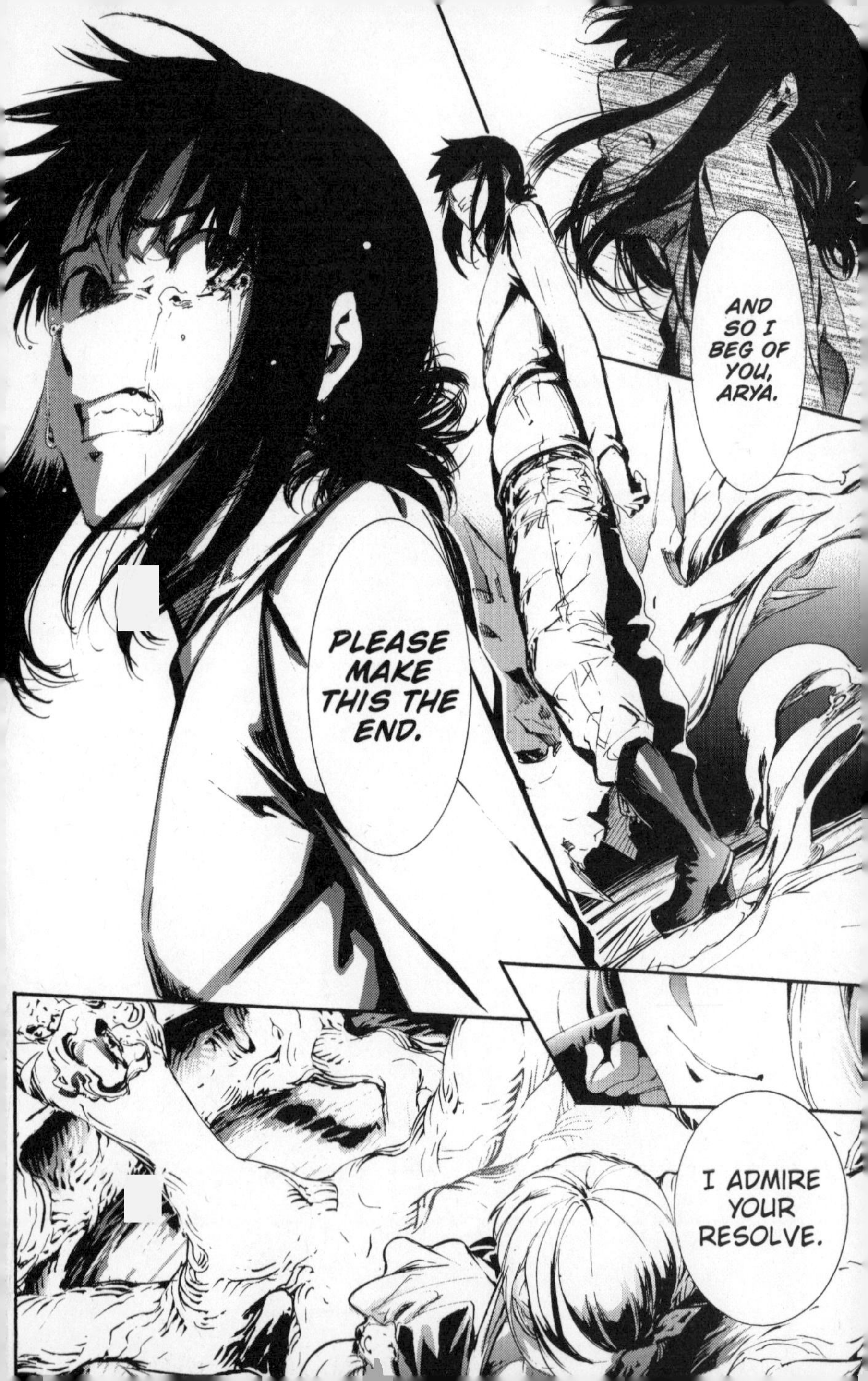
AND SO I BEG OF YOU, ARYA.
PLEASE MAKE THIS THE END.
I ADMIRE YOUR RESOLVE.

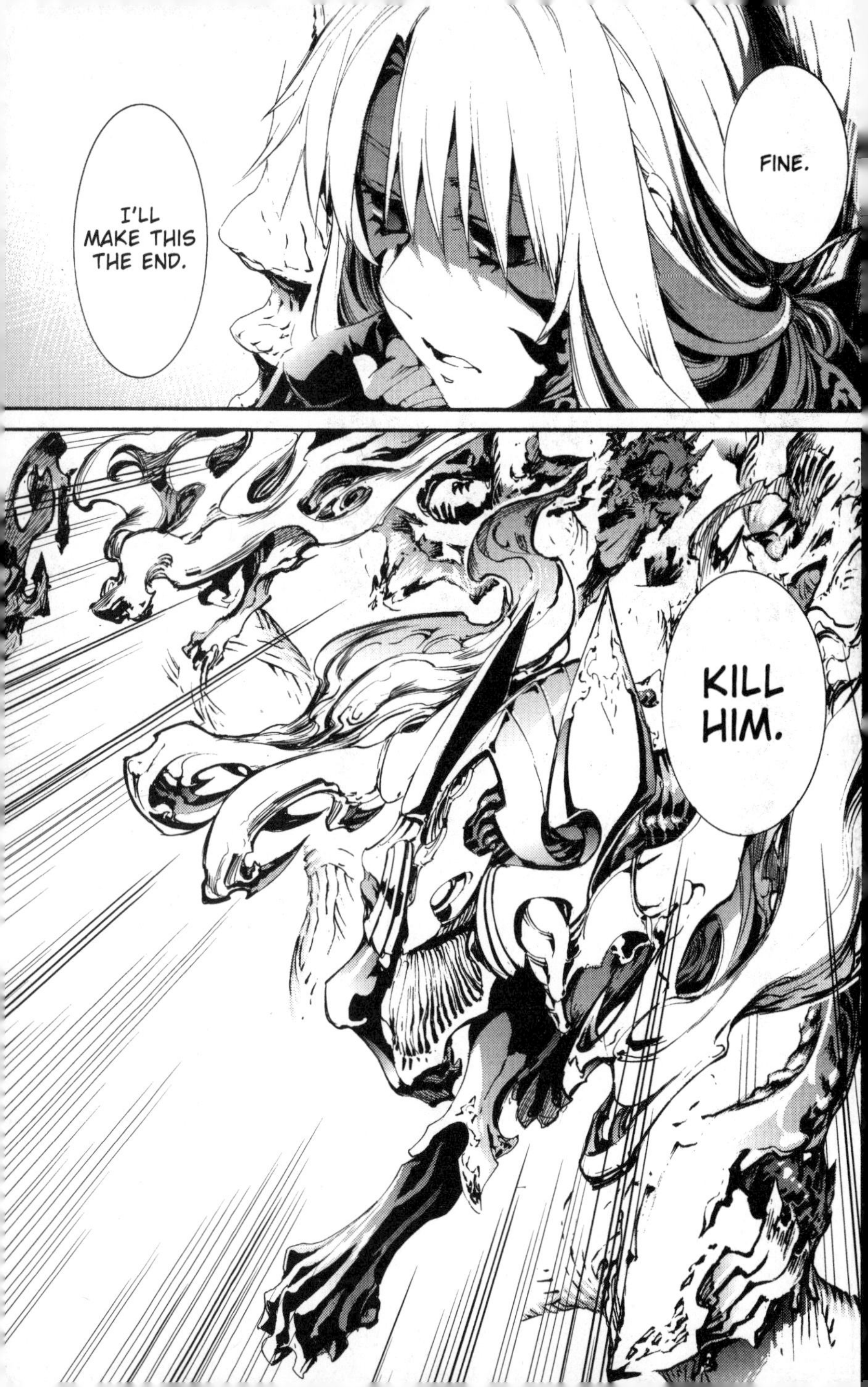
FINE.
I'LL MAKE THIS THE END.
KILL HIM.

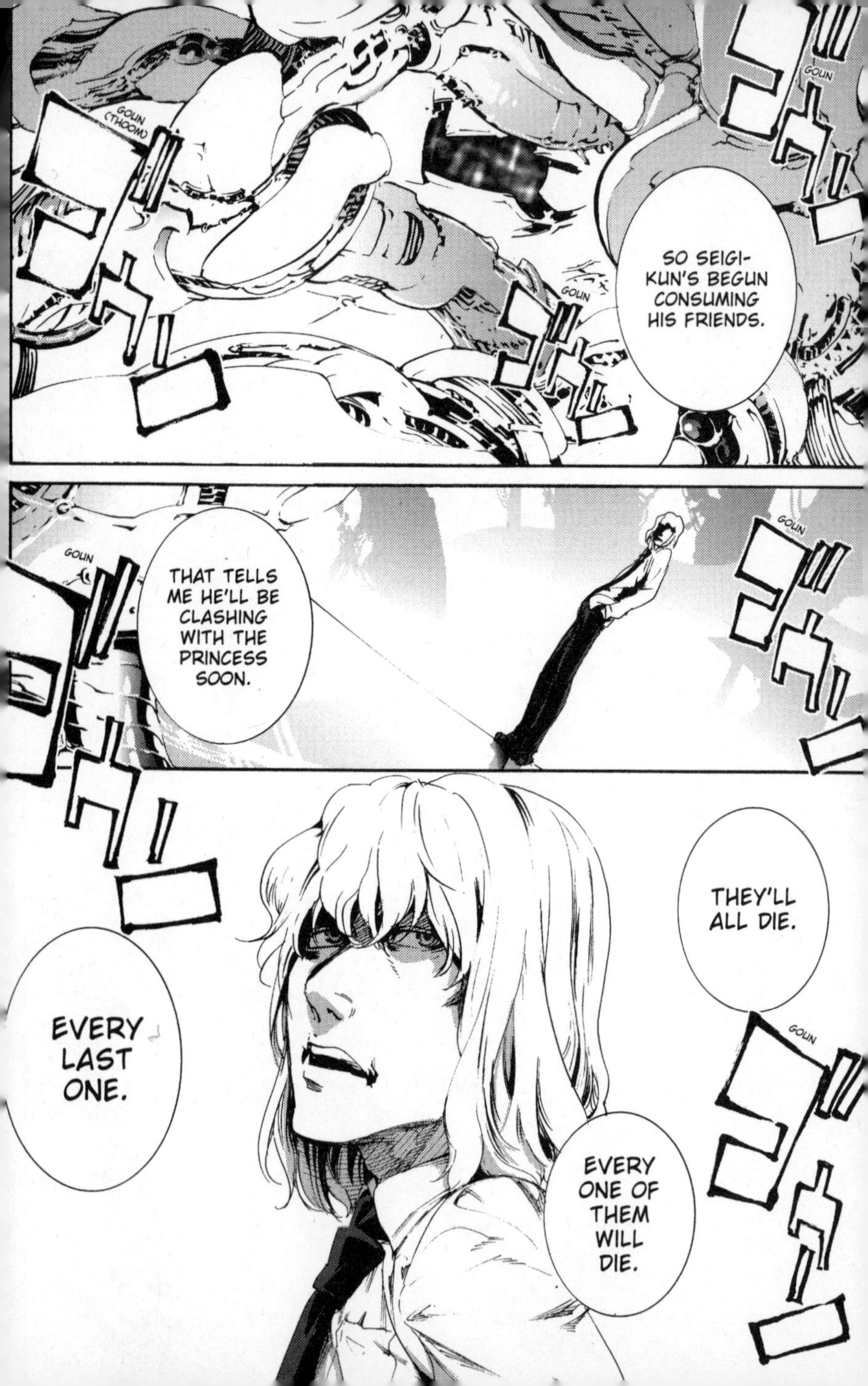
GOUN
SO SEIGI-KUN'S BEGUN CONSUMING HIS FRIENDS.
GOUN
GOUN (THOOM)
GOUN
THAT TELLS ME HE'LL BE CLASHING WITH THE PRINCESS SOON.
GOUN
THEY'LL ALL DIE.
GOUN
EVERY ONE OF THEM WILL DIE.
EVERY LAST ONE.

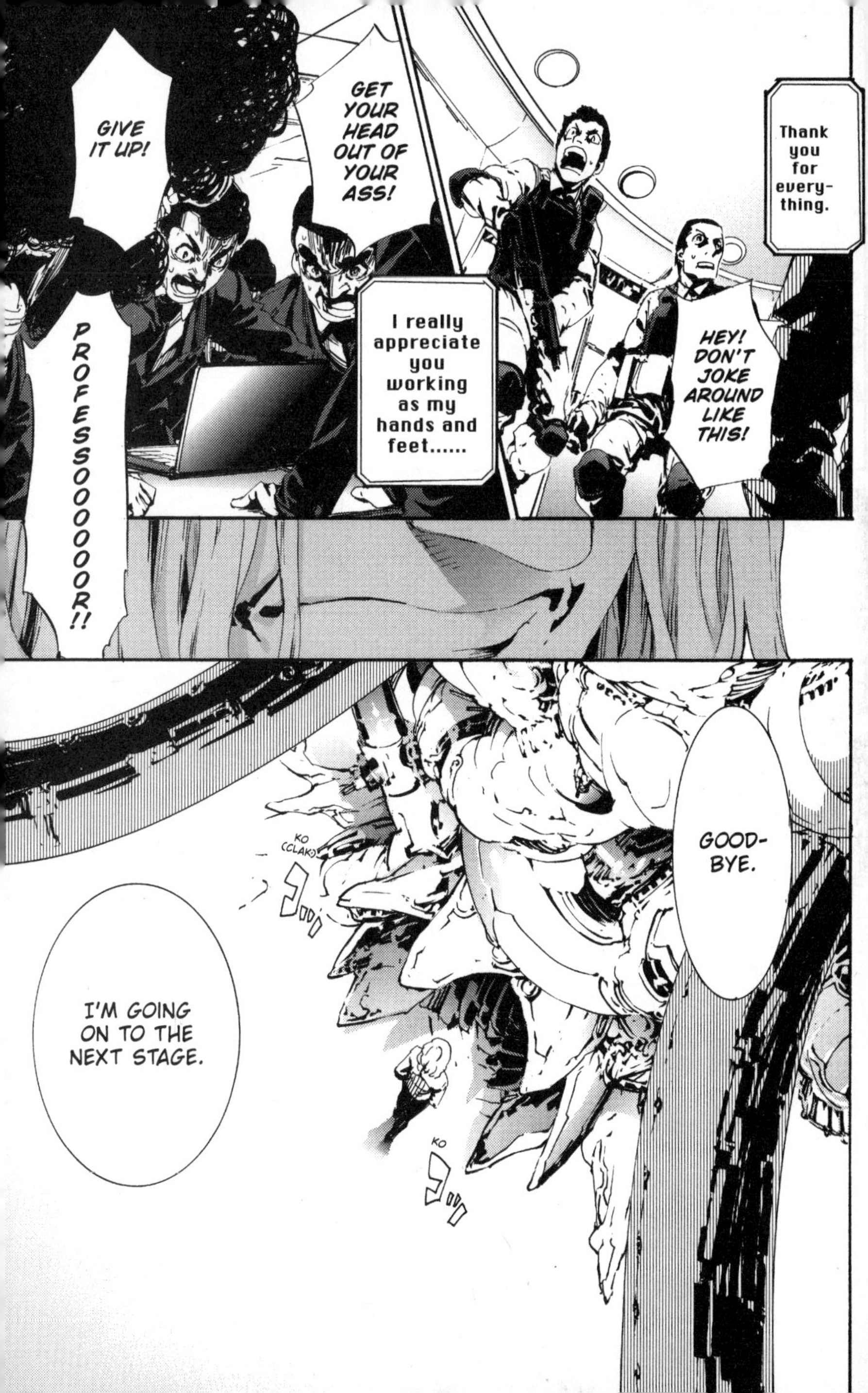
Thank you for every-thing.
HEY! DON'T JOKE AROUND LIKE THIS!
I really appreciate you working as my hands and feet......
GET YOUR HEAD OUT OF YOUR ASS!
GIVE IT UP!
PROFESSOOOOOOOR!!
GOOD-BYE.
KO (CLAK)
I'M GOING ON TO THE NEXT STAGE.
KO

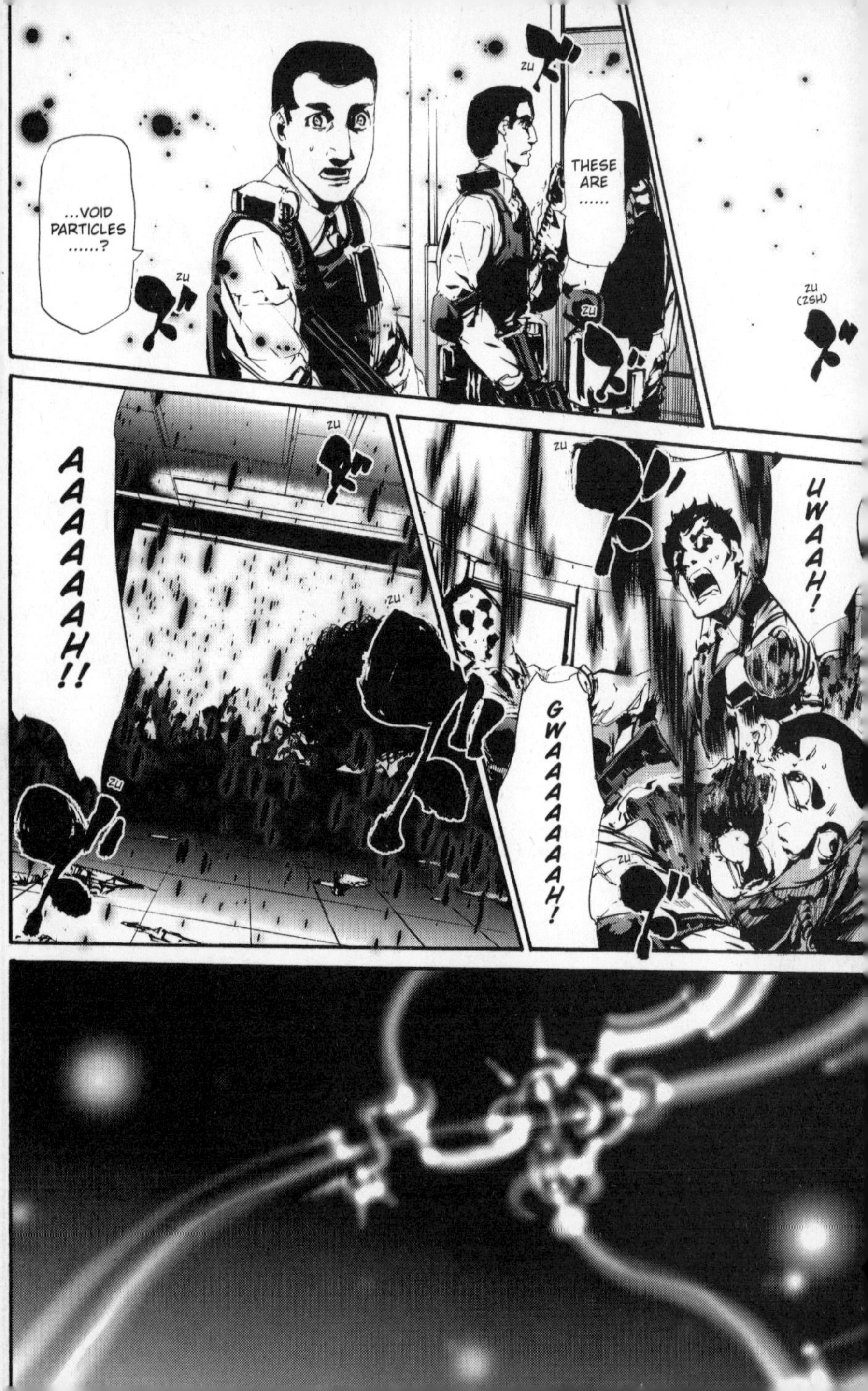
ZU
(ZSH)
ZU
THESE ARE ......
ZU
ZU
...VOID PARTICLES ......?
ZU
ZU
UWAAAH!
GWAAAAAAAAH!
ZU
ZU
AAAAAAAH!!
ZU
ZU

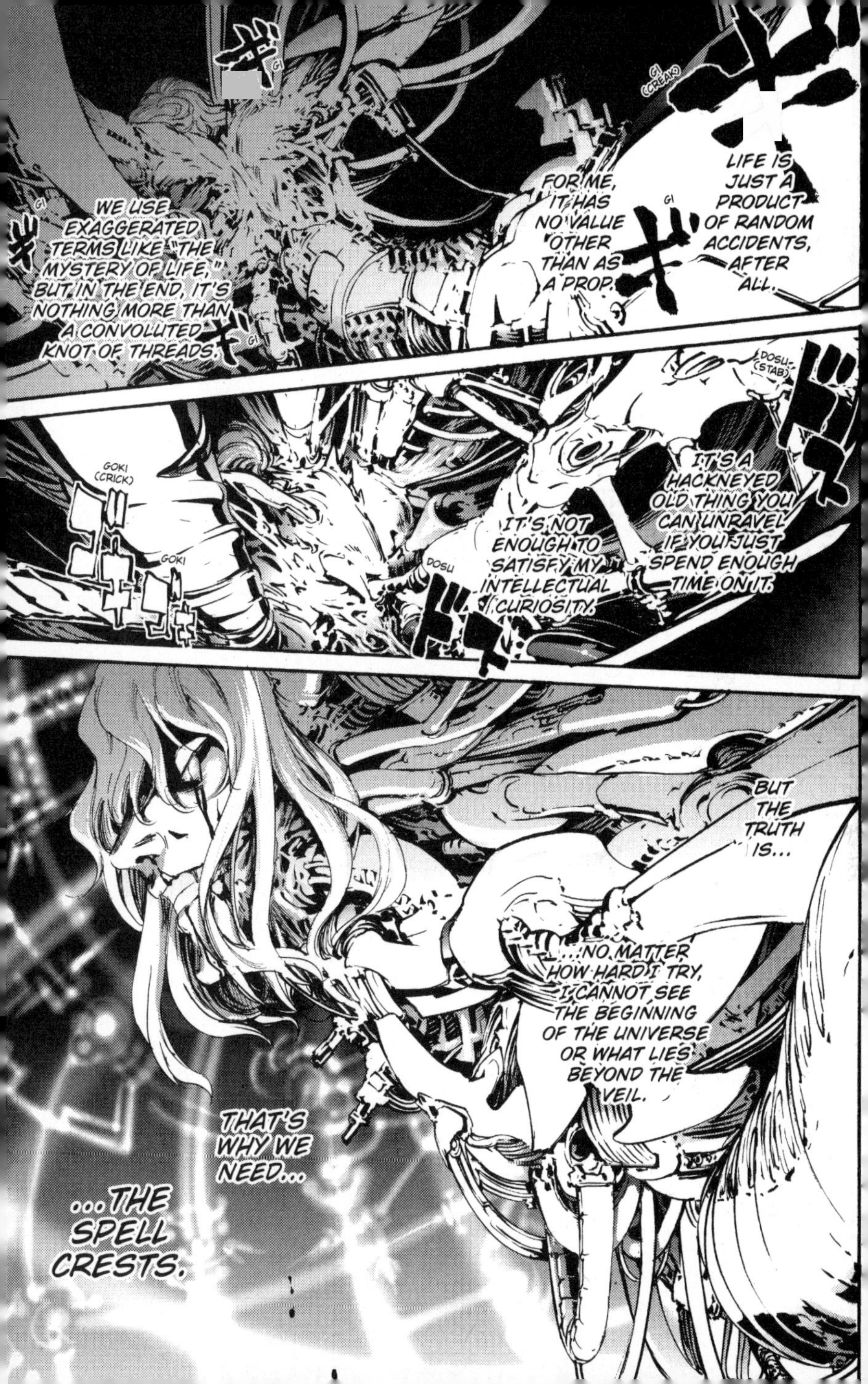
GI (CREAK)
LIFE IS JUST A PRODUCT OF RANDOM ACCIDENTS, AFTER ALL.
GI
FOR ME, IT HAS NO VALUE OTHER THAN AS A PROP.
GI
GI
WE USE EXAGGERATED TERMS LIKE "THE MYSTERY OF LIFE," BUT IN THE END, IT'S NOTHING MORE THAN A CONVOLUTED KNOT OF THREADS.
GI
DOSU (STAB)
IT'S A HACKNEYED OLD THING YOU CAN UNRAVEL IF YOU JUST SPEND ENOUGH TIME ON IT.
IT'S NOT ENOUGH TO SATISFY MY INTELLECTUAL CURIOSITY.
DOSU
GOKI (CRICK)
GOKI
BUT THE TRUTH IS...
...NO MATTER HOW HARD I TRY, I CANNOT SEE THE BEGINNING OF THE UNIVERSE OR WHAT LIES BEYOND THE VEIL.
THAT'S WHY WE NEED...
...THE SPELL CRESTS.

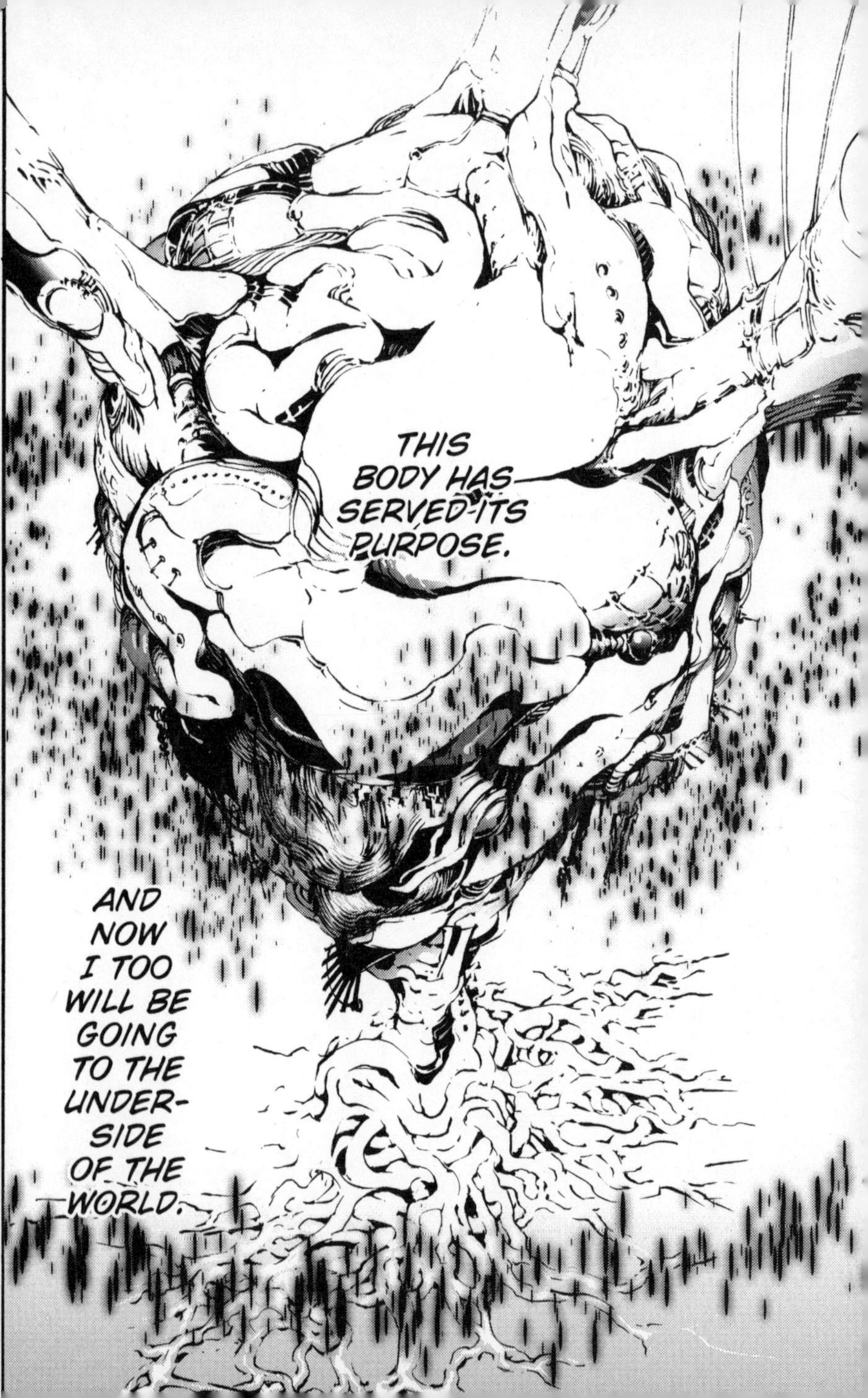

THIS BODY HAS SERVED ITS PURPOSE.
AND NOW I TOO WILL BE GOING TO THE UNDER-SIDE OF THE WORLD.

TABOO TATTOO

TABOO TATTOO

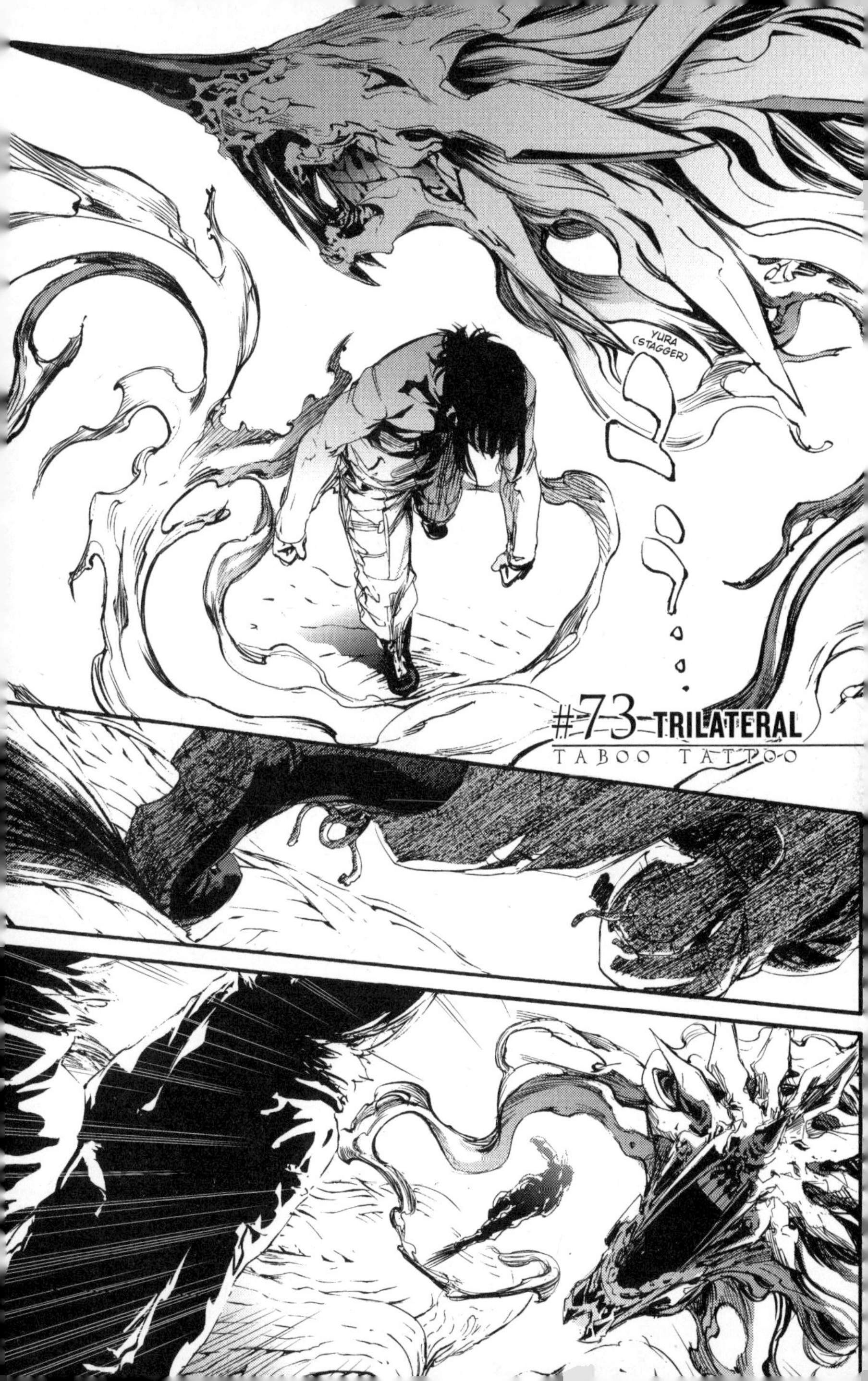
YURA
(STAGGER)
#73 TRILATERAL
TABOO TATTOO

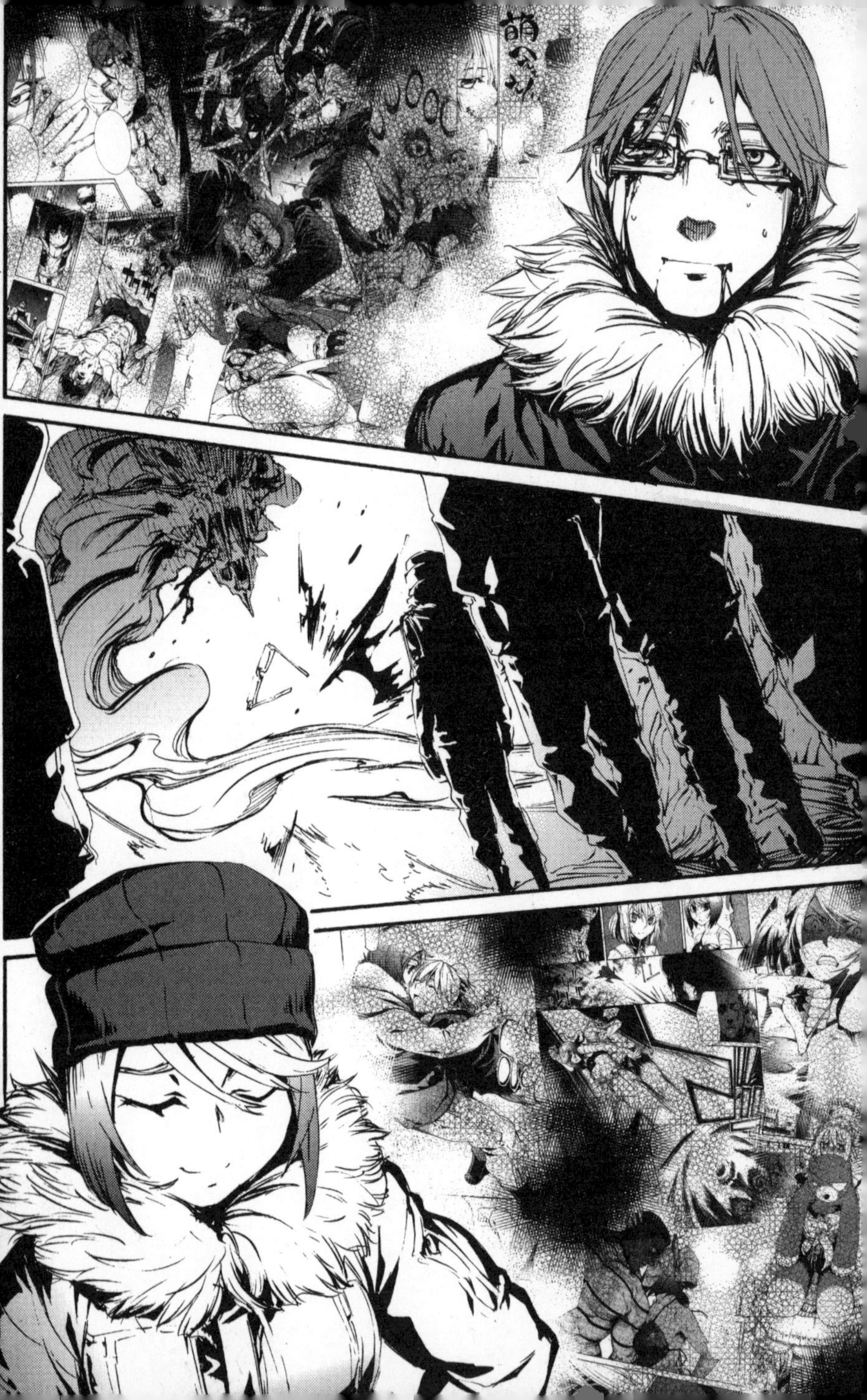

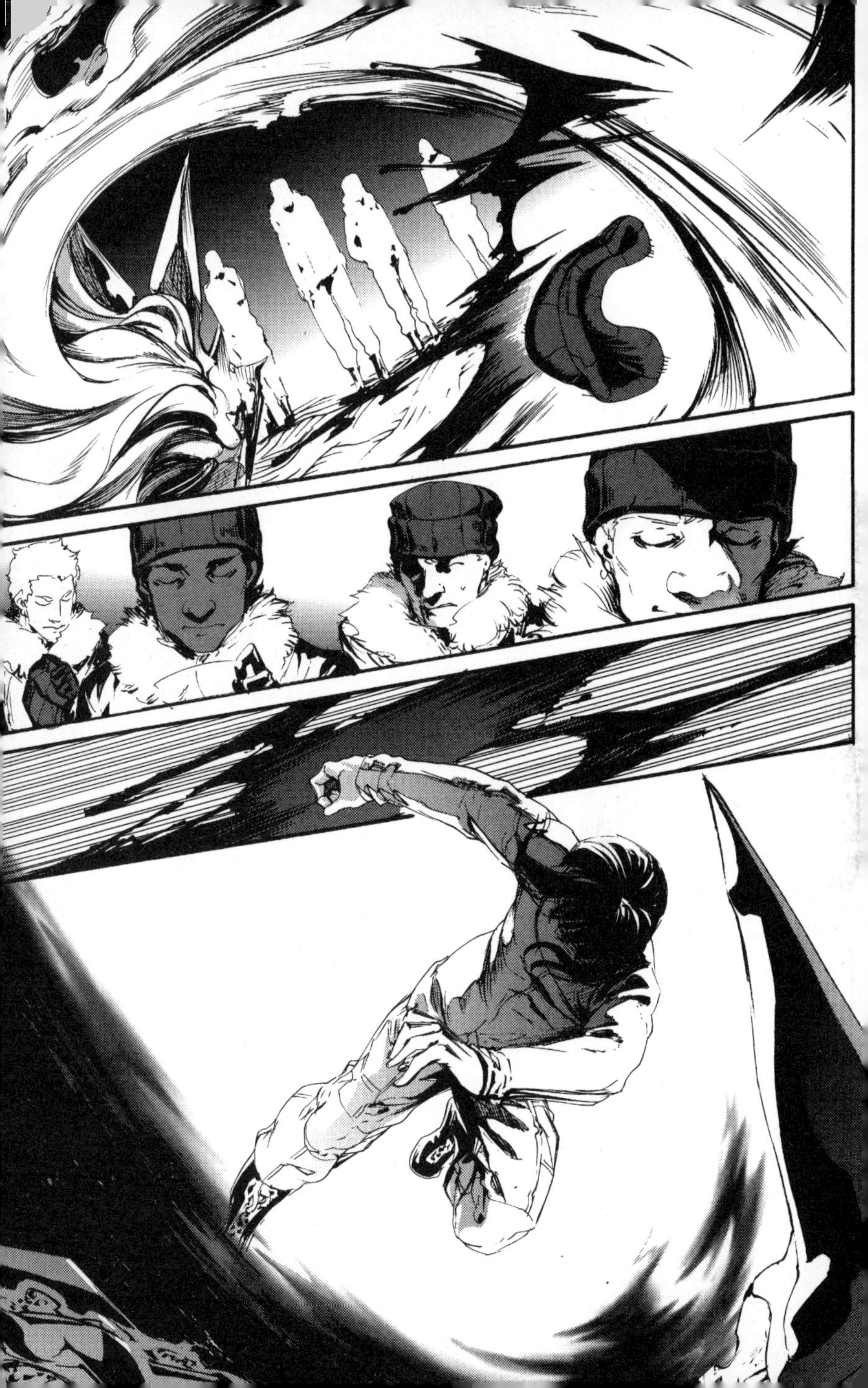

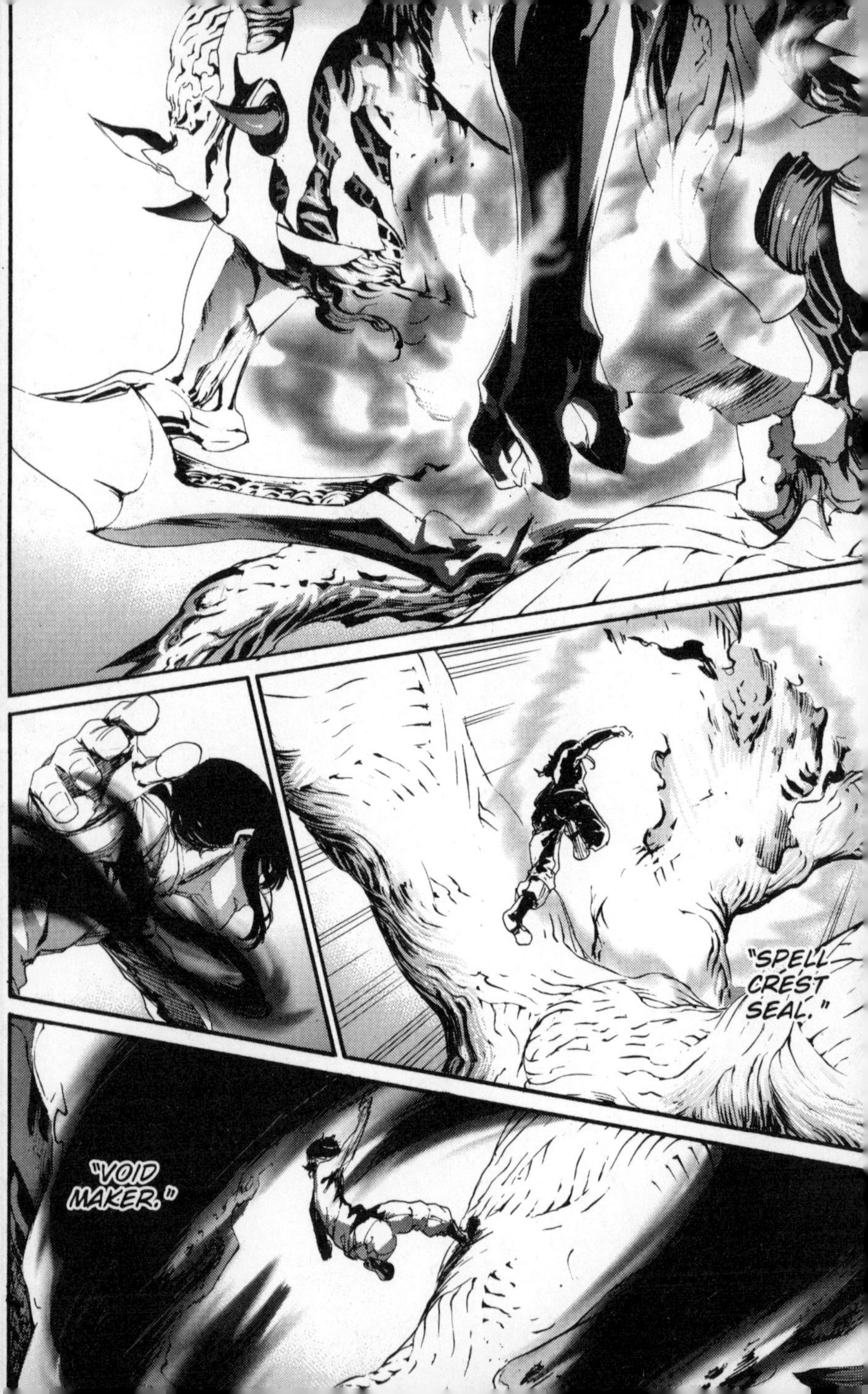
"SPELL CREST SEAL."
"VOID MAKER."

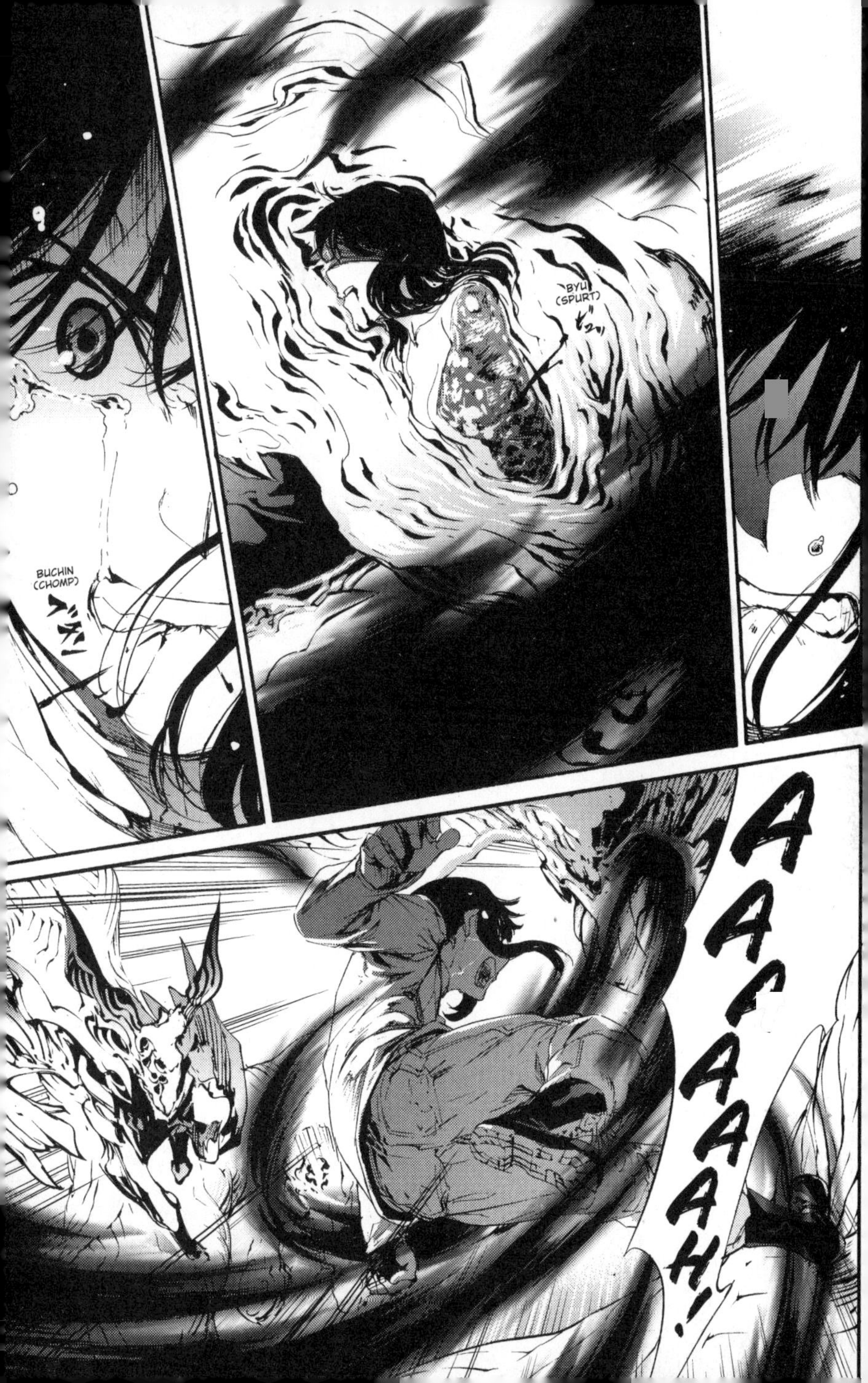

BYU (SPURT)
BUCHIN (CHOMP)
AAAAAAAH!

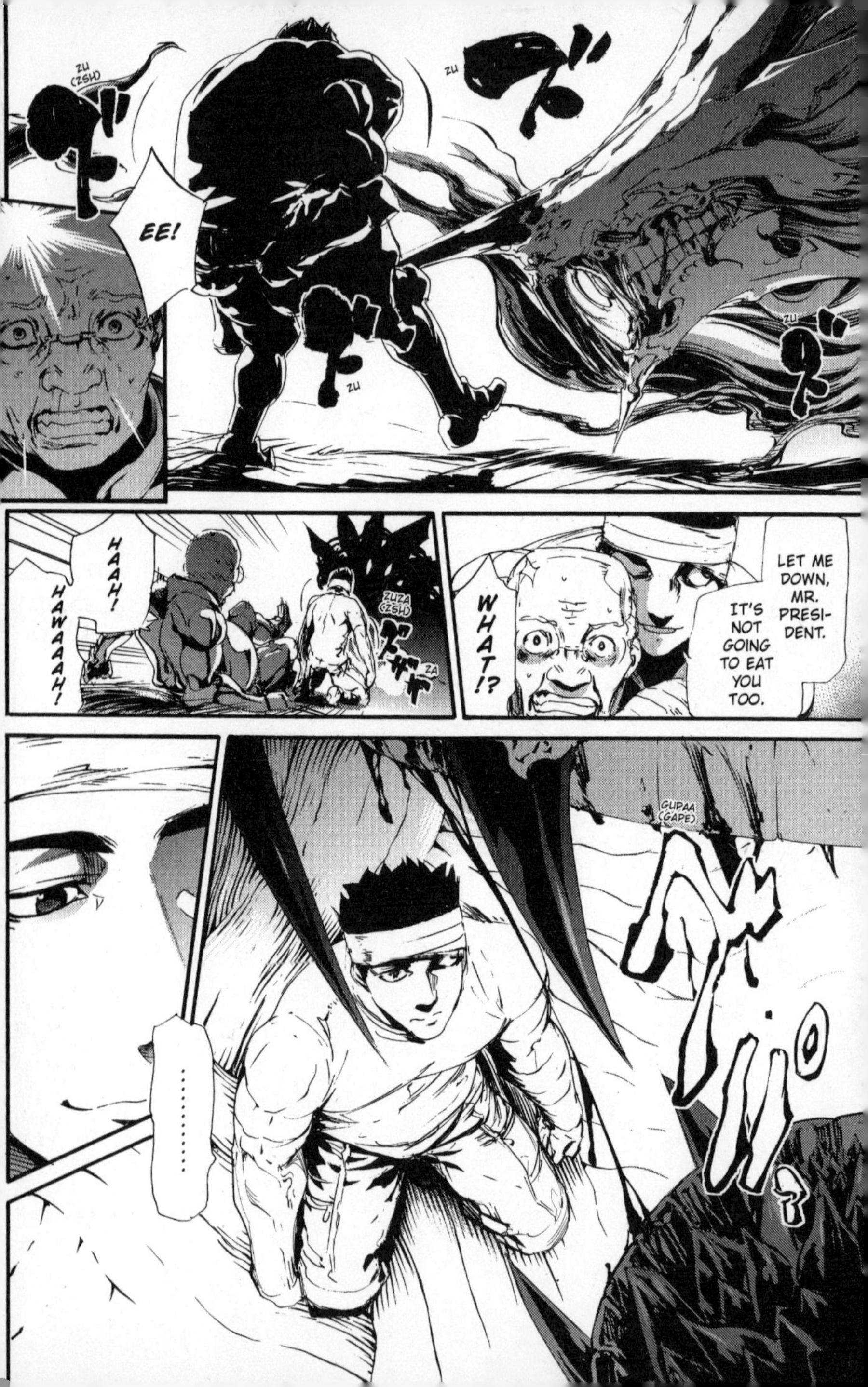
ZU
ZU
ZU
ZU (ZSH)
EE!
LET ME DOWN, MR. PRESIDENT.
IT'S NOT GOING TO EAT YOU TOO.
WHAT!?
ZUZA (ZSH)
ZA
HAAAH! HAWAAAAH!
GUPAA (GAPE)
....

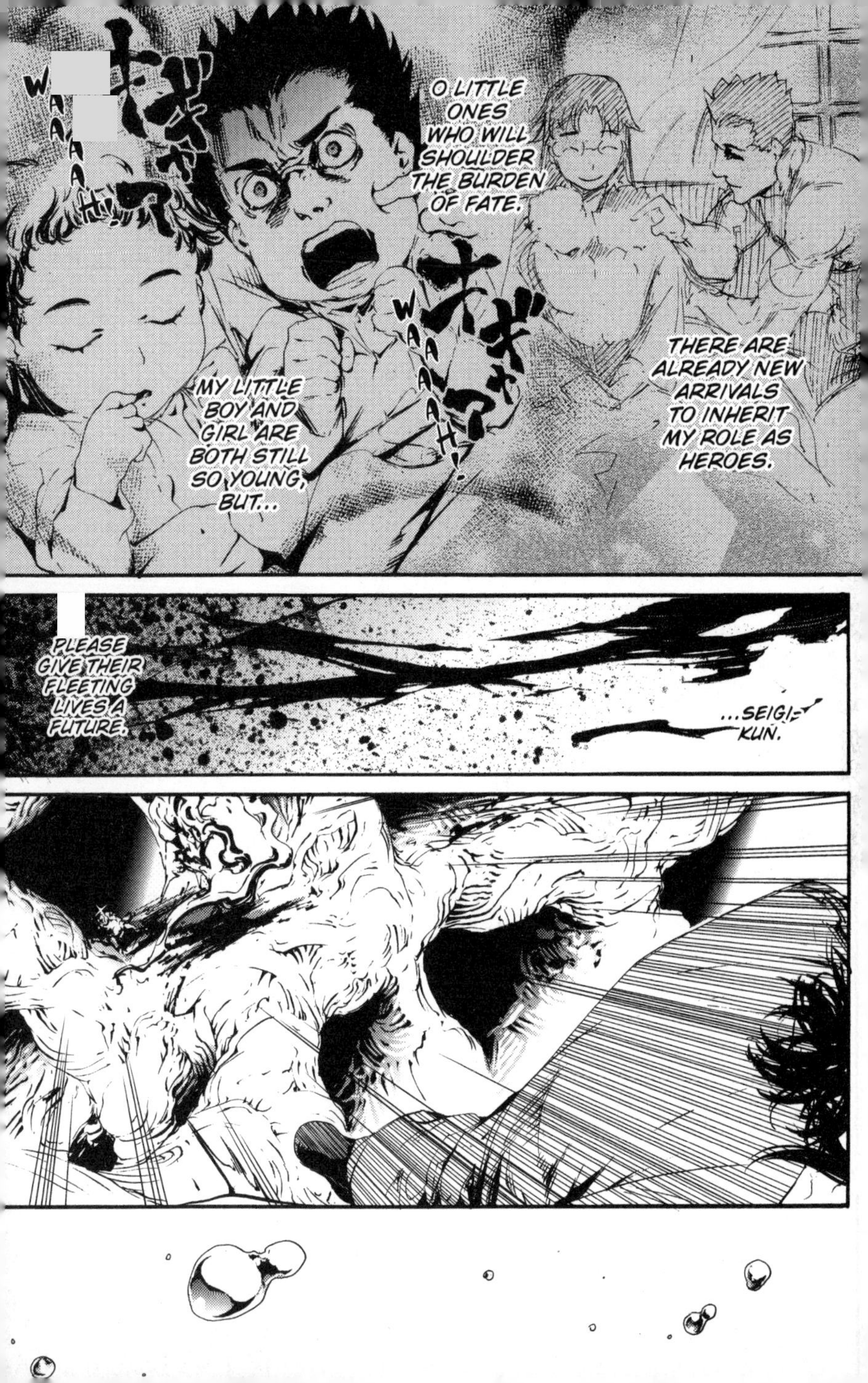
THERE ARE ALREADY NEW ARRIVALS TO INHERIT MY ROLE AS HEROES.
O LITTLE ONES WHO WILL SHOULDER THE BURDEN OF FATE.
WAAAAH!
MY LITTLE BOY AND GIRL ARE BOTH STILL SO YOUNG, BUT...
WAAAAH!
...SEIGI-KUN.
PLEASE GIVE THEIR FLEETING LIVES A FUTURE.

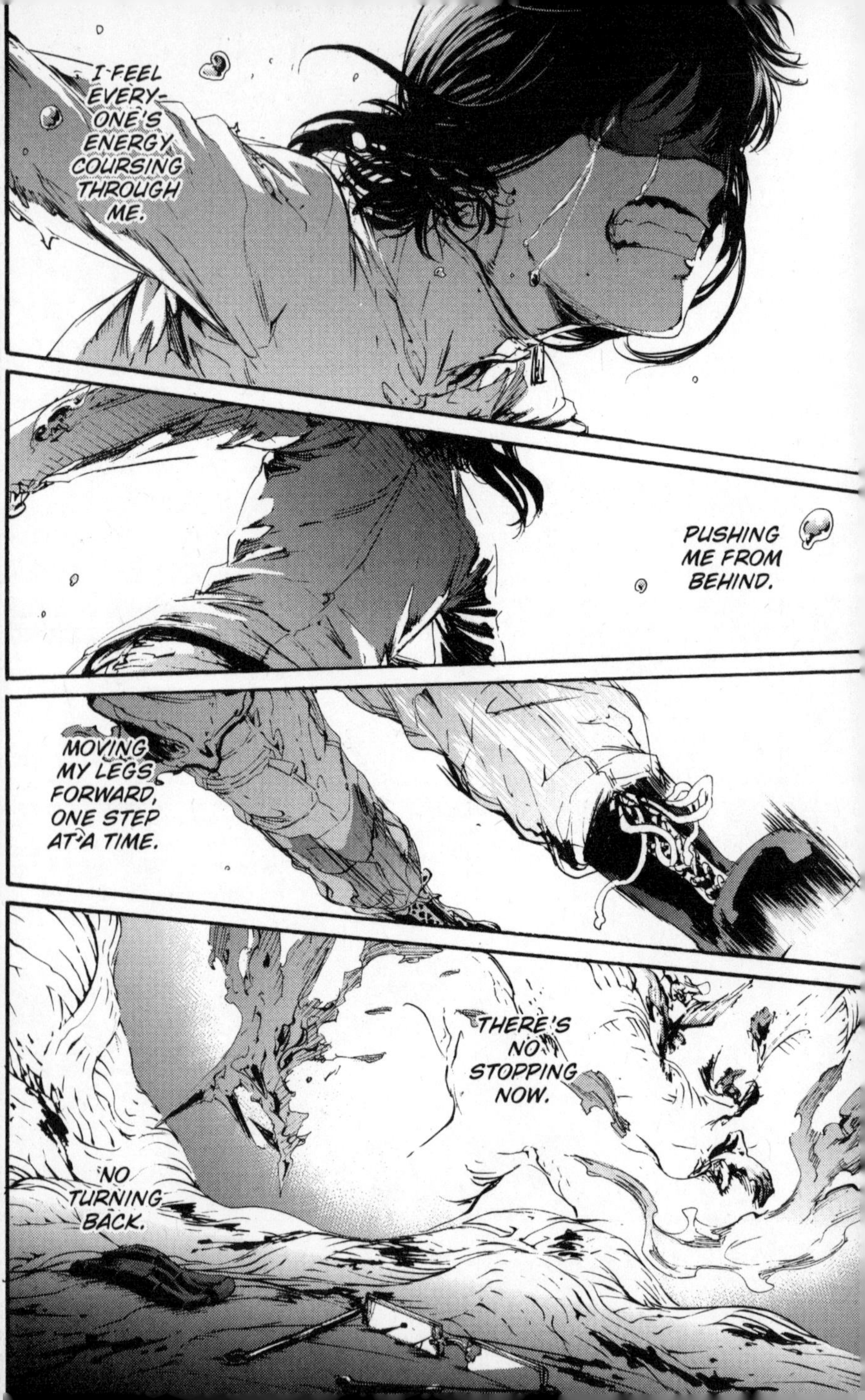
I FEEL EVERY-ONE'S ENERGY COURSING THROUGH ME.
PUSHING ME FROM BEHIND.
MOVING MY LEGS FORWARD, ONE STEP AT A TIME.
THERE'S NO STOPPING NOW.
NO TURNING BACK.

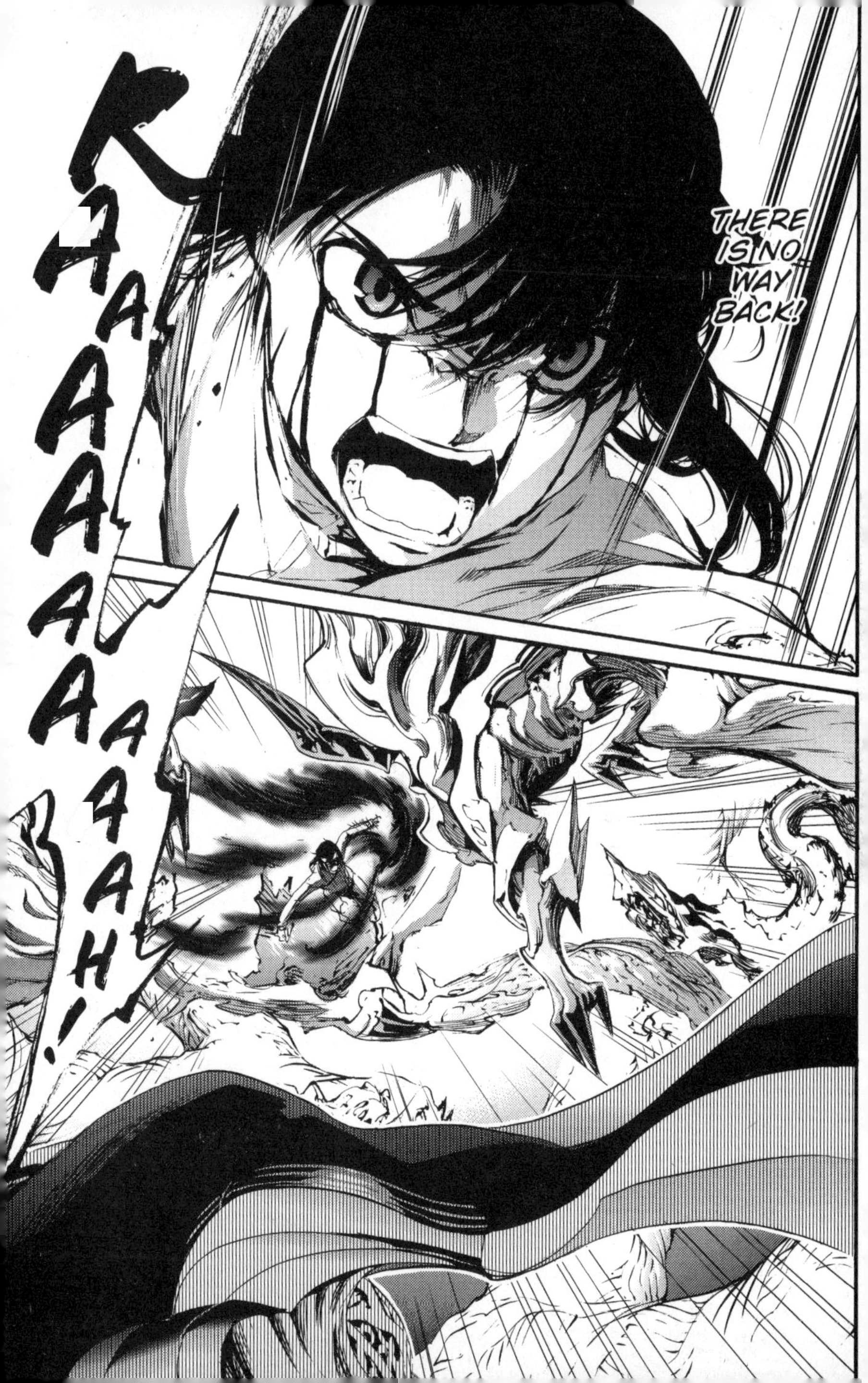
THERE IS NO WAY BACK!
KAAAAAAAAAAH!

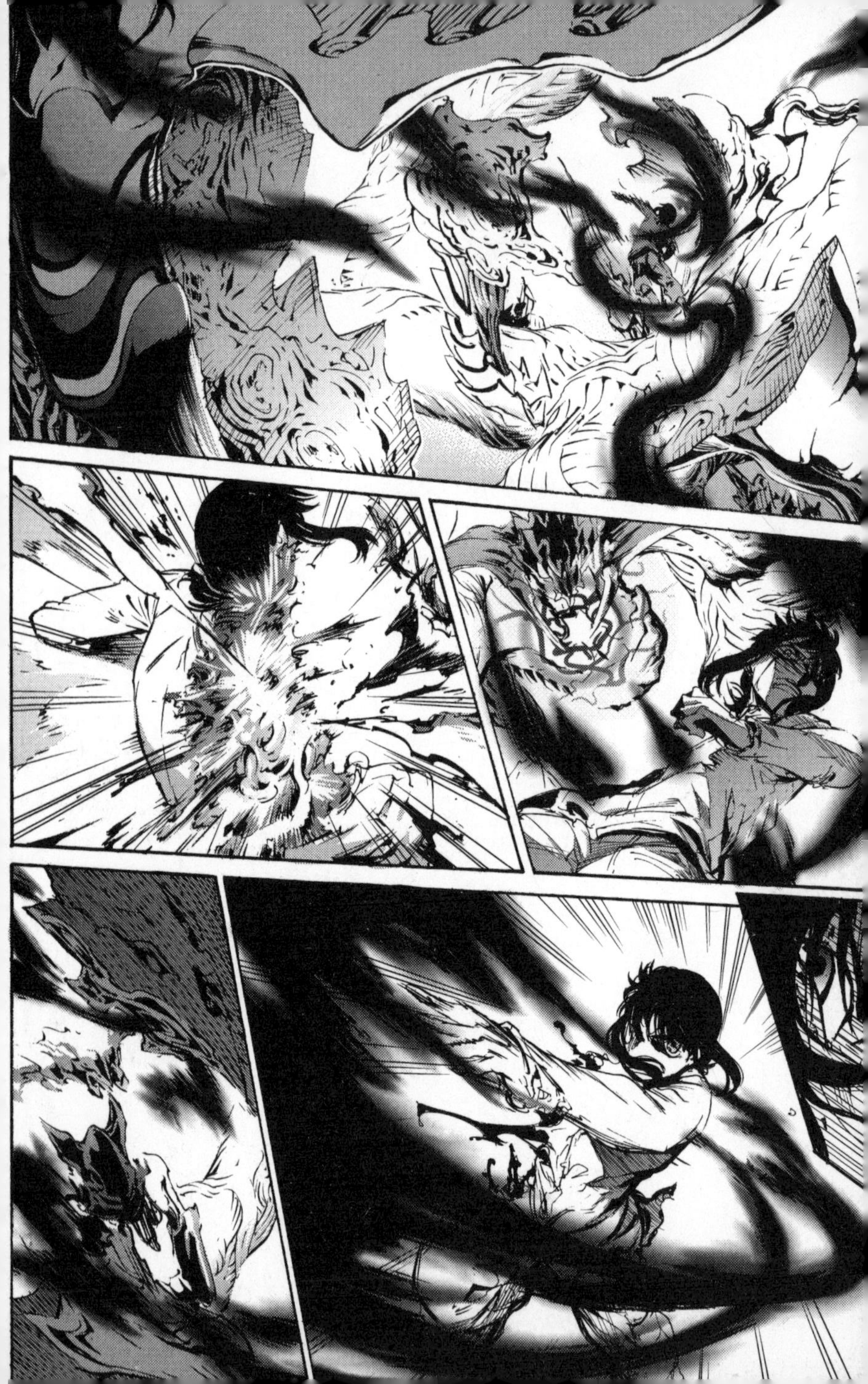

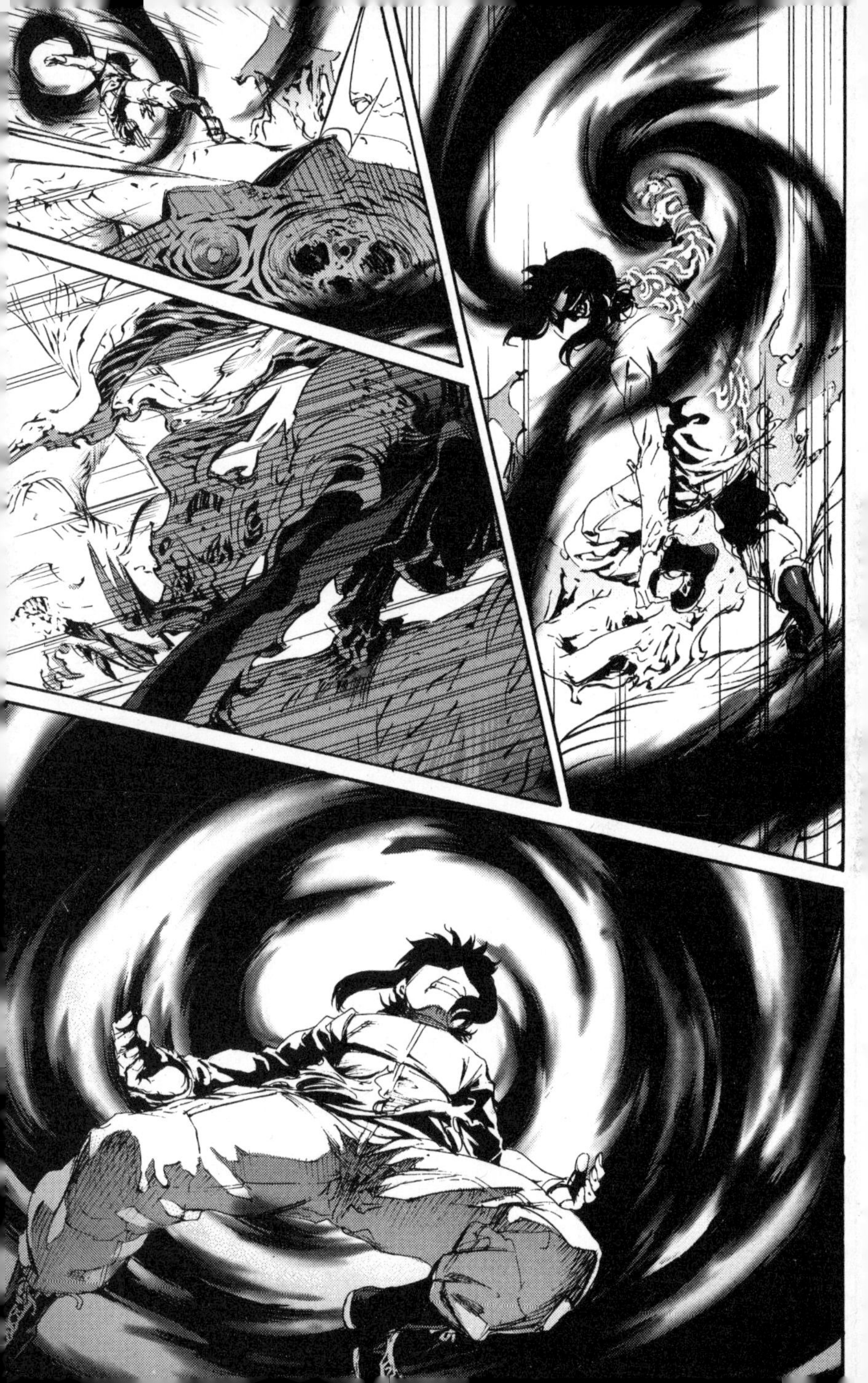

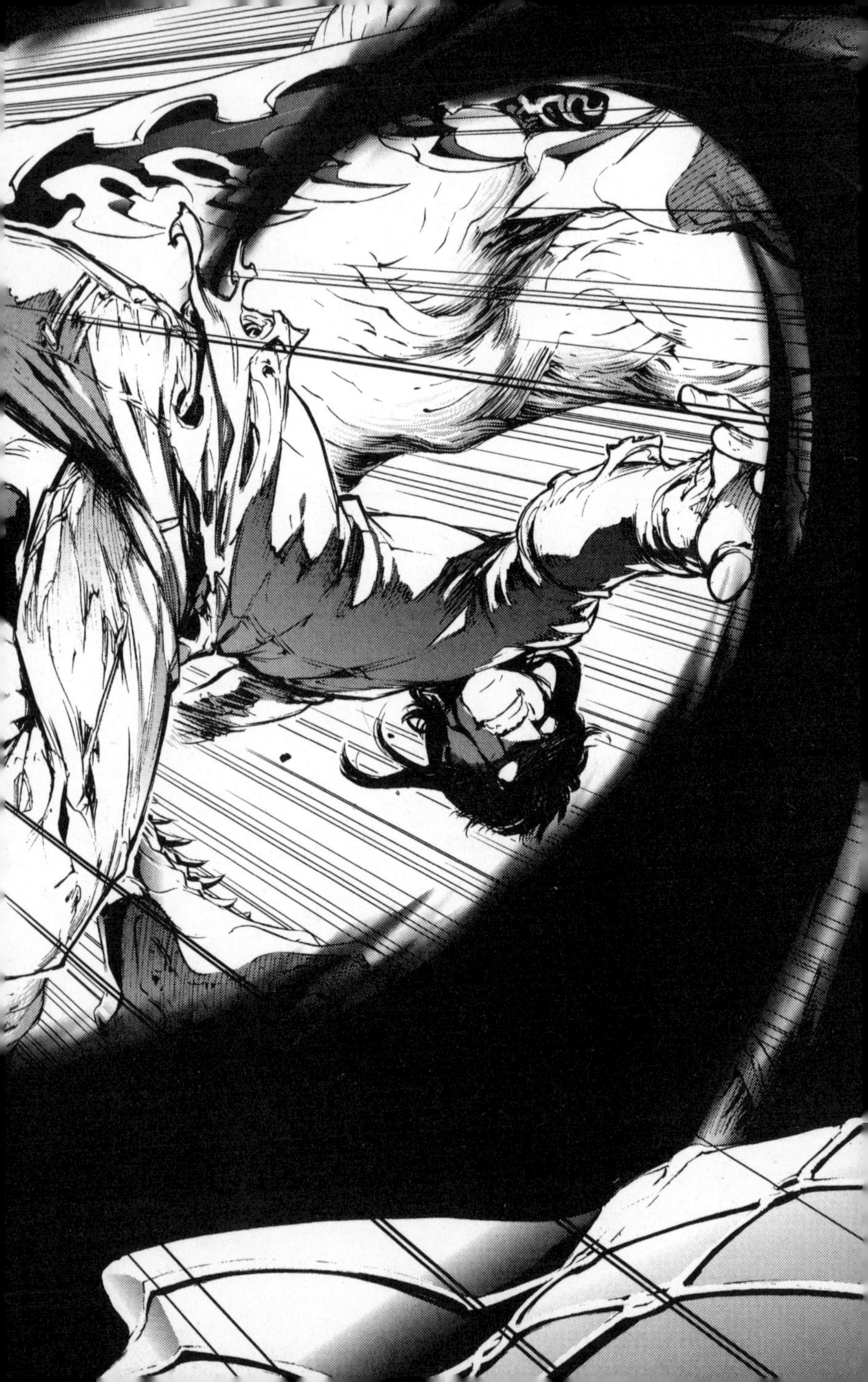

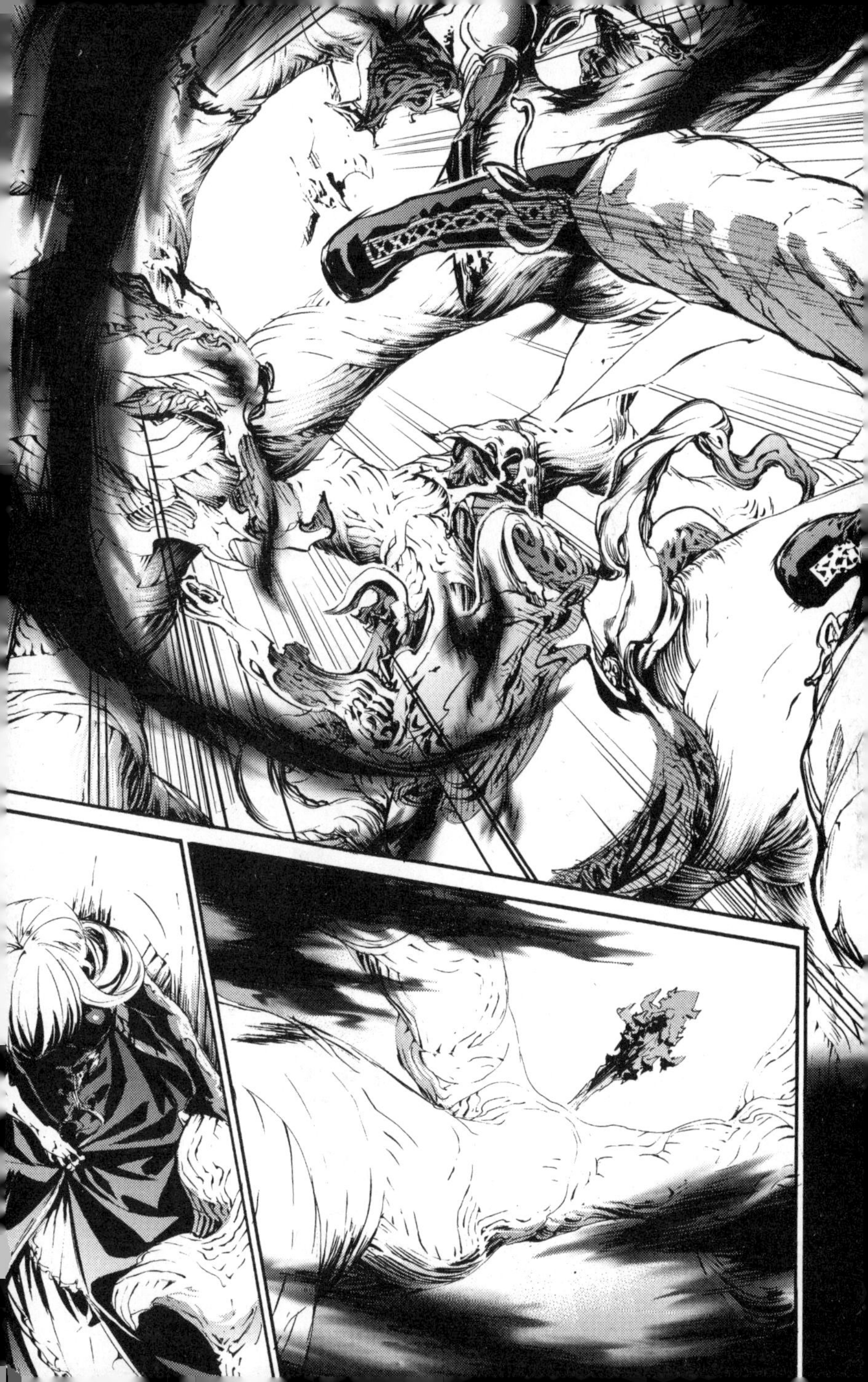

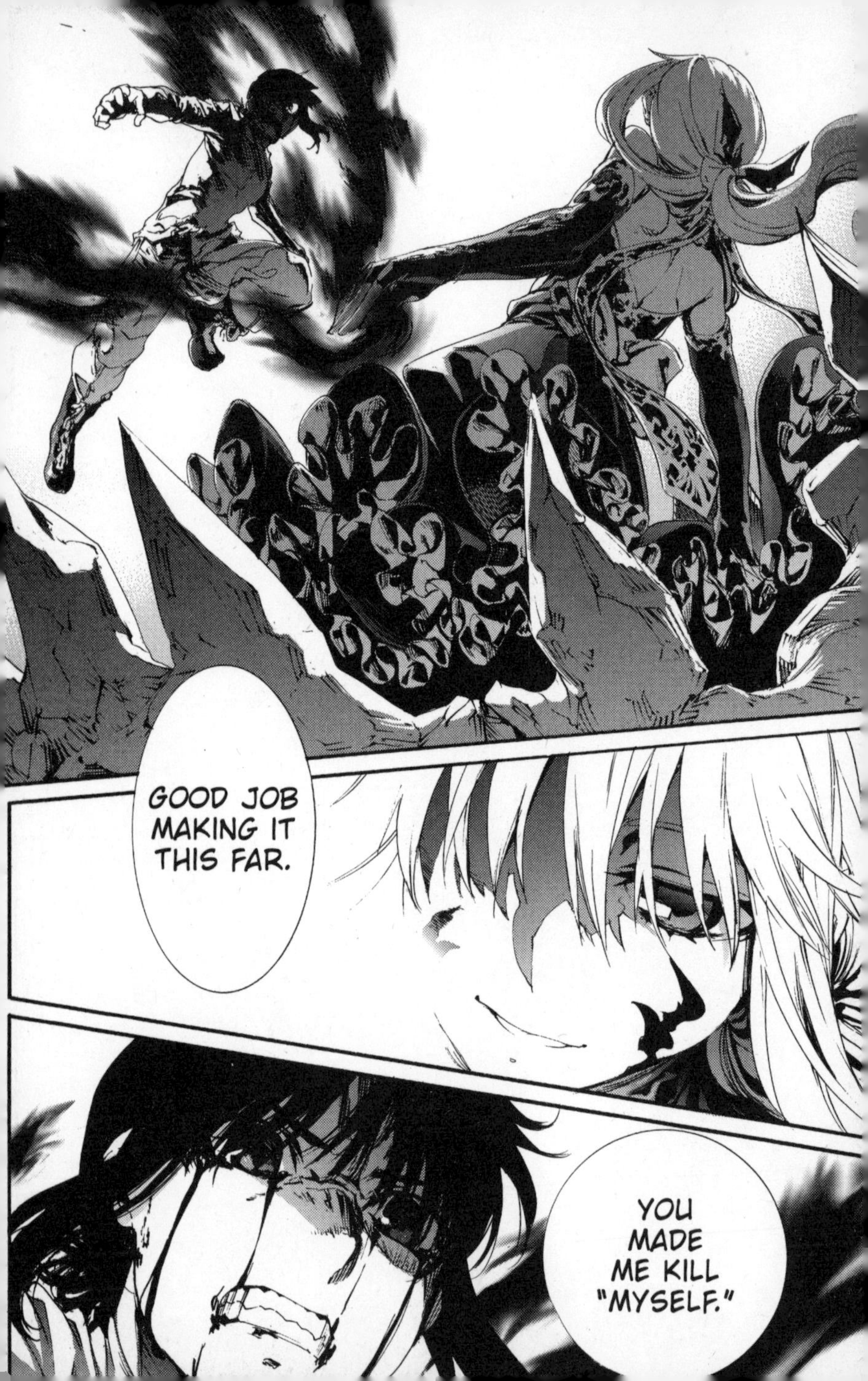
GOOD JOB MAKING IT THIS FAR.
YOU MADE ME KILL "MYSELF."

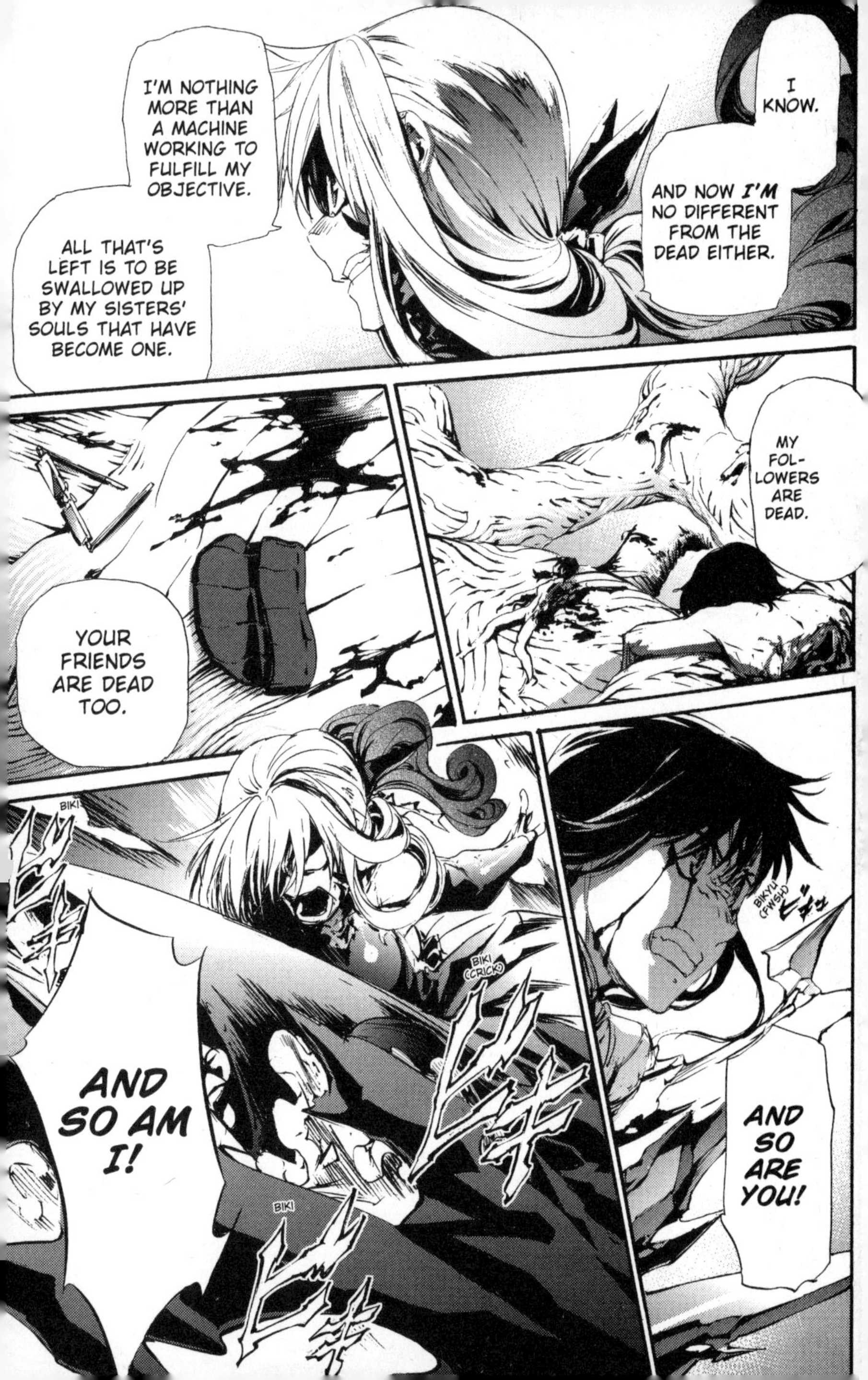
I KNOW.
AND NOW *I'M* NO DIFFERENT FROM THE DEAD EITHER.
I'M NOTHING MORE THAN A MACHINE WORKING TO FULFILL MY OBJECTIVE.
ALL THAT'S LEFT IS TO BE SWALLOWED UP BY MY SISTERS' SOULS THAT HAVE BECOME ONE.
MY FOL-LOWERS ARE DEAD.
YOUR FRIENDS ARE DEAD TOO.
BIKYU (FWSH)
AND SO ARE YOU!
BIKI
BIKI (CRICK)
AND SO AM I!
BIKI

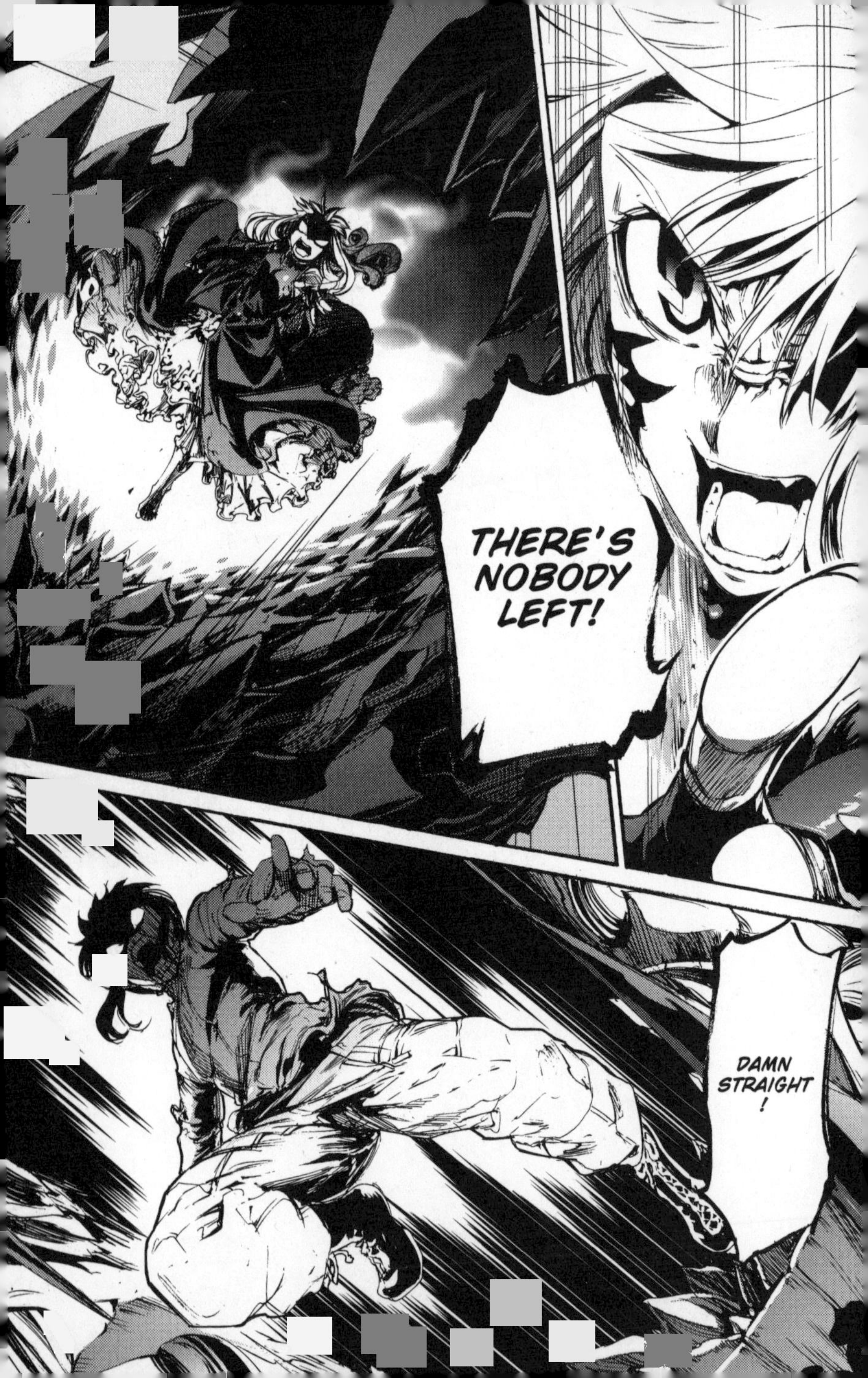
THERE'S NOBODY LEFT!
DAMN STRAIGHT!

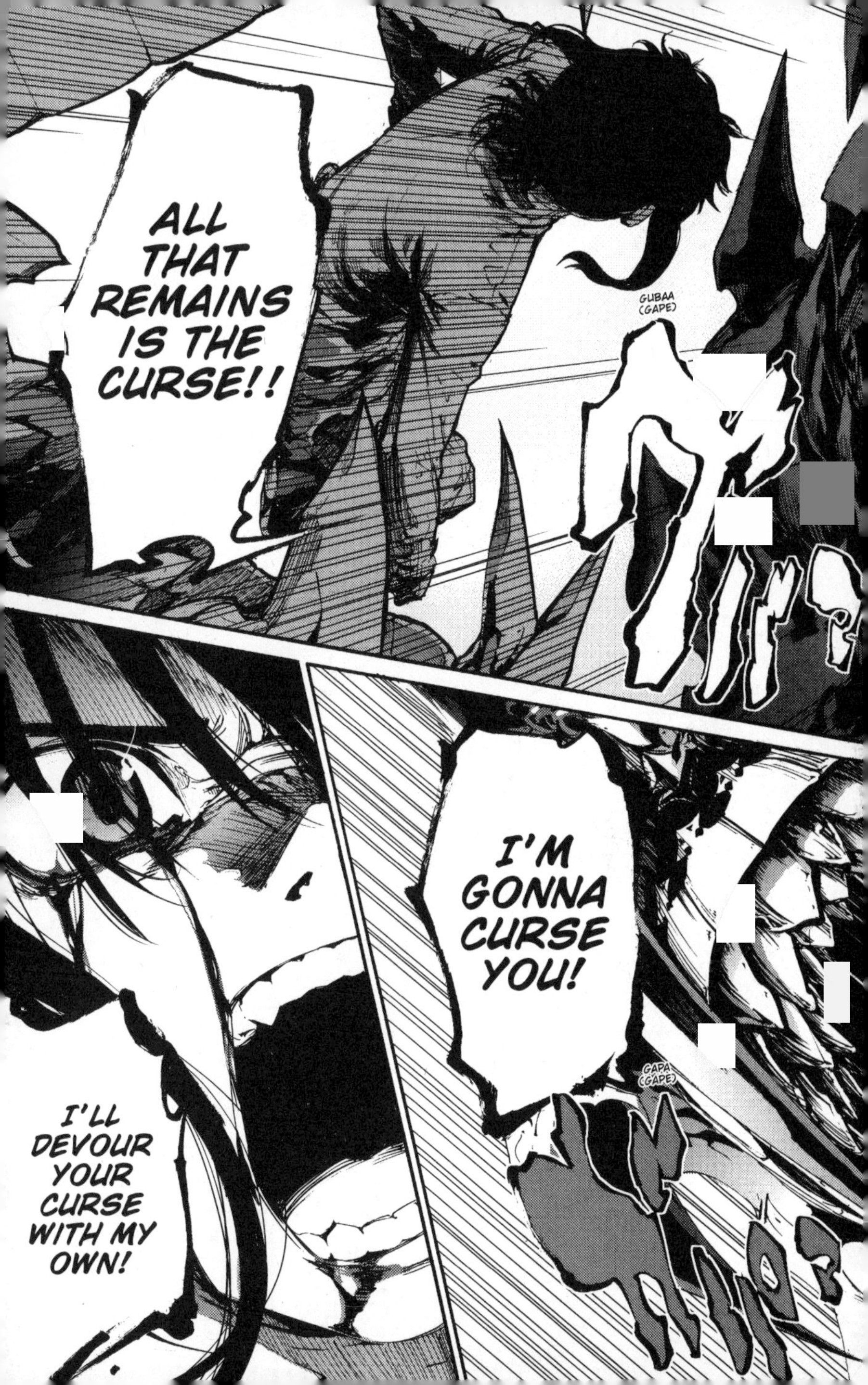
ALL THAT REMAINS IS THE CURSE!!
GUBAA (GAPE)
I'M GONNA CURSE YOU!
GAPA (GAPE)
I'LL DEVOUR YOUR CURSE WITH MY OWN!

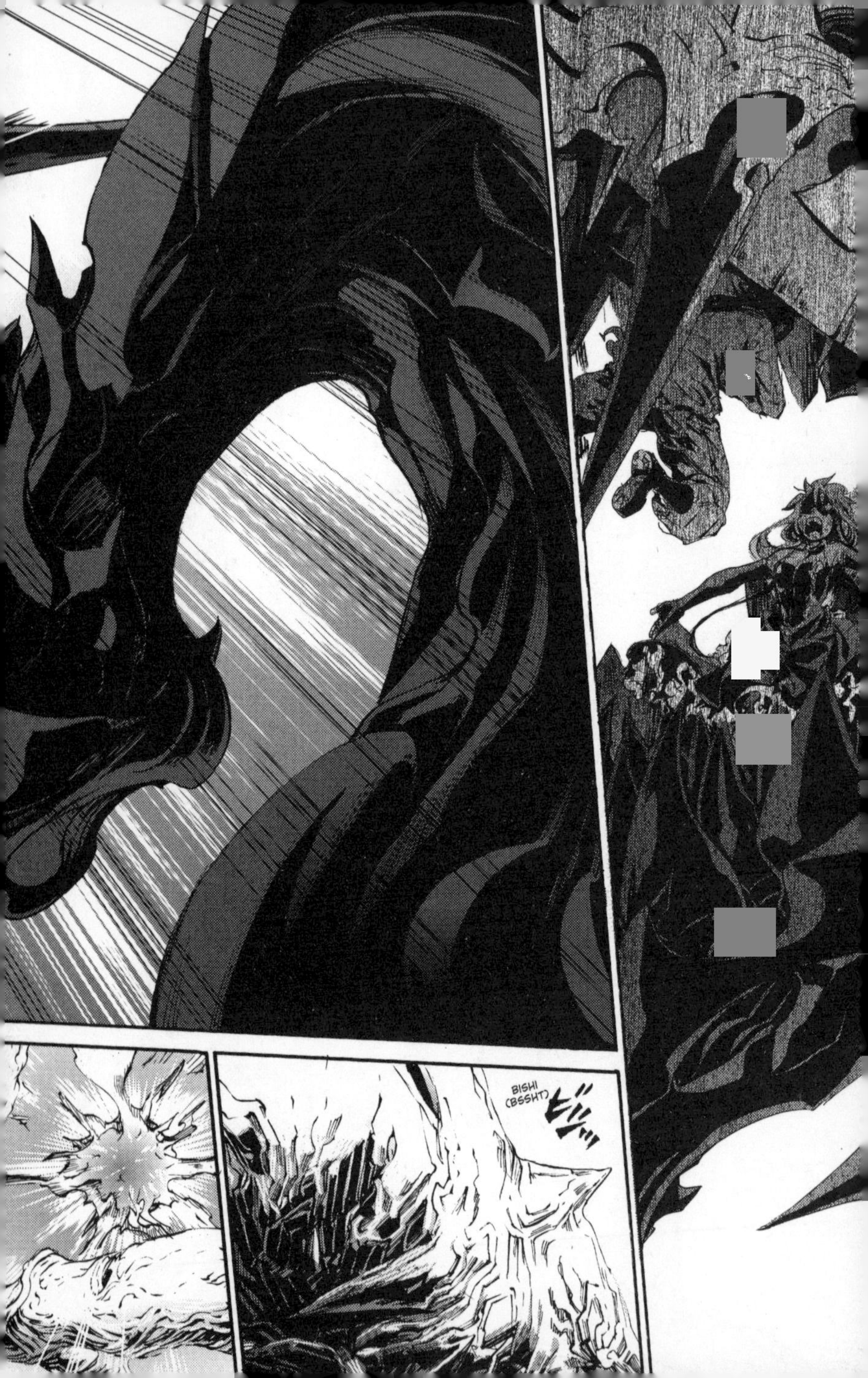
BISHI
(BSSHT)

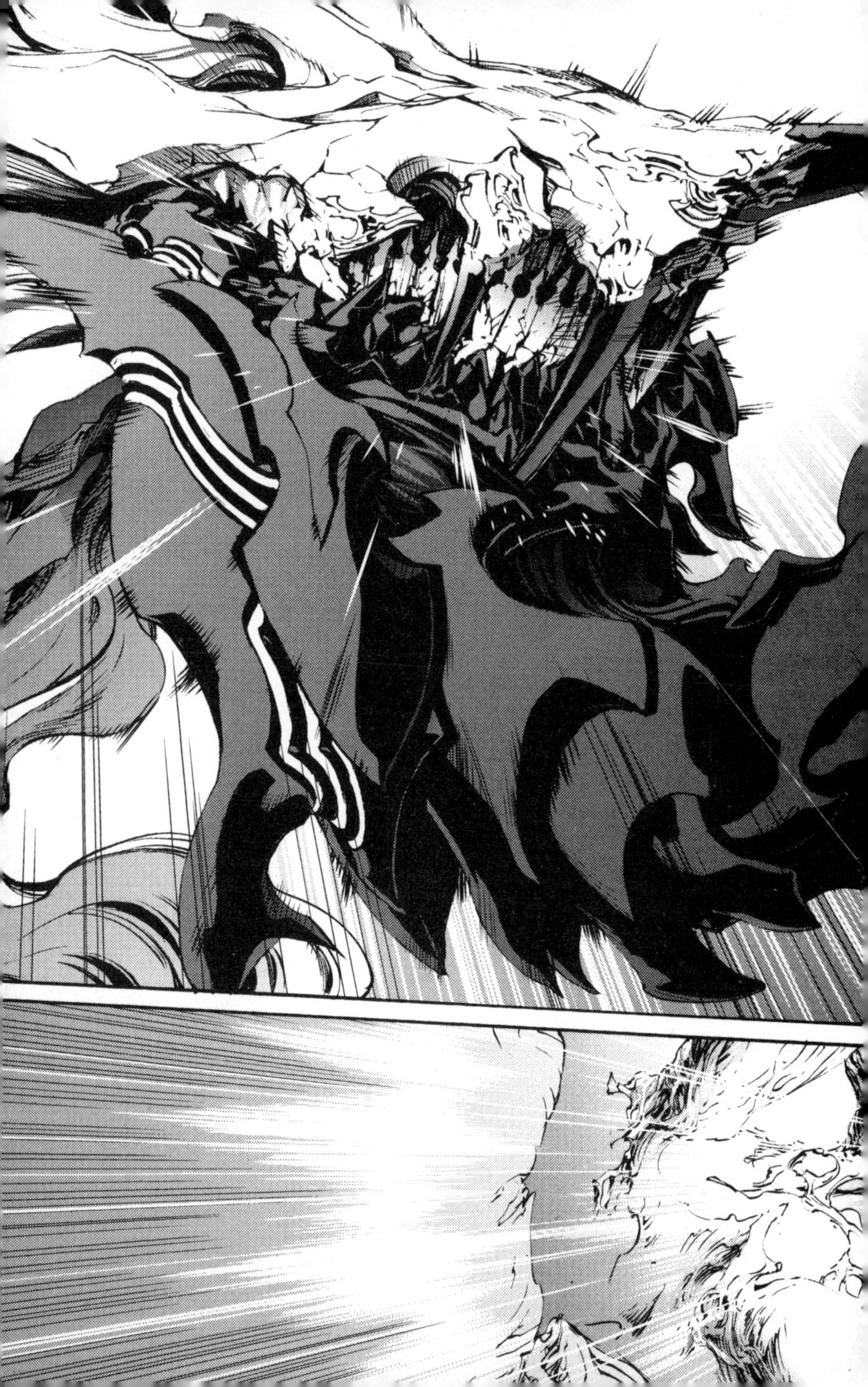

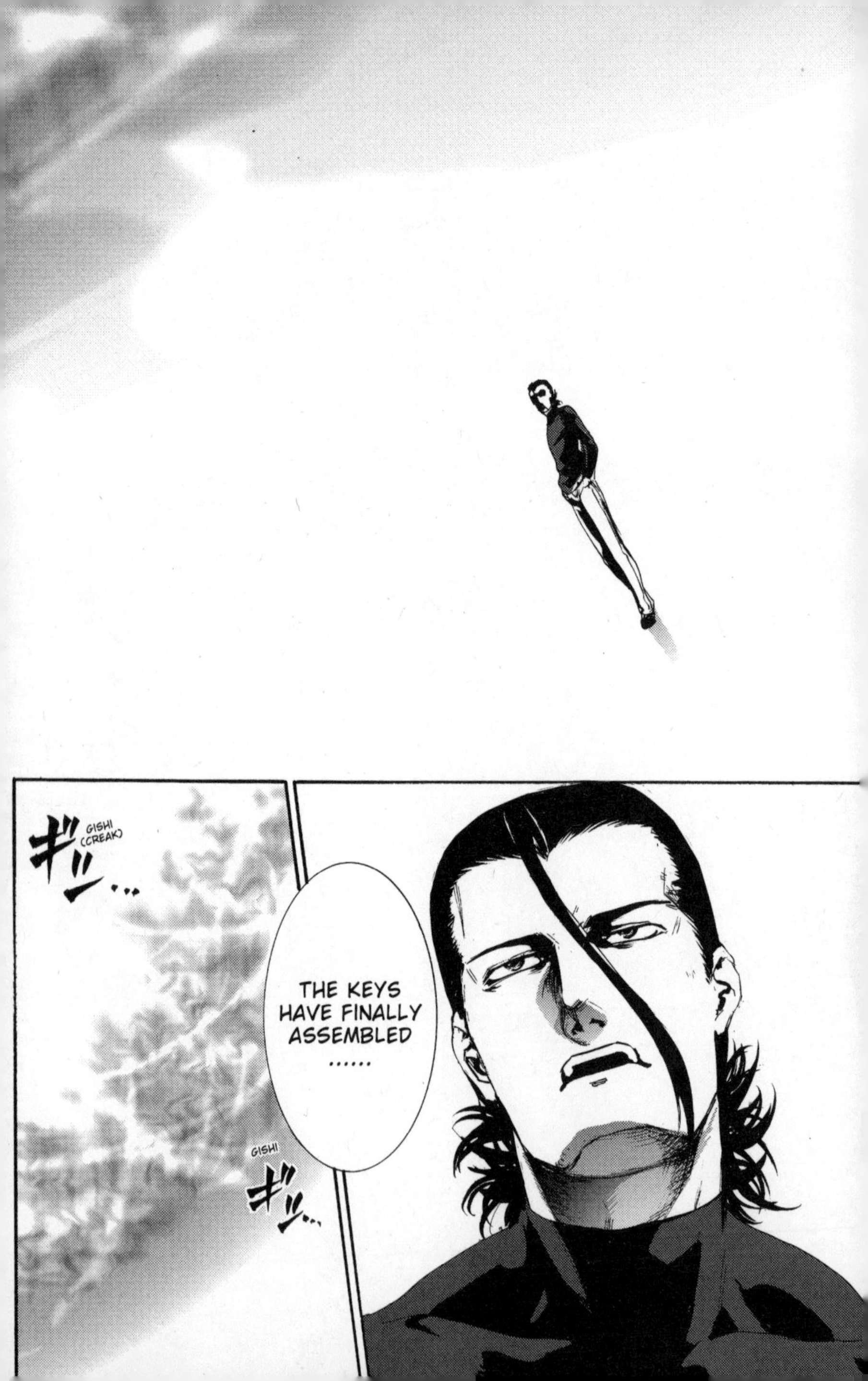
THE KEYS HAVE FINALLY ASSEMBLED ......
ギッ...
GISHI (CREAK)
ギッ...
GISHI

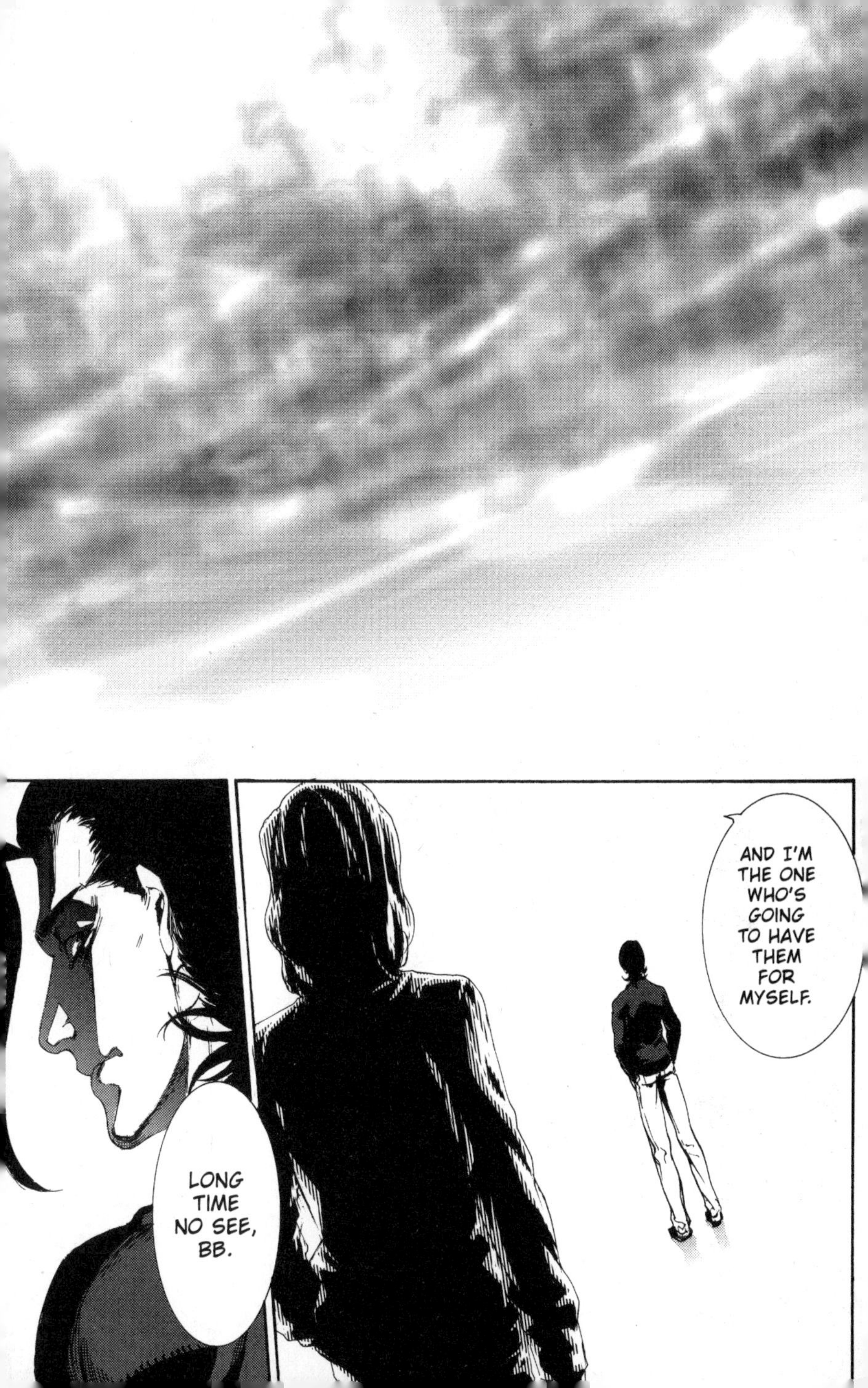
AND I'M THE ONE WHO'S GOING TO HAVE THEM FOR MYSELF.
LONG TIME NO SEE, BB.

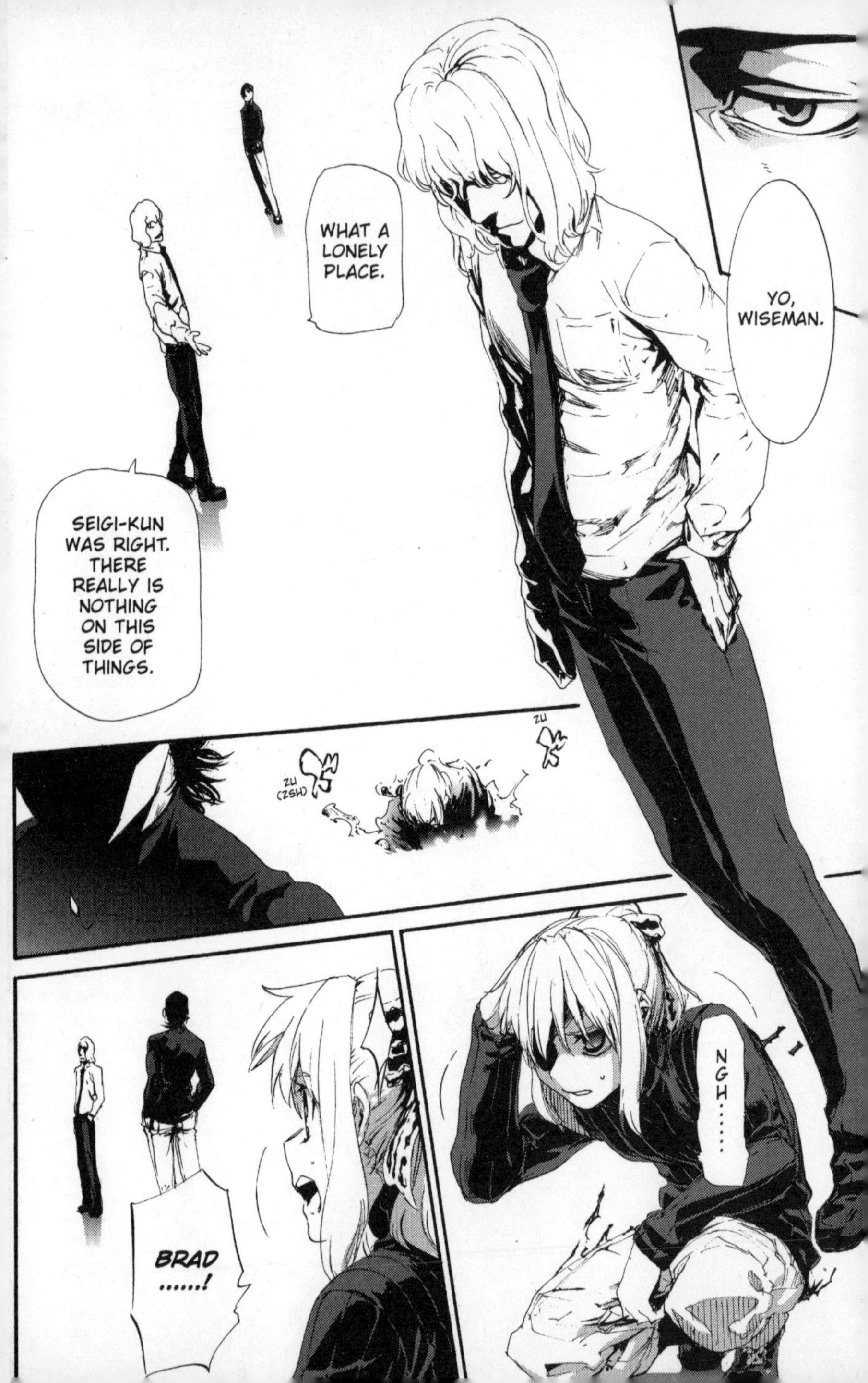
YO, WISEMAN.
WHAT A LONELY PLACE.
SEIGI-KUN WAS RIGHT. THERE REALLY IS NOTHING ON THIS SIDE OF THINGS.
ZU
ZU (ZSH)
NGH......
BRAD ......!

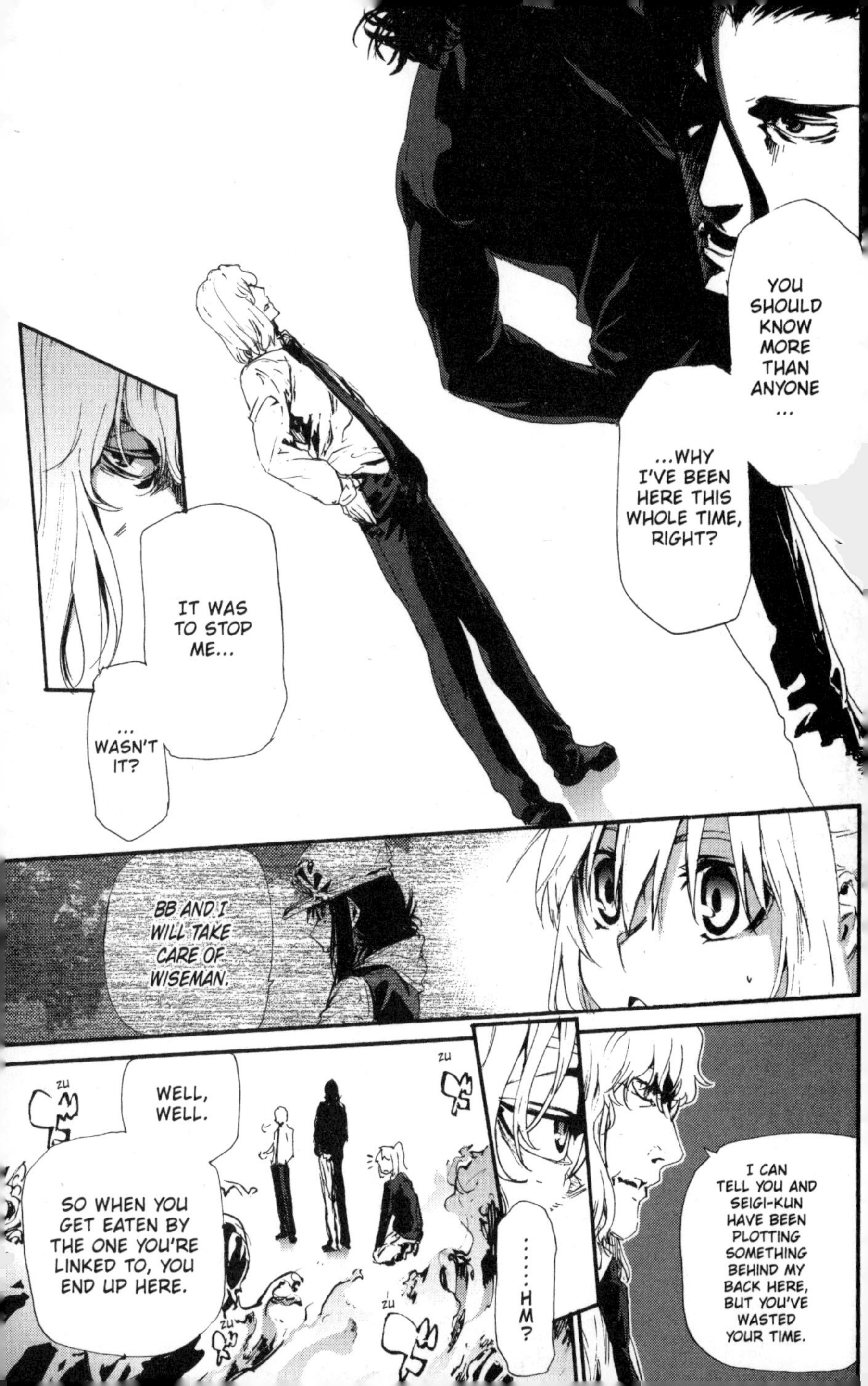
YOU SHOULD KNOW MORE THAN ANYONE ...
...WHY I'VE BEEN HERE THIS WHOLE TIME, RIGHT?
IT WAS TO STOP ME...
... WASN'T IT?
BB AND I WILL TAKE CARE OF WISEMAN.
I CAN TELL YOU AND SEIGI-KUN HAVE BEEN PLOTTING SOMETHING BEHIND MY BACK HERE, BUT YOU'VE WASTED YOUR TIME.
.....HM?
ZU
WELL, WELL.
ZU
SO WHEN YOU GET EATEN BY THE ONE YOU'RE LINKED TO, YOU END UP HERE.
ZU
ZU

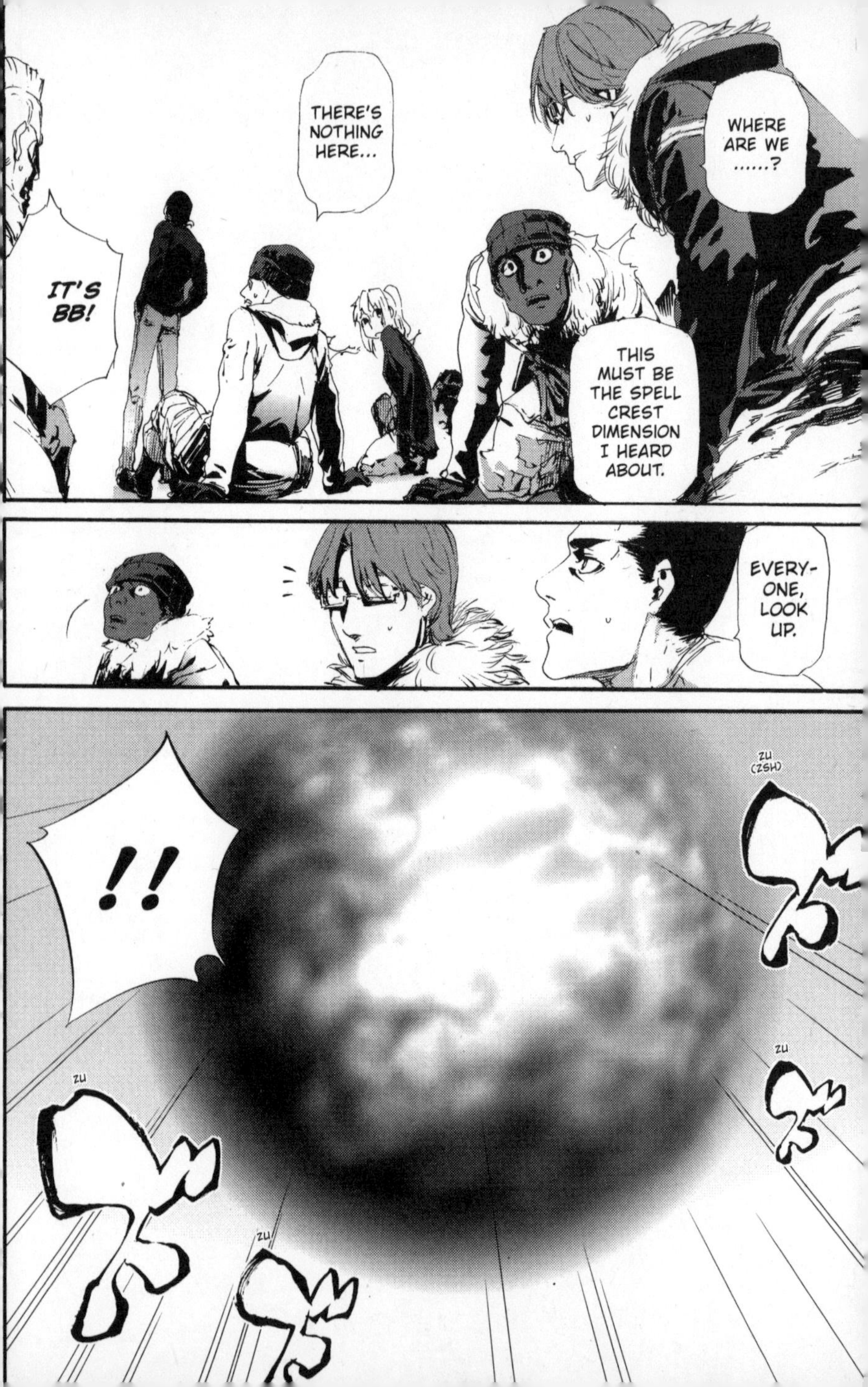
WHERE ARE WE ......?
THIS MUST BE THE SPELL CREST DIMENSION I HEARD ABOUT.
THERE'S NOTHING HERE...
IT'S BB!
EVERY-ONE, LOOK UP.
ZU (ZSH)
!!
ZU
ZU
ZU

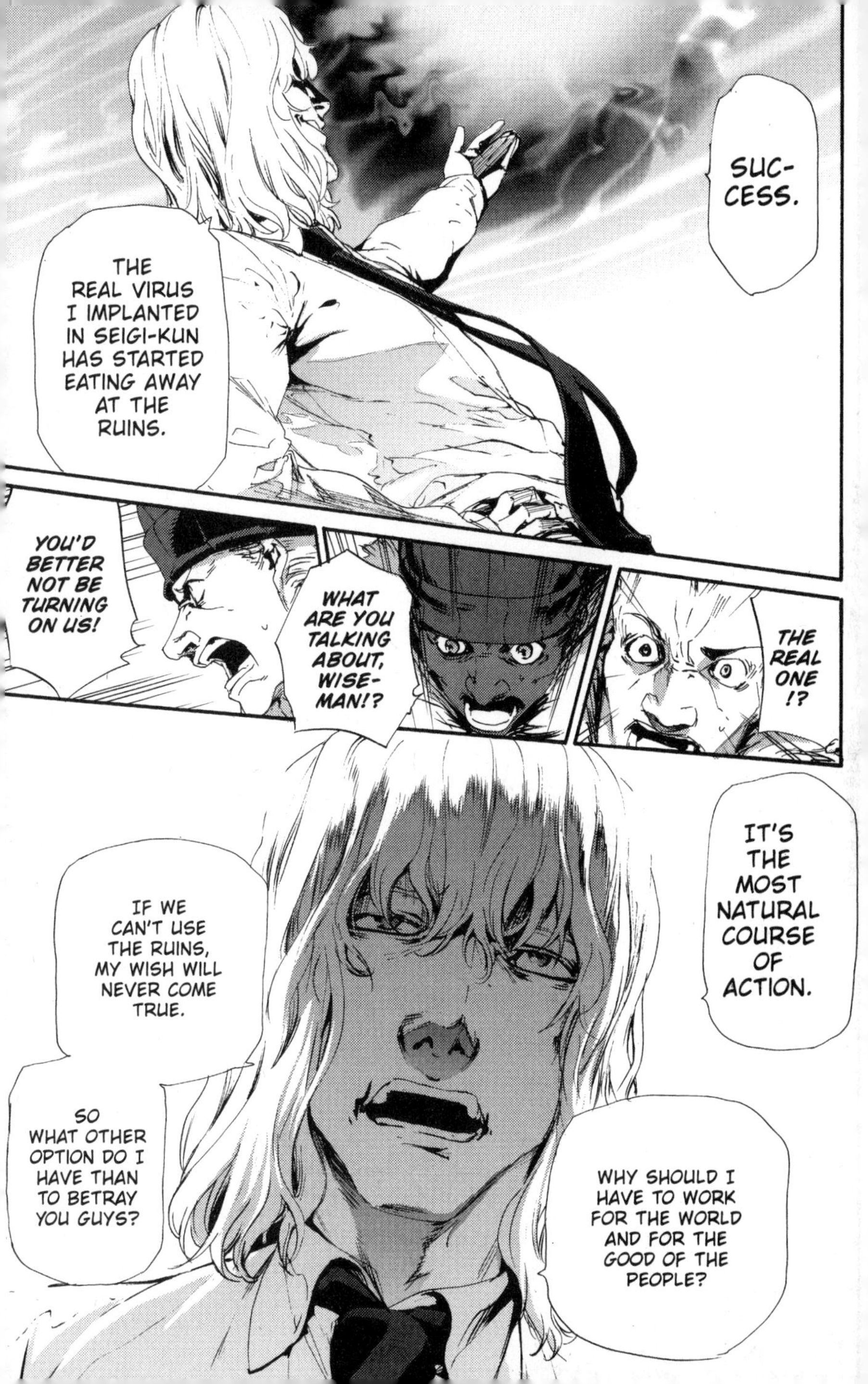
SUC-CESS.
THE REAL VIRUS I IMPLANTED IN SEIGI-KUN HAS STARTED EATING AWAY AT THE RUINS.
THE REAL ONE !?
WHAT ARE YOU TALKING ABOUT, WISE-MAN!?
YOU'D BETTER NOT BE TURNING ON US!
IT'S THE MOST NATURAL COURSE OF ACTION.
IF WE CAN'T USE THE RUINS, MY WISH WILL NEVER COME TRUE.
WHY SHOULD I HAVE TO WORK FOR THE WORLD AND FOR THE GOOD OF THE PEOPLE?
SO WHAT OTHER OPTION DO I HAVE THAN TO BETRAY YOU GUYS?

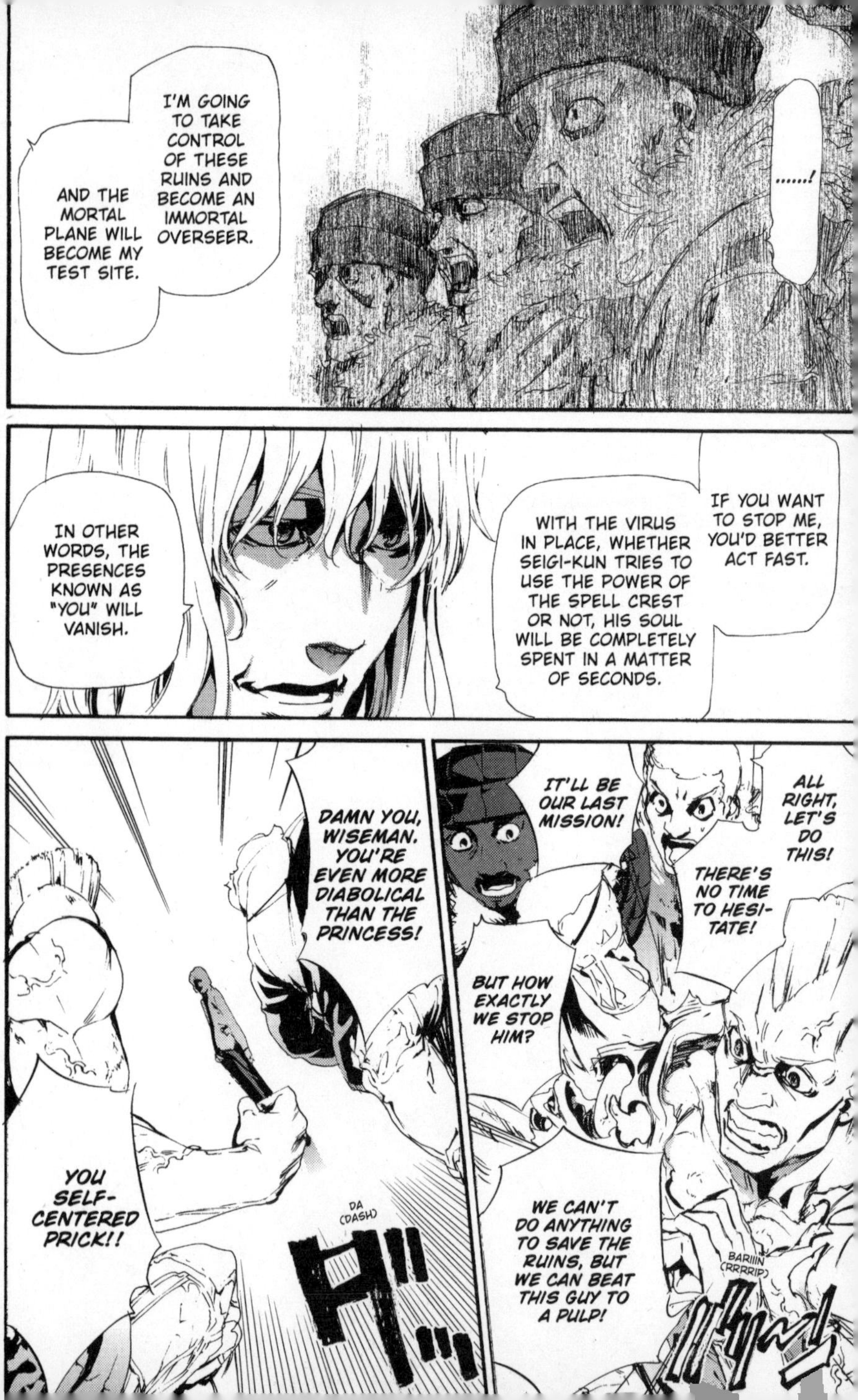

......!
I'M GOING TO TAKE CONTROL OF THESE RUINS AND BECOME AN IMMORTAL OVERSEER.
AND THE MORTAL PLANE WILL BECOME MY TEST SITE.
IF YOU WANT TO STOP ME, YOU'D BETTER ACT FAST.
WITH THE VIRUS IN PLACE, WHETHER SEIGI-KUN TRIES TO USE THE POWER OF THE SPELL CREST OR NOT, HIS SOUL WILL BE COMPLETELY SPENT IN A MATTER OF SECONDS.
IN OTHER WORDS, THE PRESENCES KNOWN AS "YOU" WILL VANISH.
ALL RIGHT, LET'S DO THIS!
IT'LL BE OUR LAST MISSION!
THERE'S NO TIME TO HESI-TATE!
BUT HOW EXACTLY WE STOP HIM?
BARIIIN (RRRRIP)
WE CAN'T DO ANYTHING TO SAVE THE RUINS, BUT WE CAN BEAT THIS GUY TO A PULP!
DAMN YOU, WISEMAN. YOU'RE EVEN MORE DIABOLICAL THAN THE PRINCESS!
DA (DASH)
YOU SELF-CENTERED PRICK!!

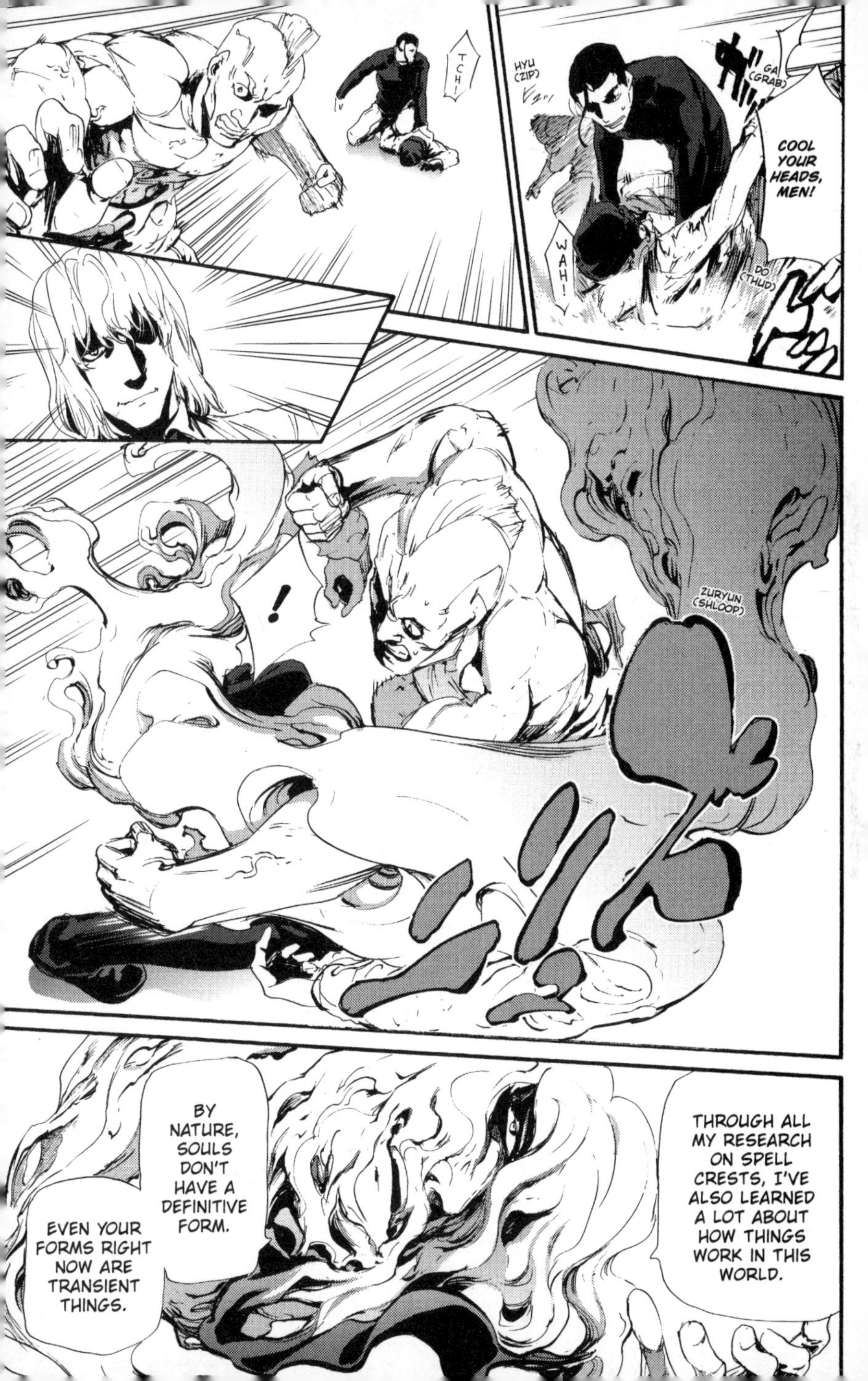
GA (GRAB)
HYU (ZIP)
COOL YOUR HEADS, MEN!
DO (THUD)
WAH!
TCH!
ZURYUN (SHLOOP)
!
THROUGH ALL MY RESEARCH ON SPELL CRESTS, I'VE ALSO LEARNED A LOT ABOUT HOW THINGS WORK IN THIS WORLD.
BY NATURE, SOULS DON'T HAVE A DEFINITIVE FORM.
EVEN YOUR FORMS RIGHT NOW ARE TRANSIENT THINGS.

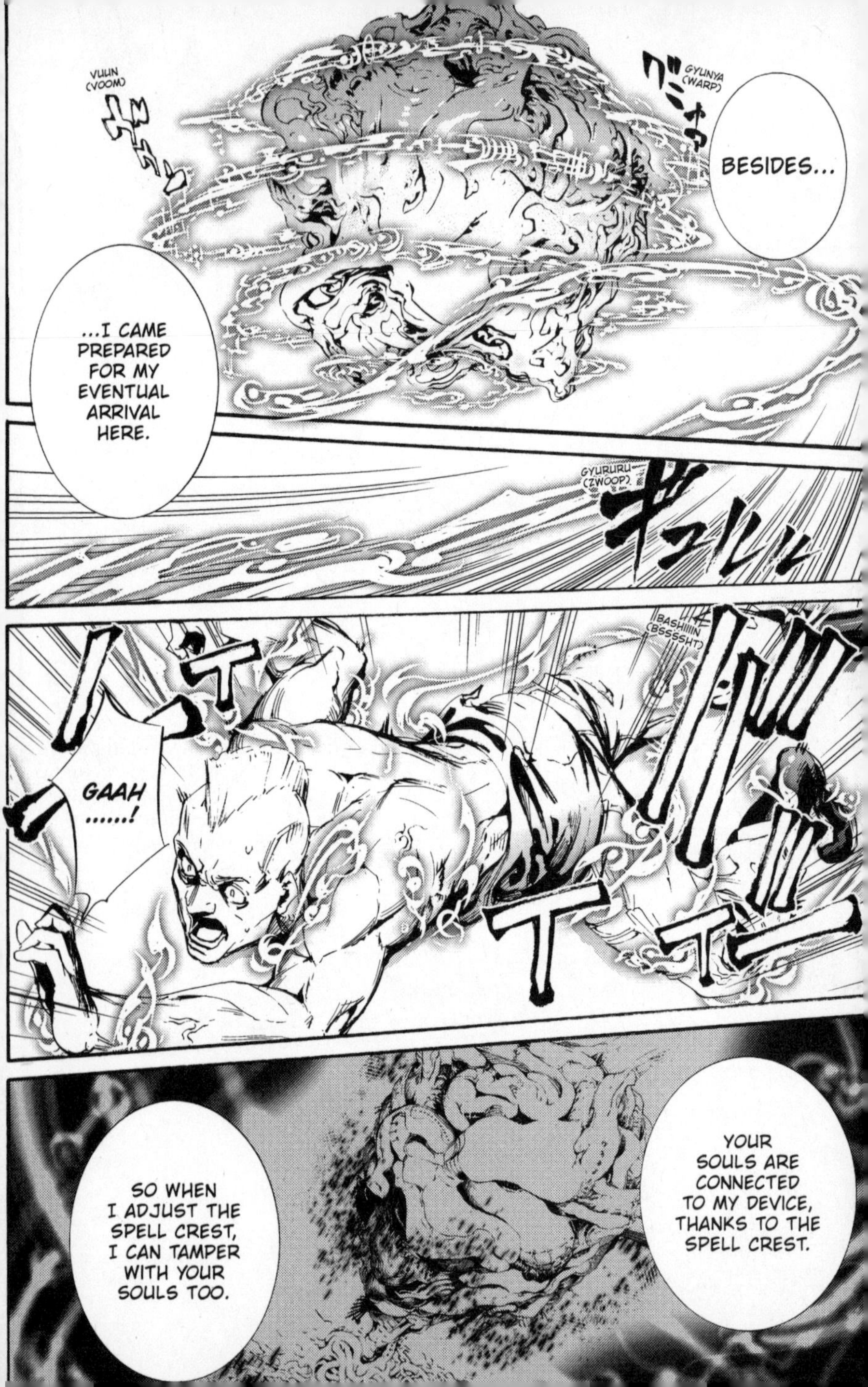
GYUNYA (WARP)
BESIDES...
VUUN (VOOM)
...I CAME PREPARED FOR MY EVENTUAL ARRIVAL HERE.
GYURURU (ZWOOP)
BASHIIIIN (BSSSSHT)
GAAH ......!
YOUR SOULS ARE CONNECTED TO MY DEVICE, THANKS TO THE SPELL CREST.
SO WHEN I ADJUST THE SPELL CREST, I CAN TAMPER WITH YOUR SOULS TOO.

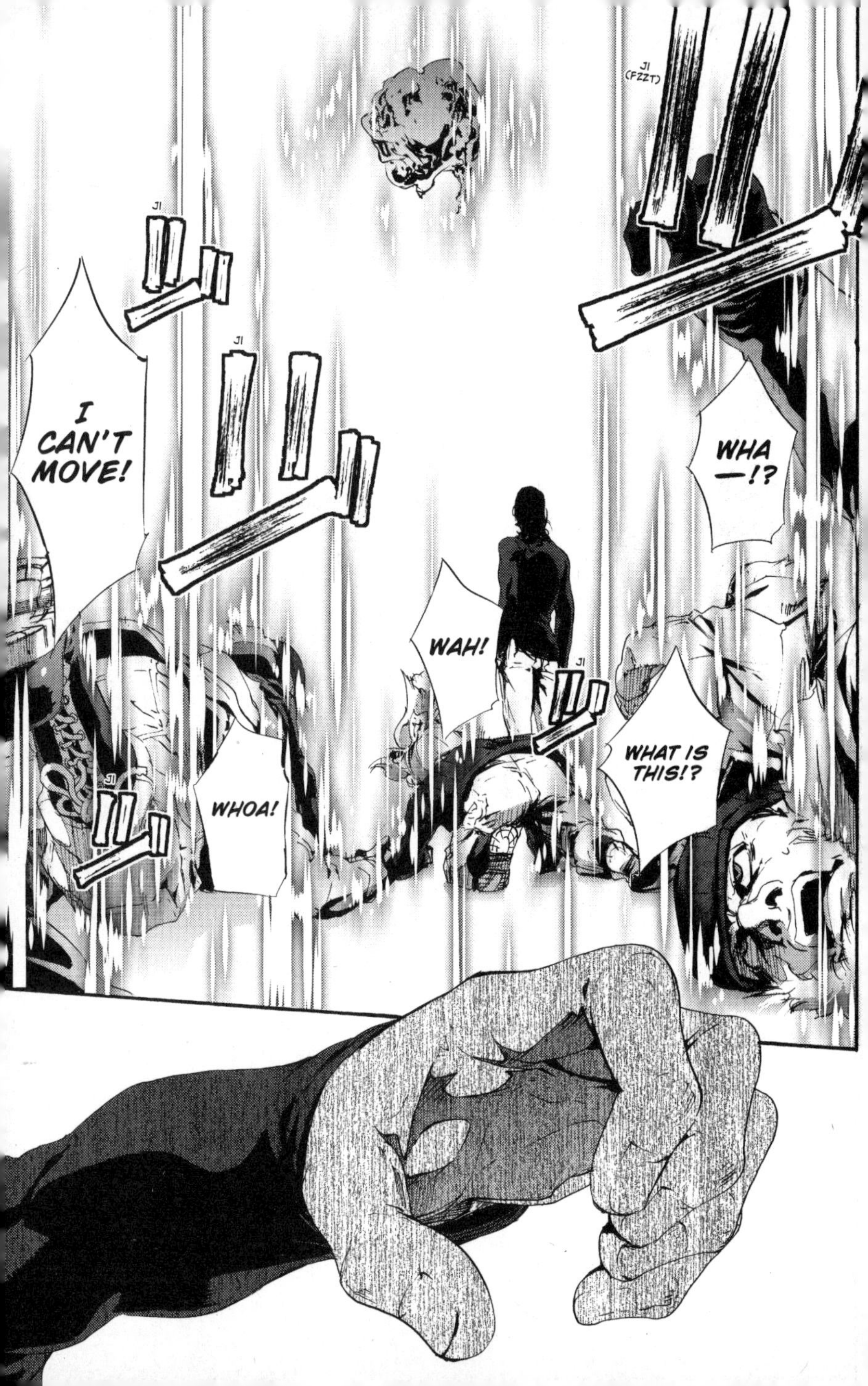
JI
(FZZT)
WHA—!?
JI
JI
I CAN'T MOVE!
WAH!
JI
WHAT IS THIS!?
JI
WHOA!

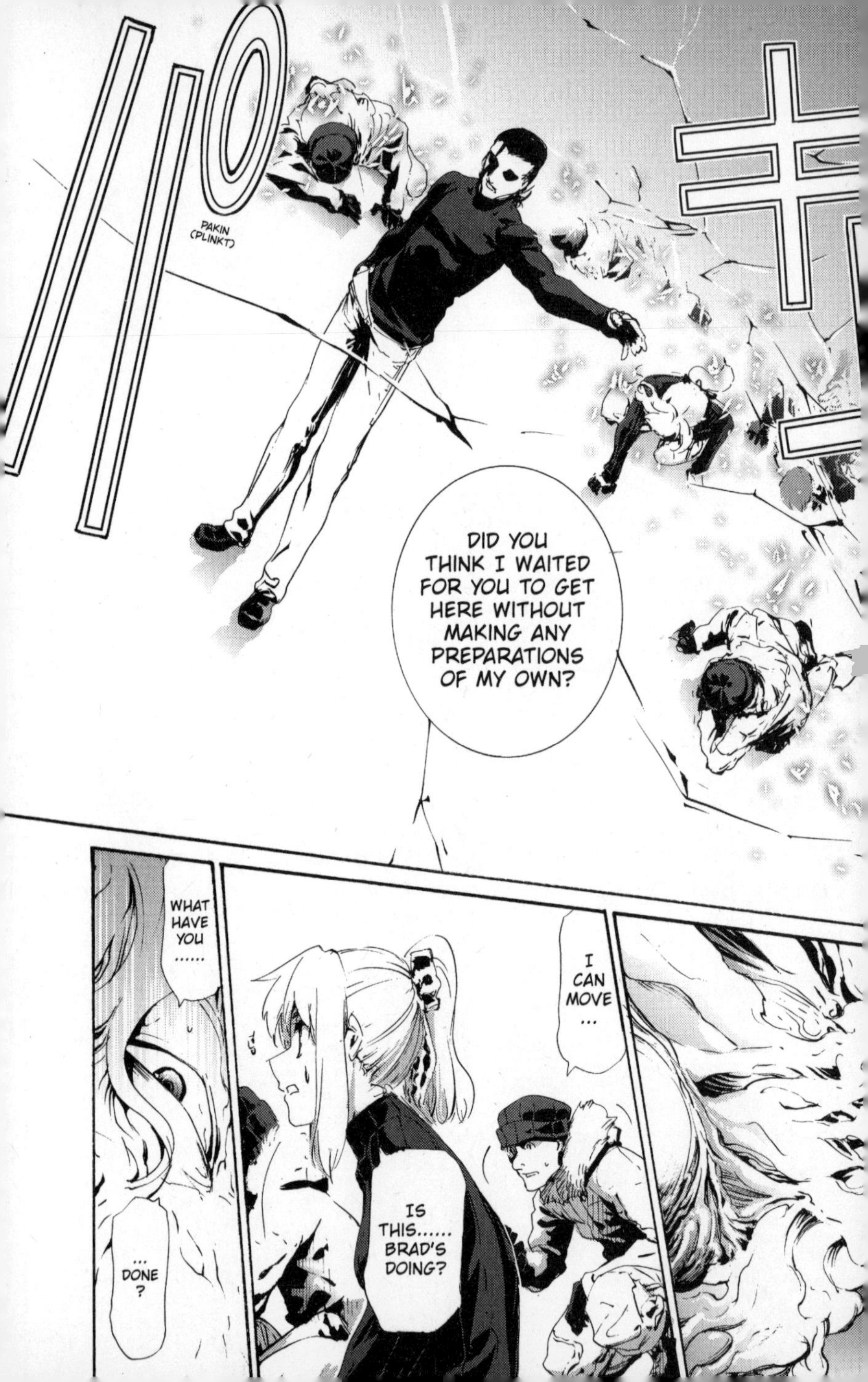
PAKIN (PLINKT)
DID YOU THINK I WAITED FOR YOU TO GET HERE WITHOUT MAKING ANY PREPARATIONS OF MY OWN?
I CAN MOVE ...
IS THIS...... BRAD'S DOING?
WHAT HAVE YOU ......
... DONE ?

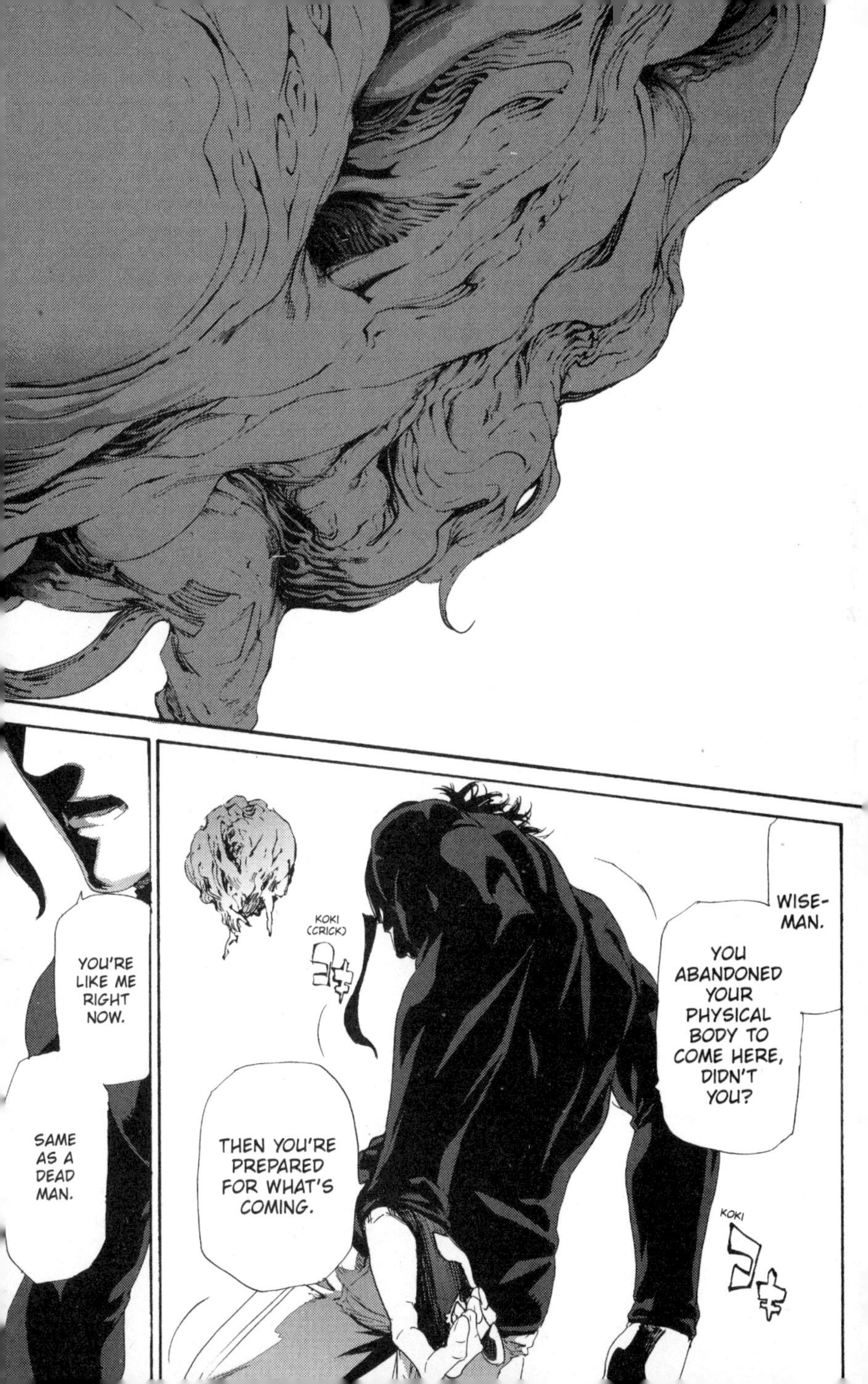
WISE-MAN.
YOU ABANDONED YOUR PHYSICAL BODY TO COME HERE, DIDN'T YOU?
KOKI (CRICK)
コキ
THEN YOU'RE PREPARED FOR WHAT'S COMING.
KOKI
コキ
YOU'RE LIKE ME RIGHT NOW.
SAME AS A DEAD MAN.

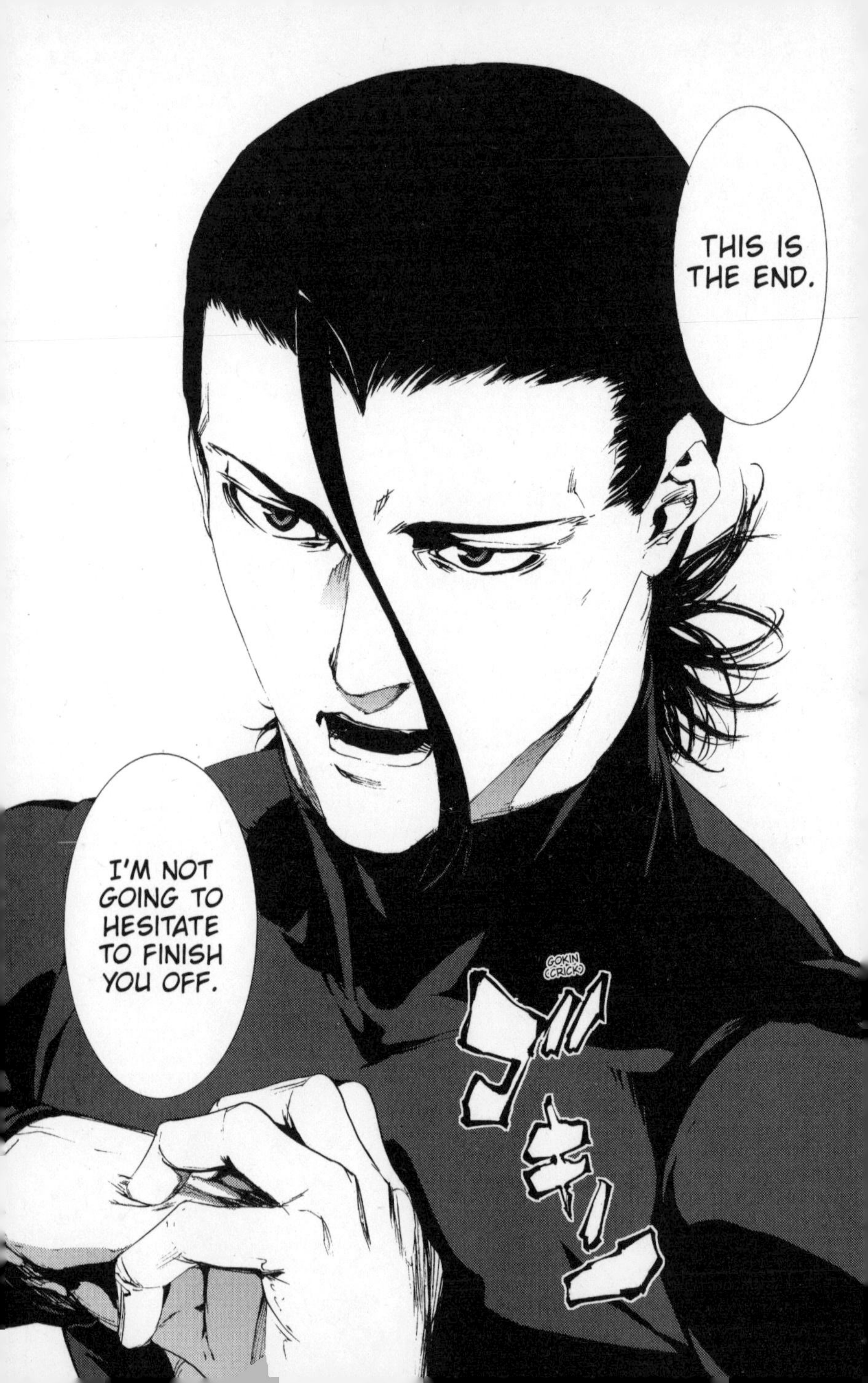
THIS IS THE END.
I'M NOT GOING TO HESITATE TO FINISH YOU OFF.
GOKIN (CRICK)

TABOO TATTOO

TABOO TATTOO

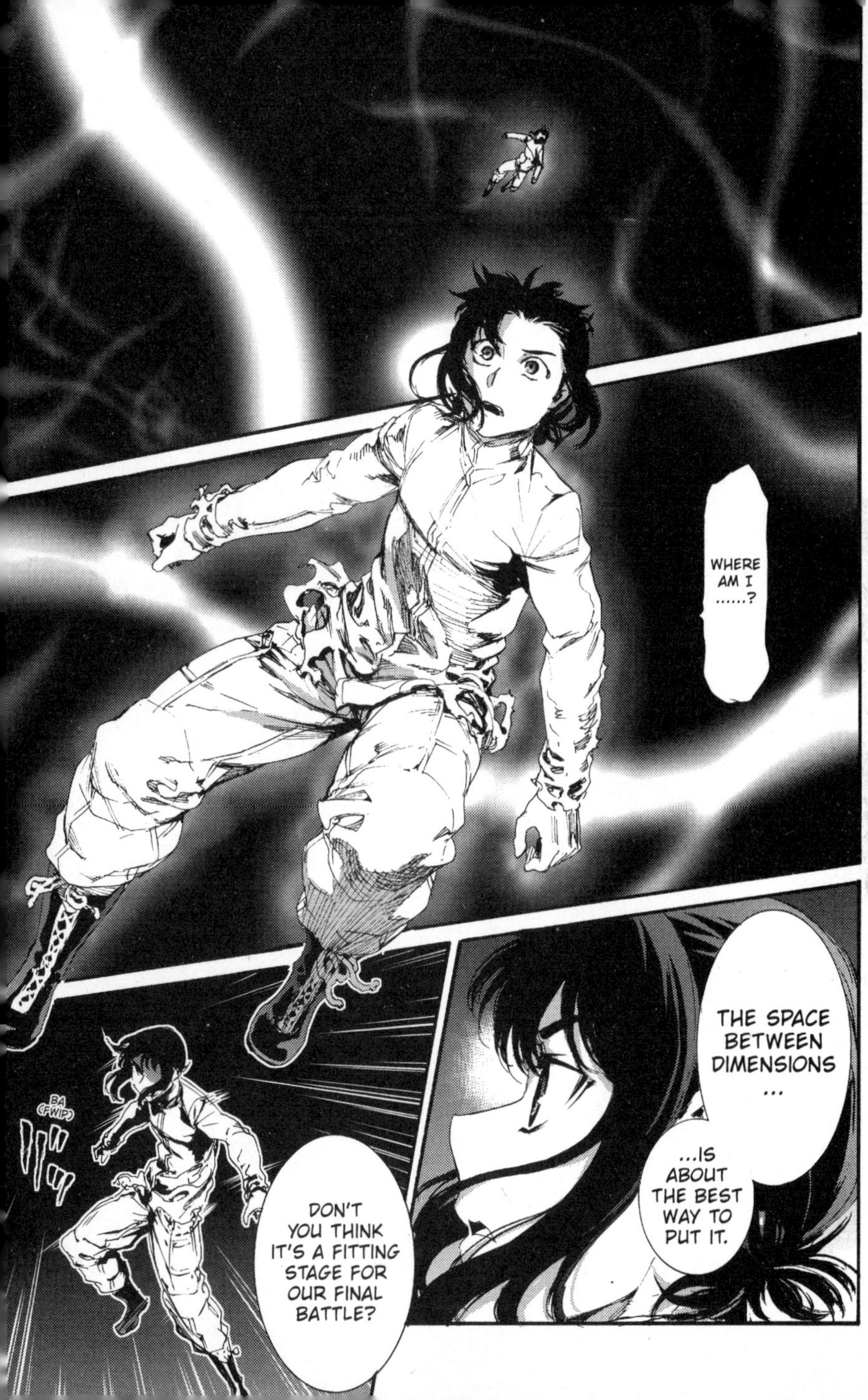
WHERE AM I ......?
THE SPACE BETWEEN DIMENSIONS ...
...IS ABOUT THE BEST WAY TO PUT IT.
DON'T YOU THINK IT'S A FITTING STAGE FOR OUR FINAL BATTLE?
BA (FWIP)

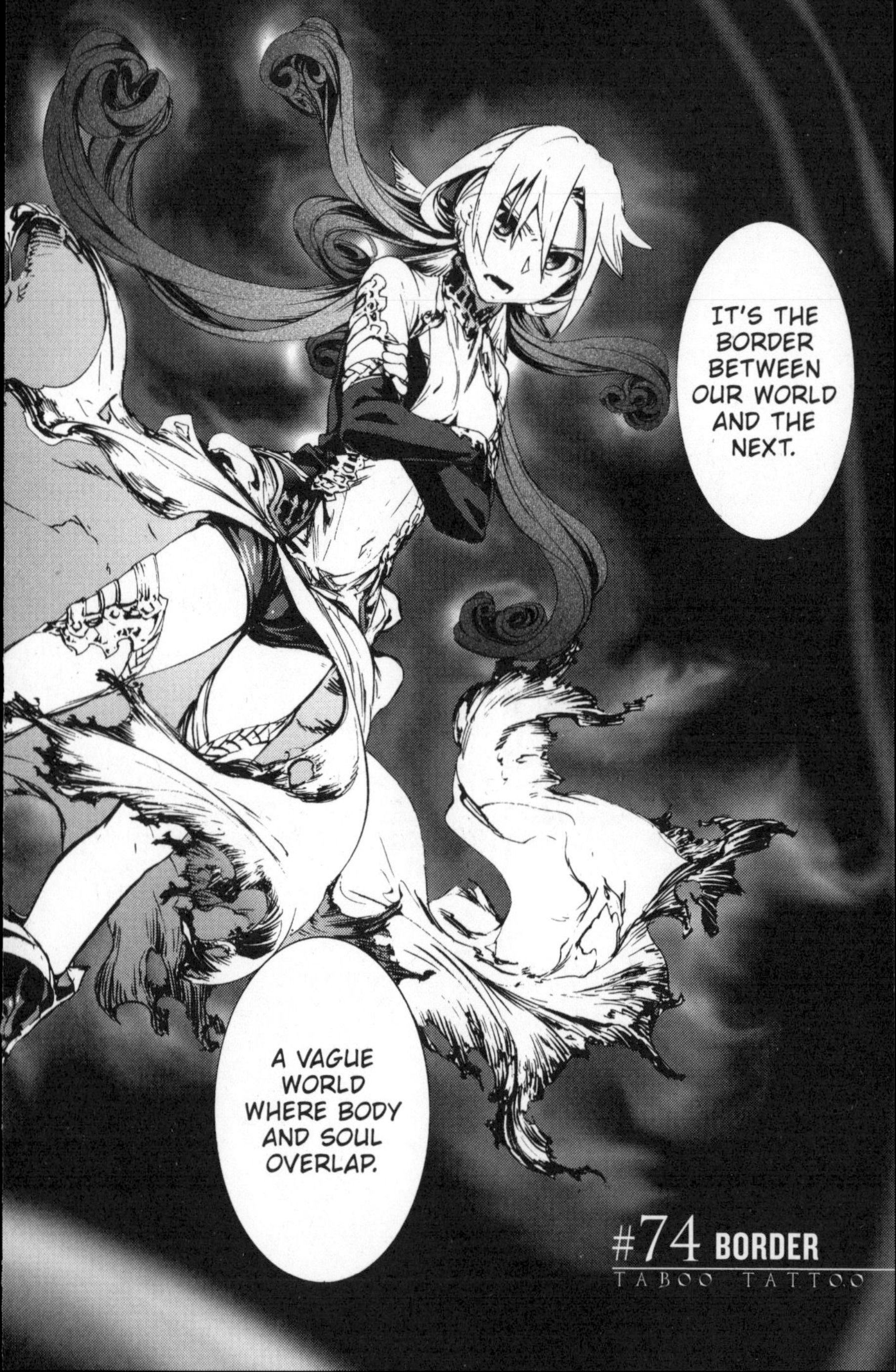
IT'S THE BORDER BETWEEN OUR WORLD AND THE NEXT.
A VAGUE WORLD WHERE BODY AND SOUL OVERLAP.
#74 BORDER
TABOO TATTOO

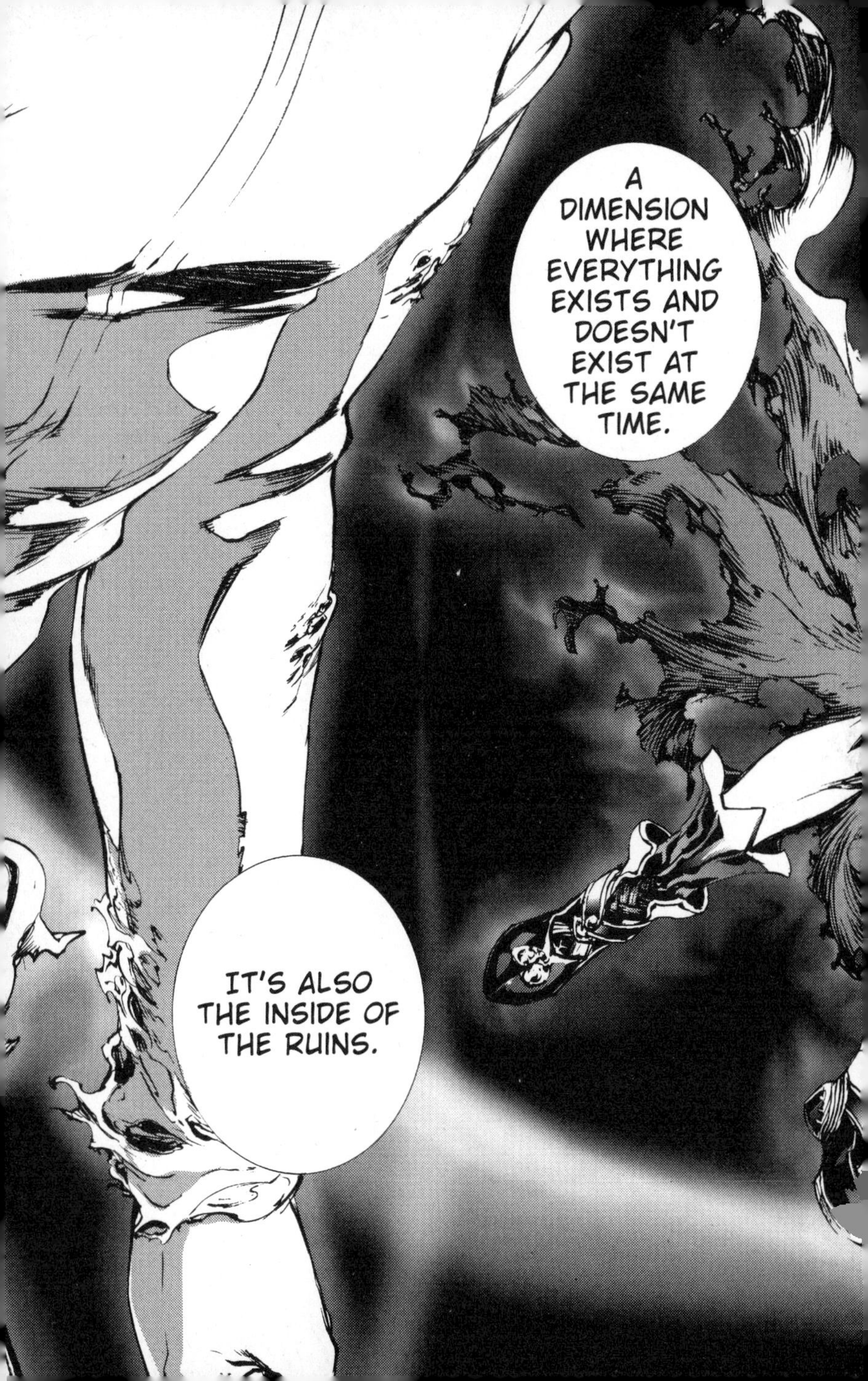
A DIMENSION WHERE EVERYTHING EXISTS AND DOESN'T EXIST AT THE SAME TIME.
IT'S ALSO THE INSIDE OF THE RUINS.

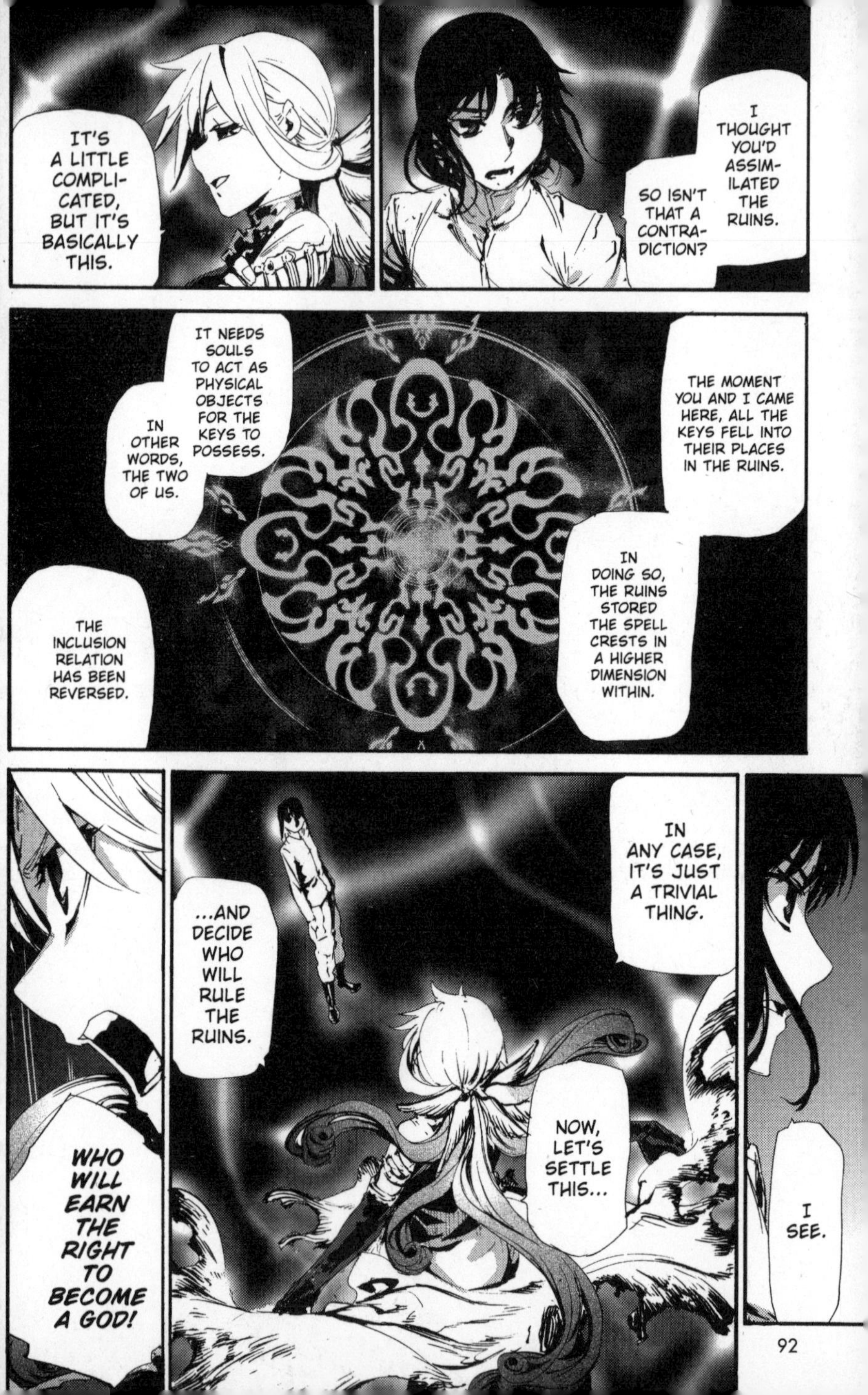

I THOUGHT YOU'D ASSIMILATED THE RUINS.
SO ISN'T THAT A CONTRADICTION?
IT'S A LITTLE COMPLICATED, BUT IT'S BASICALLY THIS.
THE MOMENT YOU AND I CAME HERE, ALL THE KEYS FELL INTO THEIR PLACES IN THE RUINS.
IN DOING SO, THE RUINS STORED THE SPELL CRESTS IN A HIGHER DIMENSION WITHIN.
IT NEEDS SOULS TO ACT AS PHYSICAL OBJECTS FOR THE KEYS TO POSSESS.
IN OTHER WORDS, THE TWO OF US.
THE INCLUSION RELATION HAS BEEN REVERSED.
I SEE.
IN ANY CASE, IT'S JUST A TRIVIAL THING.
NOW, LET'S SETTLE THIS...
...AND DECIDE WHO WILL RULE THE RUINS.
WHO WILL EARN THE RIGHT TO BECOME A GOD!

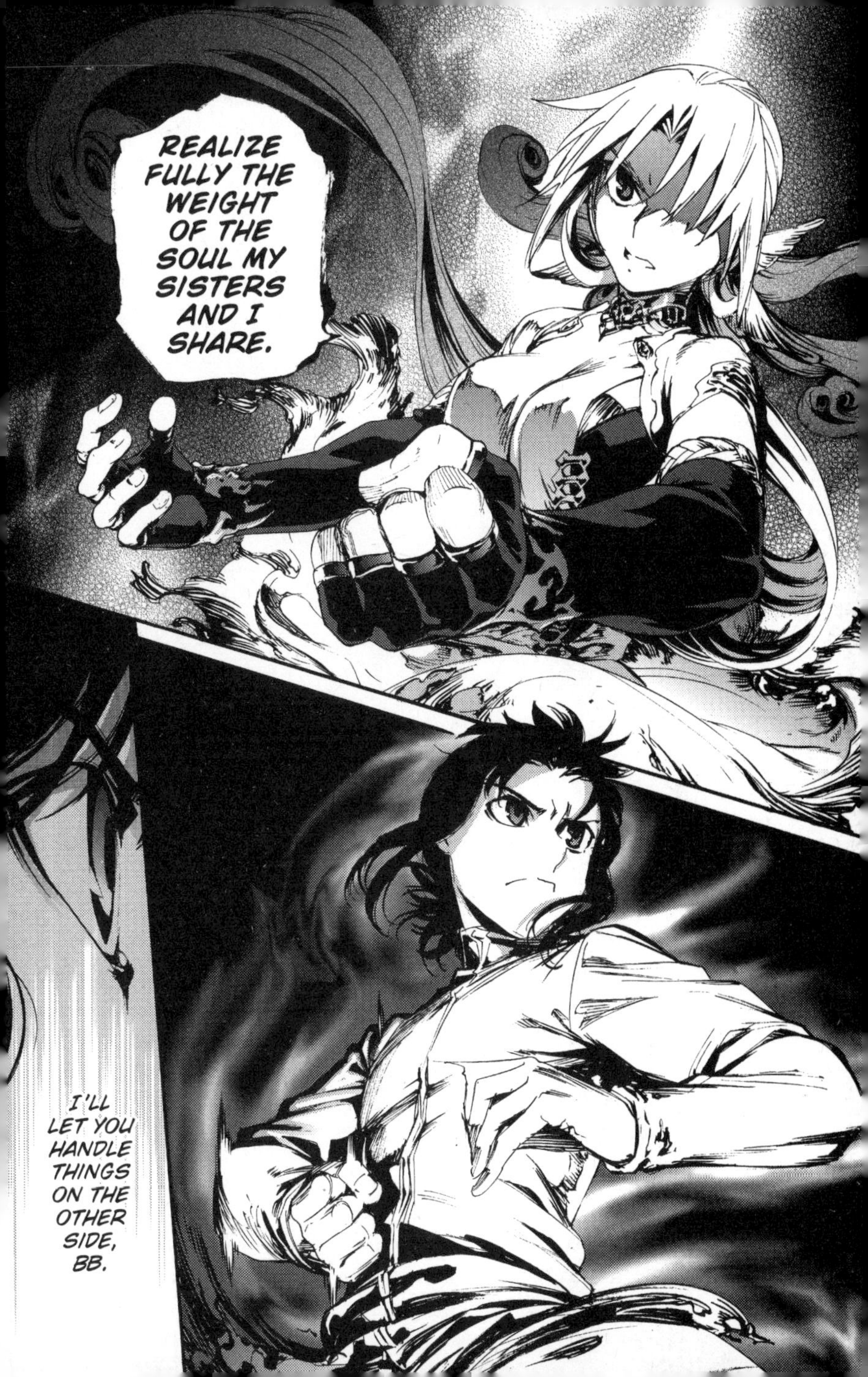
REALIZE FULLY THE WEIGHT OF THE SOUL MY SISTERS AND I SHARE.
I'LL LET YOU HANDLE THINGS ON THE OTHER SIDE, BB.

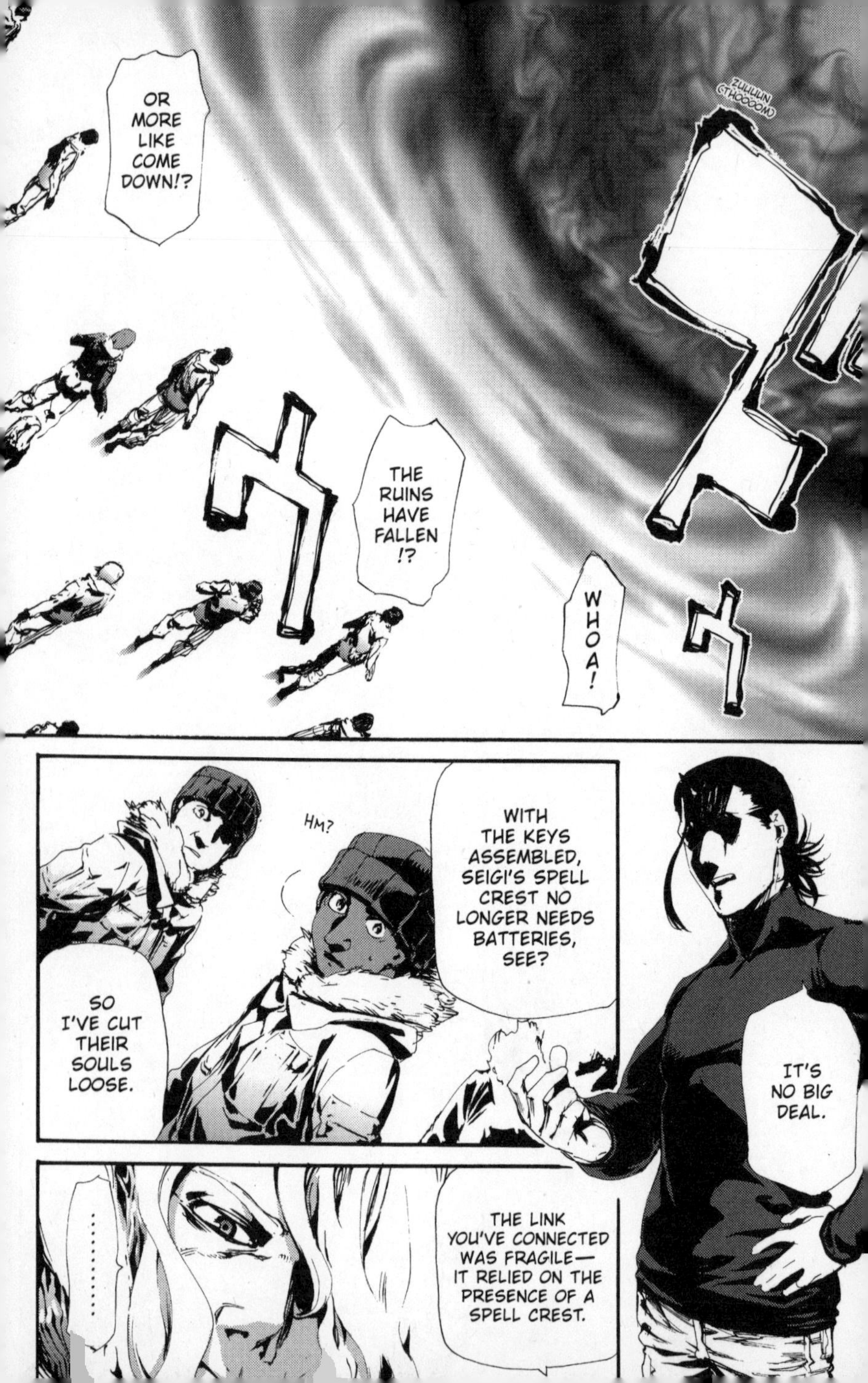
ZUUUUUN (THOOOOOM)
WHOA!
THE RUINS HAVE FALLEN!?
OR MORE LIKE COME DOWN!?
WITH THE KEYS ASSEMBLED, SEIGI'S SPELL CREST NO LONGER NEEDS BATTERIES, SEE?
HM?
SO I'VE CUT THEIR SOULS LOOSE.
IT'S NO BIG DEAL.
THE LINK YOU'VE CONNECTED WAS FRAGILE—IT RELIED ON THE PRESENCE OF A SPELL CREST.
……

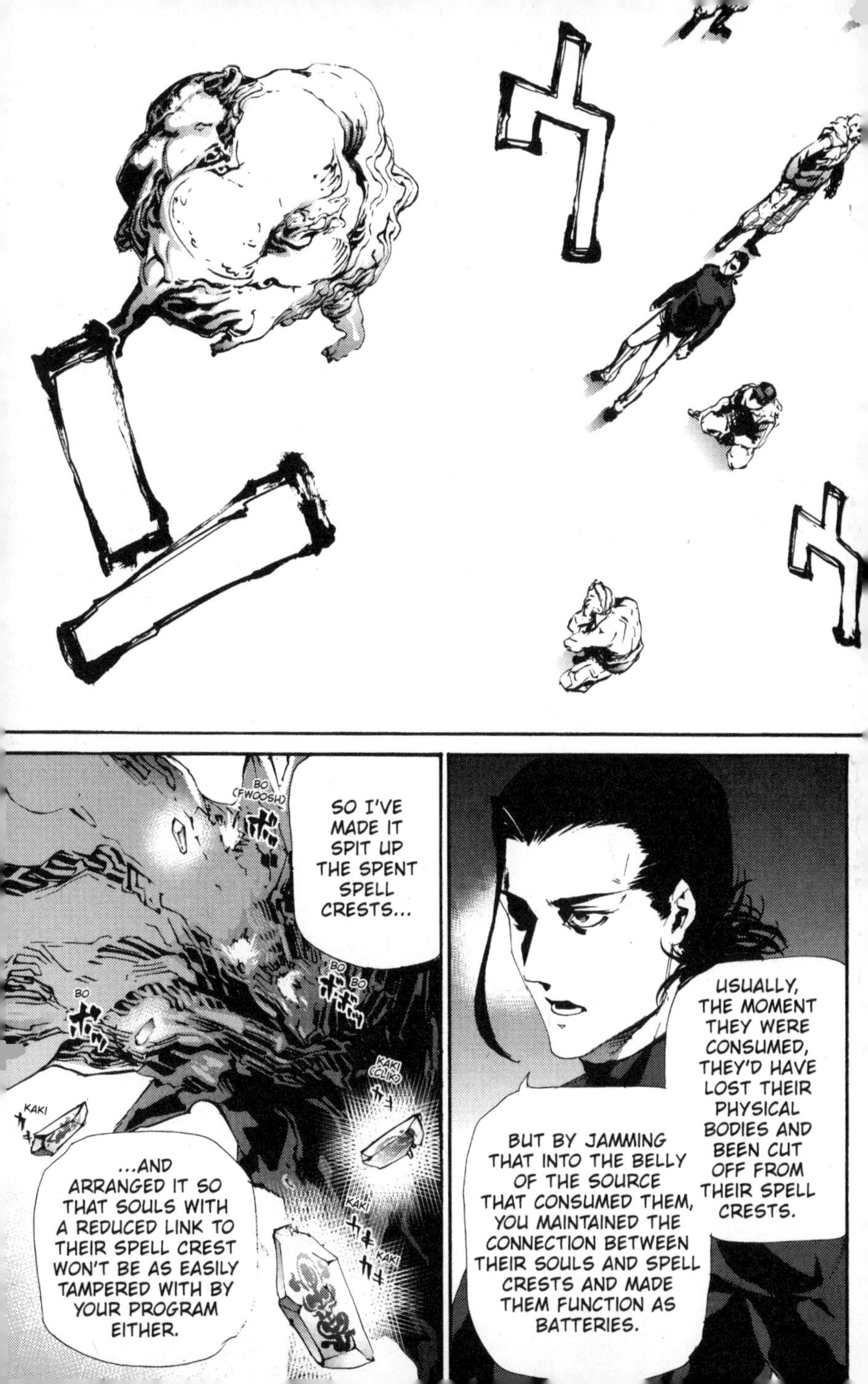
USUALLY, THE MOMENT THEY WERE CONSUMED, THEY'D HAVE LOST THEIR PHYSICAL BODIES AND BEEN CUT OFF FROM THEIR SPELL CRESTS.
BUT BY JAMMING THAT INTO THE BELLY OF THE SOURCE THAT CONSUMED THEM, YOU MAINTAINED THE CONNECTION BETWEEN THEIR SOULS AND SPELL CRESTS AND MADE THEM FUNCTION AS BATTERIES.
SO I'VE MADE IT SPIT UP THE SPENT SPELL CRESTS...
BO (FWOOSH)
BO BO
BO
KAKI (CLIK)
KAKI
KAKI
KAKI
...AND ARRANGED IT SO THAT SOULS WITH A REDUCED LINK TO THEIR SPELL CREST WON'T BE AS EASILY TAMPERED WITH BY YOUR PROGRAM EITHER.

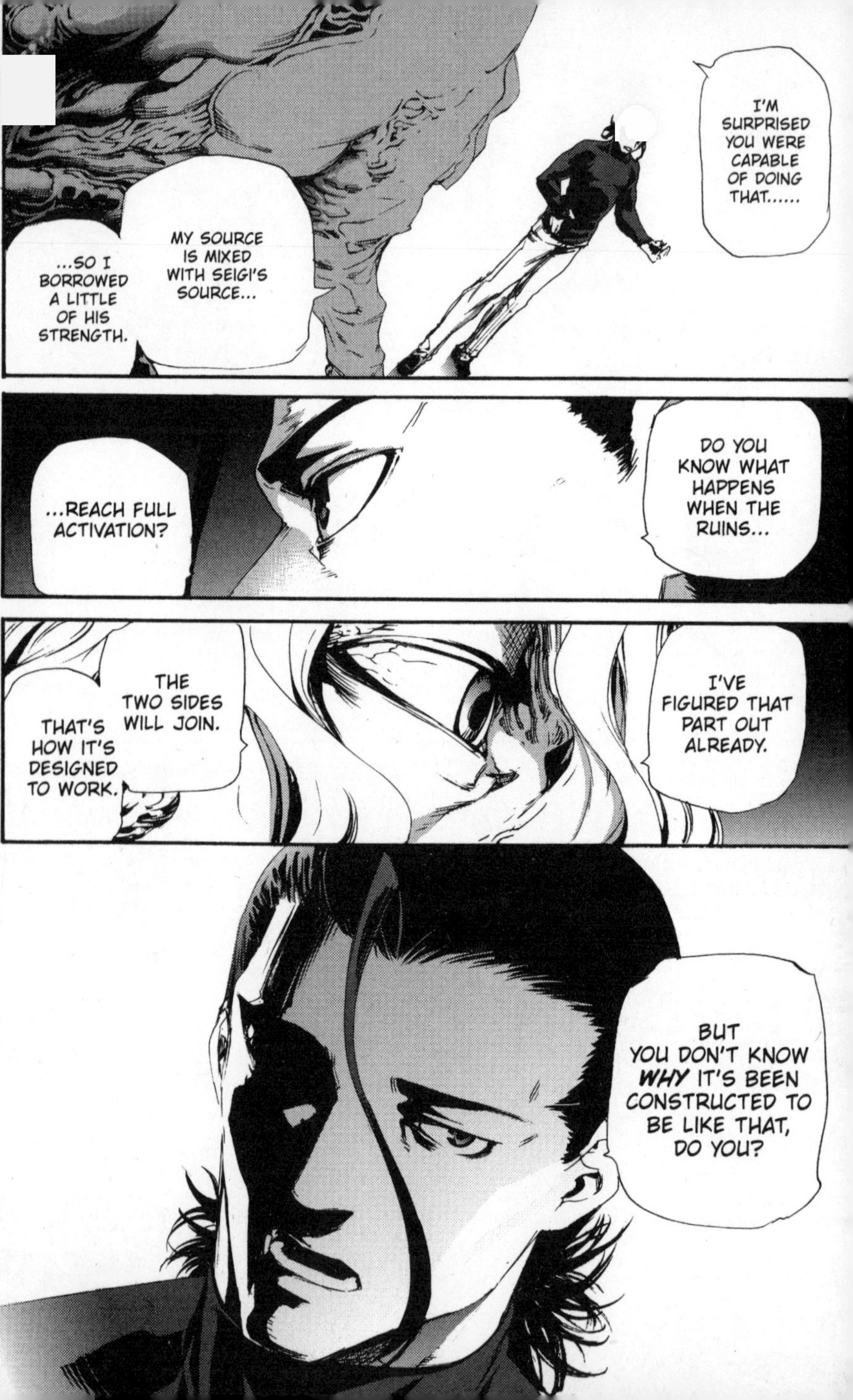
I'M SURPRISED YOU WERE CAPABLE OF DOING THAT......
MY SOURCE IS MIXED WITH SEIGI'S SOURCE...
...SO I BORROWED A LITTLE OF HIS STRENGTH.
DO YOU KNOW WHAT HAPPENS WHEN THE RUINS...
...REACH FULL ACTIVATION?
I'VE FIGURED THAT PART OUT ALREADY.
THE TWO SIDES WILL JOIN.
THAT'S HOW IT'S DESIGNED TO WORK.
BUT YOU DON'T KNOW *WHY* IT'S BEEN CONSTRUCTED TO BE LIKE THAT, DO YOU?

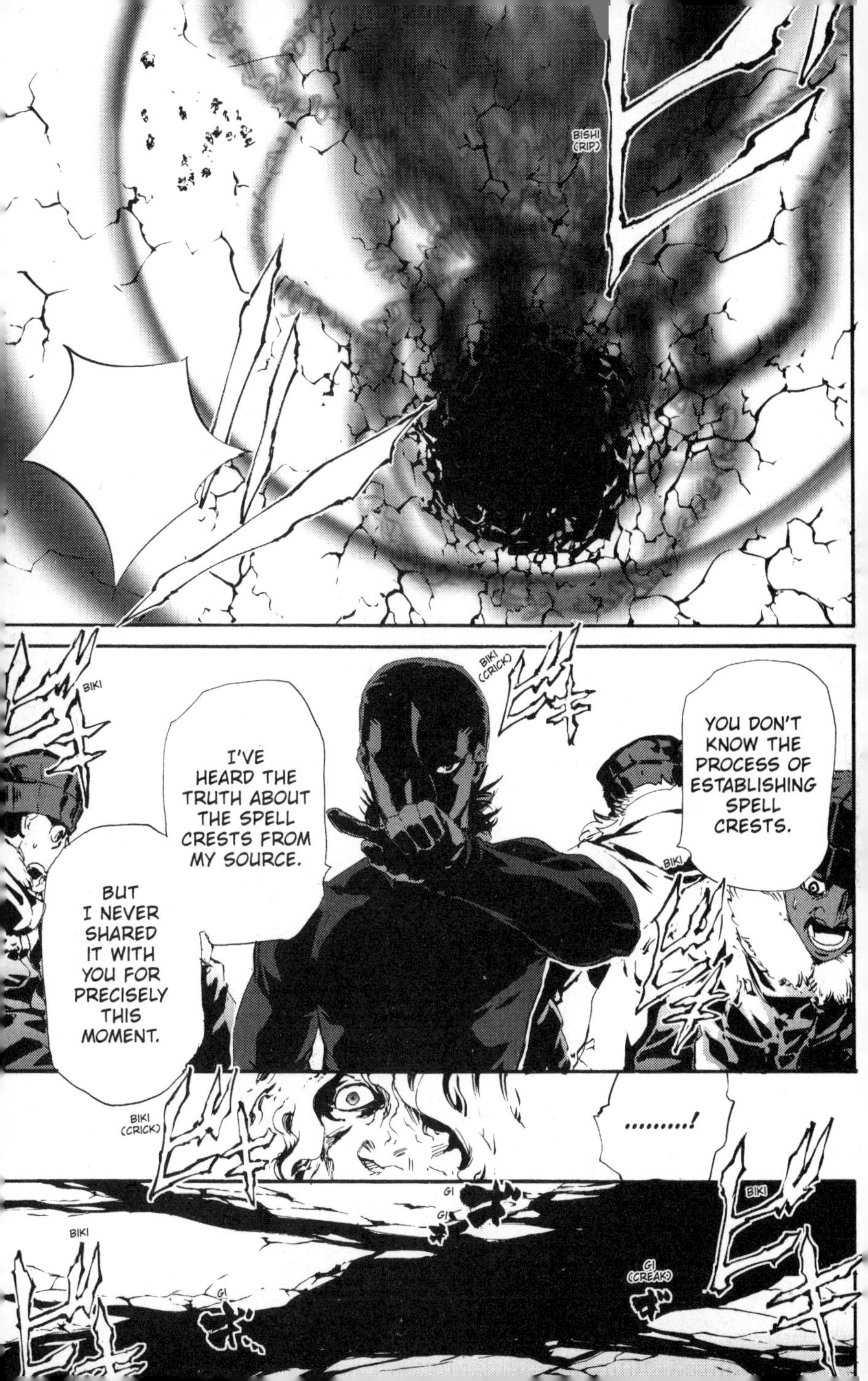
BISHI (RIP)
YOU DON'T KNOW THE PROCESS OF ESTABLISHING SPELL CRESTS.
BIKI (CRICK)
BIKI
I'VE HEARD THE TRUTH ABOUT THE SPELL CRESTS FROM MY SOURCE.
BUT I NEVER SHARED IT WITH YOU FOR PRECISELY THIS MOMENT.
BIKI
..........!
BIKI (CRICK)
BIKI
GI (CREAK)
GI
GI
GI
BIKI

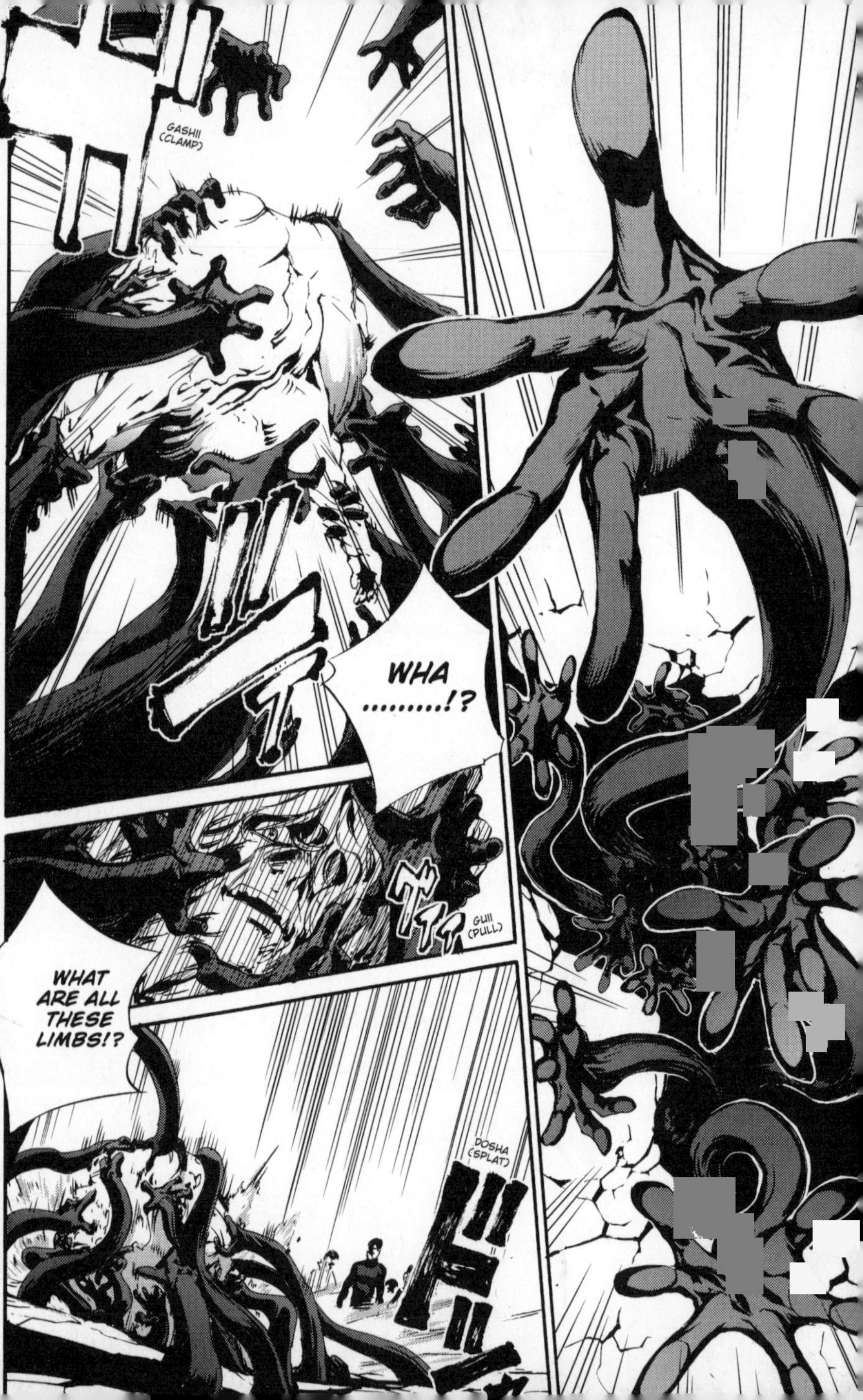
GASHII (CLAMP)
WHA ....!?
GUII (PULL)
WHAT ARE ALL THESE LIMBS!?
DOSHA (SPLAT)

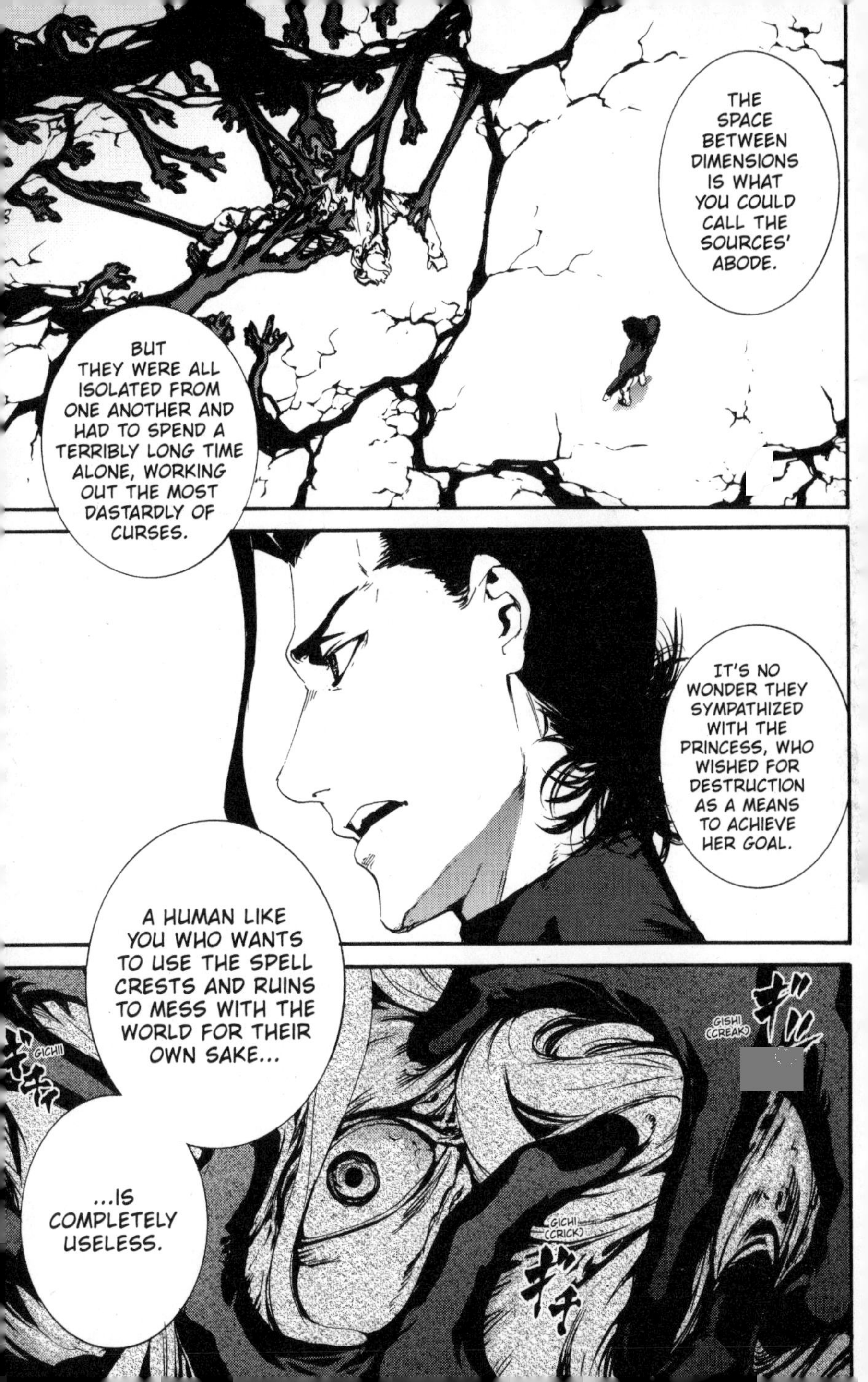
THE SPACE BETWEEN DIMENSIONS IS WHAT YOU COULD CALL THE SOURCES' ABODE.
BUT THEY WERE ALL ISOLATED FROM ONE ANOTHER AND HAD TO SPEND A TERRIBLY LONG TIME ALONE, WORKING OUT THE MOST DASTARDLY OF CURSES.
IT'S NO WONDER THEY SYMPATHIZED WITH THE PRINCESS, WHO WISHED FOR DESTRUCTION AS A MEANS TO ACHIEVE HER GOAL.
GISHI (CREAK)
A HUMAN LIKE YOU WHO WANTS TO USE THE SPELL CRESTS AND RUINS TO MESS WITH THE WORLD FOR THEIR OWN SAKE...
GICHII
GICHI (CRICK)
...IS COMPLETELY USELESS.

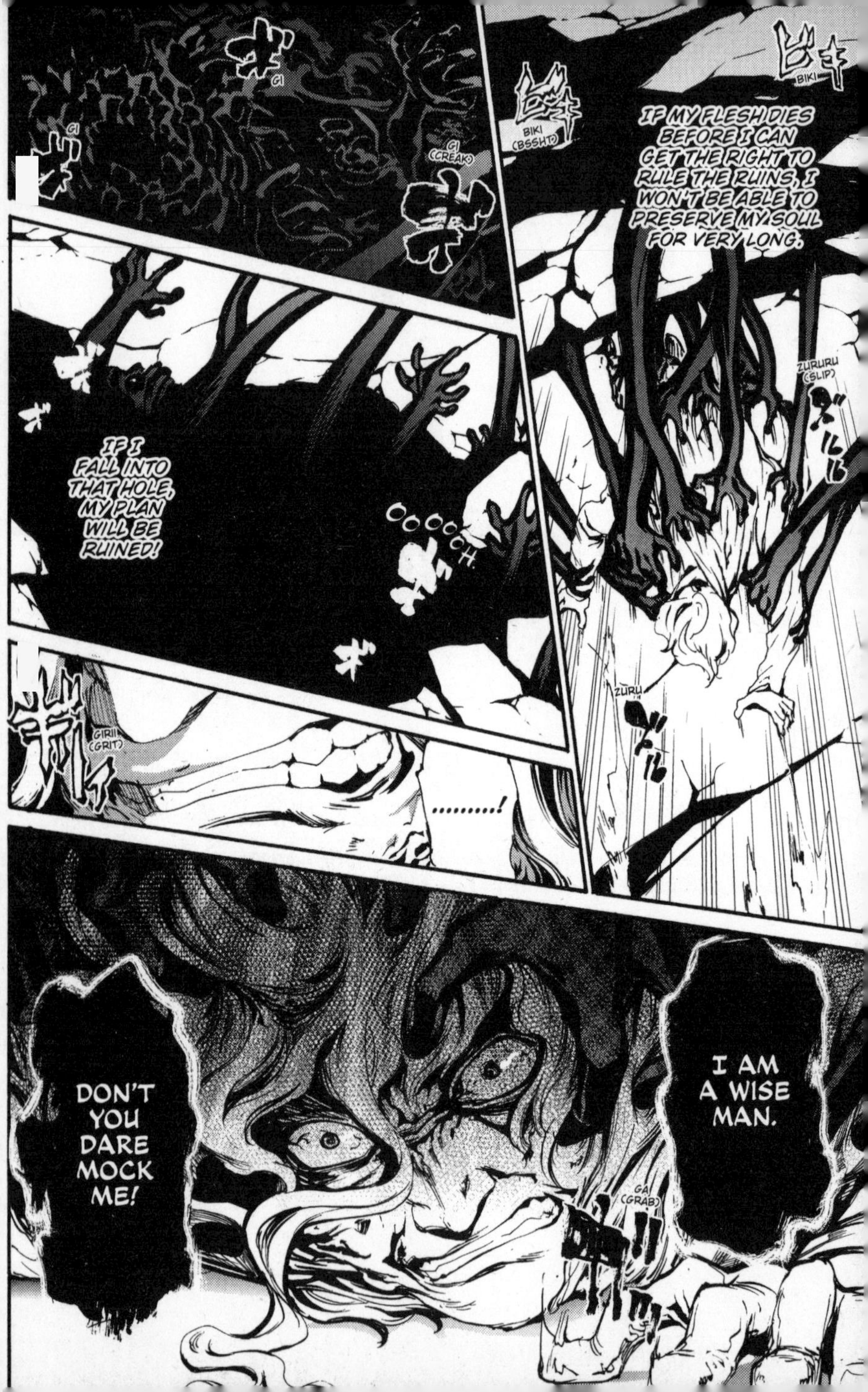
BIKI
BIKI (BSSHT)
IF MY FLESH DIES BEFORE I CAN GET THE RIGHT TO RULE THE RUINS, I WON'T BE ABLE TO PRESERVE MY SOUL FOR VERY LONG.
ZURURU (SLIP)
ZURU
GI (CREAK)
GI
GI
OOOOCH.
IF I FALL INTO THAT HOLE, MY PLAN WILL BE RUINED!
..........!
GIRII (GRIT)
I AM A WISE MAN.
GA (GRAB)
DON'T YOU DARE MOCK ME!

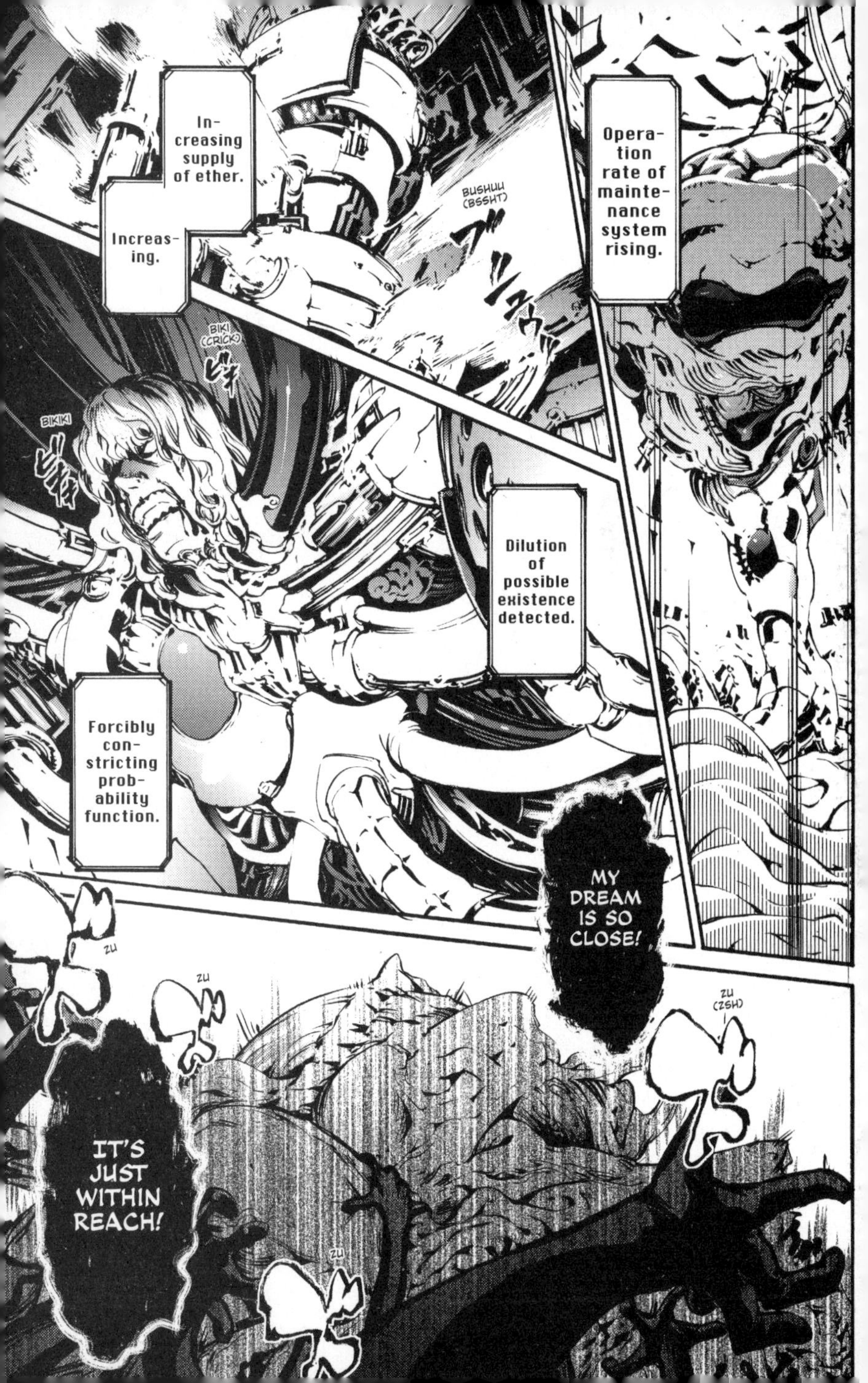
Operation rate of maintenance system rising.
Increasing supply of ether.
Increasing.
BUSHUU (BSSHT)
BIKI (CRICK)
BIKIKI
Dilution of possible existence detected.
Forcibly constricting probability function.
MY DREAM IS SO CLOSE!
ZU (ZSH)
ZU
ZU
IT'S JUST WITHIN REACH!
ZU

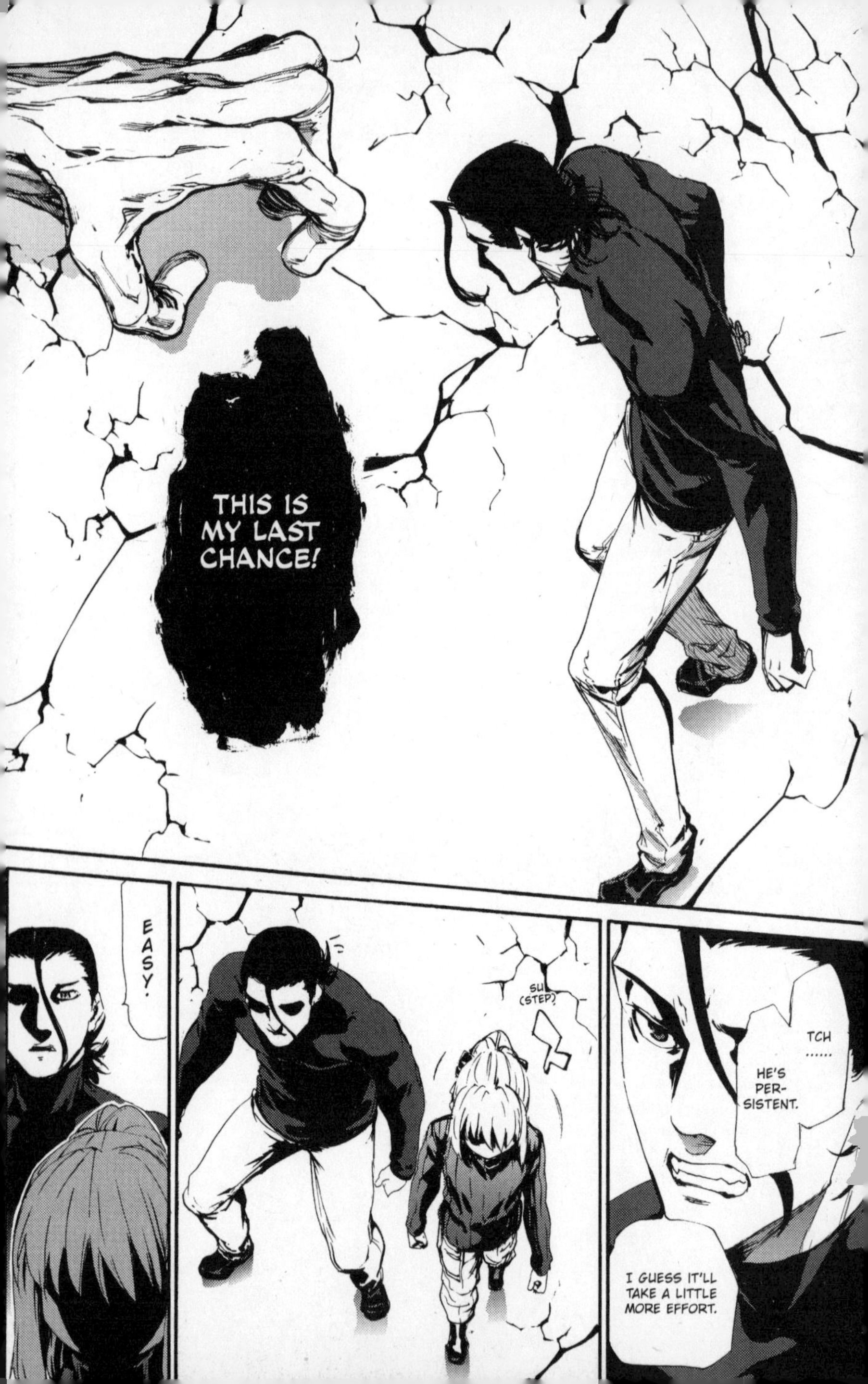
THIS IS MY LAST CHANCE!
TCH ......
HE'S PER-SISTENT.
I GUESS IT'LL TAKE A LITTLE MORE EFFORT.
SU (STEP)
EASY.

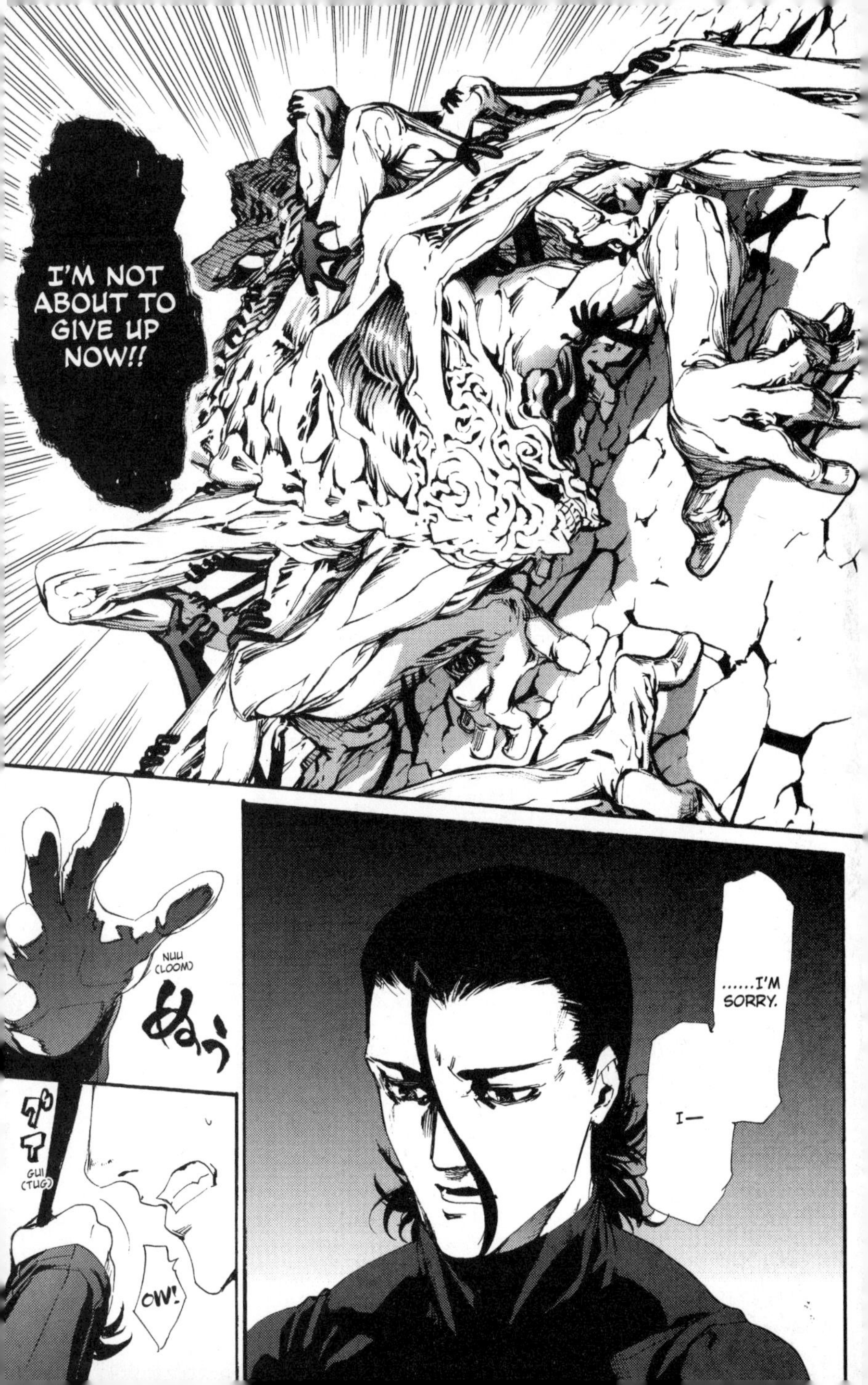
I'M NOT ABOUT TO GIVE UP NOW!!
......I'M SORRY.
I—
NUU (LOOM)
GUI (TUG)
OW!

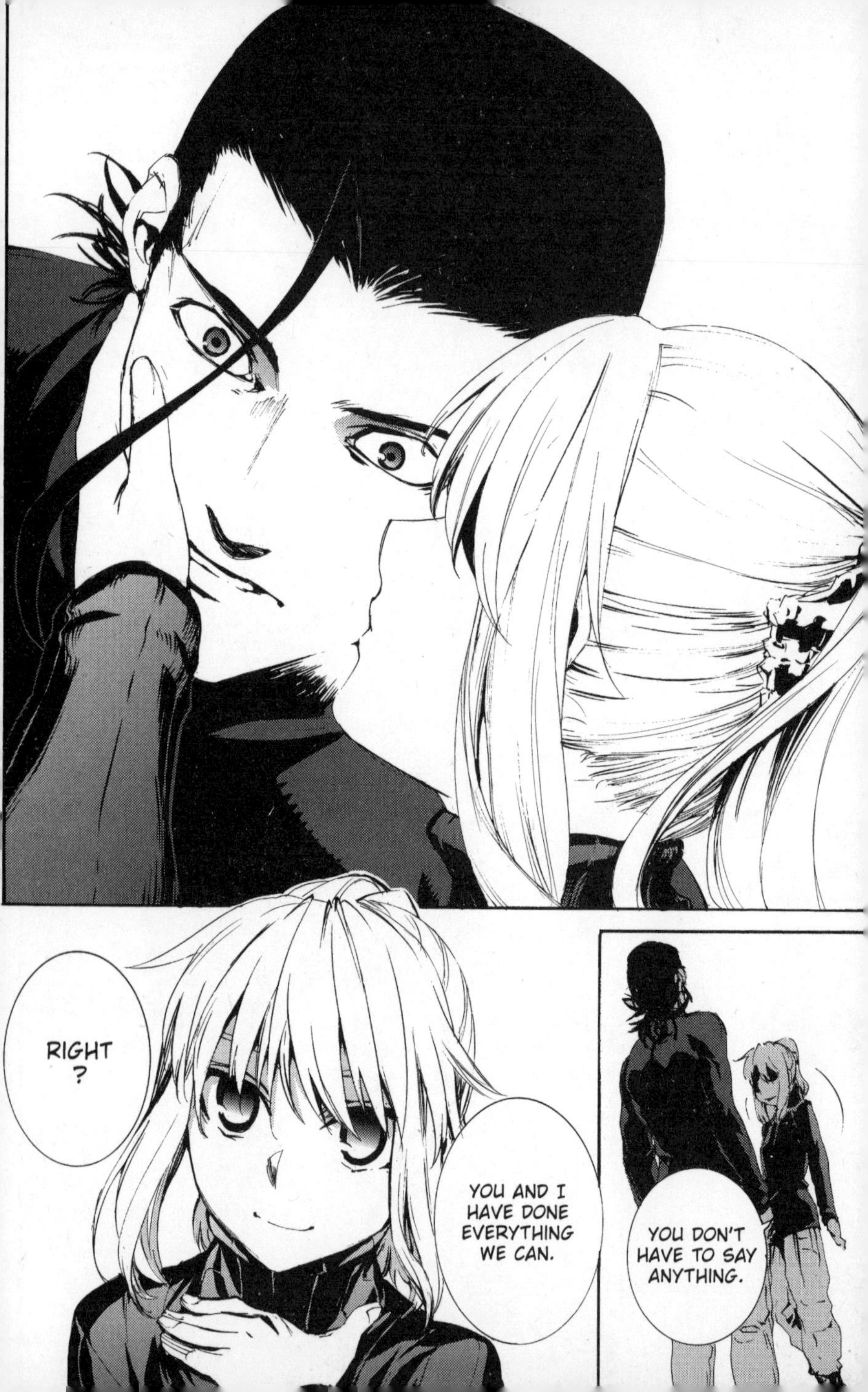
YOU DON'T HAVE TO SAY ANYTHING.
YOU AND I HAVE DONE EVERYTHING WE CAN.
RIGHT?

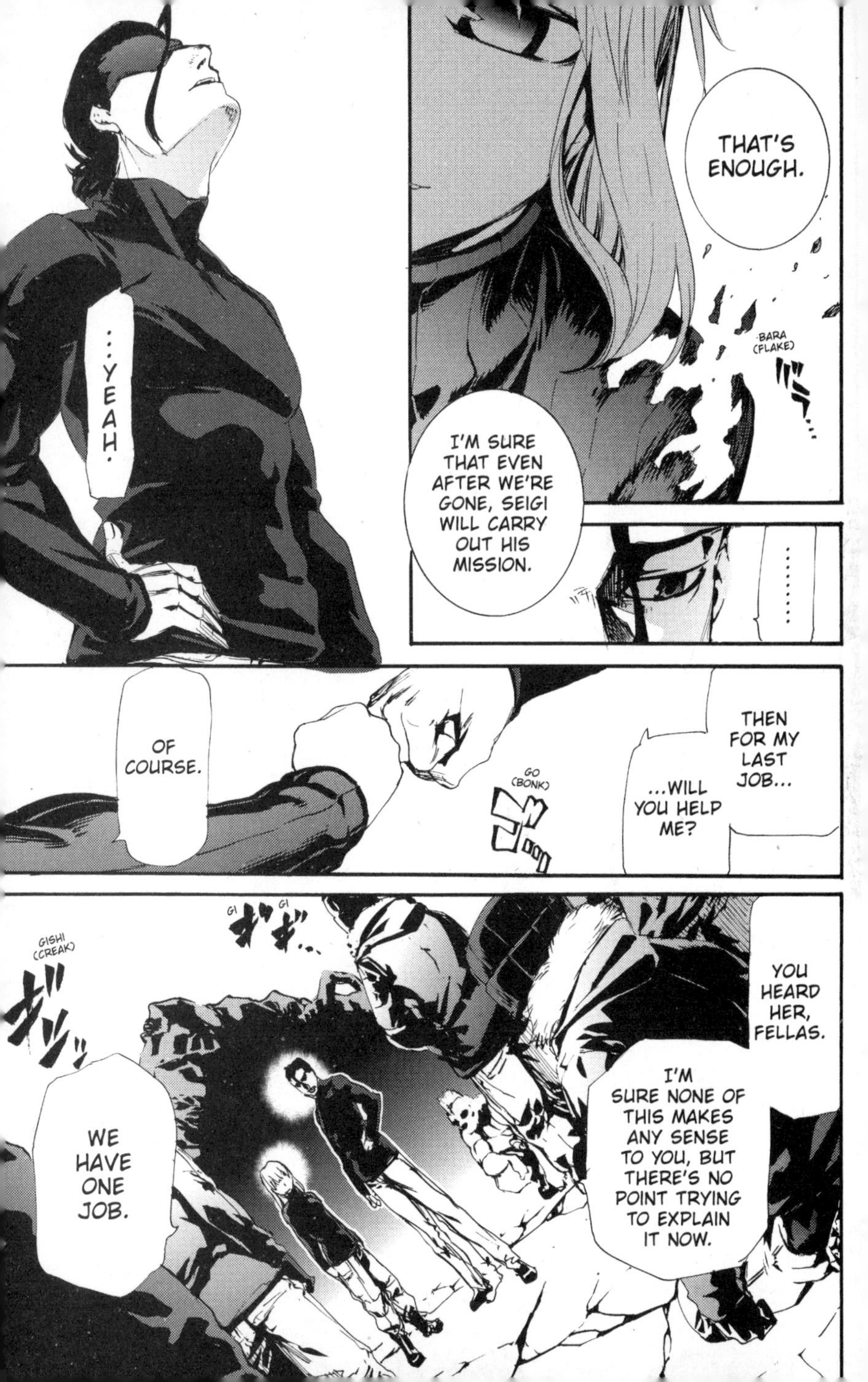
THAT'S ENOUGH.
BARA (FLAKE)
I'M SURE THAT EVEN AFTER WE'RE GONE, SEIGI WILL CARRY OUT HIS MISSION.
....
...YEAH.
THEN FOR MY LAST JOB...
...WILL YOU HELP ME?
GO (BONK)
OF COURSE.
GI GI
YOU HEARD HER, FELLAS.
I'M SURE NONE OF THIS MAKES ANY SENSE TO YOU, BUT THERE'S NO POINT TRYING TO EXPLAIN IT NOW.
GISHI (CREAK)
WE HAVE ONE JOB.

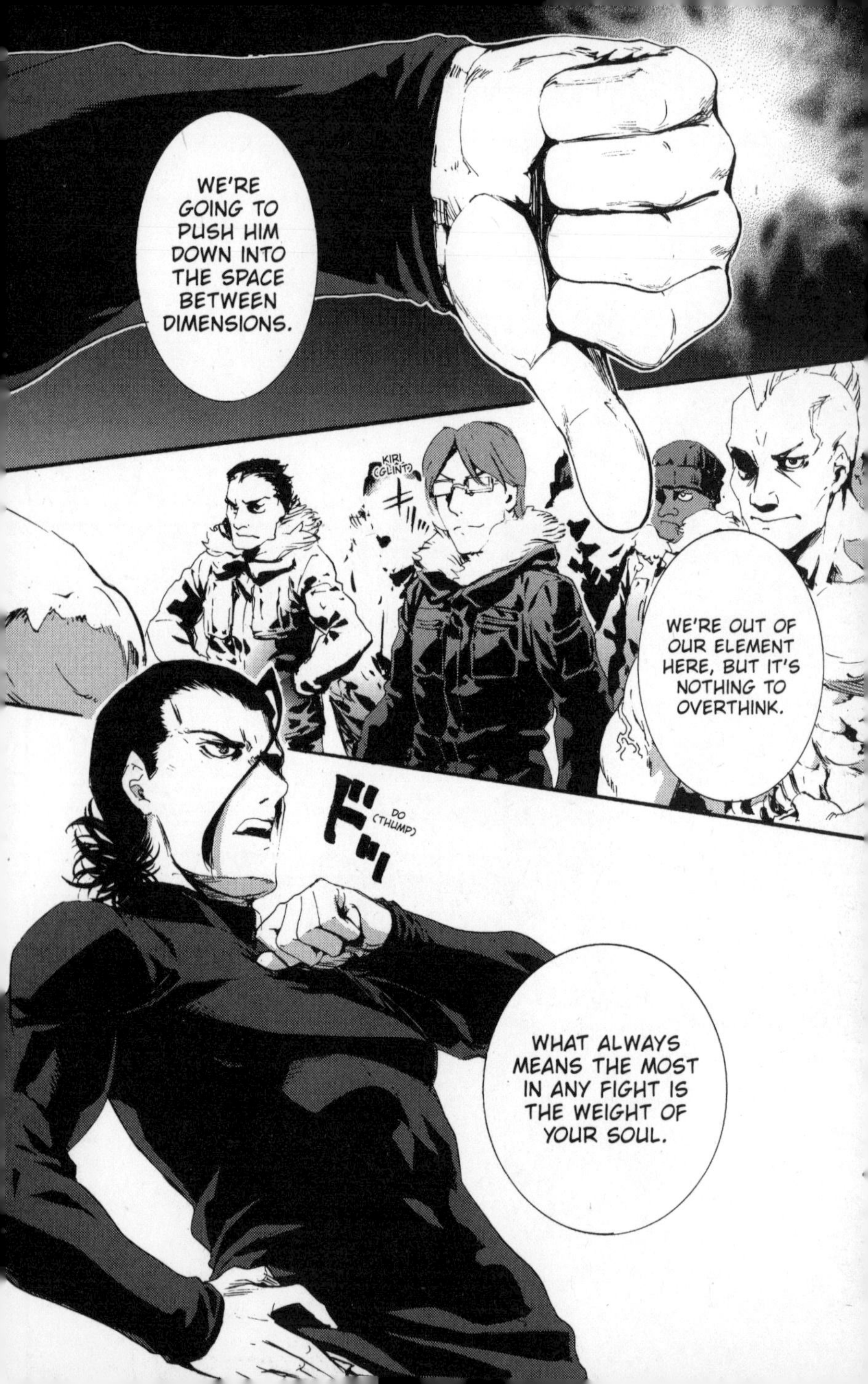
WE'RE GOING TO PUSH HIM DOWN INTO THE SPACE BETWEEN DIMENSIONS.
KIRI (GLINT)
WE'RE OUT OF OUR ELEMENT HERE, BUT IT'S NOTHING TO OVERTHINK.
ドッ
DO (THUMP)
WHAT ALWAYS MEANS THE MOST IN ANY FIGHT IS THE WEIGHT OF YOUR SOUL.

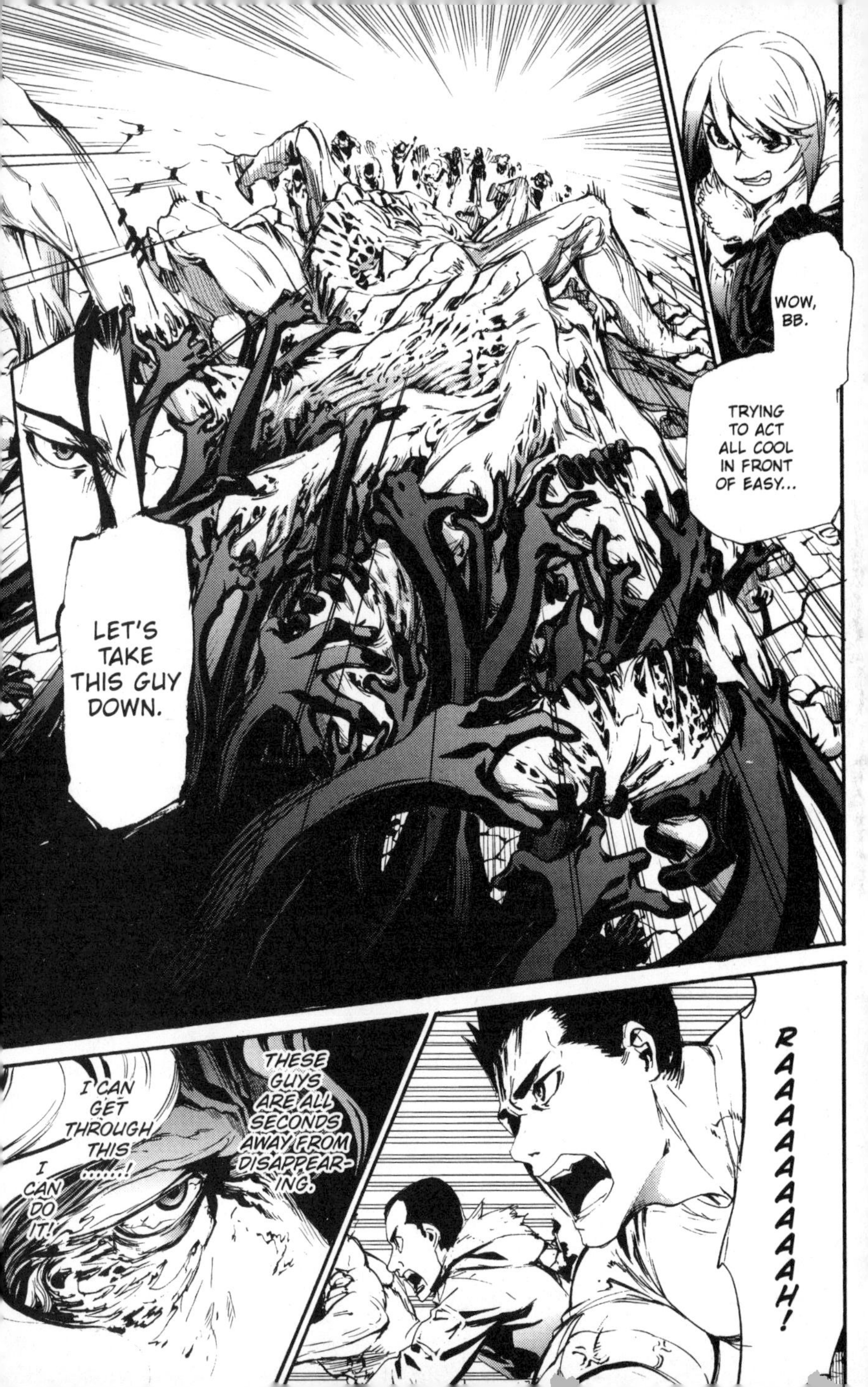
WOW, BB.
TRYING TO ACT ALL COOL IN FRONT OF EASY...
LET'S TAKE THIS GUY DOWN.
RAAAAAAAAAAH!
THESE GUYS ARE ALL SECONDS AWAY FROM DISAPPEARING.
I CAN GET THROUGH THIS ......!
I CAN DO IT!

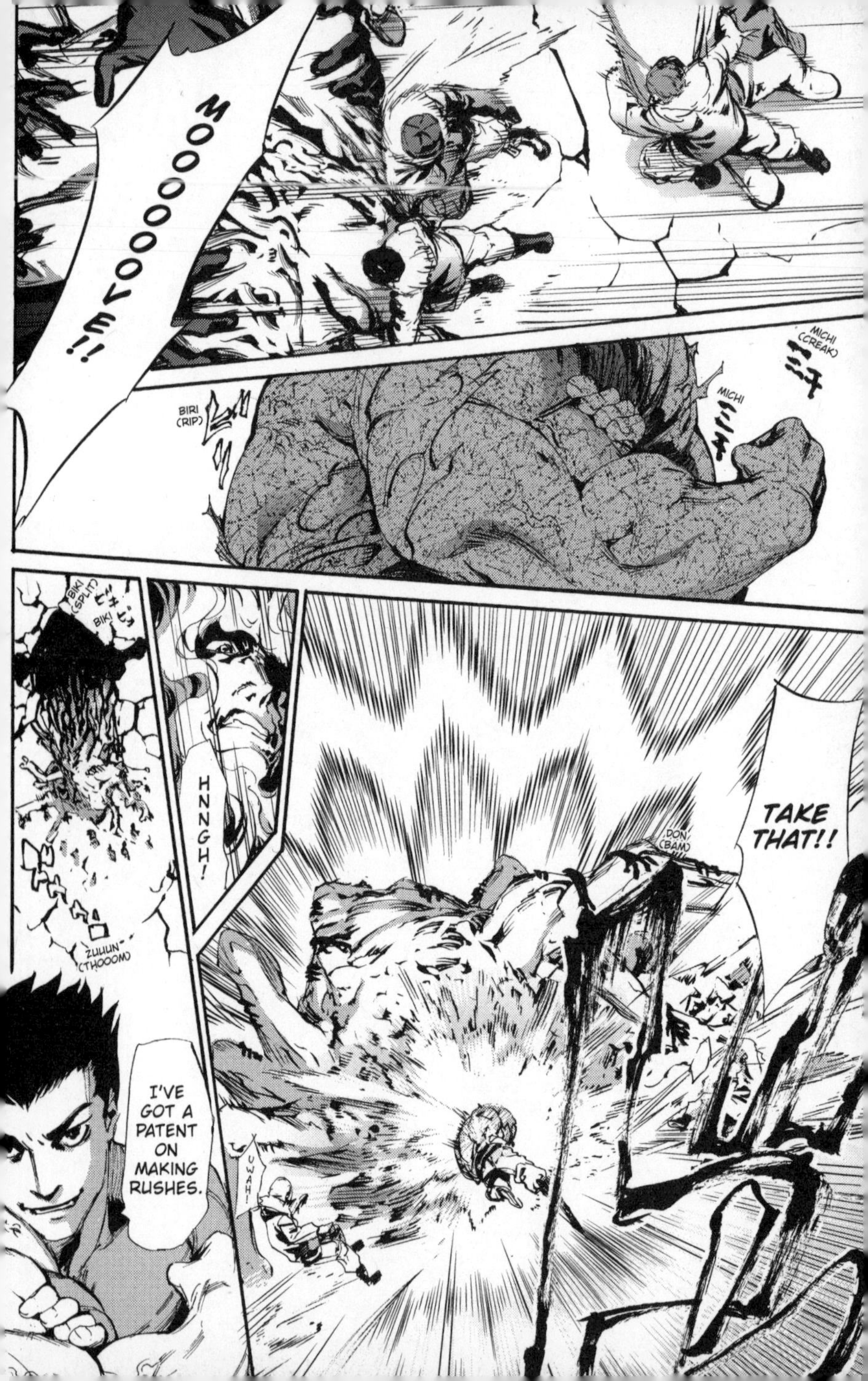
MOOOOOOOVE!!
MICHI (CREAK)
MICHI
BIRI (RIP)
TAKE THAT!!
DON (BAM)
UWAH!
HNNGH!
BIKI (SPLIT) BIKI
ZUUUN (THOOOM)
I'VE GOT A PATENT ON MAKING RUSHES.

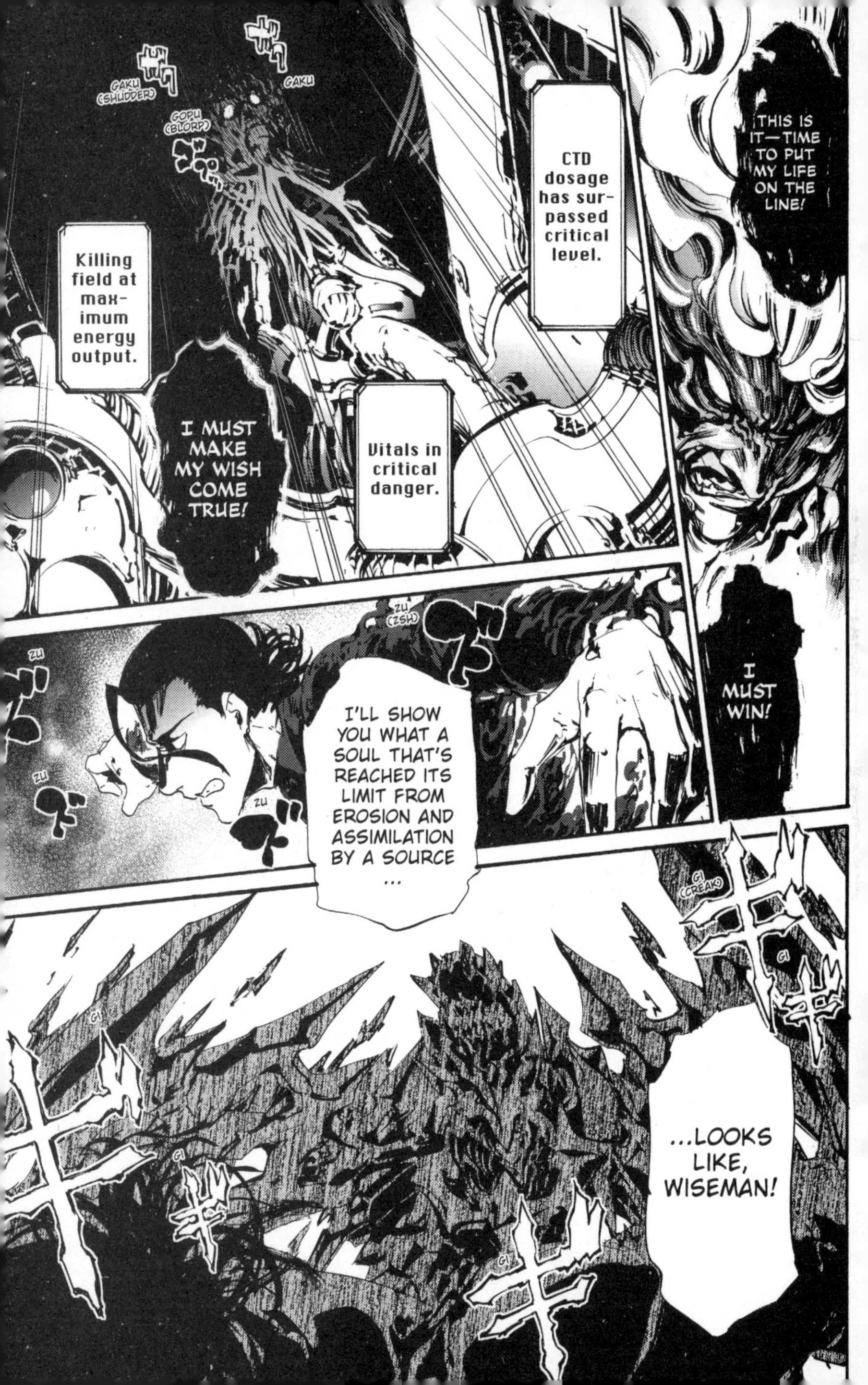
THIS IS IT—TIME TO PUT MY LIFE ON THE LINE!
I MUST WIN!
GAKU
GAKU (SHUDDER)
GOPU (BLORP)
CTD dosage has surpassed critical level.
Killing field at maximum energy output.
Vitals in critical danger.
I MUST MAKE MY WISH COME TRUE!
ZU (ZSH)
I'LL SHOW YOU WHAT A SOUL THAT'S REACHED ITS LIMIT FROM EROSION AND ASSIMILATION BY A SOURCE ...
ZU
ZU
ZU
GI (CREAK)
GI
GI
GI
GI
...LOOKS LIKE, WISEMAN!

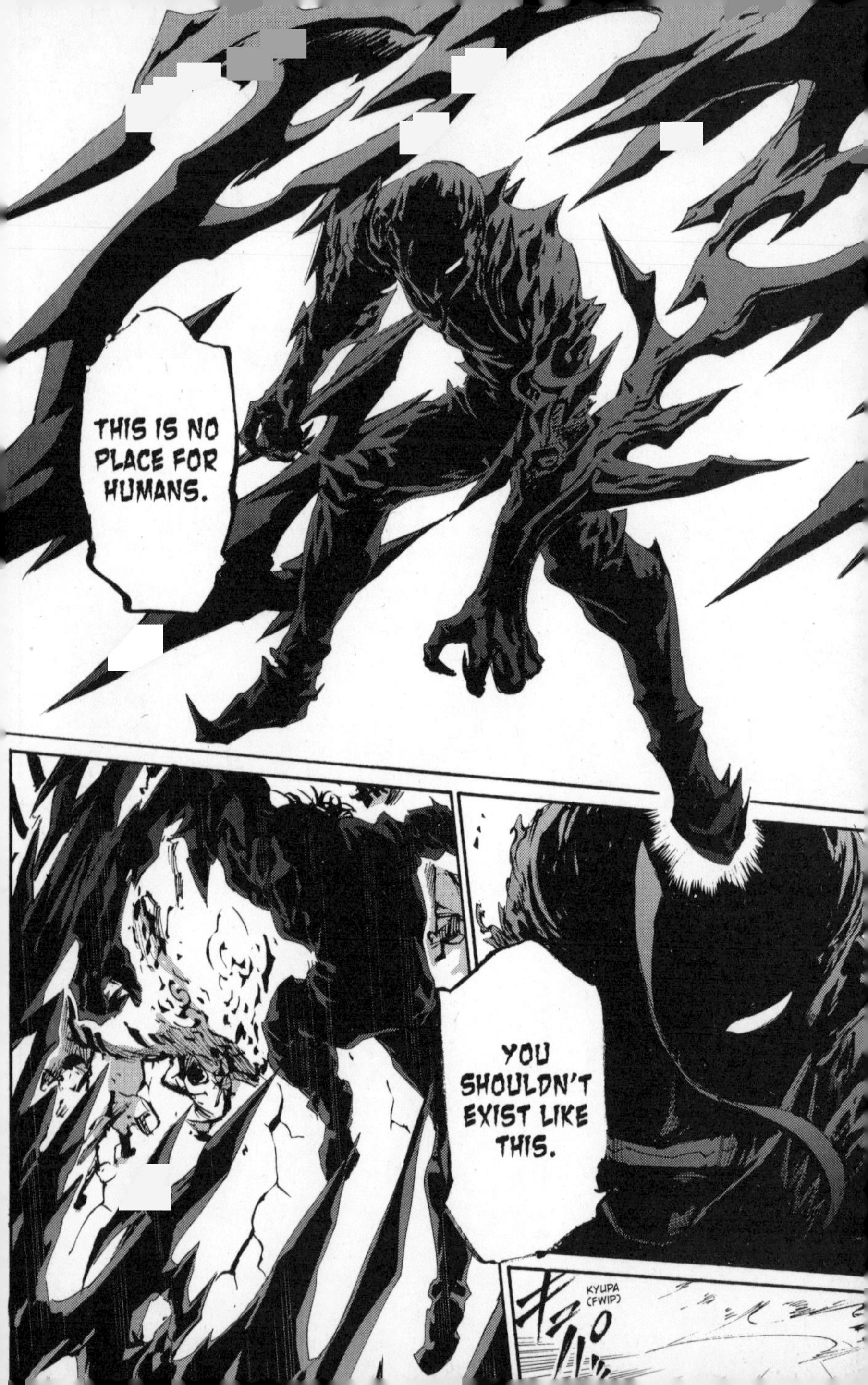
THIS IS NO PLACE FOR HUMANS.
YOU SHOULDN'T EXIST LIKE THIS.
KYUPA (FWIP)

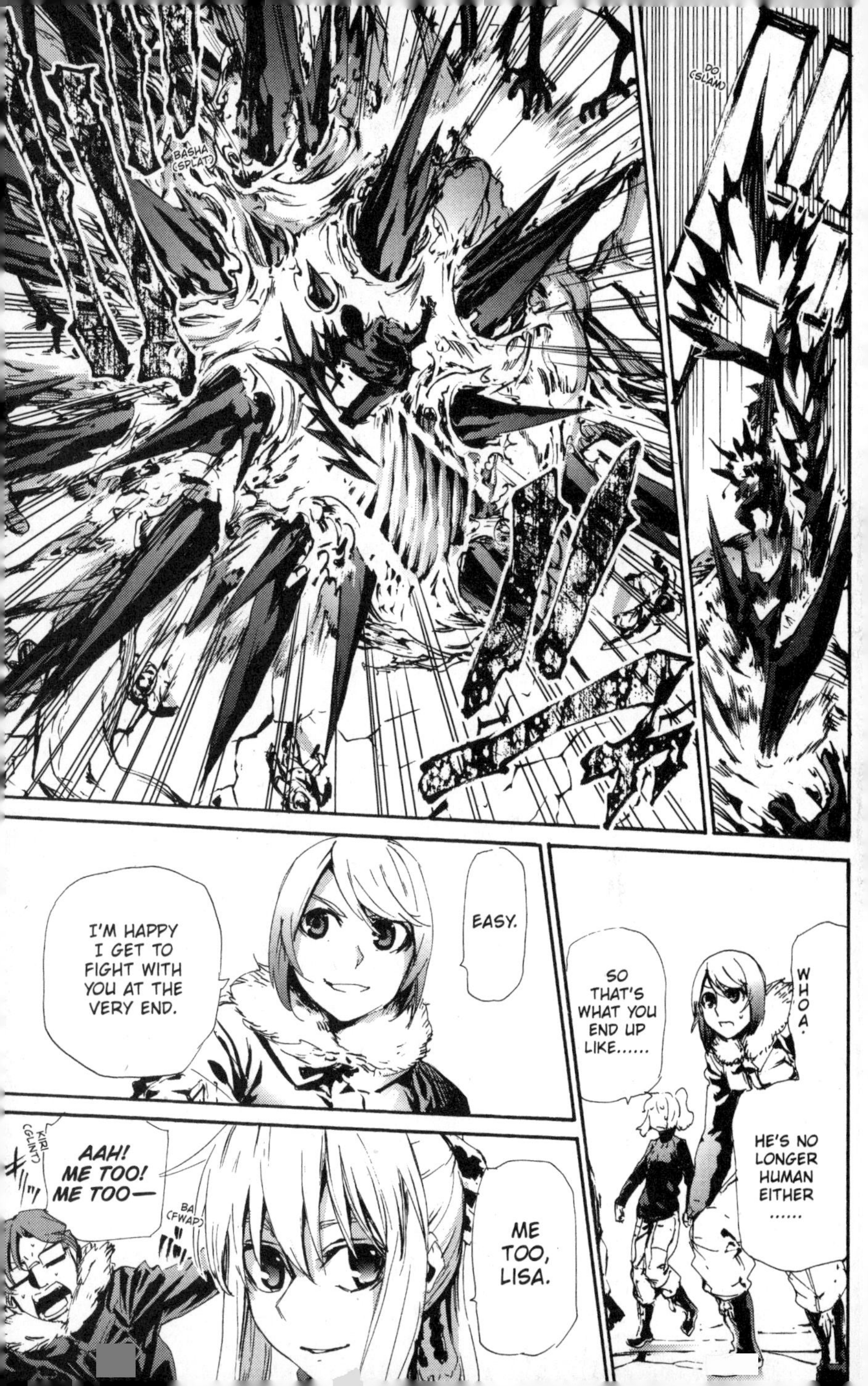
DO (SLAM)
BASHA (SPLAT)
WHOA.
SO THAT'S WHAT YOU END UP LIKE......
HE'S NO LONGER HUMAN EITHER......
EASY.
I'M HAPPY I GET TO FIGHT WITH YOU AT THE VERY END.
ME TOO, LISA.
BA (FWAP)
AAH! ME TOO! ME TOO—
KIRI (GLINT)

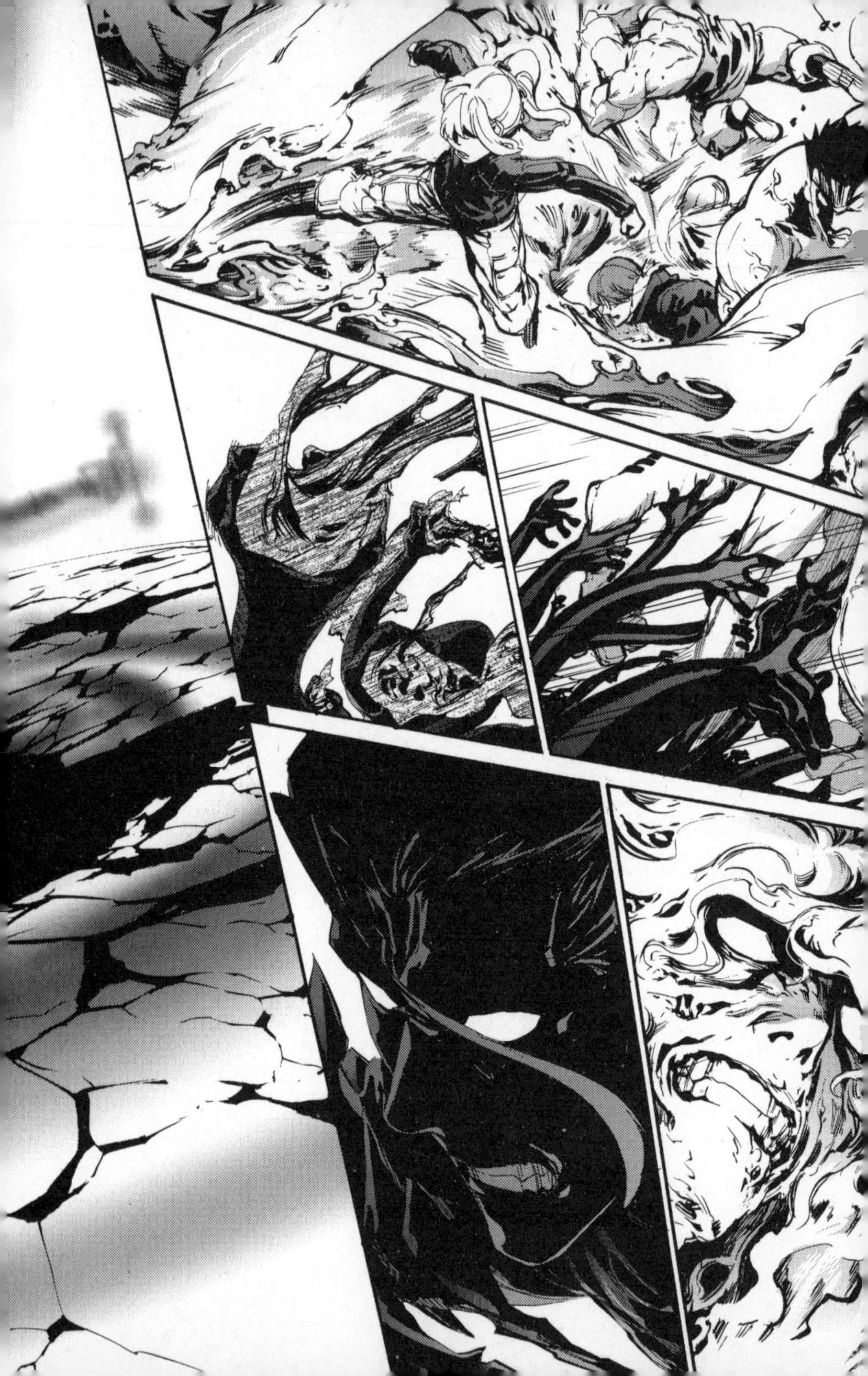

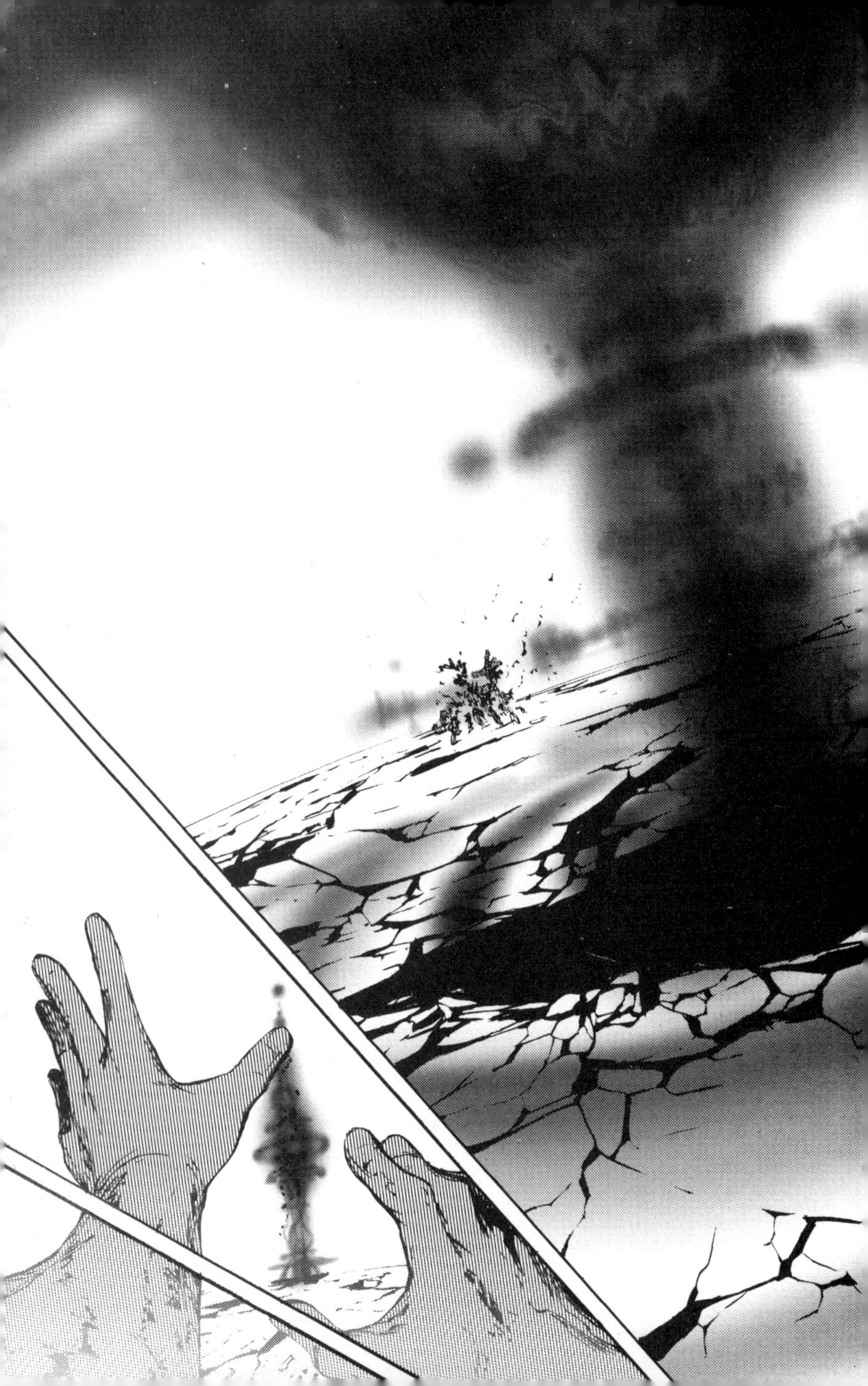

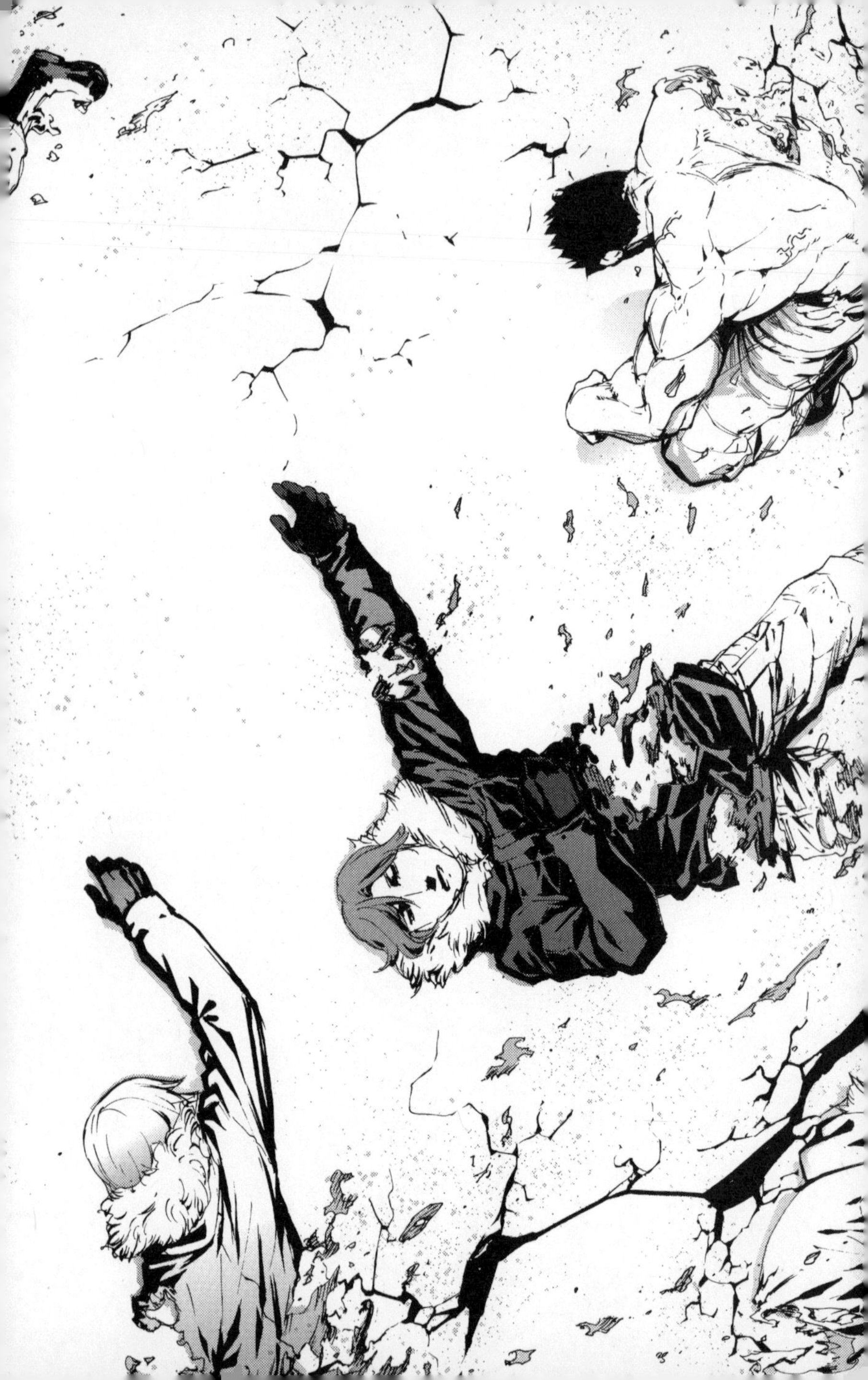

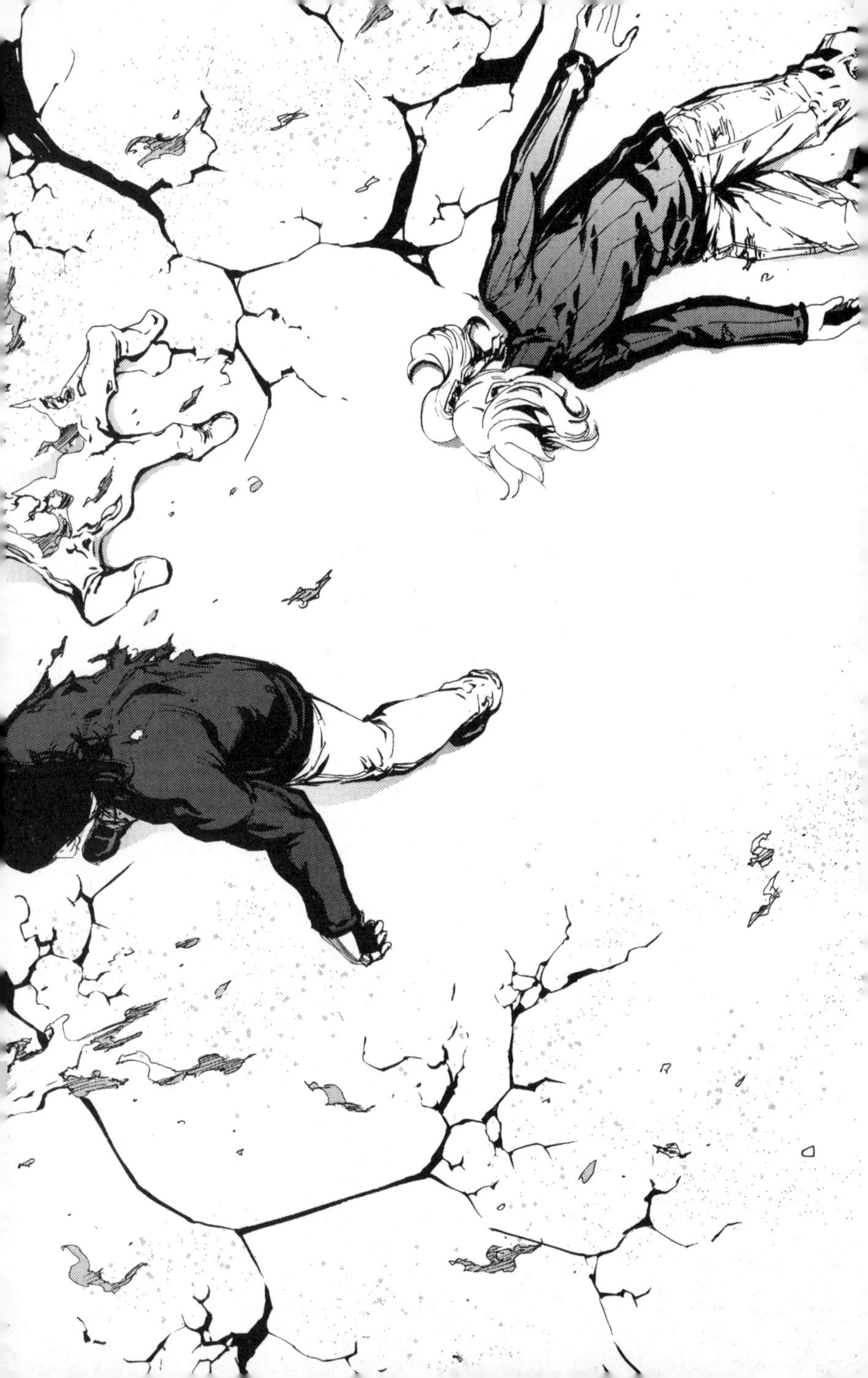

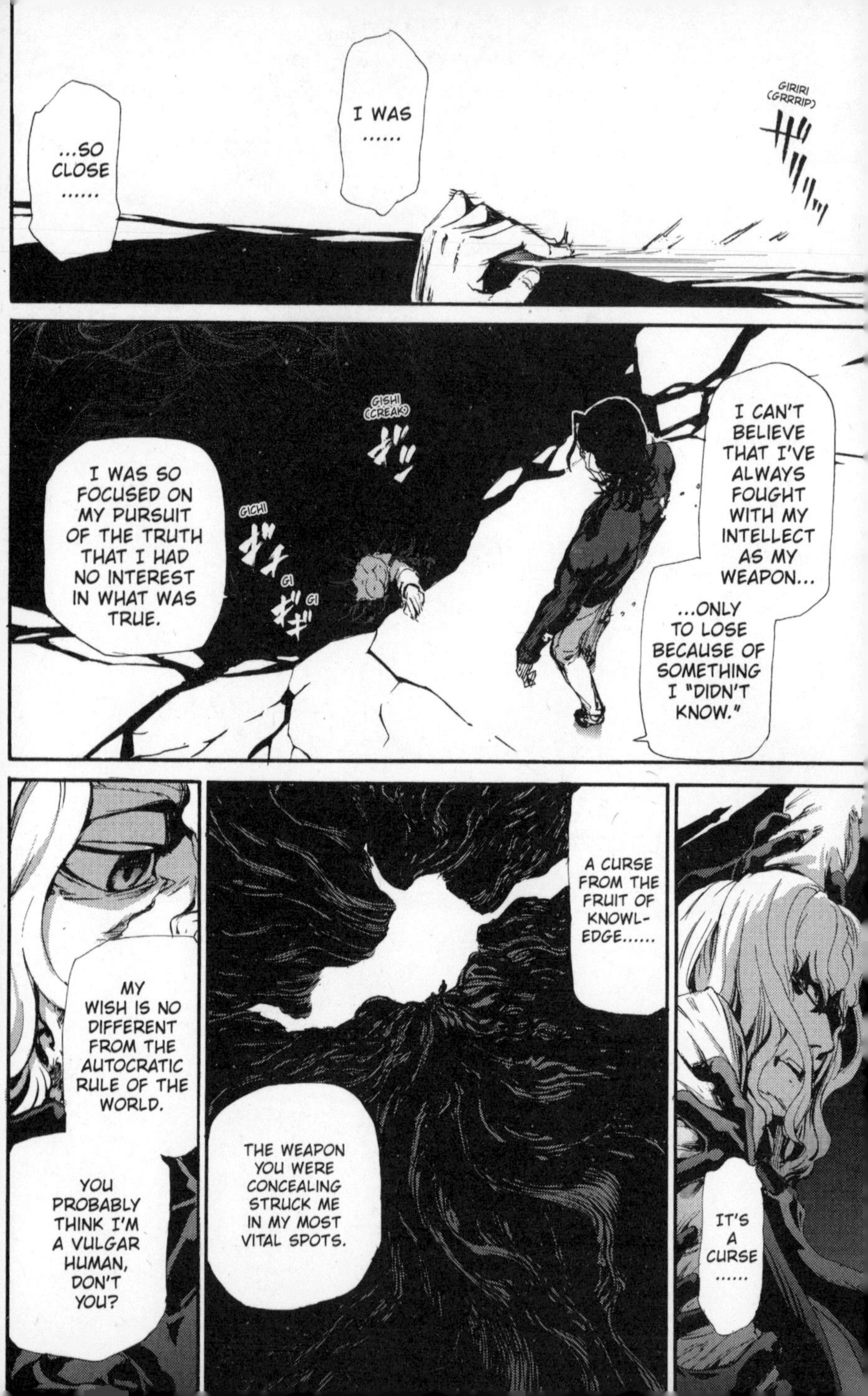GIRIRI (GRRRIP)
I WAS ......
...SO CLOSE ......
I CAN'T BELIEVE THAT I'VE ALWAYS FOUGHT WITH MY INTELLECT AS MY WEAPON...
...ONLY TO LOSE BECAUSE OF SOMETHING I "DIDN'T KNOW."
GISHI (CREAK)
GICHI
GI
GI
I WAS SO FOCUSED ON MY PURSUIT OF THE TRUTH THAT I HAD NO INTEREST IN WHAT WAS TRUE.
IT'S A CURSE ......
A CURSE FROM THE FRUIT OF KNOWL-EDGE......
THE WEAPON YOU WERE CONCEALING STRUCK ME IN MY MOST VITAL SPOTS.
MY WISH IS NO DIFFERENT FROM THE AUTOCRATIC RULE OF THE WORLD.
YOU PROBABLY THINK I'M A VULGAR HUMAN, DON'T YOU?

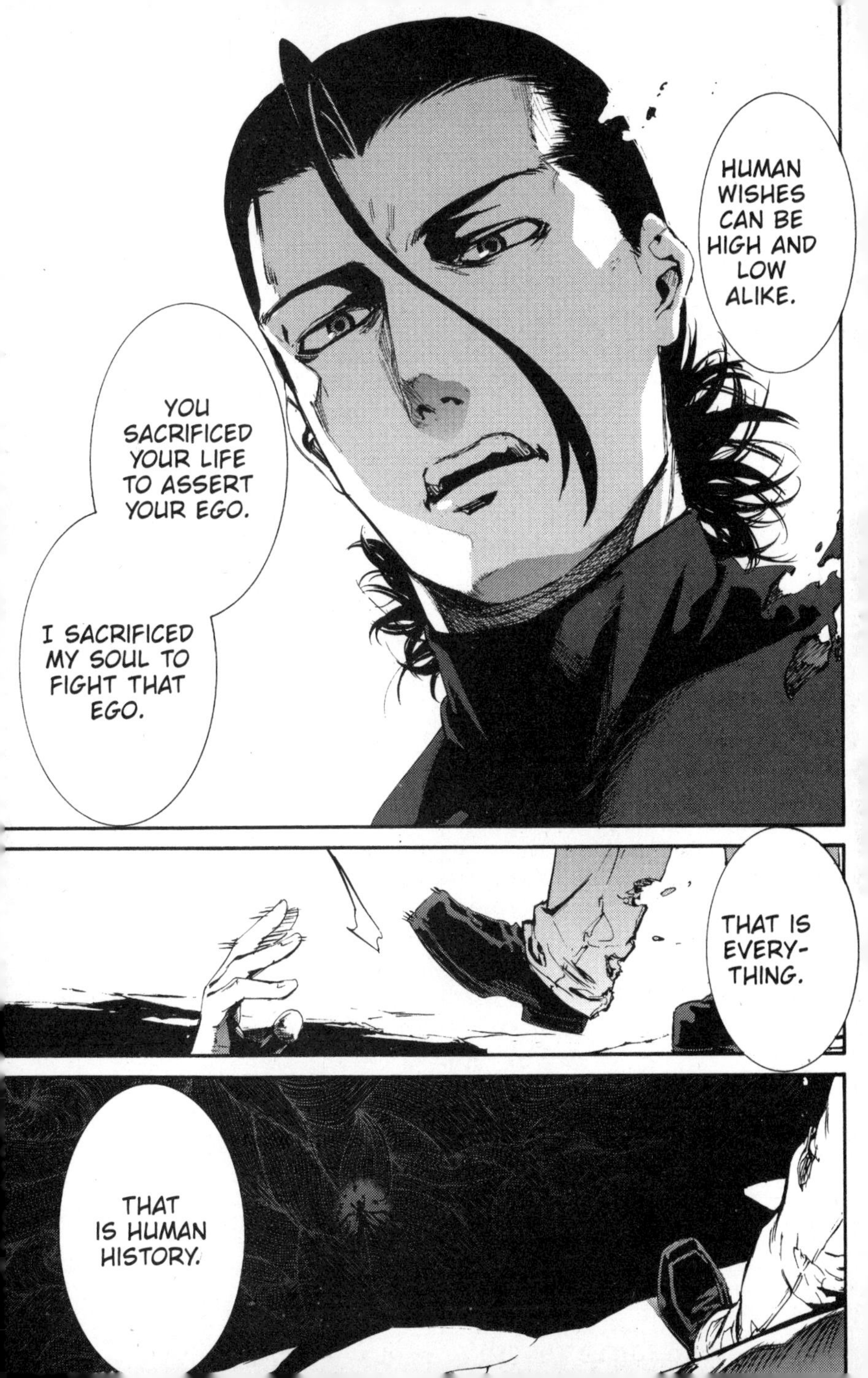
HUMAN WISHES CAN BE HIGH AND LOW ALIKE.
YOU SACRIFICED YOUR LIFE TO ASSERT YOUR EGO.
I SACRIFICED MY SOUL TO FIGHT THAT EGO.
THAT IS EVERY-THING.
THAT IS HUMAN HISTORY.

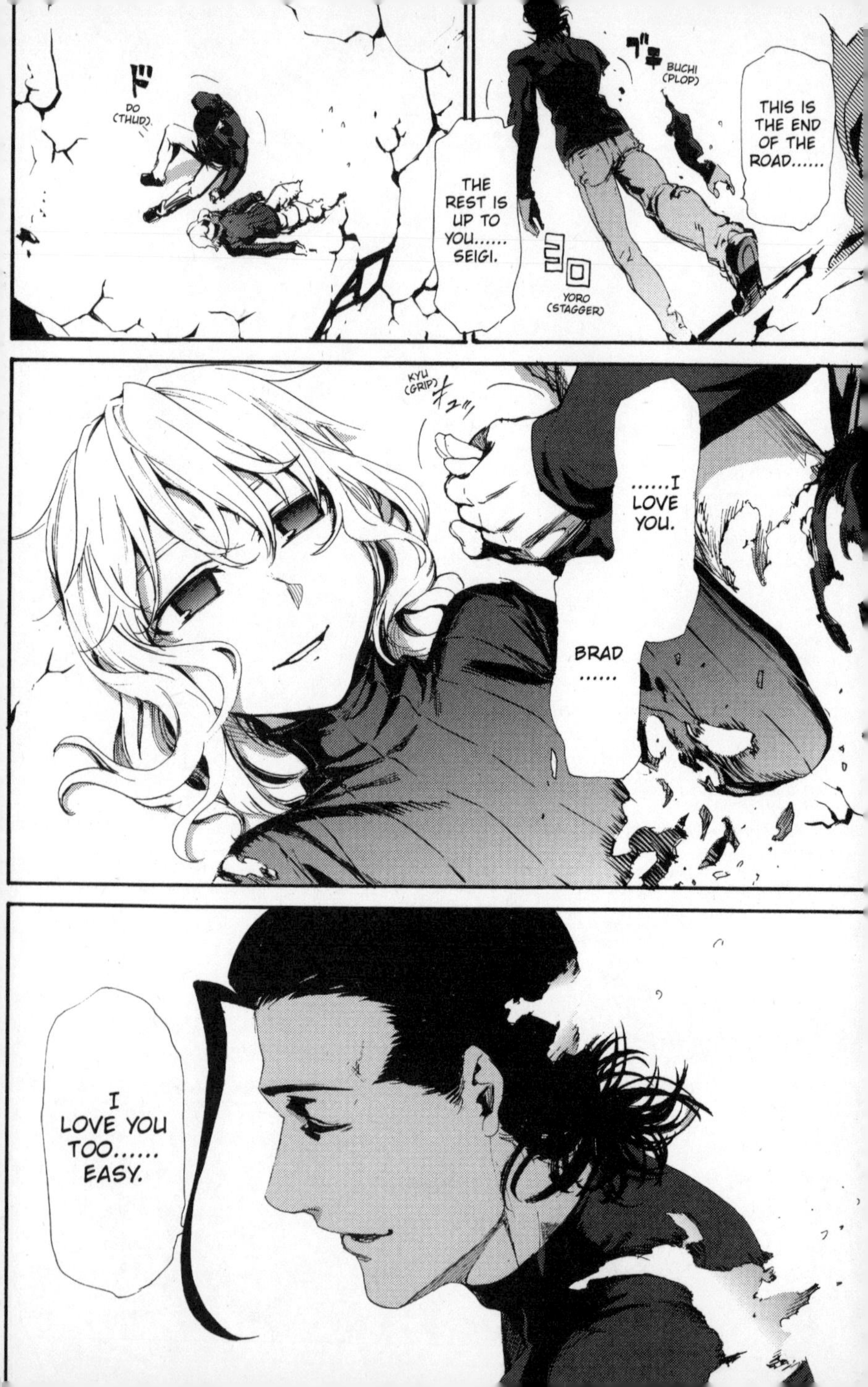
THIS IS THE END OF THE ROAD......
BUCHI (PLOP)
YORO (STAGGER)
THE REST IS UP TO YOU...... SEIGI.
ド
DO (THUD)
KYU (GRIP)
......I LOVE YOU.
BRAD ......
I LOVE YOU TOO...... EASY.

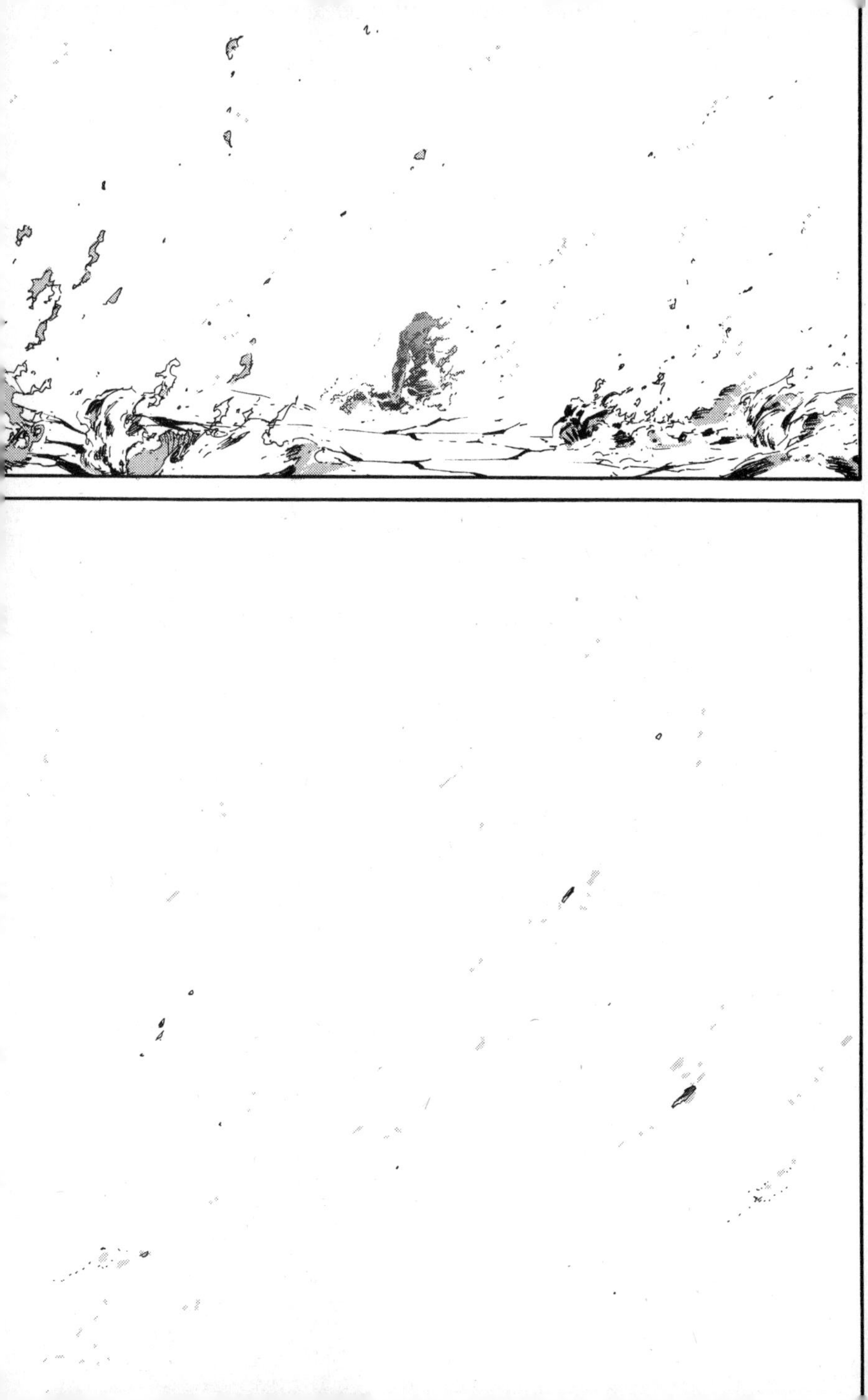

TABOO TATTOO

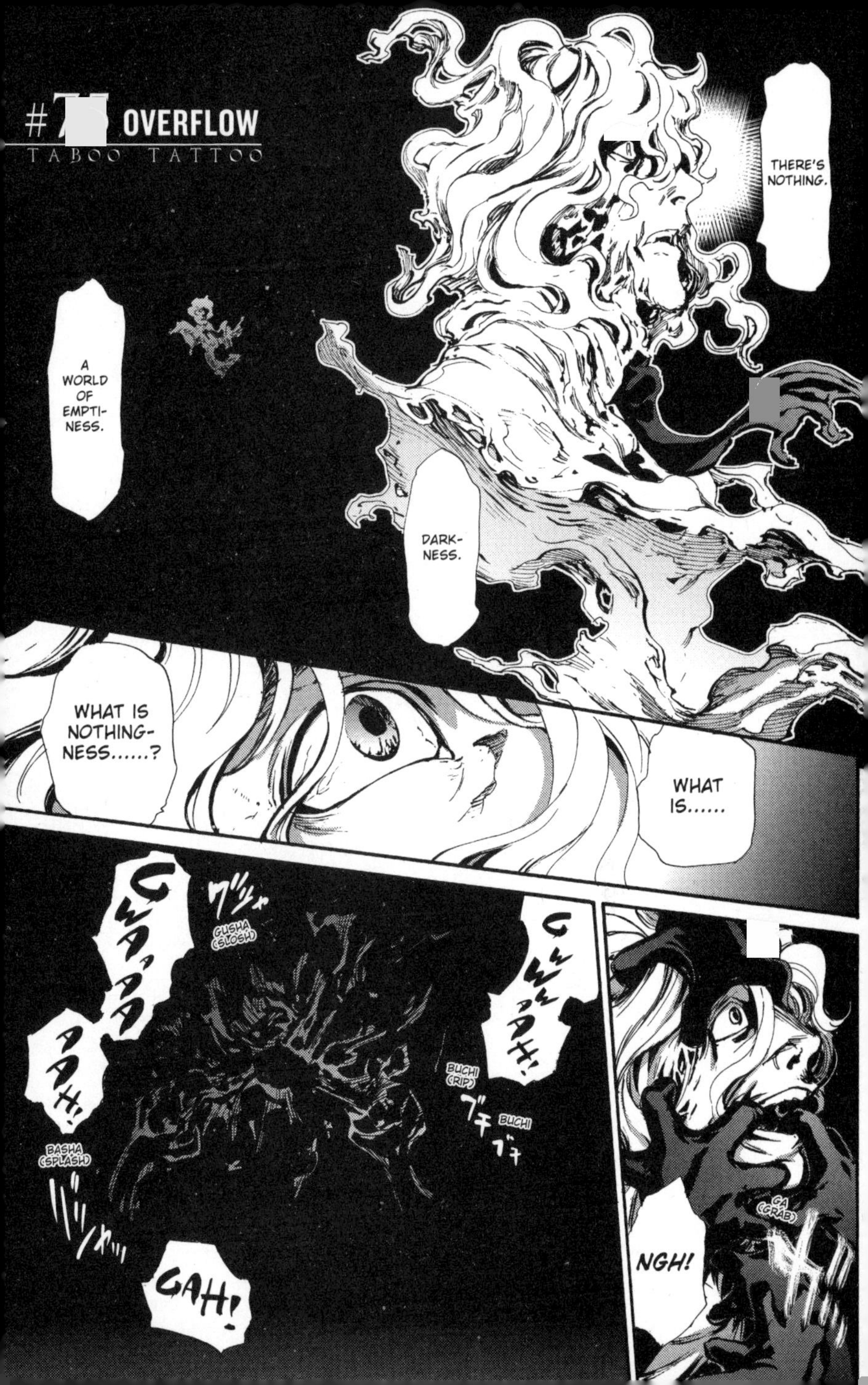
OVERFLOW
TABOO TATTOO
THERE'S NOTHING.
A WORLD OF EMPTI-NESS.
DARK-NESS.
WHAT IS......
WHAT IS NOTHING-NESS......?
GA (GRAB)
NGH!
GWWWAAH!
BUCHI (RIP)
BUCHI
GUSHA (SLOSH)
GWAAAAAAH!
BASHA (SPLASH)
GAH!

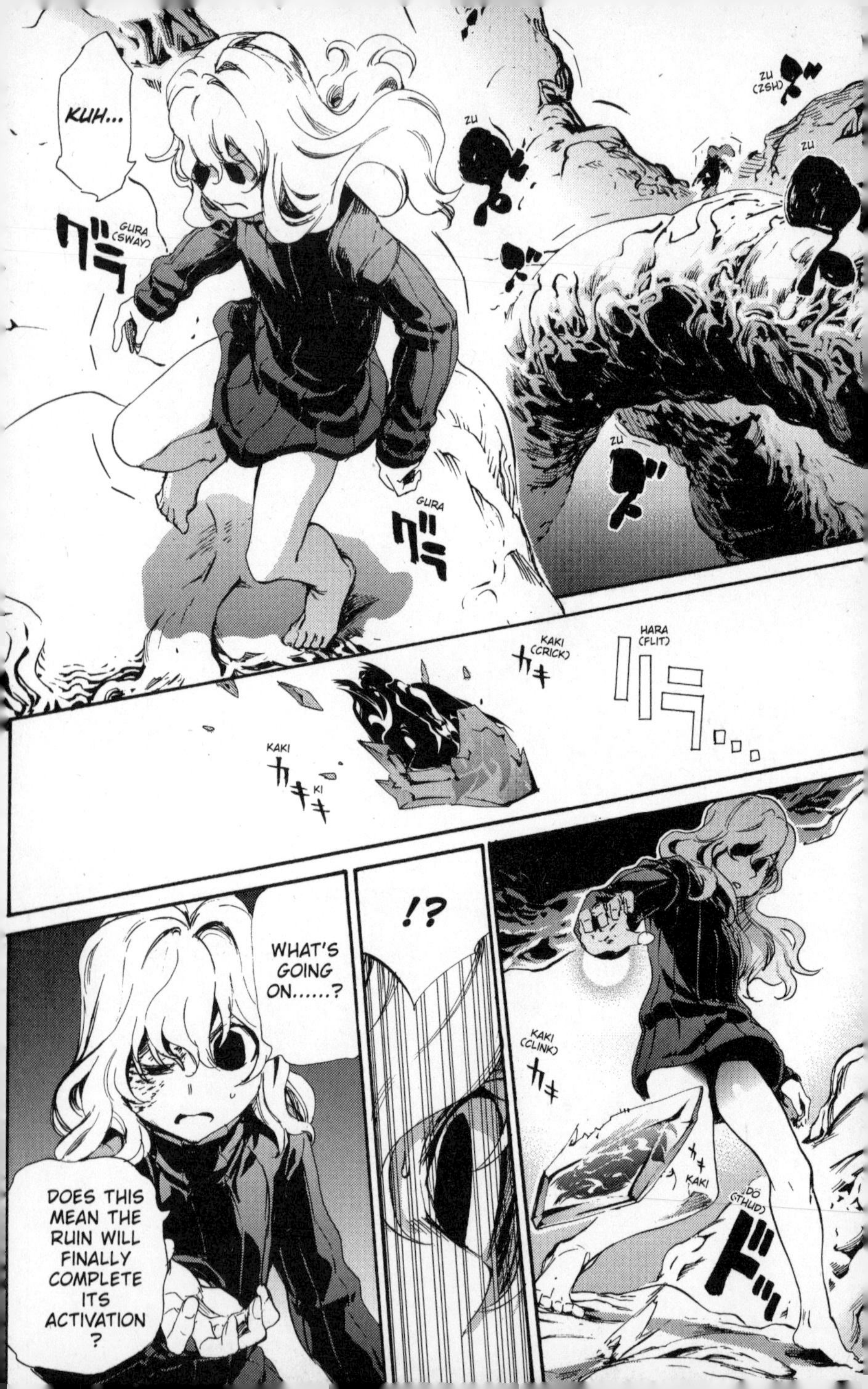

ZU (ZSH)
ズ
ZU
ズ
ZU
ZU
ズ
KUH...
GURA (SWAY)
グラ
GURA
グラ
HARA (FLIT)
ハラ...
KAKI (CRICK)
カキ
KAKI
KI
カキキ
KAKI (CLINK)
カキ
KAKI
カキ
DŌ (THUD)
ドッ
!?
WHAT'S GOING ON......?
DOES THIS MEAN THE RUIN WILL FINALLY COMPLETE ITS ACTIVATION?

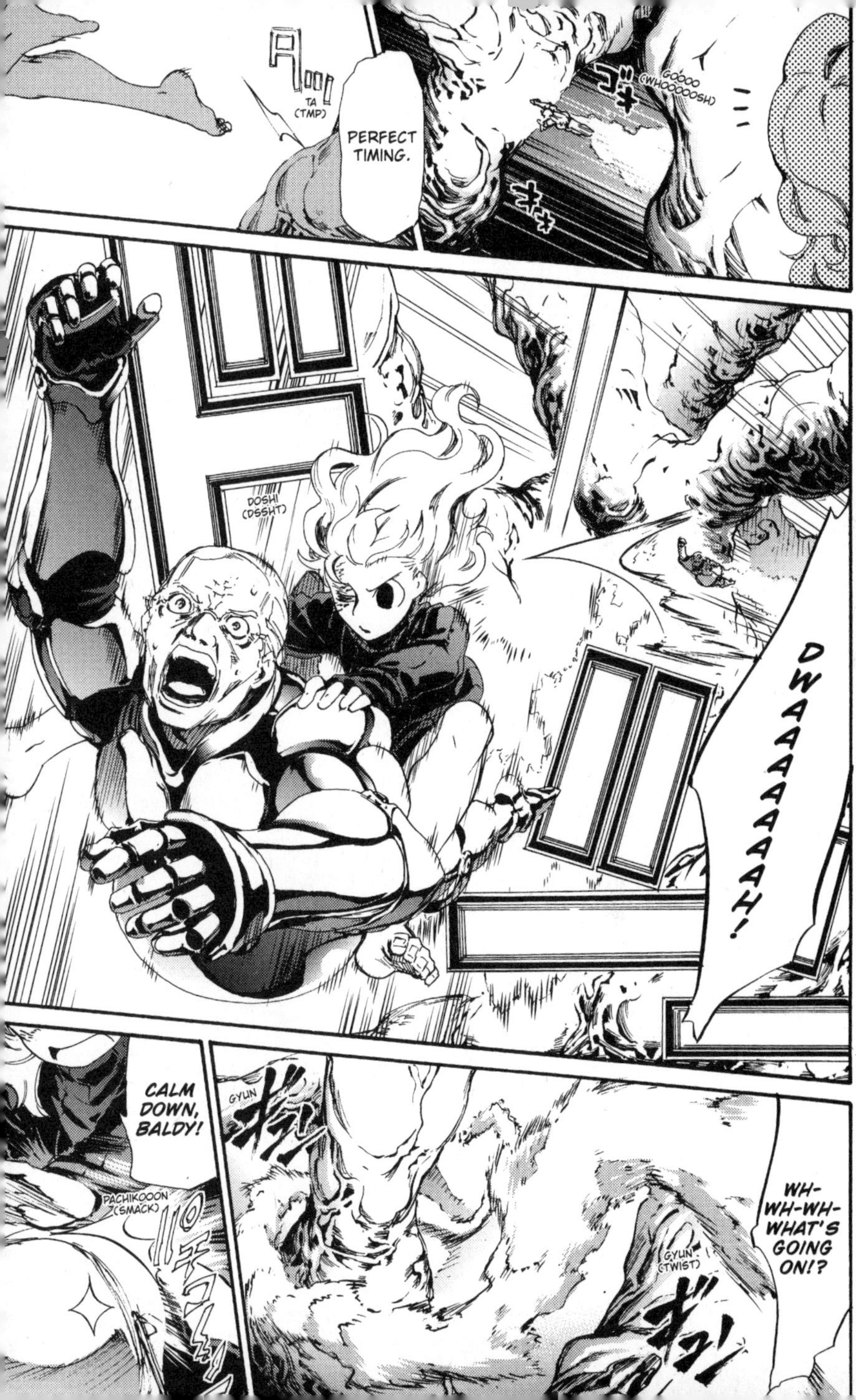
GOOOO (WHOOOOOSH)
PERFECT TIMING.
TA (TMP)
DWAAAAAAAH!
DOSHI (DSSHT)
WH-WH-WH-WHAT'S GOING ON!?
GYUN (TWIST)
GYUN
CALM DOWN, BALDY!
PACHIKOOON (SMACK)

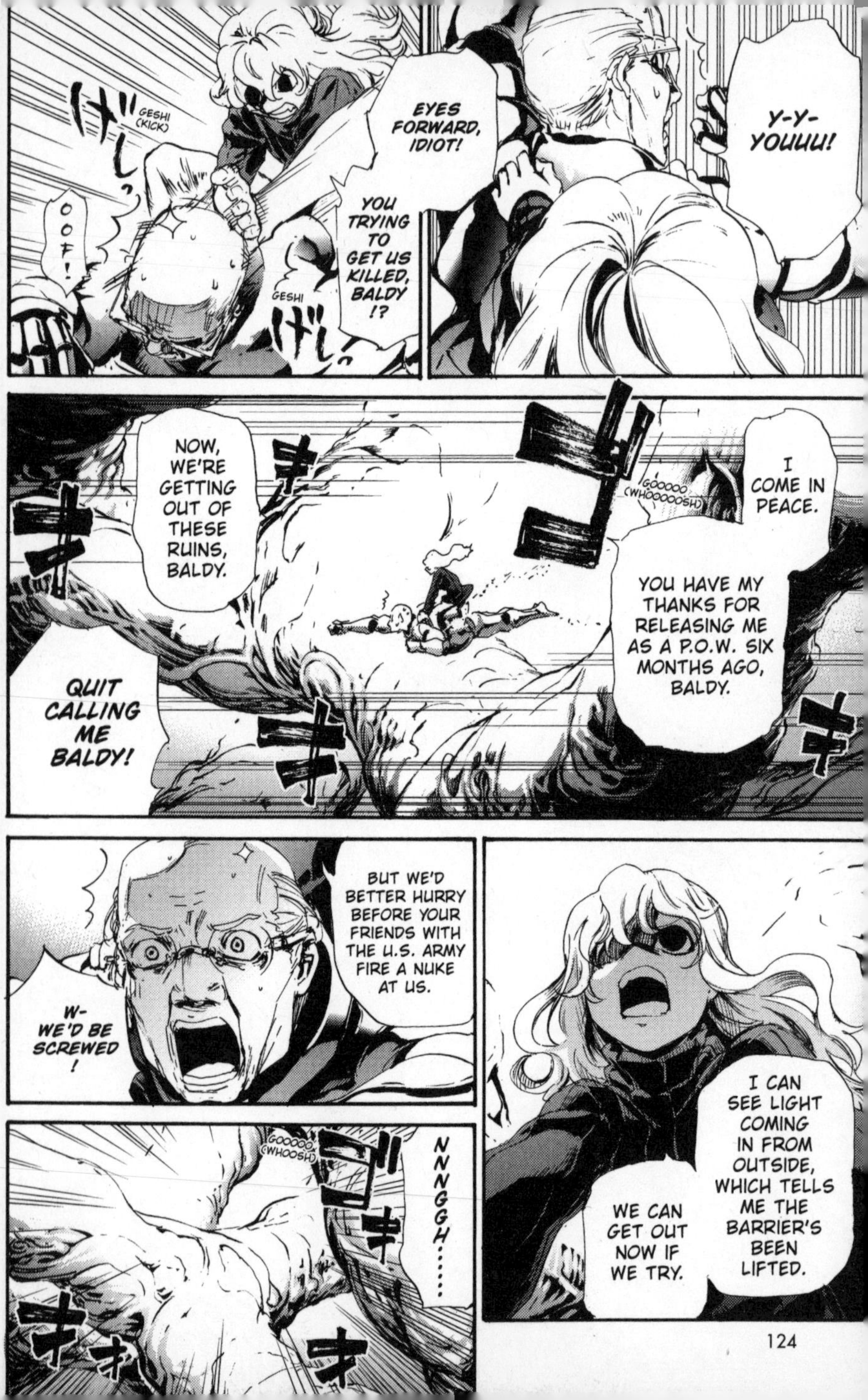
Y-Y-YOUUU!
EYES FORWARD, IDIOT!
GESHI (KICK)
YOU TRYING TO GET US KILLED, BALDY!?
OOF!
GESHI
I COME IN PEACE.
GOOOOO (WHOOOOOSH)
YOU HAVE MY THANKS FOR RELEASING ME AS A P.O.W. SIX MONTHS AGO, BALDY.
NOW, WE'RE GETTING OUT OF THESE RUINS, BALDY.
QUIT CALLING ME BALDY!
I CAN SEE LIGHT COMING IN FROM OUTSIDE, WHICH TELLS ME THE BARRIER'S BEEN LIFTED.
WE CAN GET OUT NOW IF WE TRY.
BUT WE'D BETTER HURRY BEFORE YOUR FRIENDS WITH THE U.S. ARMY FIRE A NUKE AT US.
W- WE'D BE SCREWED!
NNNGGH......
GOOOOO (WHOOSH)

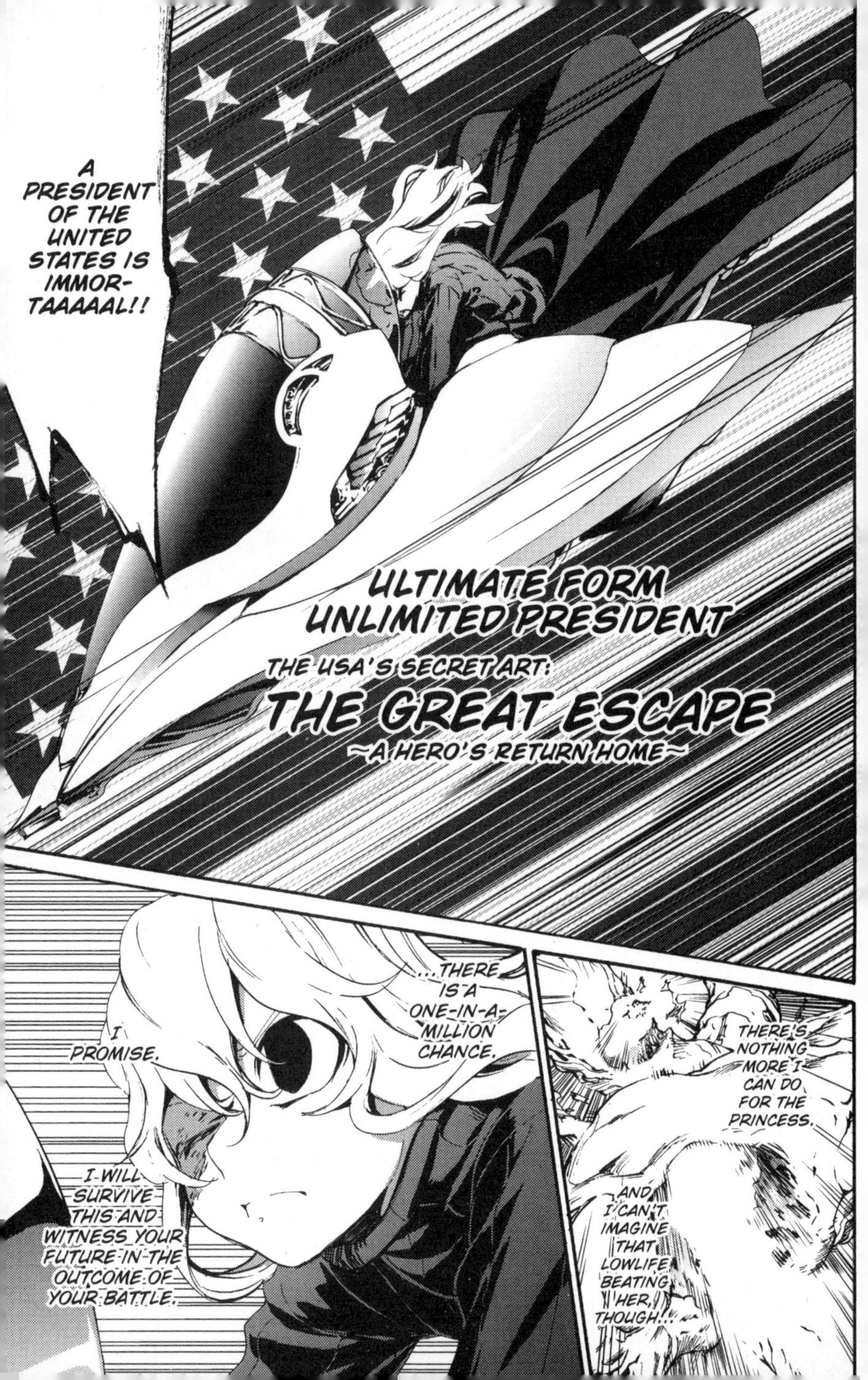
A PRESIDENT OF THE UNITED STATES IS IMMOR-TAAAAAL!!
ULTIMATE FORM UNLIMITED PRESIDENT
THE USA'S SECRET ART:
THE GREAT ESCAPE
~A HERO'S RETURN HOME~
THERE'S NOTHING MORE I CAN DO FOR THE PRINCESS.
AND I CAN'T IMAGINE THAT LOWLIFE BEATING HER, THOUGH...
...THERE IS A ONE-IN-A-MILLION CHANCE.
I PROMISE.
I WILL SURVIVE THIS AND WITNESS YOUR FUTURE IN THE OUTCOME OF YOUR BATTLE.

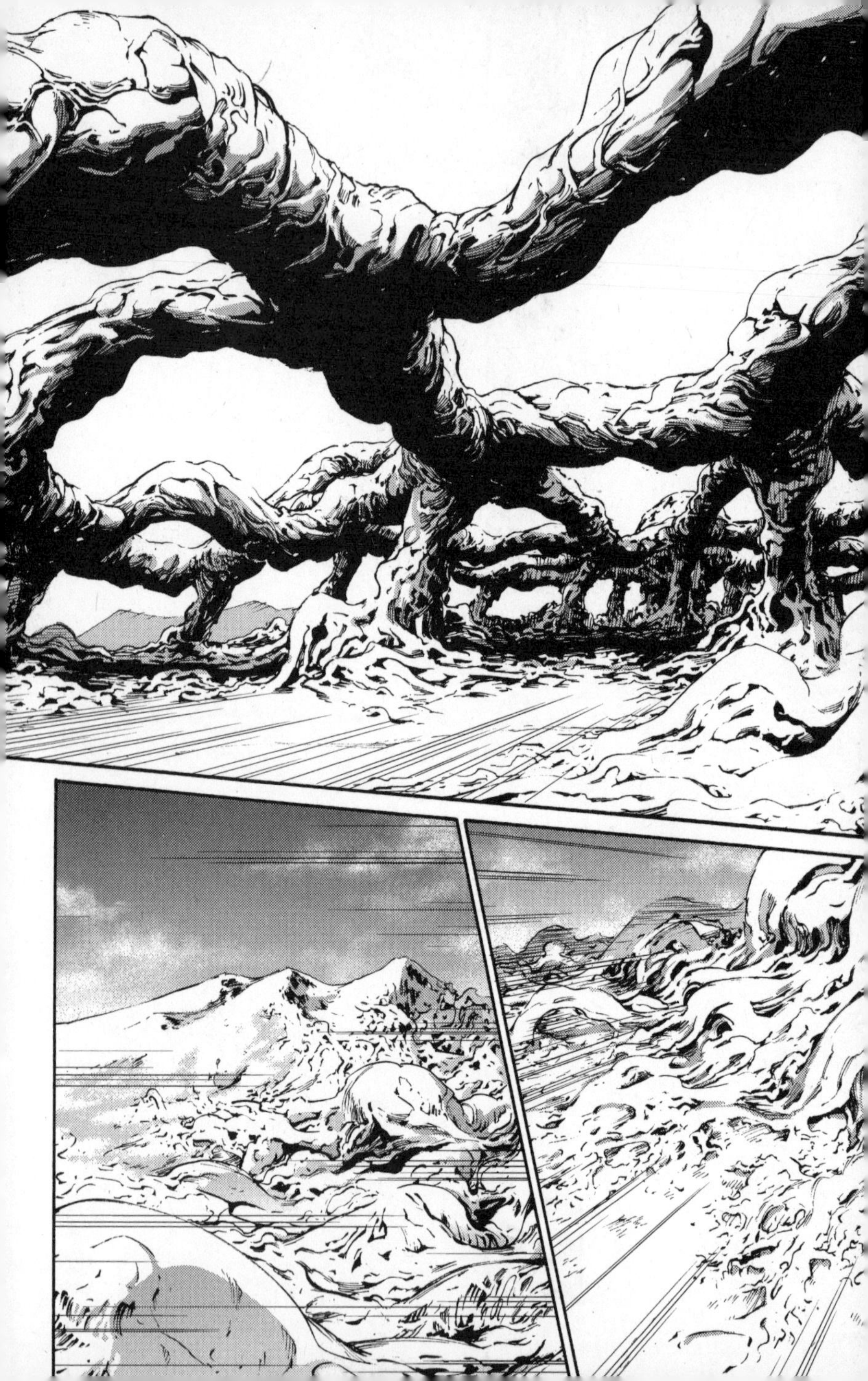

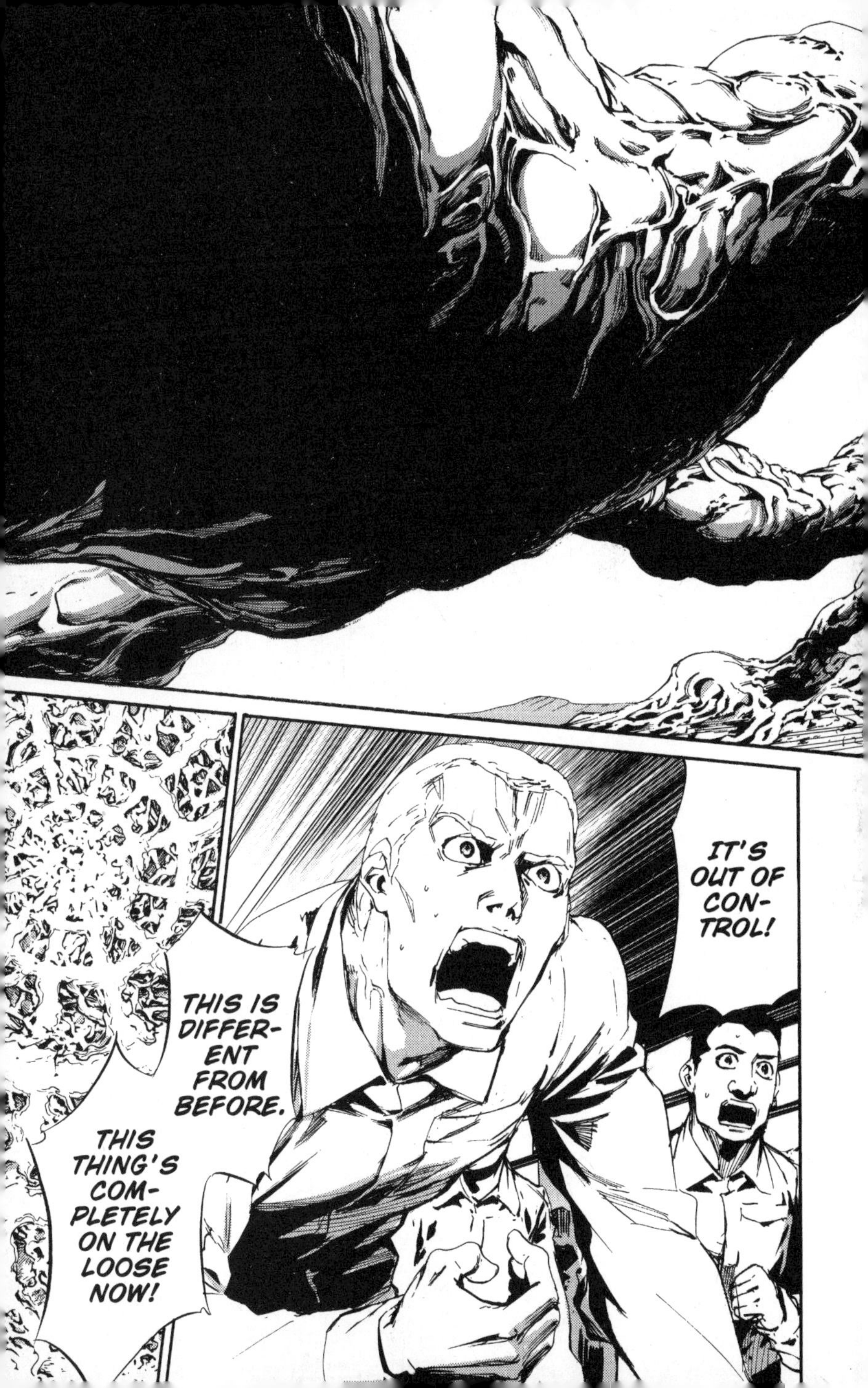
IT'S OUT OF CON-TROL!
THIS IS DIFFER-ENT FROM BEFORE.
THIS THING'S COM-PLETELY ON THE LOOSE NOW!

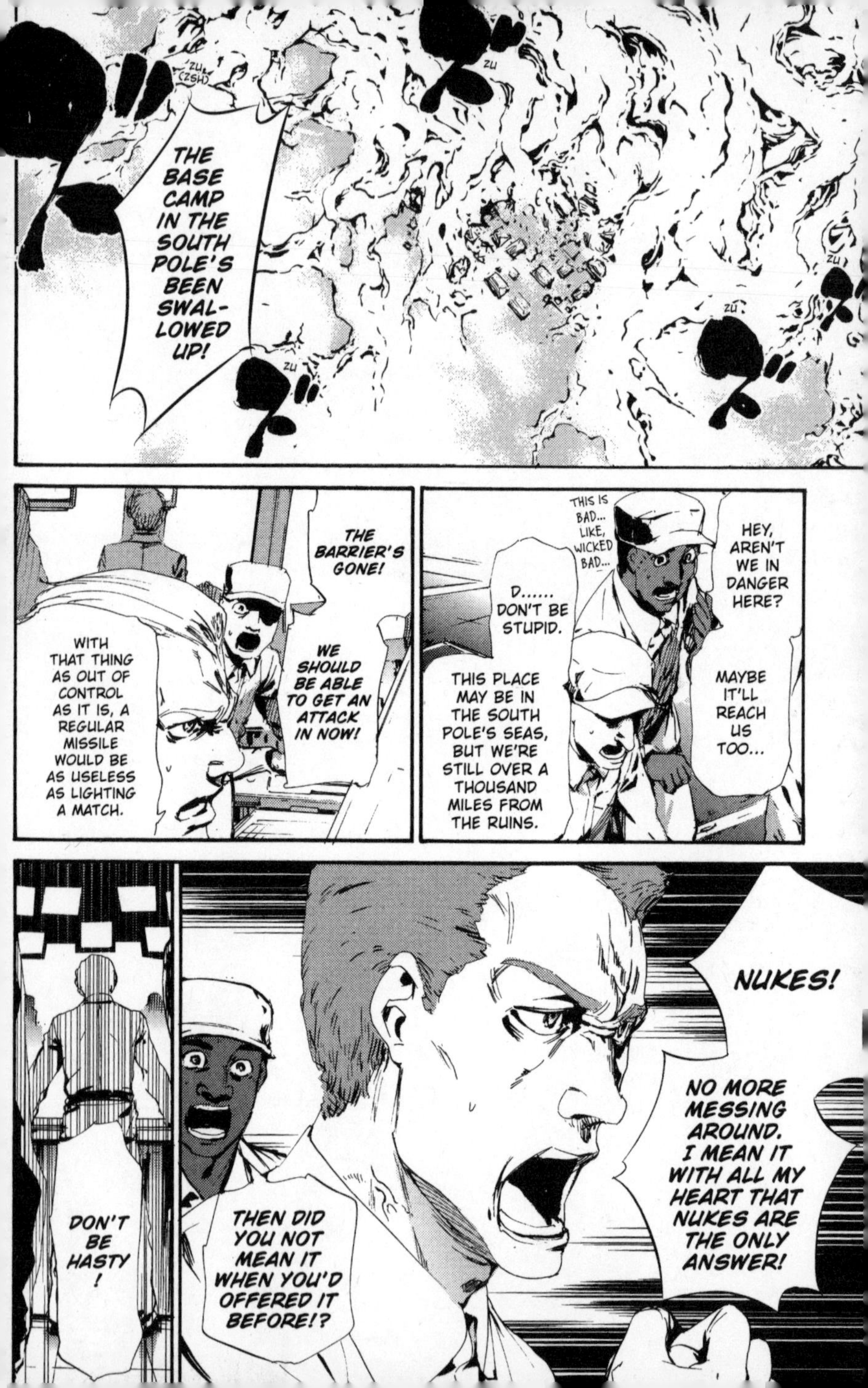
ZU
ZU
ZU
ZU (ZSH)
THE BASE CAMP IN THE SOUTH POLE'S BEEN SWAL-LOWED UP!
ZU
HEY, AREN'T WE IN DANGER HERE?
MAYBE IT'LL REACH US TOO...
THIS IS BAD... LIKE, WICKED BAD...
D...... DON'T BE STUPID.
THIS PLACE MAY BE IN THE SOUTH POLE'S SEAS, BUT WE'RE STILL OVER A THOUSAND MILES FROM THE RUINS.
THE BARRIER'S GONE!
WE SHOULD BE ABLE TO GET AN ATTACK IN NOW!
WITH THAT THING AS OUT OF CONTROL AS IT IS, A REGULAR MISSILE WOULD BE AS USELESS AS LIGHTING A MATCH.
NUKES!
NO MORE MESSING AROUND. I MEAN IT WITH ALL MY HEART THAT NUKES ARE THE ONLY ANSWER!
THEN DID YOU NOT MEAN IT WHEN YOU'D OFFERED IT BEFORE!?
DON'T BE HASTY!

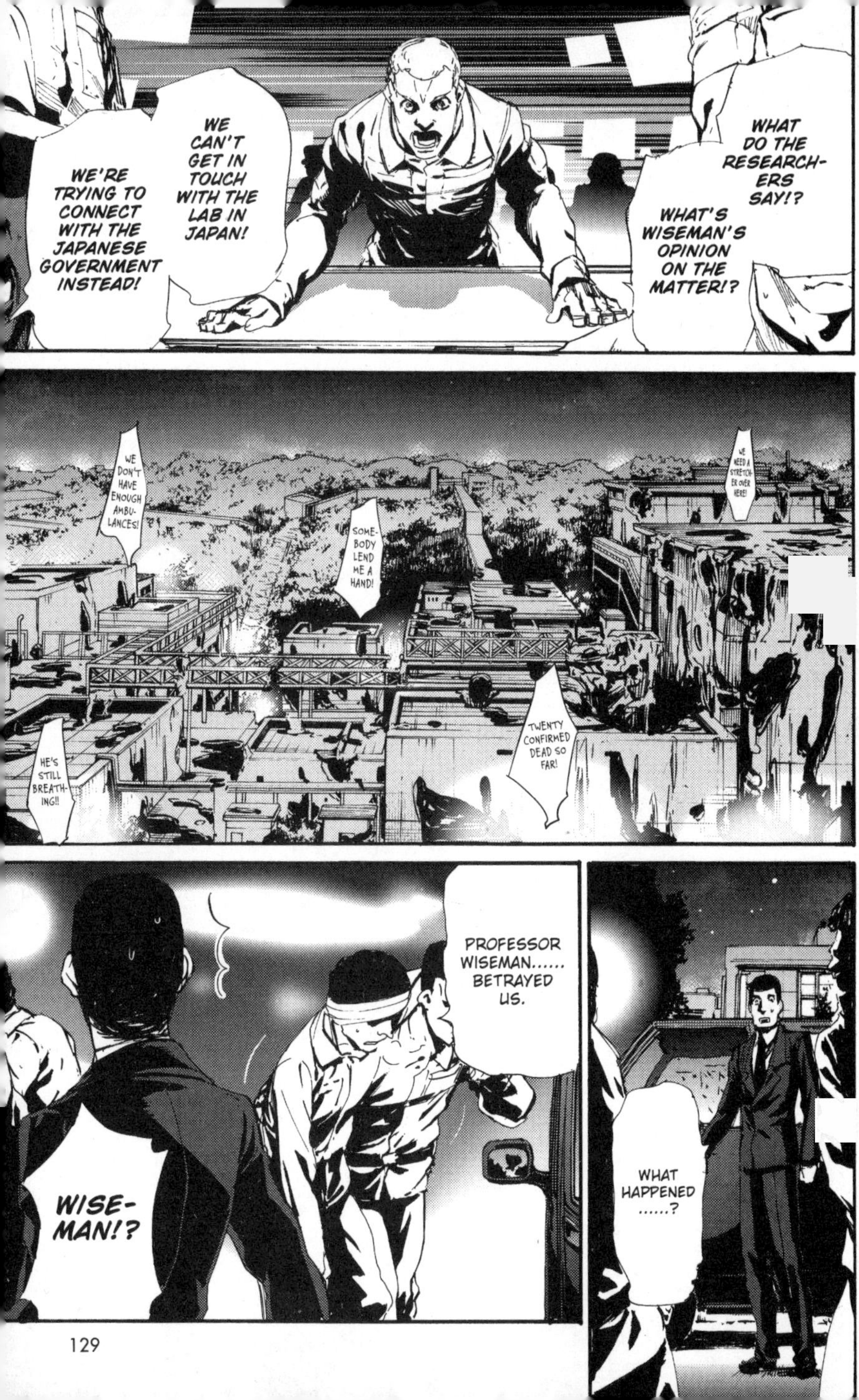

WHAT DO THE RESEARCHERS SAY!?
WHAT'S WISEMAN'S OPINION ON THE MATTER!?
WE CAN'T GET IN TOUCH WITH THE LAB IN JAPAN!
WE'RE TRYING TO CONNECT WITH THE JAPANESE GOVERNMENT INSTEAD!
WE NEED A STRETCHER OVER HERE!
WE DON'T HAVE ENOUGH AMBULANCES!
SOMEBODY LEND ME A HAND!
TWENTY CONFIRMED DEAD SO FAR!
HE'S STILL BREATHING!!
WHAT HAPPENED......?
PROFESSOR WISEMAN...... BETRAYED US.
WISE-MAN!?

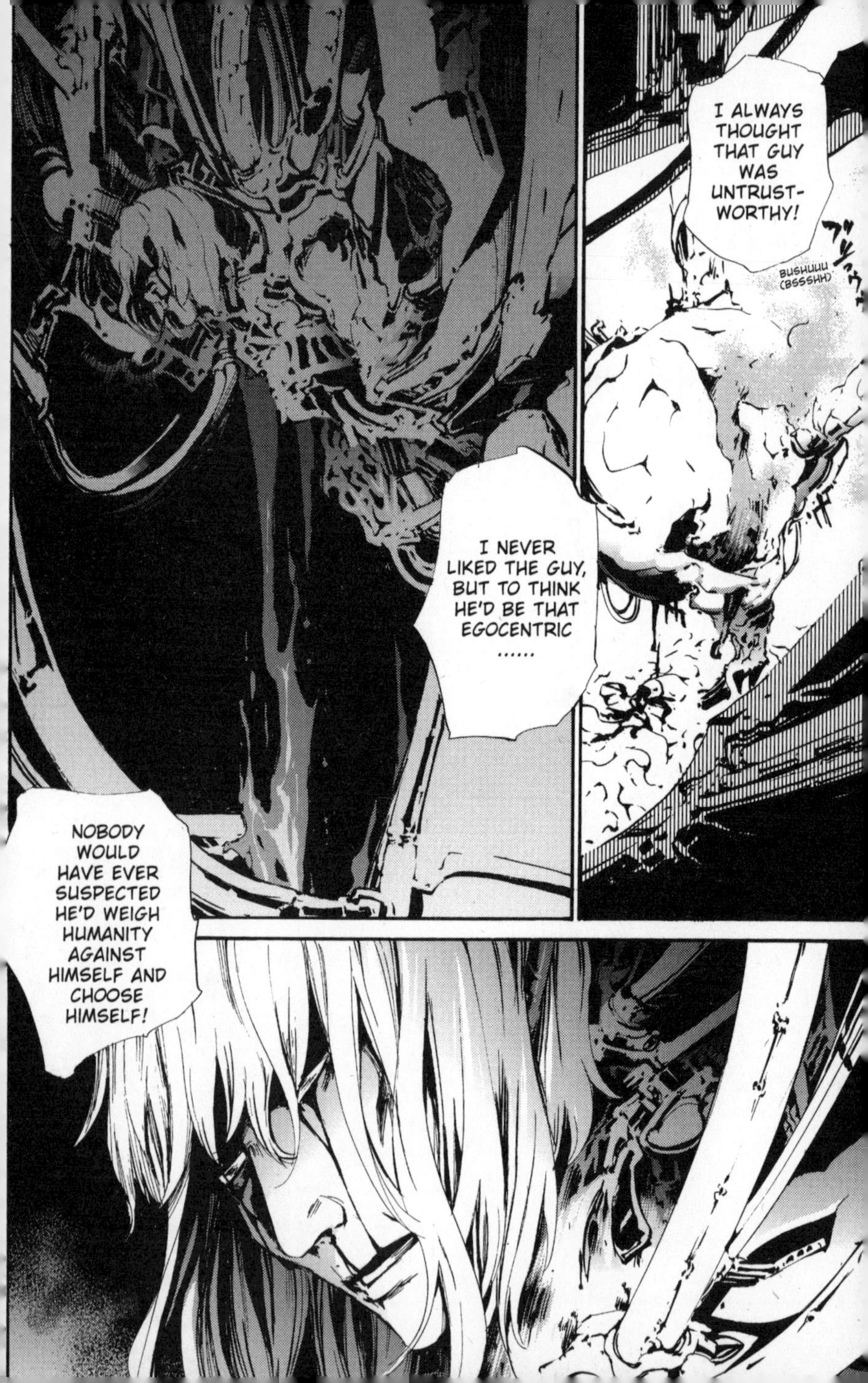
I ALWAYS THOUGHT THAT GUY WAS UNTRUST-WORTHY!
BUSHUUU (BSSSHH)
I NEVER LIKED THE GUY, BUT TO THINK HE'D BE THAT EGOCENTRIC ......
NOBODY WOULD HAVE EVER SUSPECTED HE'D WEIGH HUMANITY AGAINST HIMSELF AND CHOOSE HIMSELF!

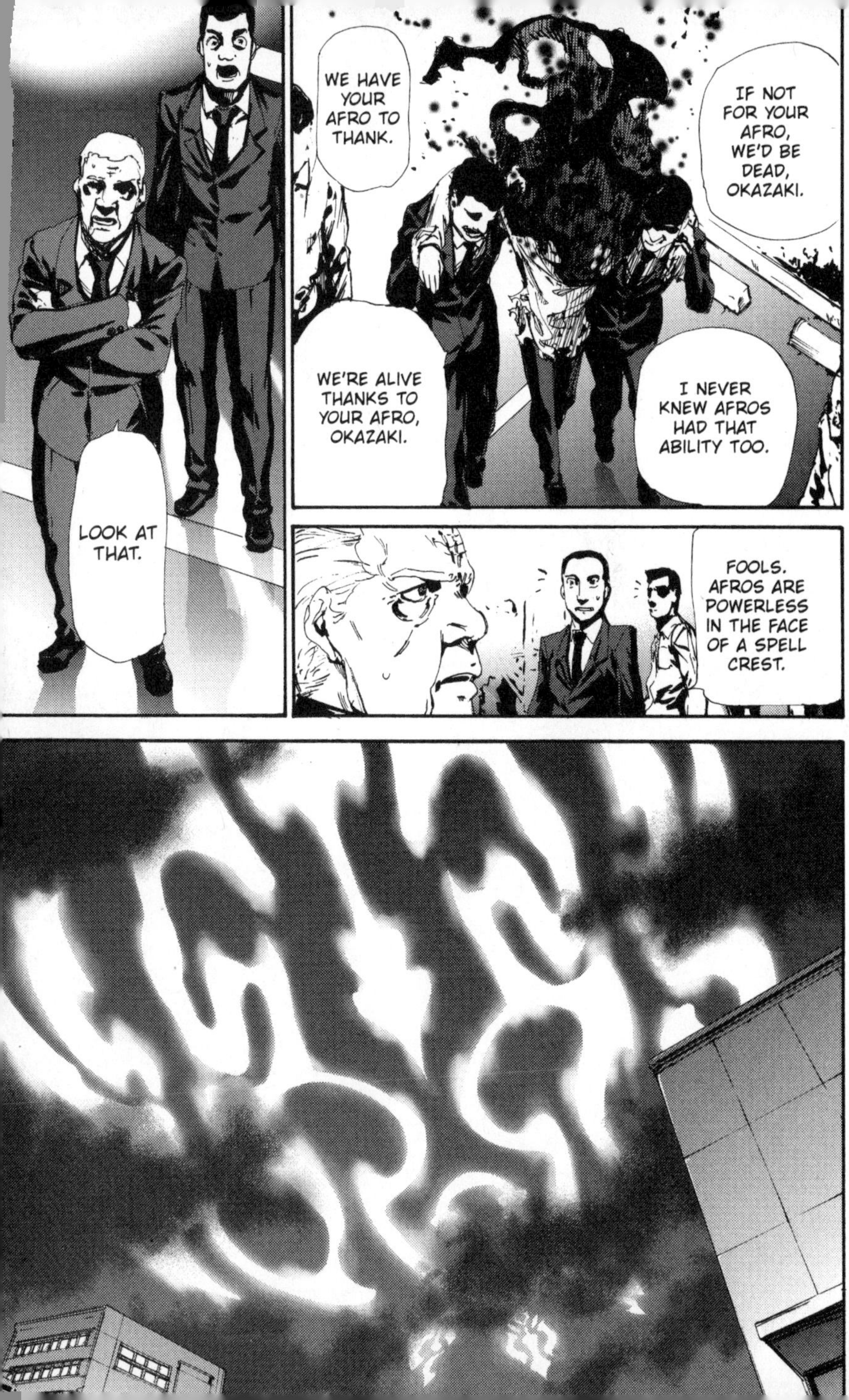
IF NOT FOR YOUR AFRO, WE'D BE DEAD, OKAZAKI.
WE HAVE YOUR AFRO TO THANK.
I NEVER KNEW AFROS HAD THAT ABILITY TOO.
WE'RE ALIVE THANKS TO YOUR AFRO, OKAZAKI.
FOOLS. AFROS ARE POWERLESS IN THE FACE OF A SPELL CREST.
LOOK AT THAT.

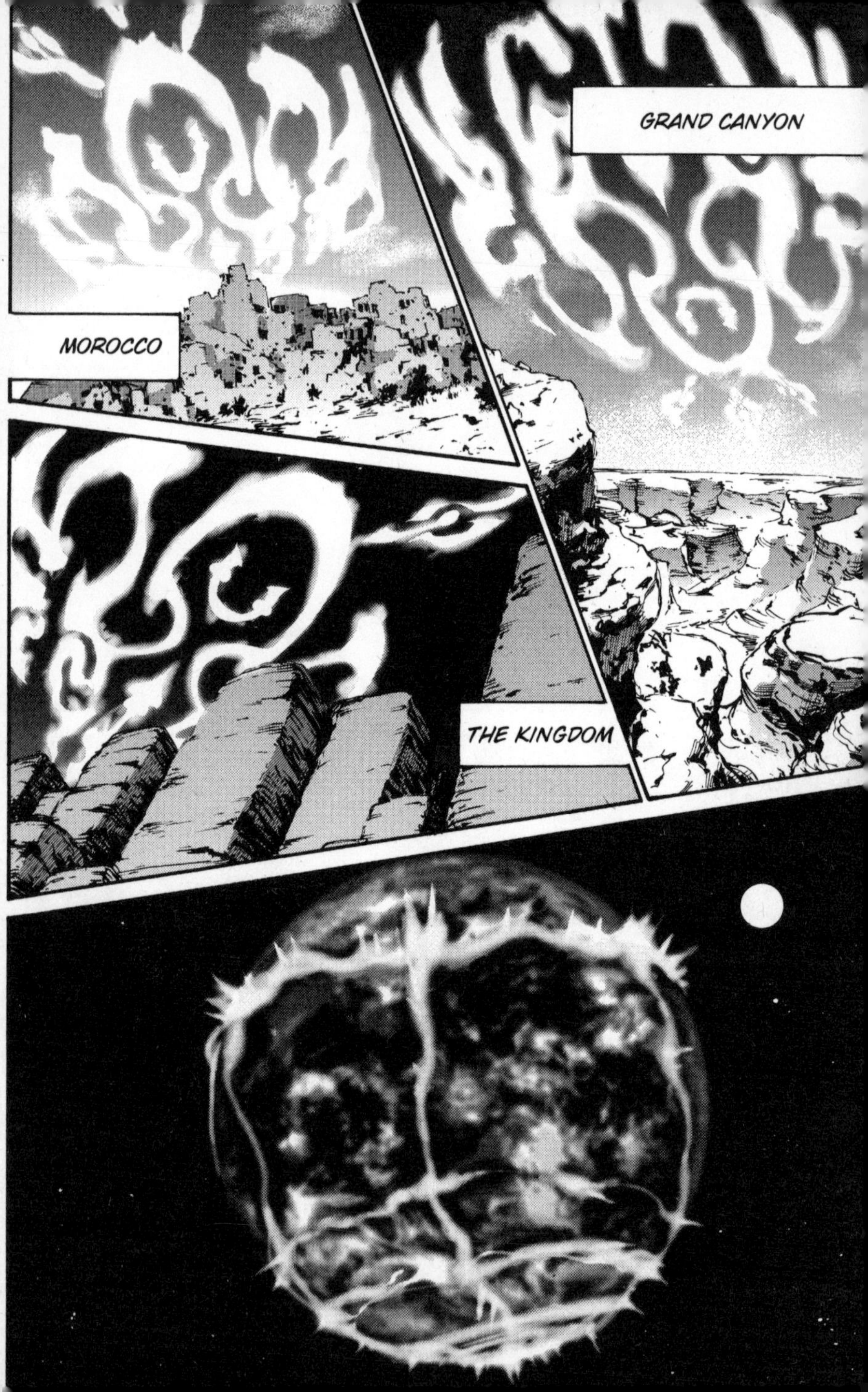
GRAND CANYON
MOROCCO
THE KINGDOM

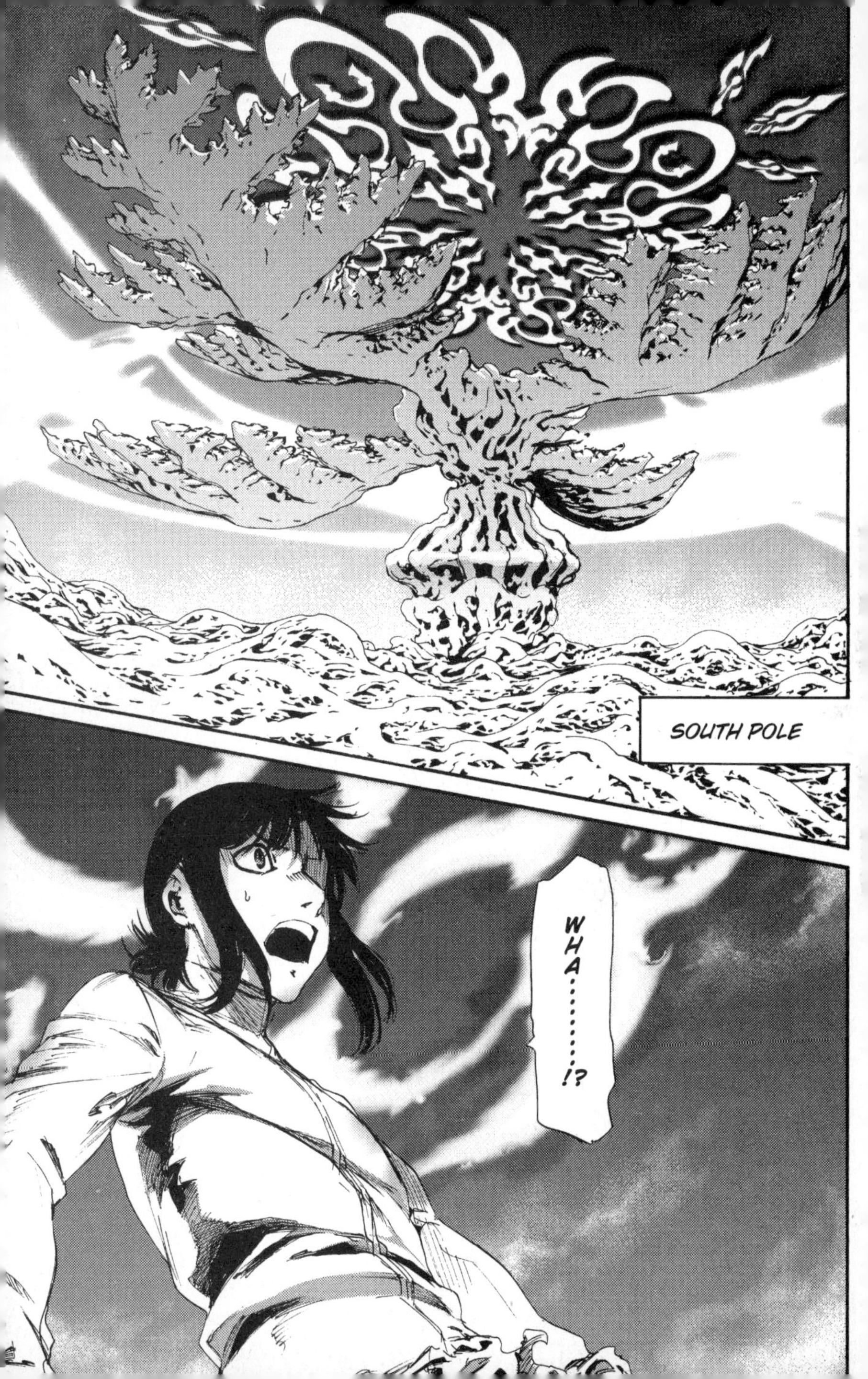
SOUTH POLE
WHA.........!?

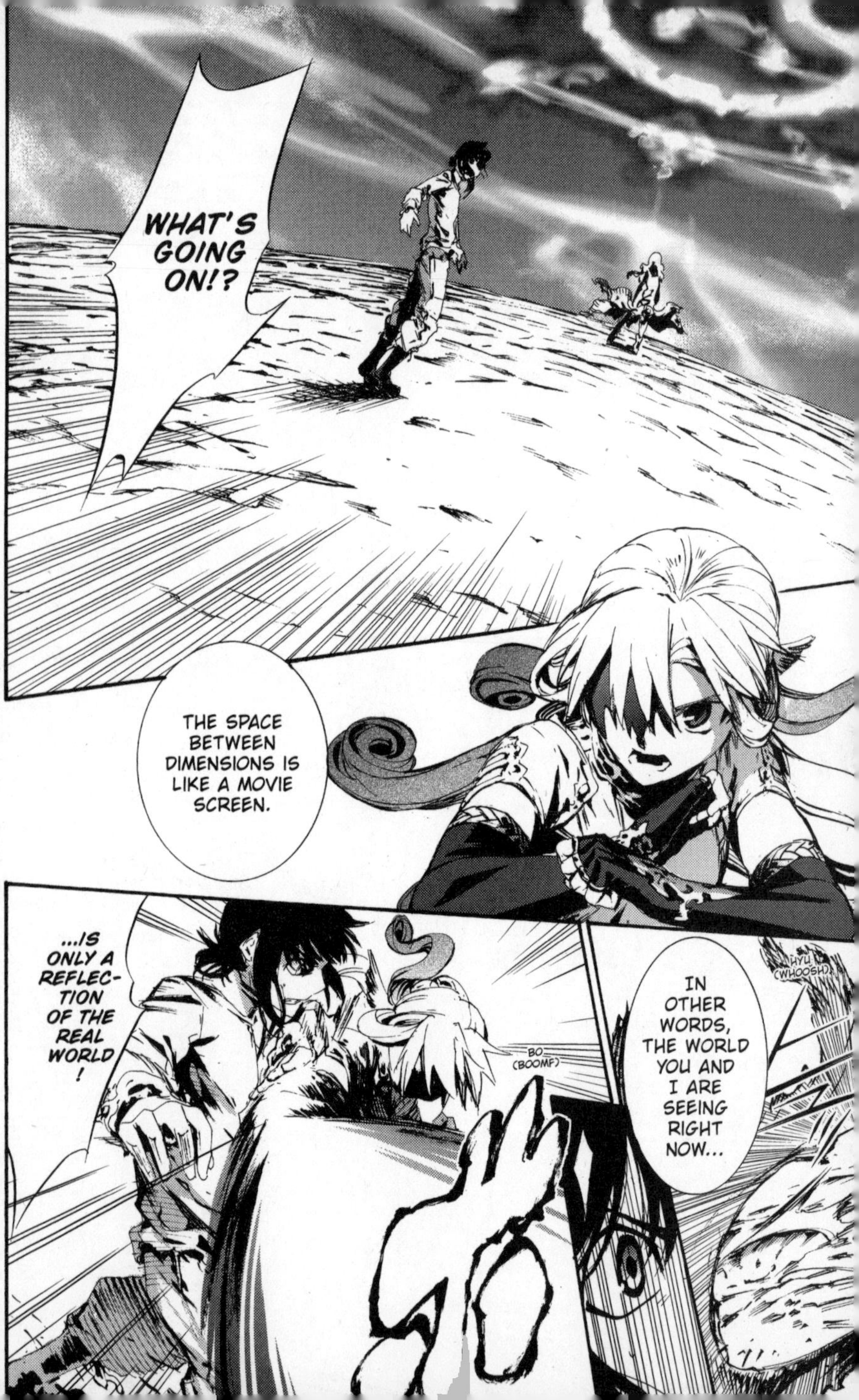
WHAT'S GOING ON!?
THE SPACE BETWEEN DIMENSIONS IS LIKE A MOVIE SCREEN.
HYU (WHOOSH)
IN OTHER WORDS, THE WORLD YOU AND I ARE SEEING RIGHT NOW...
BO (BOOMF)
...IS ONLY A REFLECTION OF THE REAL WORLD!

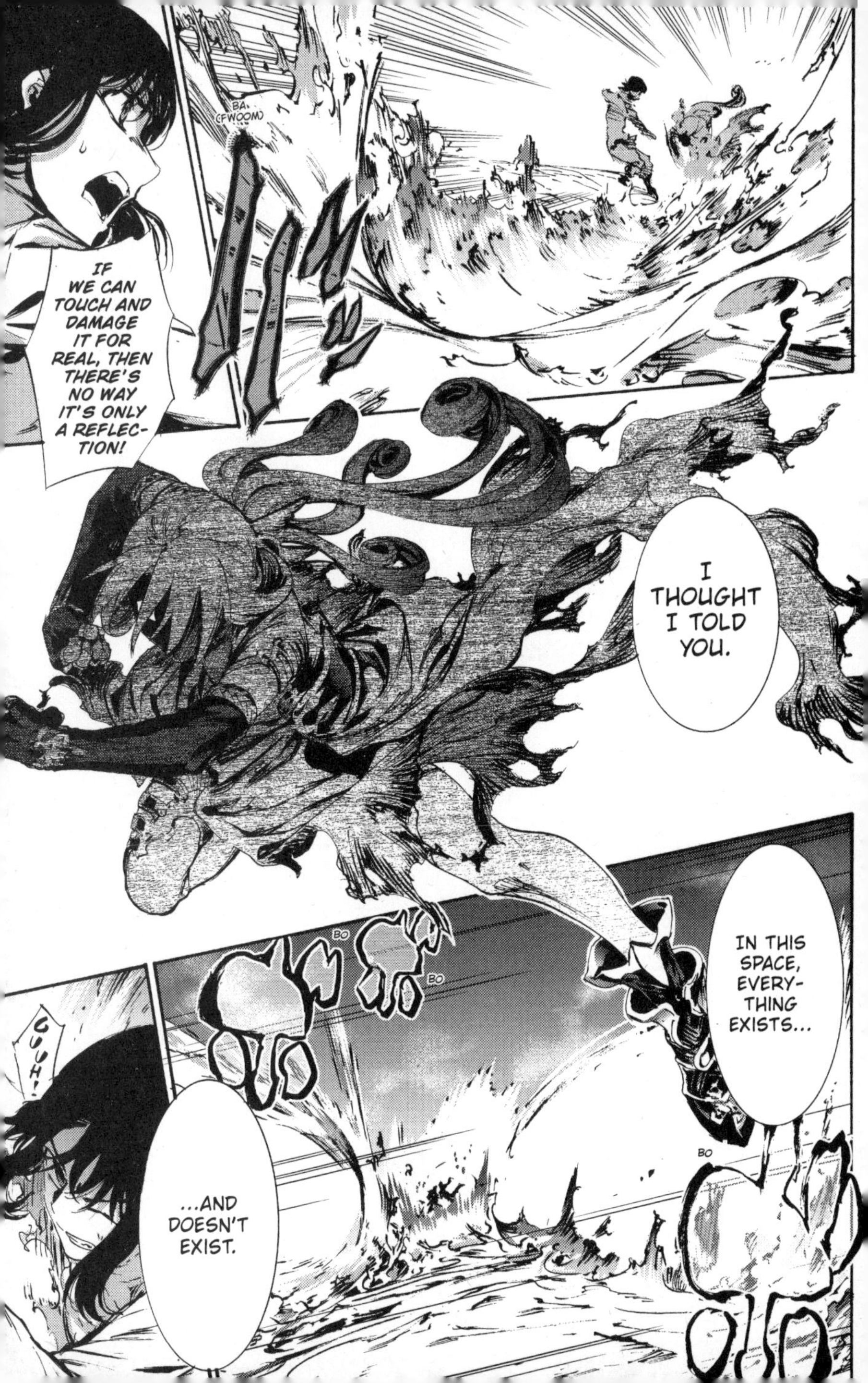
BA
(FWOOM)
IF WE CAN TOUCH AND DAMAGE IT FOR REAL, THEN THERE'S NO WAY IT'S ONLY A REFLECTION!
I THOUGHT I TOLD YOU.
BO
BO
IN THIS SPACE, EVERYTHING EXISTS...
BO
GUUH!
...AND DOESN'T EXIST.

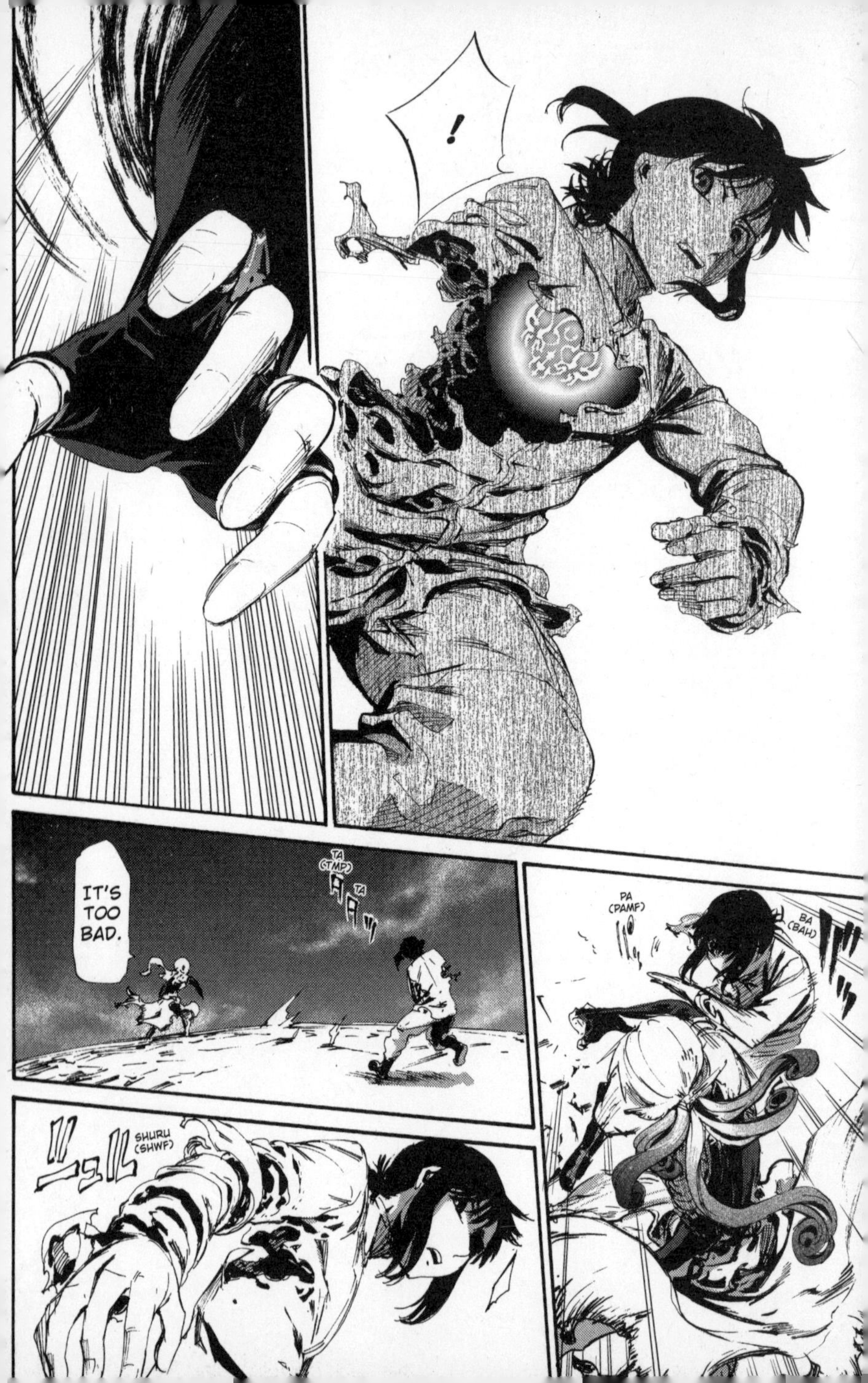
!
PA (PAMF)
BA (BAH)
IT'S TOO BAD.
TA (TMP) TA
SHURU (SHWF)

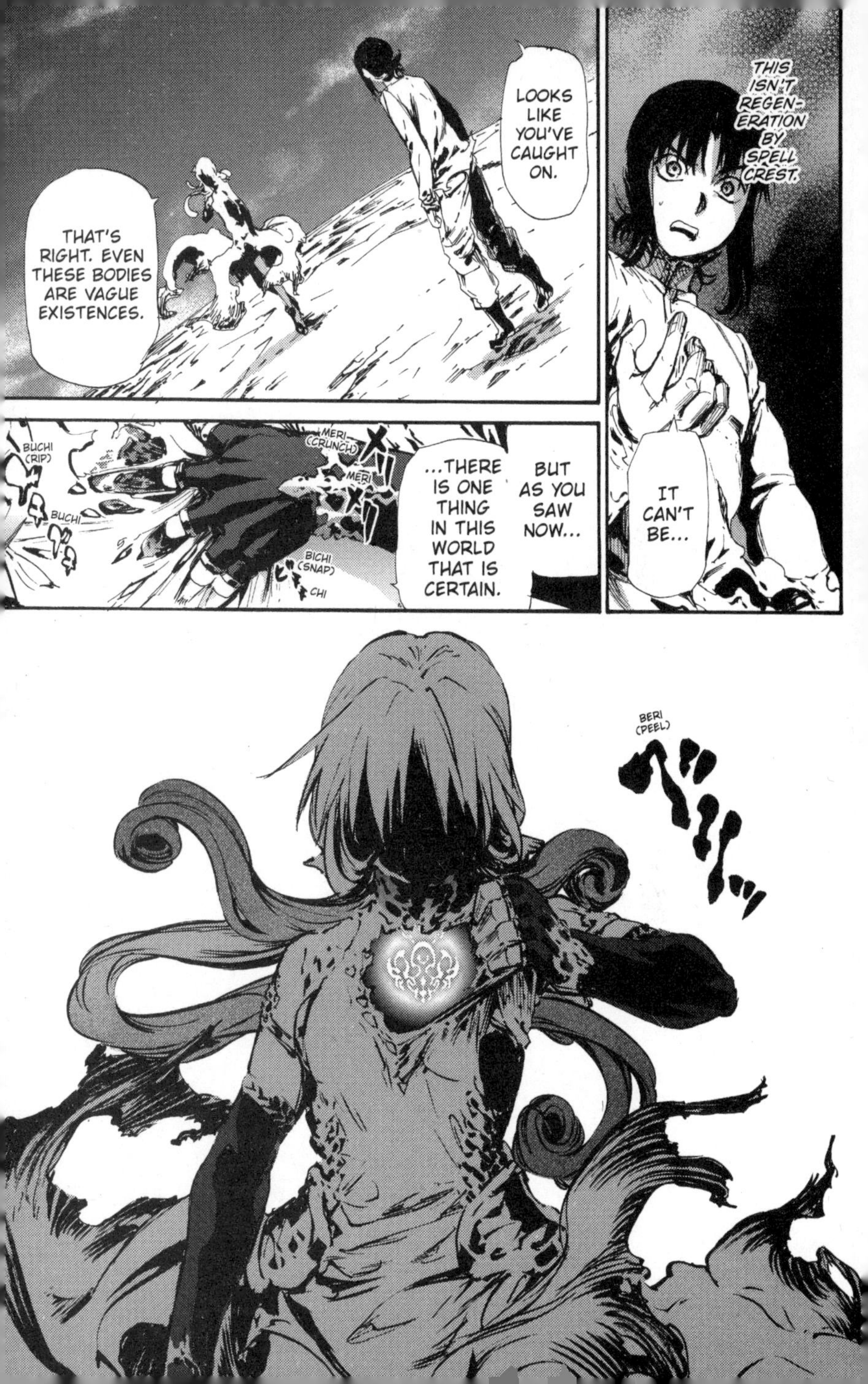

THIS ISN'T REGENERATION BY SPELL CREST.
IT CAN'T BE...
LOOKS LIKE YOU'VE CAUGHT ON.
THAT'S RIGHT. EVEN THESE BODIES ARE VAGUE EXISTENCES.
BUT AS YOU SAW NOW...
...THERE IS ONE THING IN THIS WORLD THAT IS CERTAIN.
MERI (CRUNCH)
MERI
BUCHI (RIP)
BUCHI
BICHI (SNAP)
CHI
BERI (PEEL)

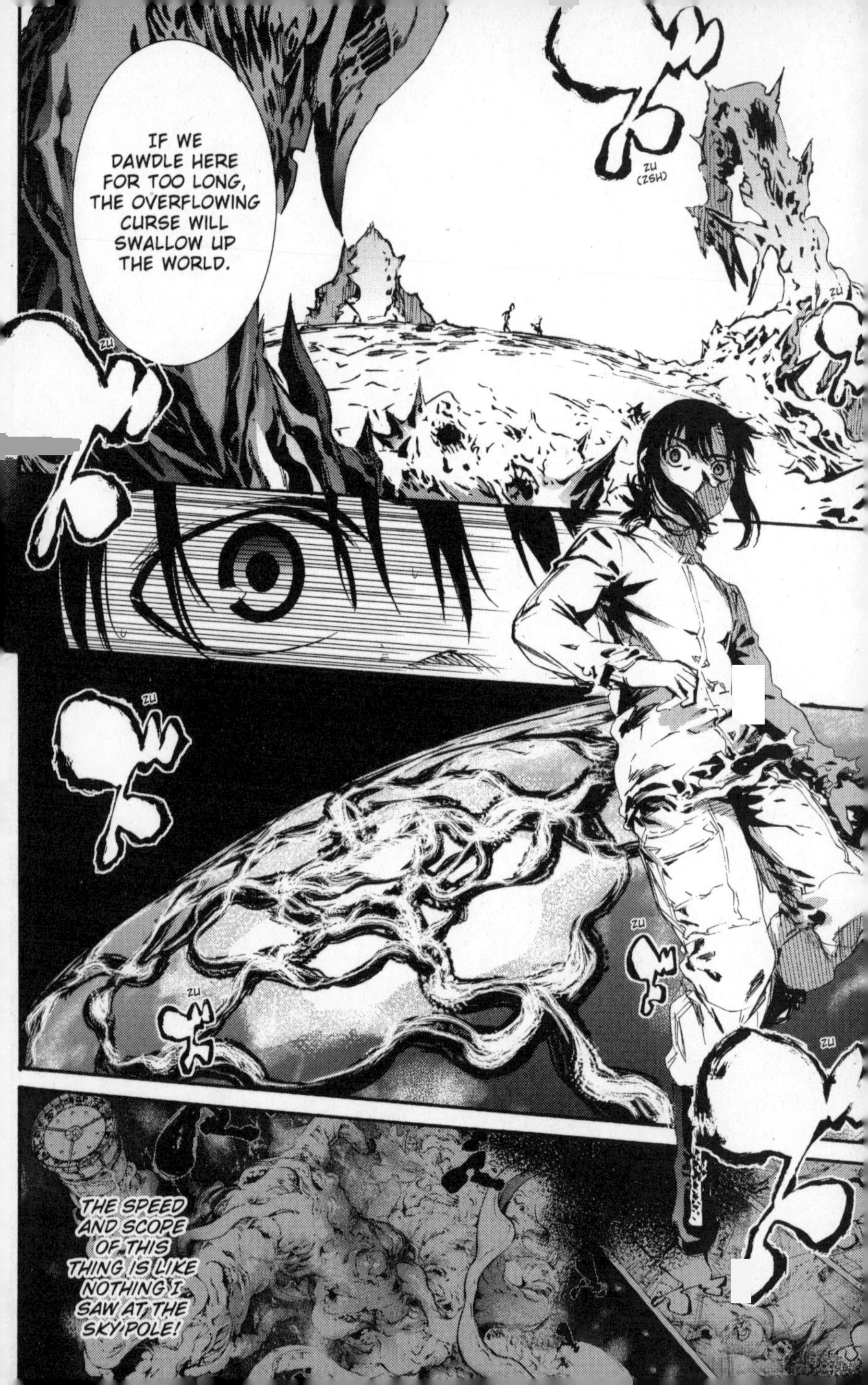
ZU
(ZSH)
ZU
IF WE DAWDLE HERE FOR TOO LONG, THE OVERFLOWING CURSE WILL SWALLOW UP THE WORLD.
ZU
ZU
ZU
ZU
ZU
THE SPEED AND SCOPE OF THIS THING IS LIKE NOTHING I SAW AT THE SKY POLE!

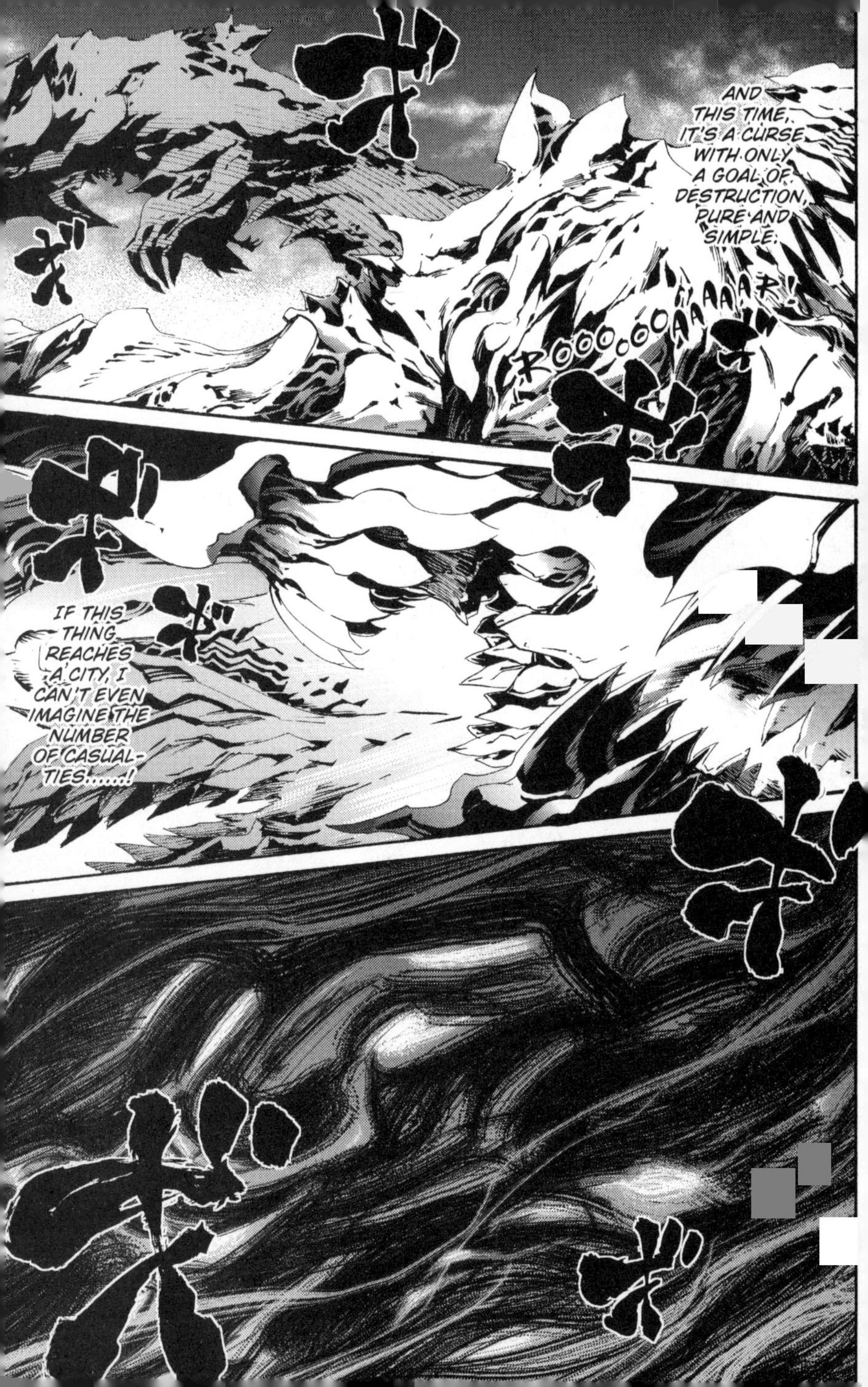
AND THIS TIME, IT'S A CURSE WITH ONLY A GOAL OF DESTRUCTION, PURE AND SIMPLE.
ROOOOOOOAAAAAAR!
IF THIS THING REACHES A CITY, I CAN'T EVEN IMAGINE THE NUMBER OF CASUALTIES......!

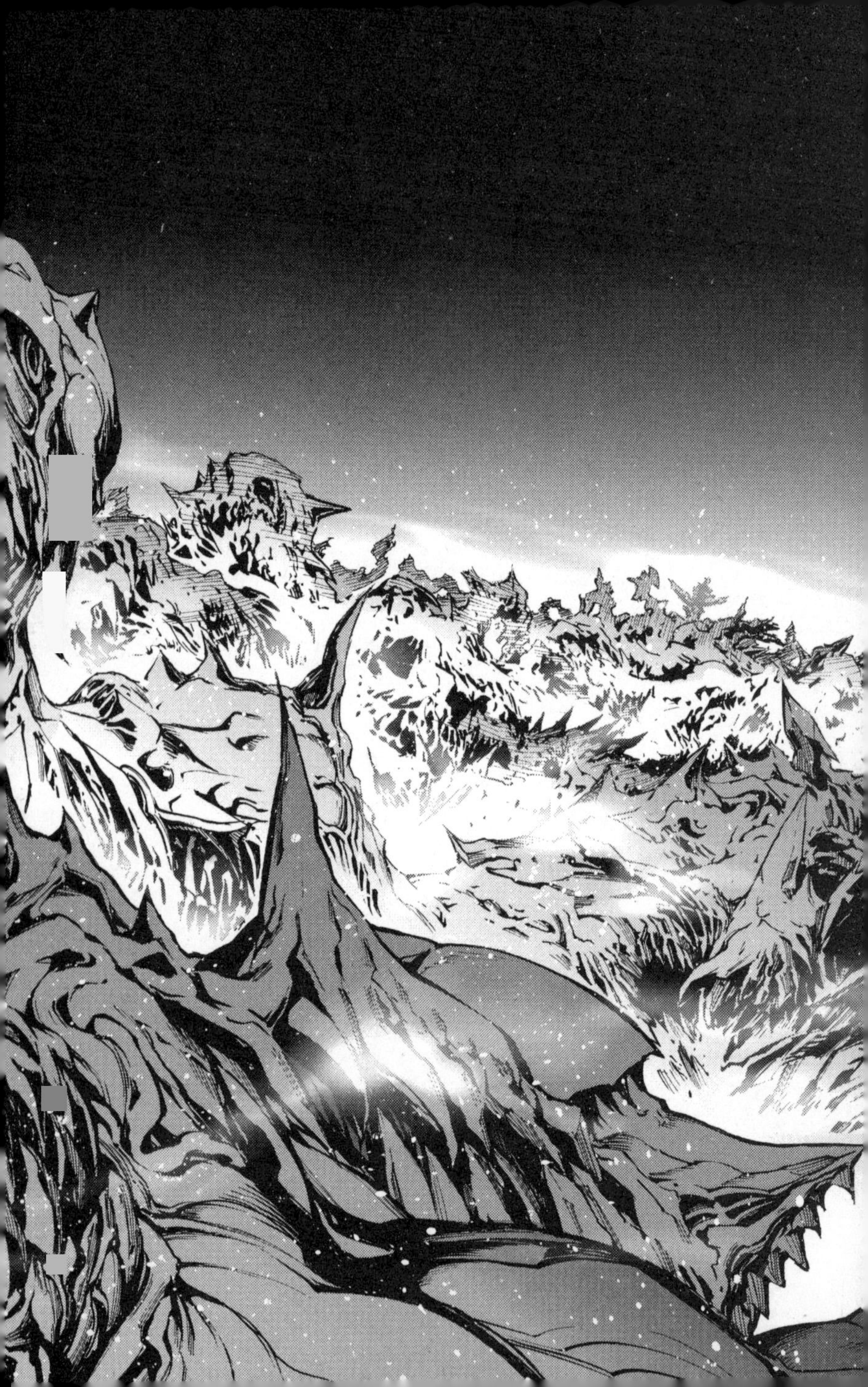

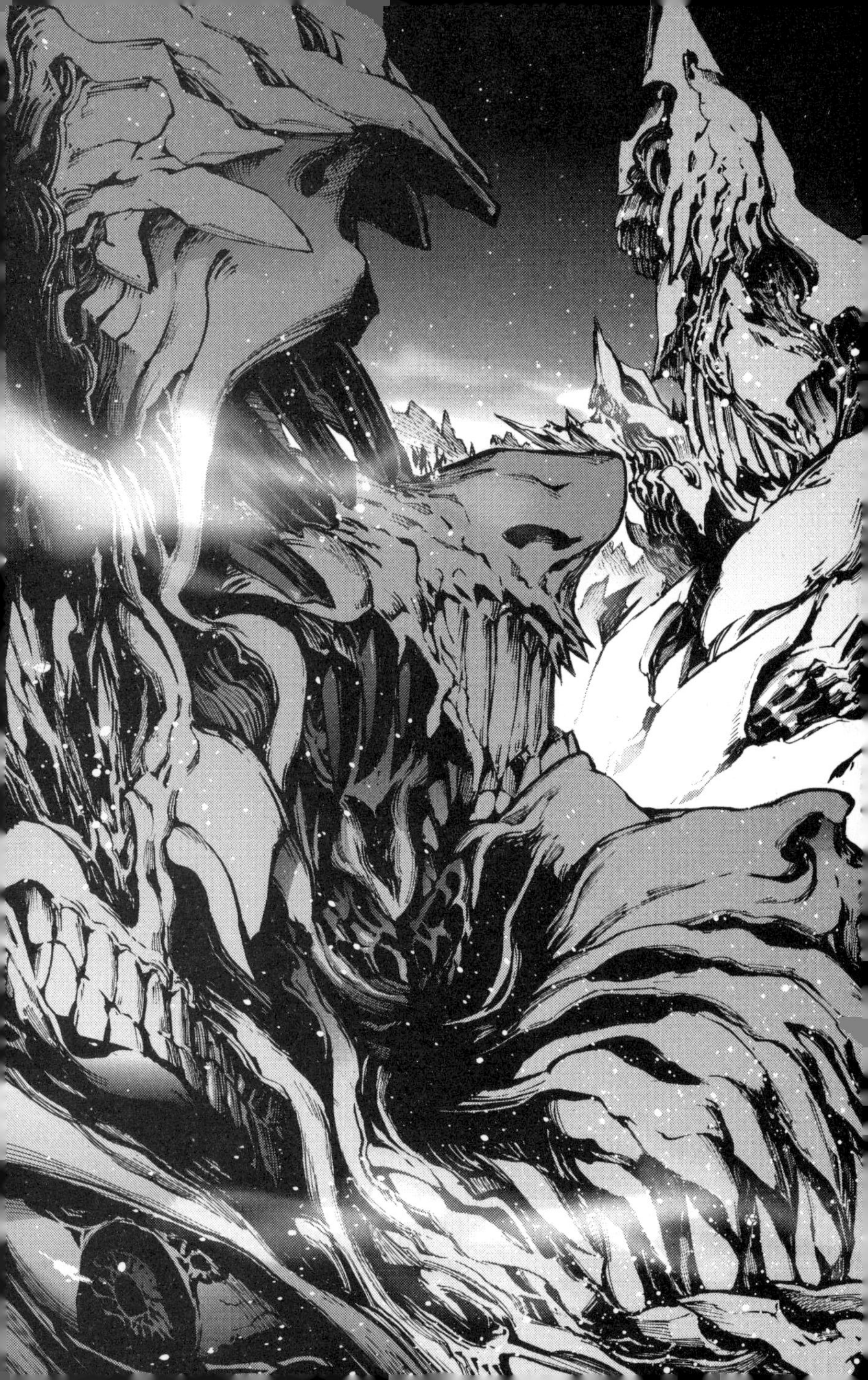

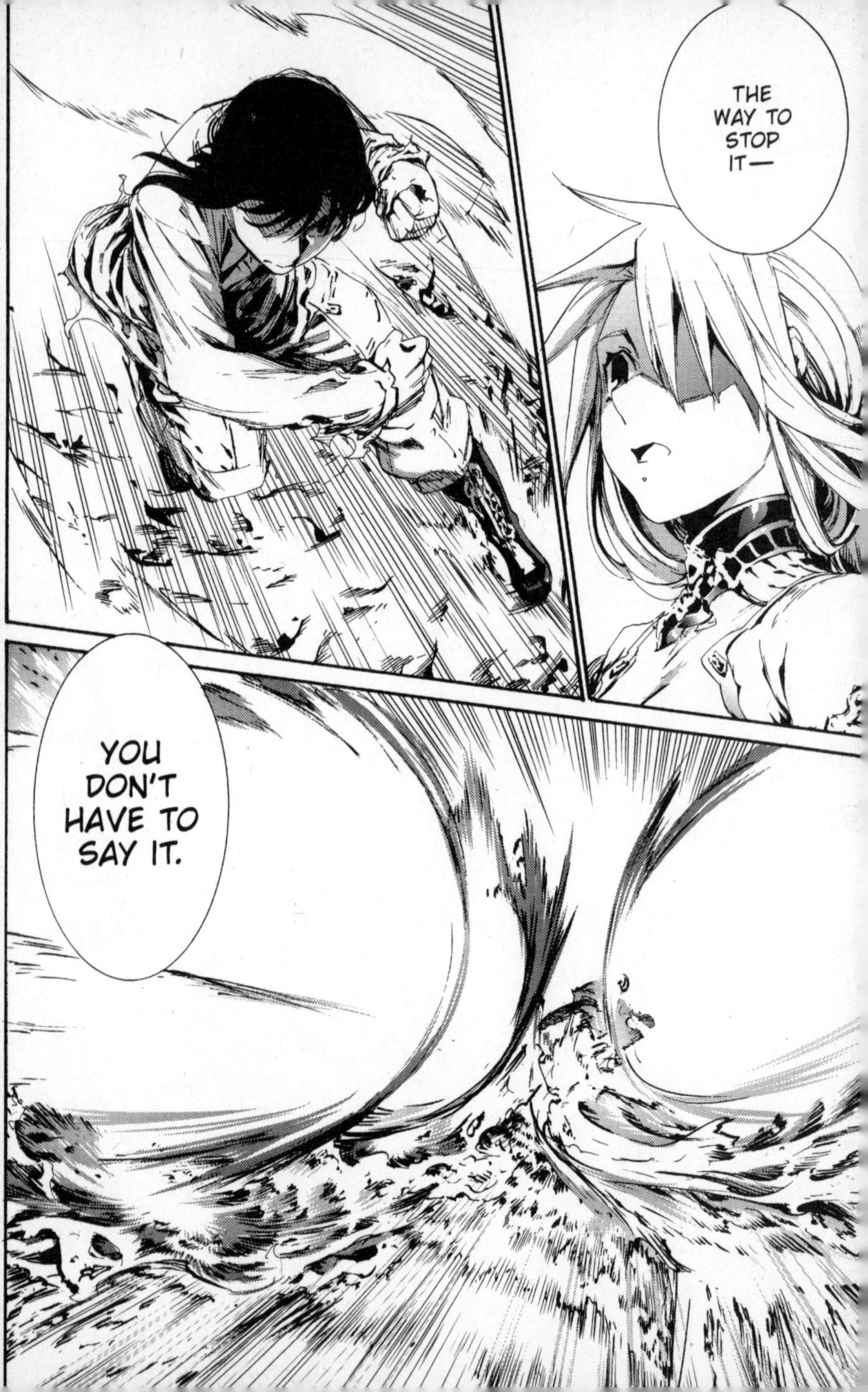
THE WAY TO STOP IT—
YOU DON'T HAVE TO SAY IT.

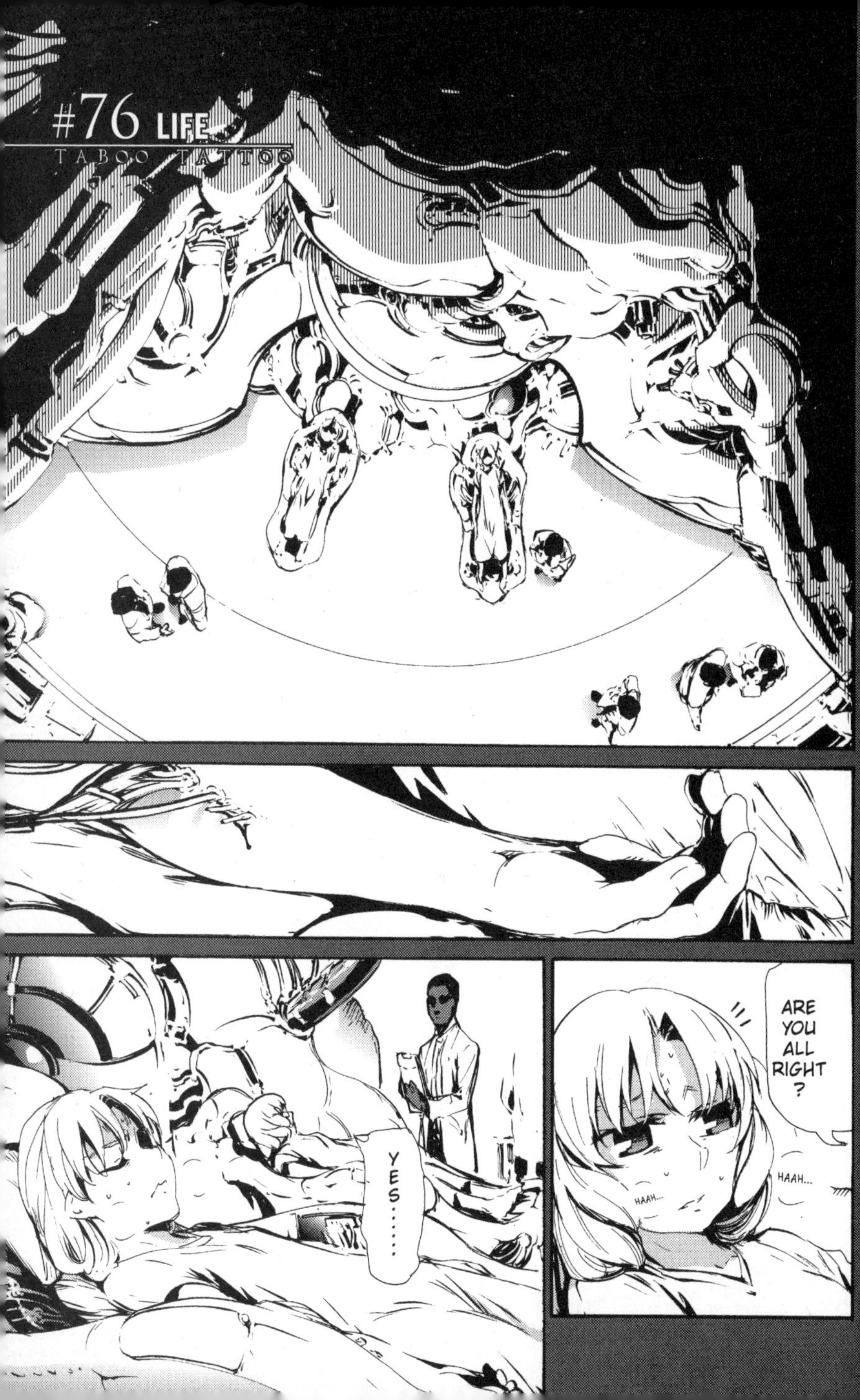
#76 LIFE
TABOO TATTOO
ARE YOU ALL RIGHT?
HAAH...
HAAH...
YES......

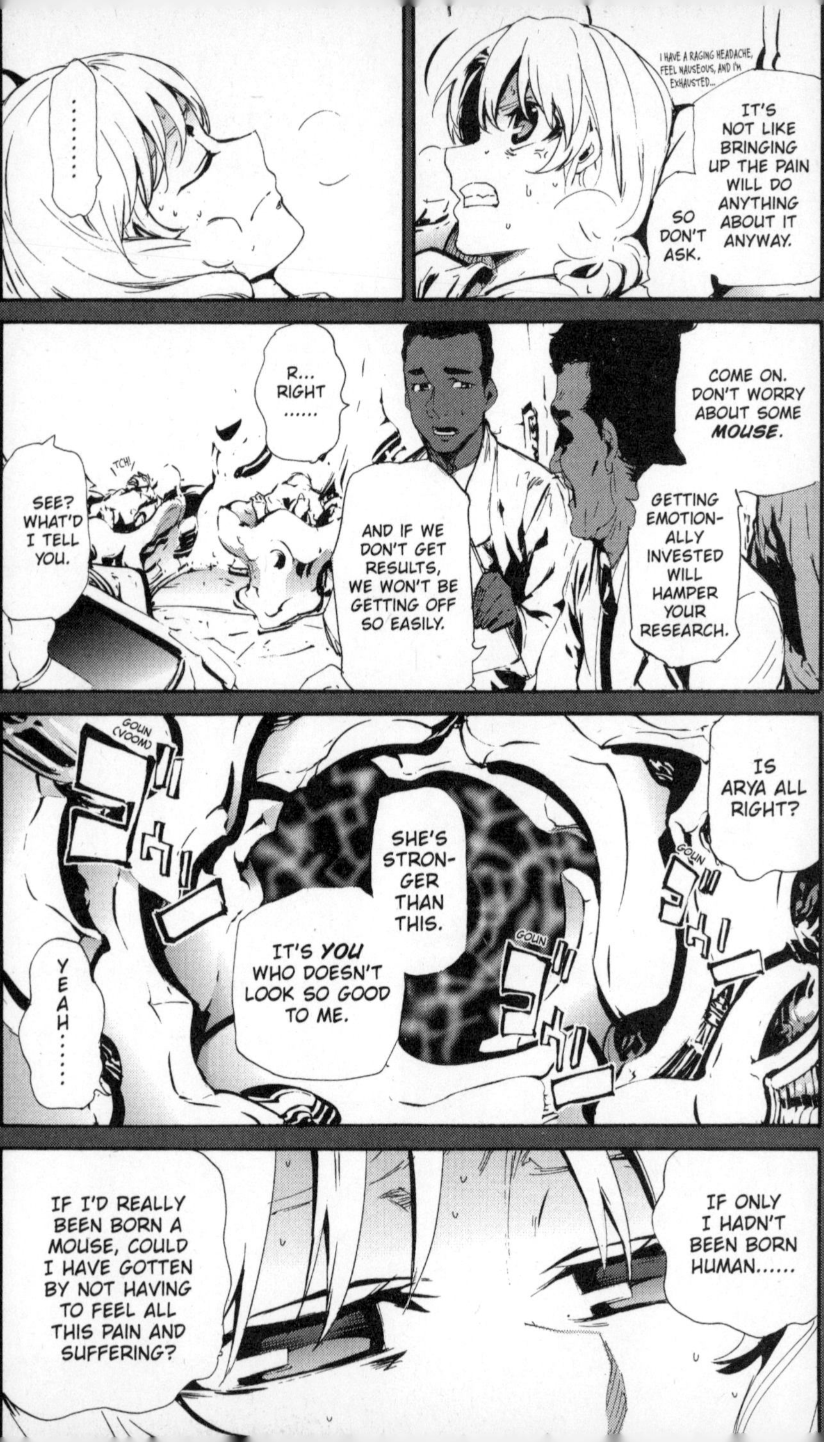
I HAVE A RAGING HEADACHE, FEEL NAUSEOUS, AND I'M EXHAUSTED...
IT'S NOT LIKE BRINGING UP THE PAIN WILL DO ANYTHING ABOUT IT ANYWAY.
SO DON'T ASK.
......
COME ON. DON'T WORRY ABOUT SOME MOUSE.
GETTING EMOTIONALLY INVESTED WILL HAMPER YOUR RESEARCH.
R... RIGHT ......
AND IF WE DON'T GET RESULTS, WE WON'T BE GETTING OFF SO EASILY.
TCH!
SEE? WHAT'D I TELL YOU.
IS ARYA ALL RIGHT?
GOUN
GOUN
SHE'S STRONGER THAN THIS.
IT'S YOU WHO DOESN'T LOOK SO GOOD TO ME.
GOUN (VOOM)
YEAH......
IF ONLY I HADN'T BEEN BORN HUMAN......
IF I'D REALLY BEEN BORN A MOUSE, COULD I HAVE GOTTEN BY NOT HAVING TO FEEL ALL THIS PAIN AND SUFFERING?

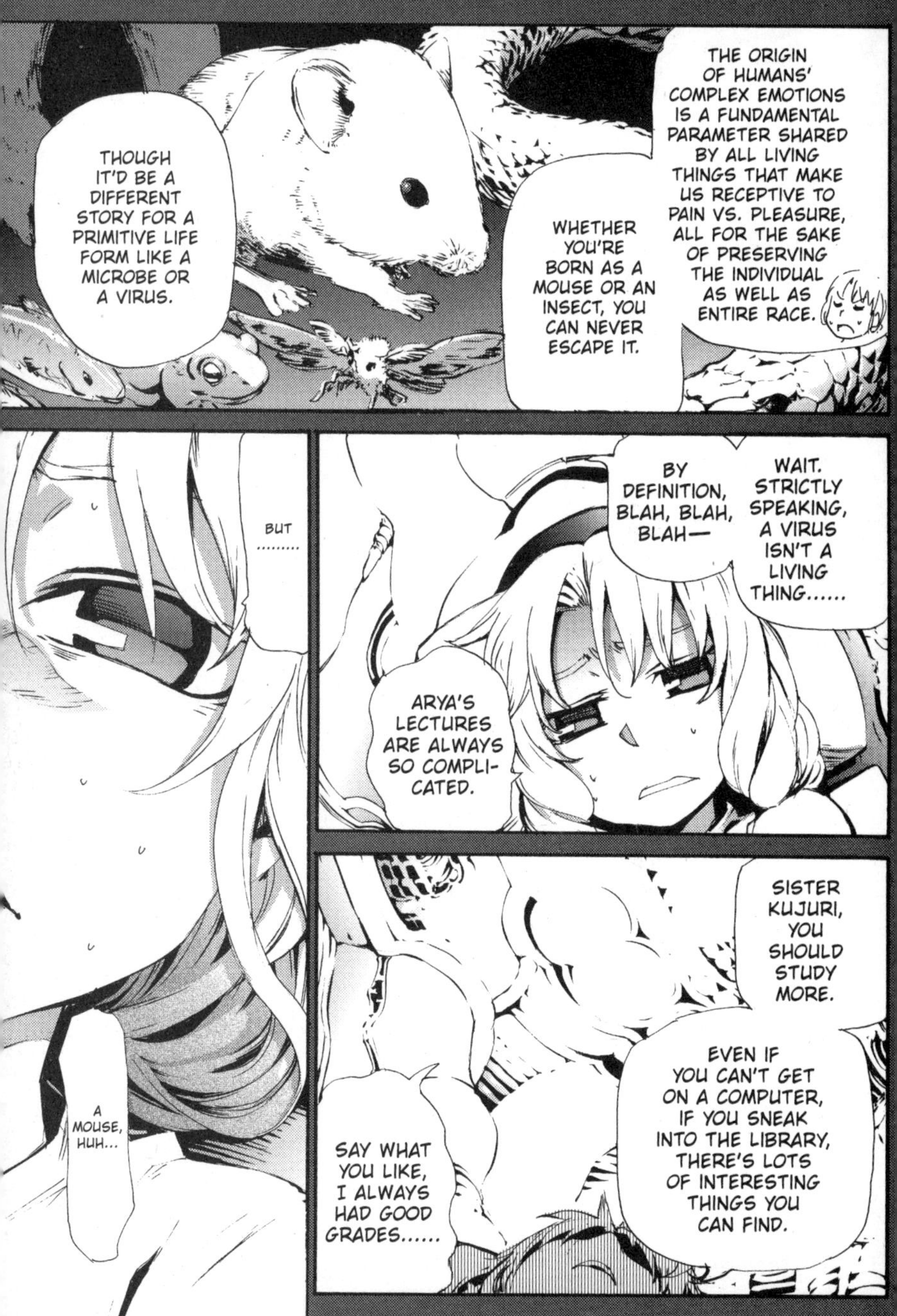
THE ORIGIN OF HUMANS' COMPLEX EMOTIONS IS A FUNDAMENTAL PARAMETER SHARED BY ALL LIVING THINGS THAT MAKE US RECEPTIVE TO PAIN VS. PLEASURE, ALL FOR THE SAKE OF PRESERVING THE INDIVIDUAL AS WELL AS ENTIRE RACE.
WHETHER YOU'RE BORN AS A MOUSE OR AN INSECT, YOU CAN NEVER ESCAPE IT.
THOUGH IT'D BE A DIFFERENT STORY FOR A PRIMITIVE LIFE FORM LIKE A MICROBE OR A VIRUS.
WAIT. STRICTLY SPEAKING, A VIRUS ISN'T A LIVING THING......
BY DEFINITION, BLAH, BLAH, BLAH—
ARYA'S LECTURES ARE ALWAYS SO COMPLICATED.
SISTER KUJURI, YOU SHOULD STUDY MORE.
EVEN IF YOU CAN'T GET ON A COMPUTER, IF YOU SNEAK INTO THE LIBRARY, THERE'S LOTS OF INTERESTING THINGS YOU CAN FIND.
SAY WHAT YOU LIKE, I ALWAYS HAD GOOD GRADES......
BUT ....
A MOUSE, HUH...

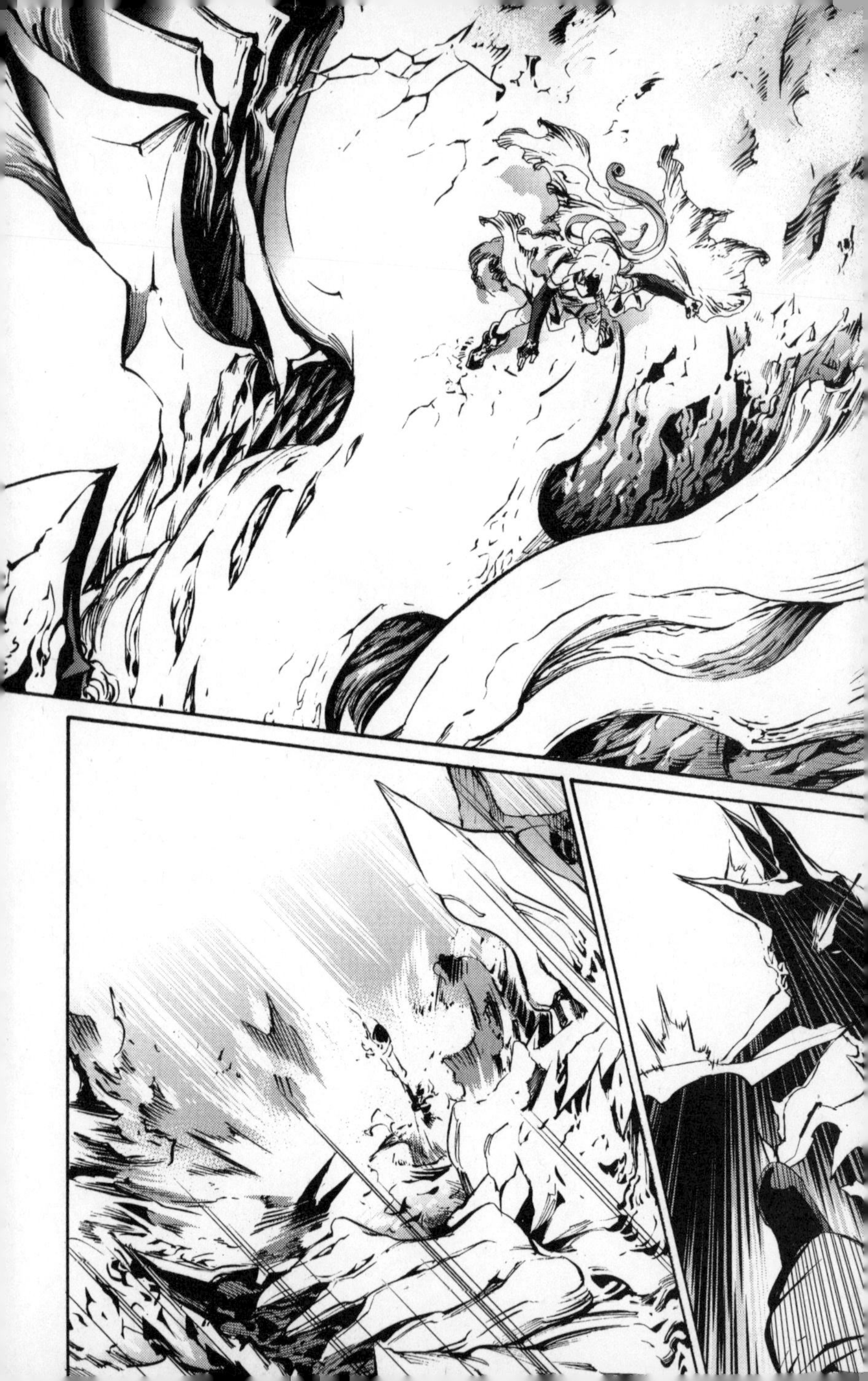

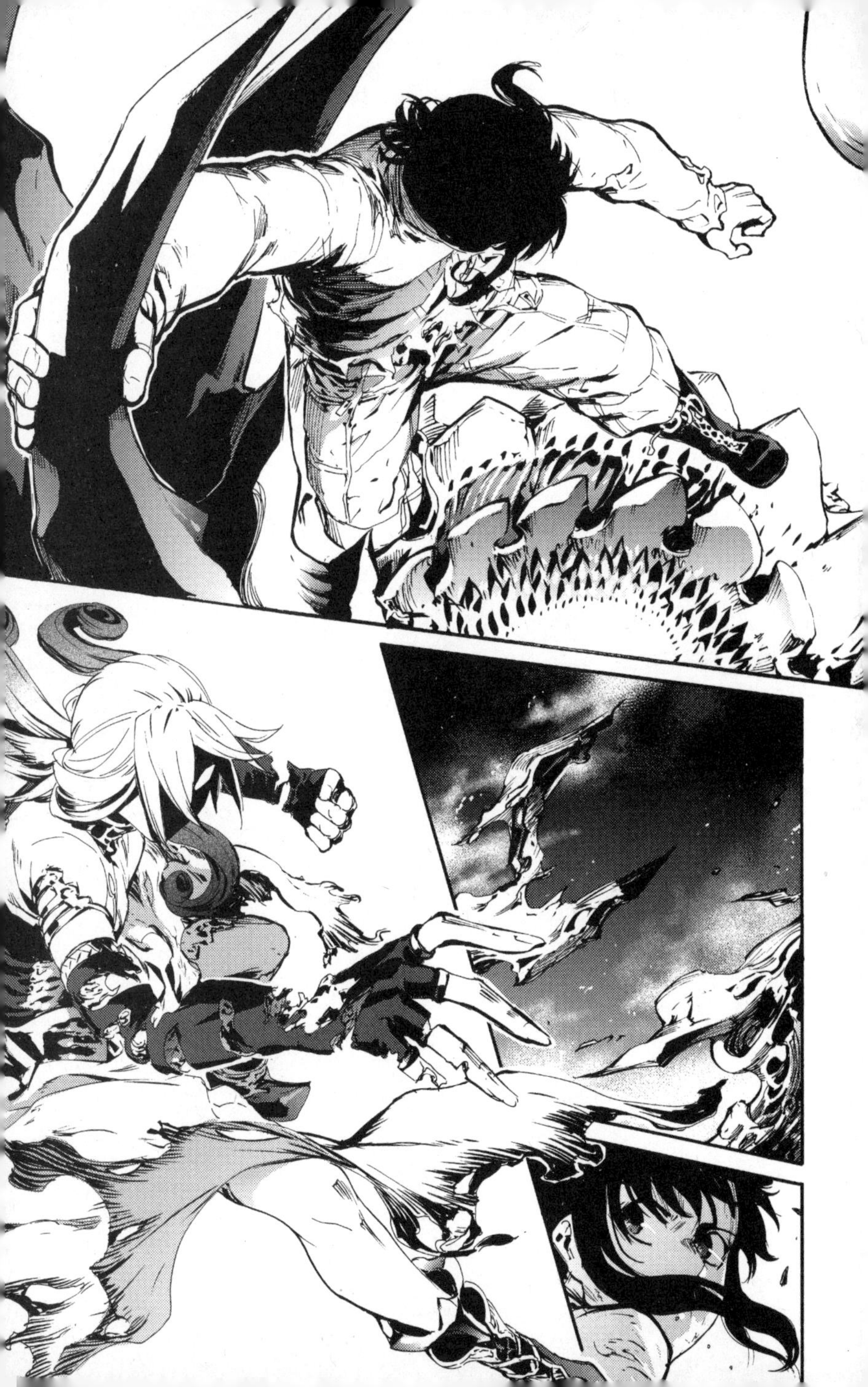

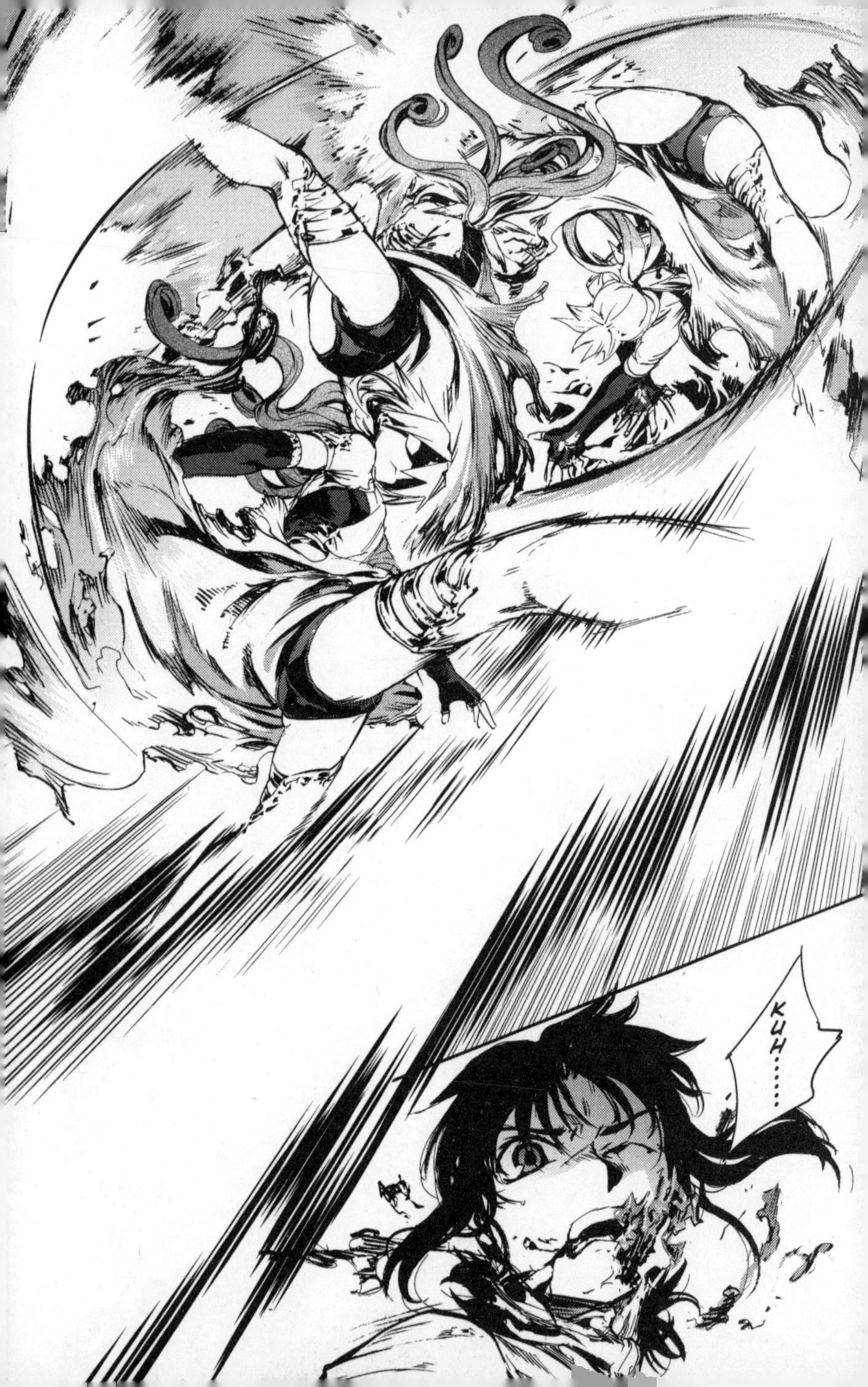
KUH......

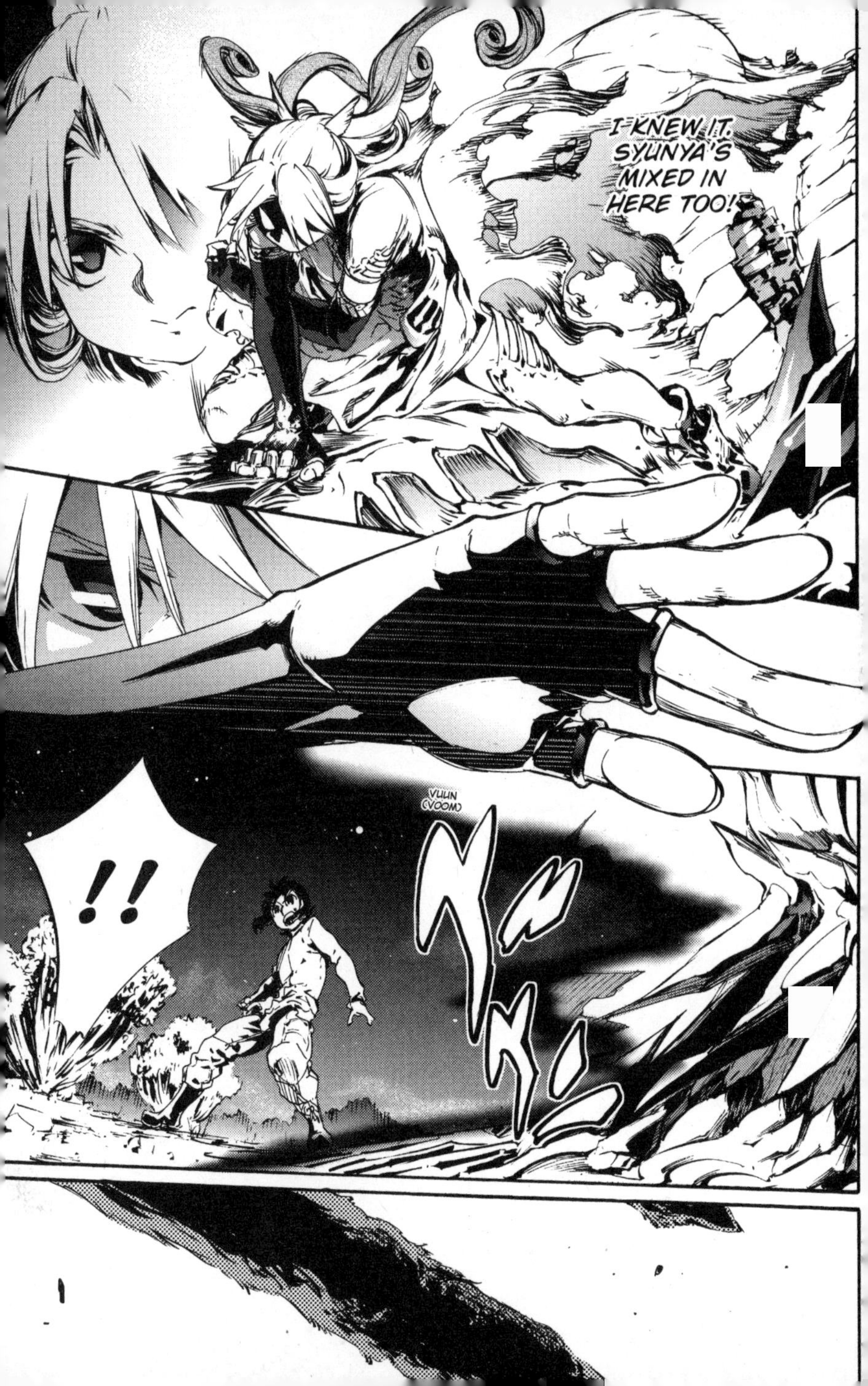
I KNEW IT. SYUNYA'S MIXED IN HERE TOO!
VUUN (VOOM)
!!

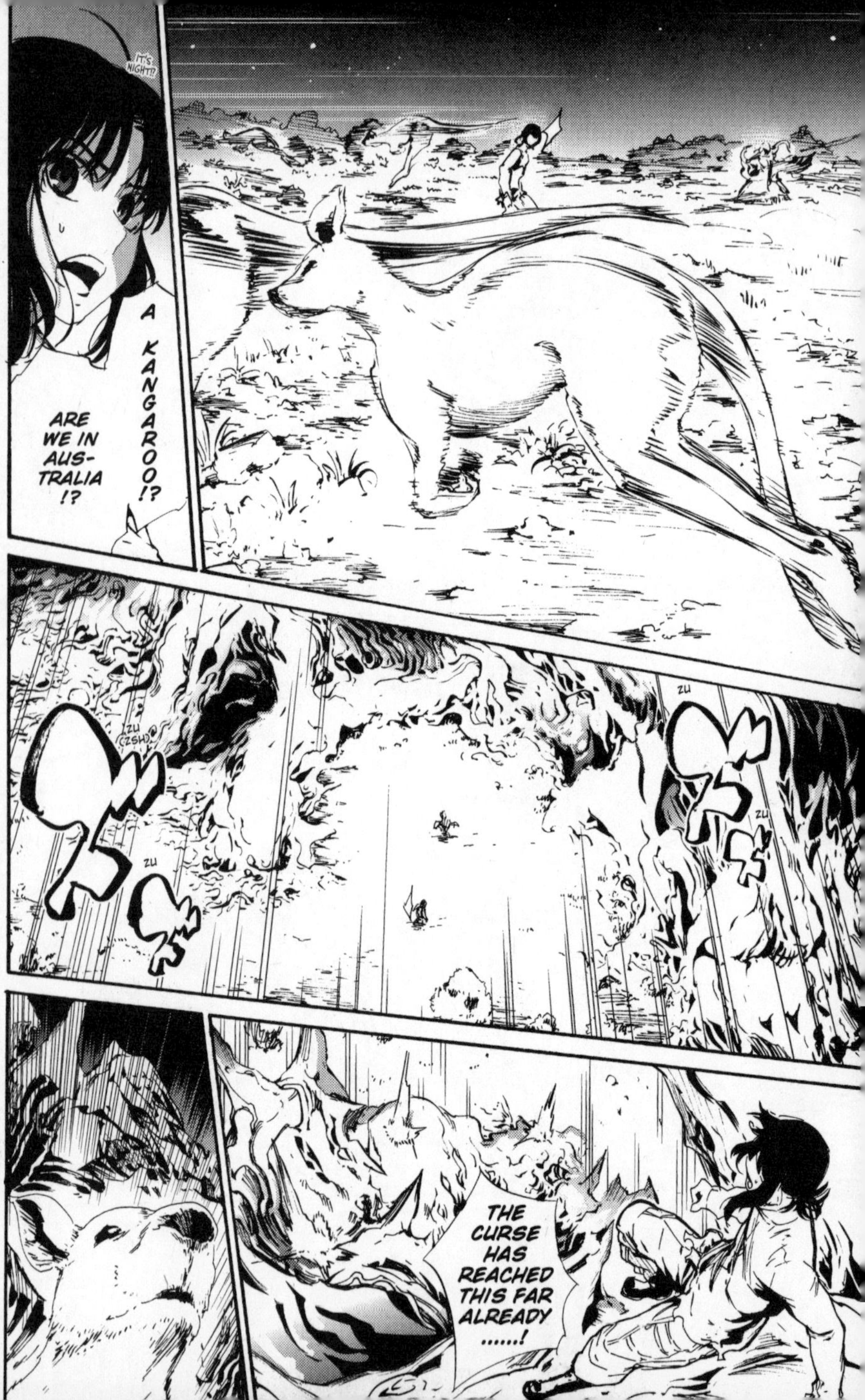
IT'S NIGHT!?
A KANGAROO!?
ARE WE IN AUS-TRALIA !?
ZU
ZU
ZU (CZSH)
ZU
THE CURSE HAS REACHED THIS FAR ALREADY ......!

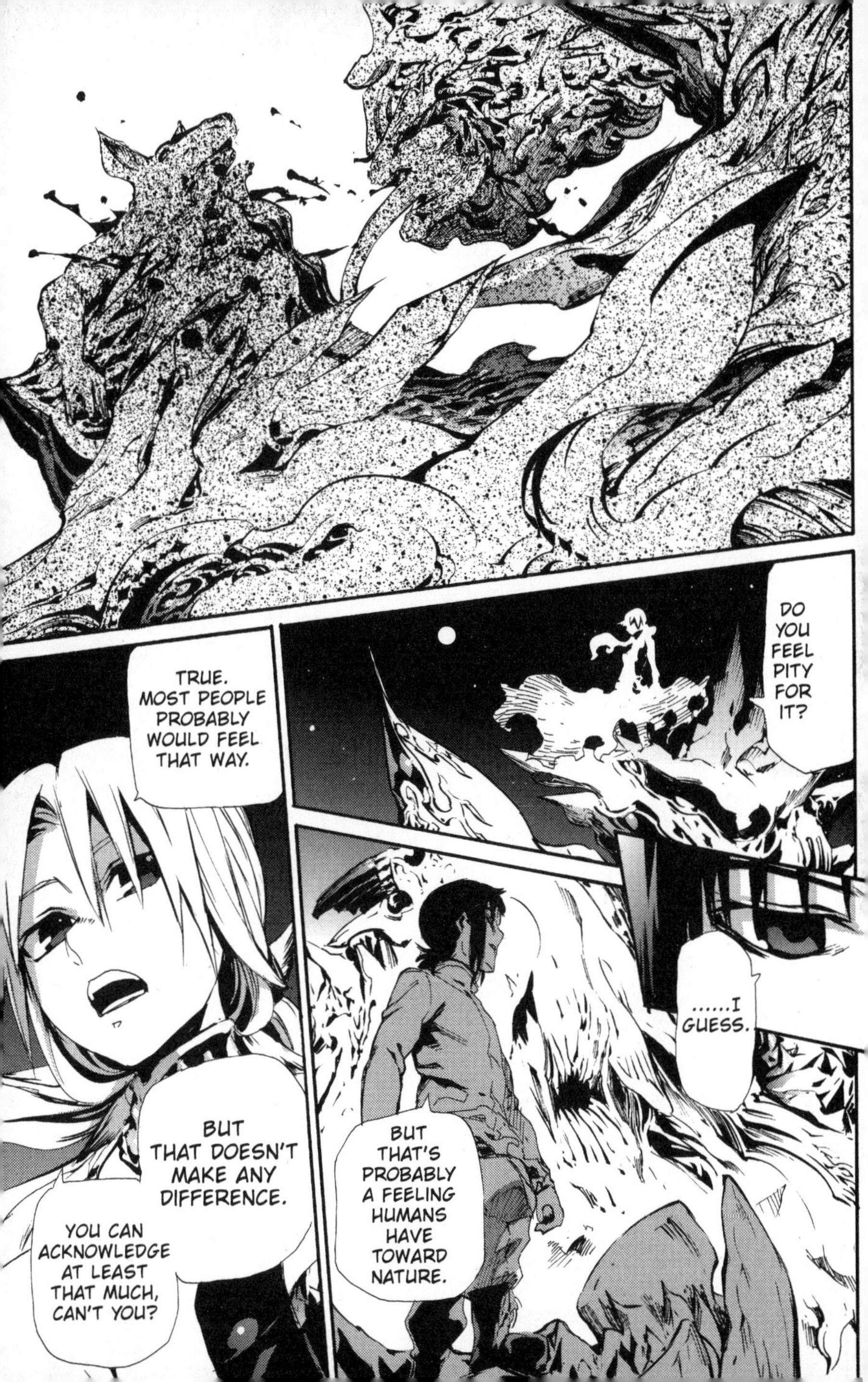
DO YOU FEEL PITY FOR IT?
......I GUESS.
BUT THAT'S PROBABLY A FEELING HUMANS HAVE TOWARD NATURE.
TRUE. MOST PEOPLE PROBABLY WOULD FEEL THAT WAY.
BUT THAT DOESN'T MAKE ANY DIFFERENCE.
YOU CAN ACKNOWLEDGE AT LEAST THAT MUCH, CAN'T YOU?

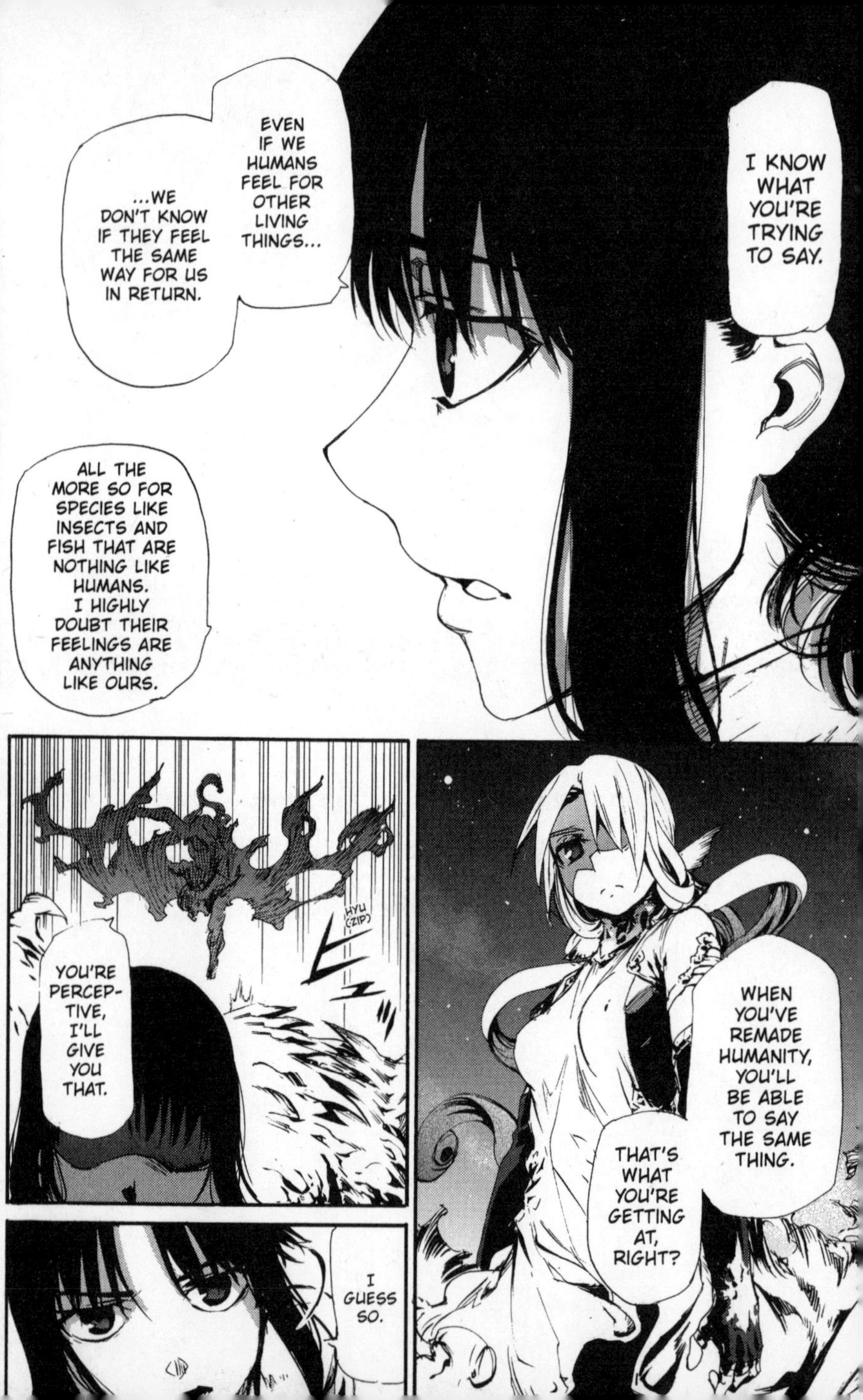
I KNOW WHAT YOU'RE TRYING TO SAY.
EVEN IF WE HUMANS FEEL FOR OTHER LIVING THINGS...
...WE DON'T KNOW IF THEY FEEL THE SAME WAY FOR US IN RETURN.
ALL THE MORE SO FOR SPECIES LIKE INSECTS AND FISH THAT ARE NOTHING LIKE HUMANS. I HIGHLY DOUBT THEIR FEELINGS ARE ANYTHING LIKE OURS.
WHEN YOU'VE REMADE HUMANITY, YOU'LL BE ABLE TO SAY THE SAME THING.
THAT'S WHAT YOU'RE GETTING AT, RIGHT?
HYU (ZIP)
YOU'RE PERCEPTIVE, I'LL GIVE YOU THAT.
I GUESS SO.

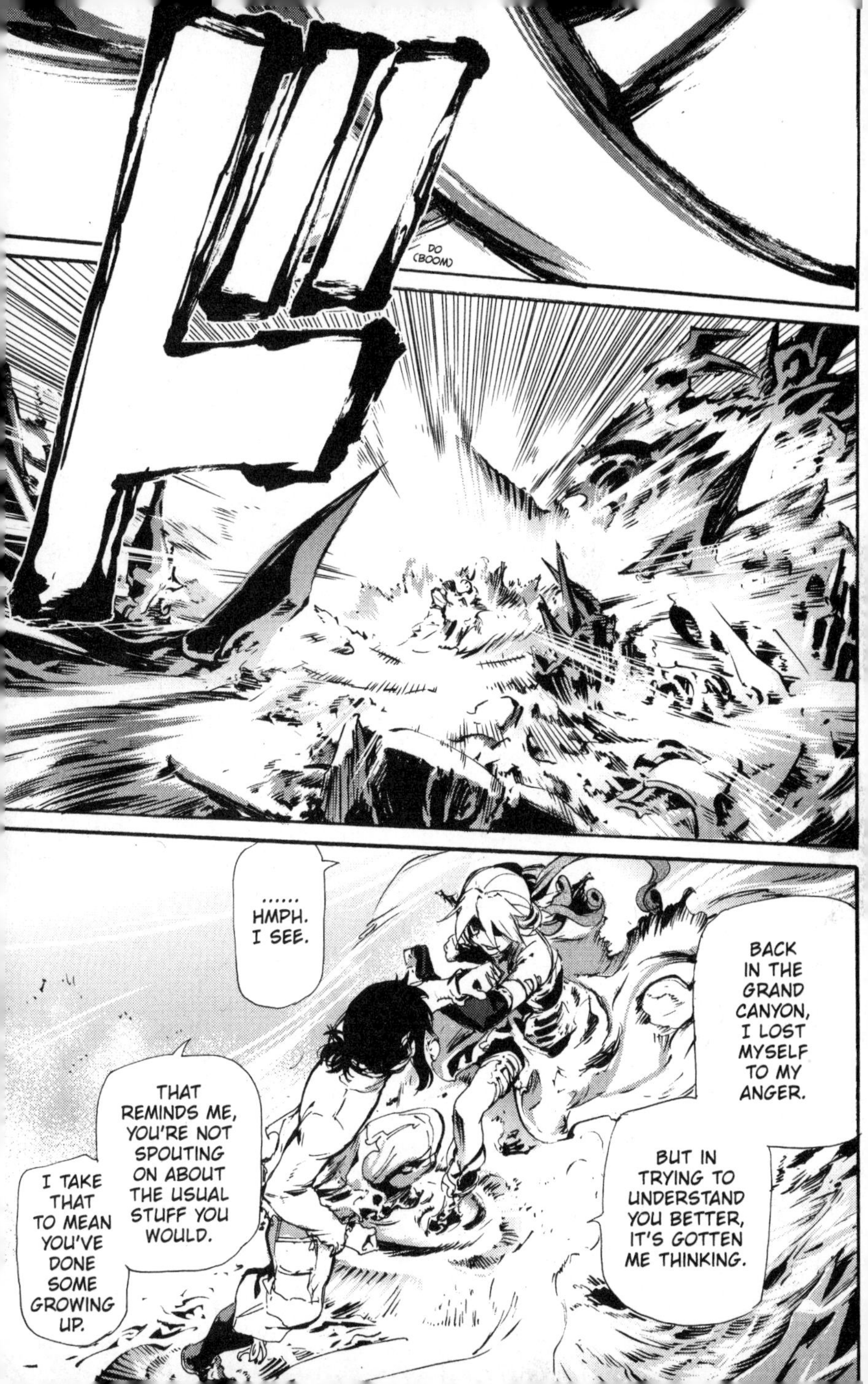
DO (BOOM)
BACK IN THE GRAND CANYON, I LOST MYSELF TO MY ANGER.
BUT IN TRYING TO UNDERSTAND YOU BETTER, IT'S GOTTEN ME THINKING.
...... HMPH. I SEE.
THAT REMINDS ME, YOU'RE NOT SPOUTING ON ABOUT THE USUAL STUFF YOU WOULD.
I TAKE THAT TO MEAN YOU'VE DONE SOME GROWING UP.

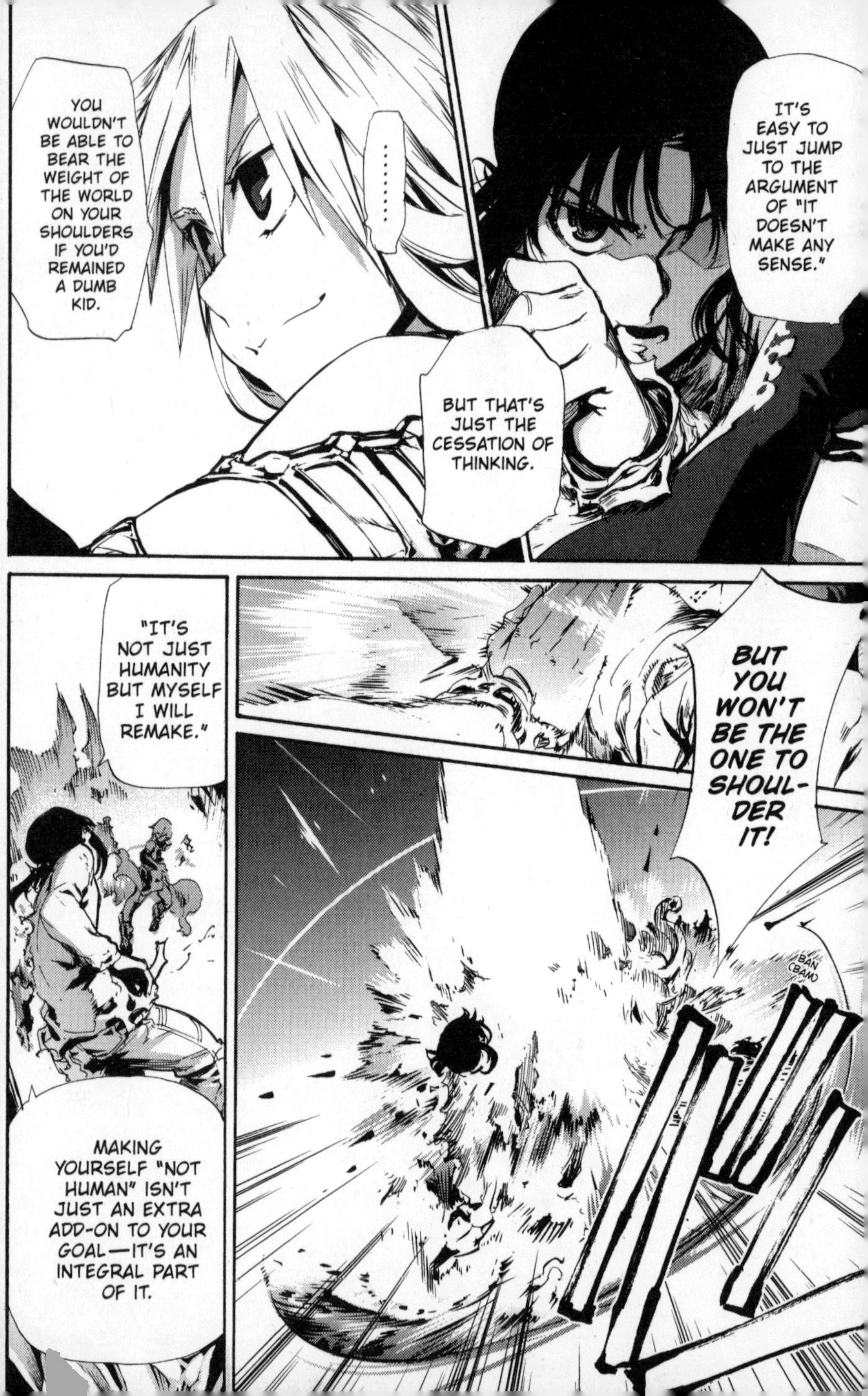
IT'S EASY TO JUST JUMP TO THE ARGUMENT OF "IT DOESN'T MAKE ANY SENSE."
BUT THAT'S JUST THE CESSATION OF THINKING.
......
YOU WOULDN'T BE ABLE TO BEAR THE WEIGHT OF THE WORLD ON YOUR SHOULDERS IF YOU'D REMAINED A DUMB KID.
BUT YOU WON'T BE THE ONE TO SHOUL-DER IT!
BAN (BAM)
"IT'S NOT JUST HUMANITY BUT MYSELF I WILL REMAKE."
MAKING YOURSELF "NOT HUMAN" ISN'T JUST AN EXTRA ADD-ON TO YOUR GOAL—IT'S AN INTEGRAL PART OF IT.

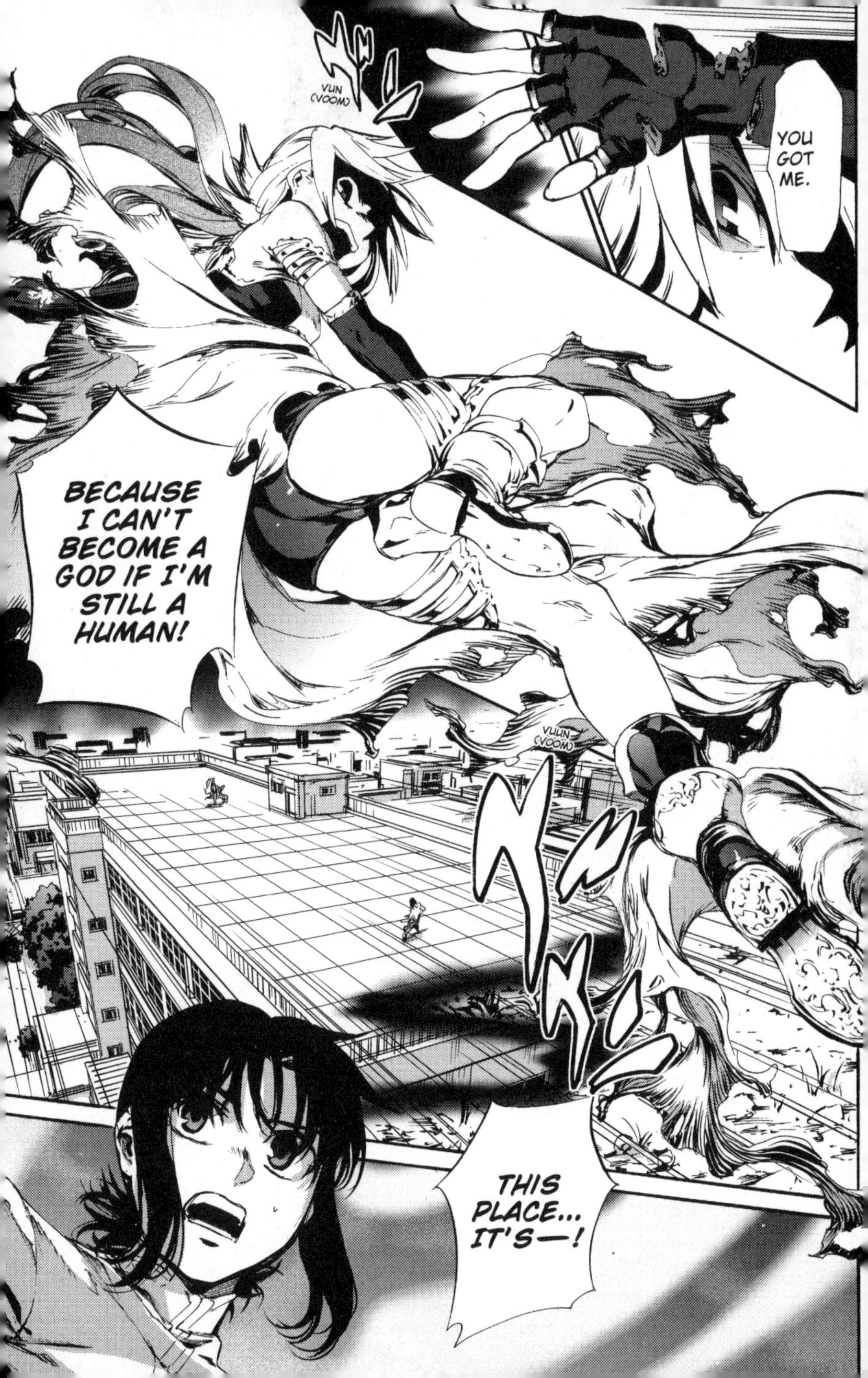
VUN (VOOM)
YOU GOT ME.
BECAUSE I CAN'T BECOME A GOD IF I'M STILL A HUMAN!
VUN (VOOM)
THIS PLACE... IT'S—!

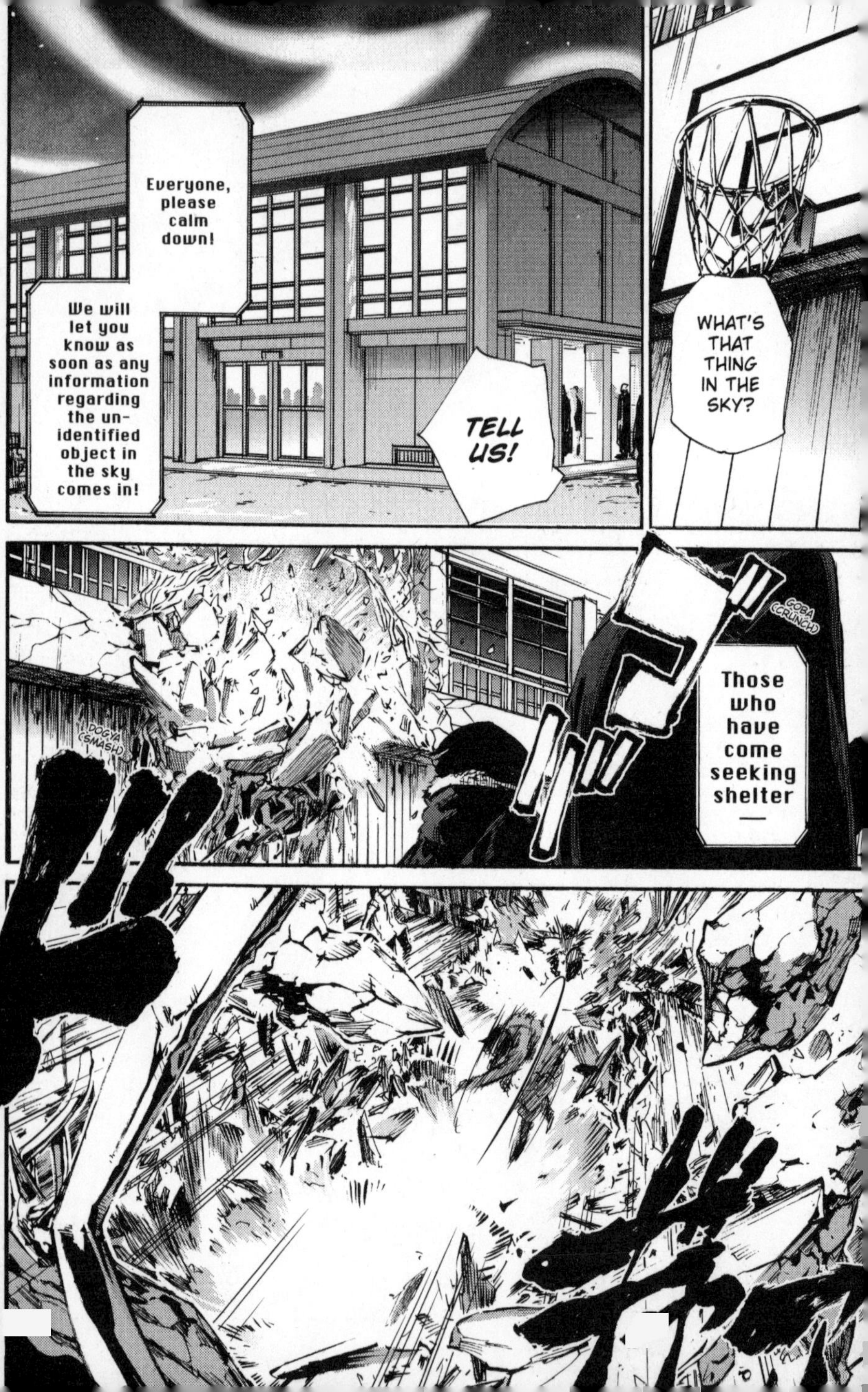
WHAT'S THAT THING IN THE SKY?
TELL US!
Everyone, please calm down!
We will let you know as soon as any information regarding the un-identified object in the sky comes in!
GOBA (CRUNCH)
Those who have come seeking shelter —
DOGYA (SMASH)

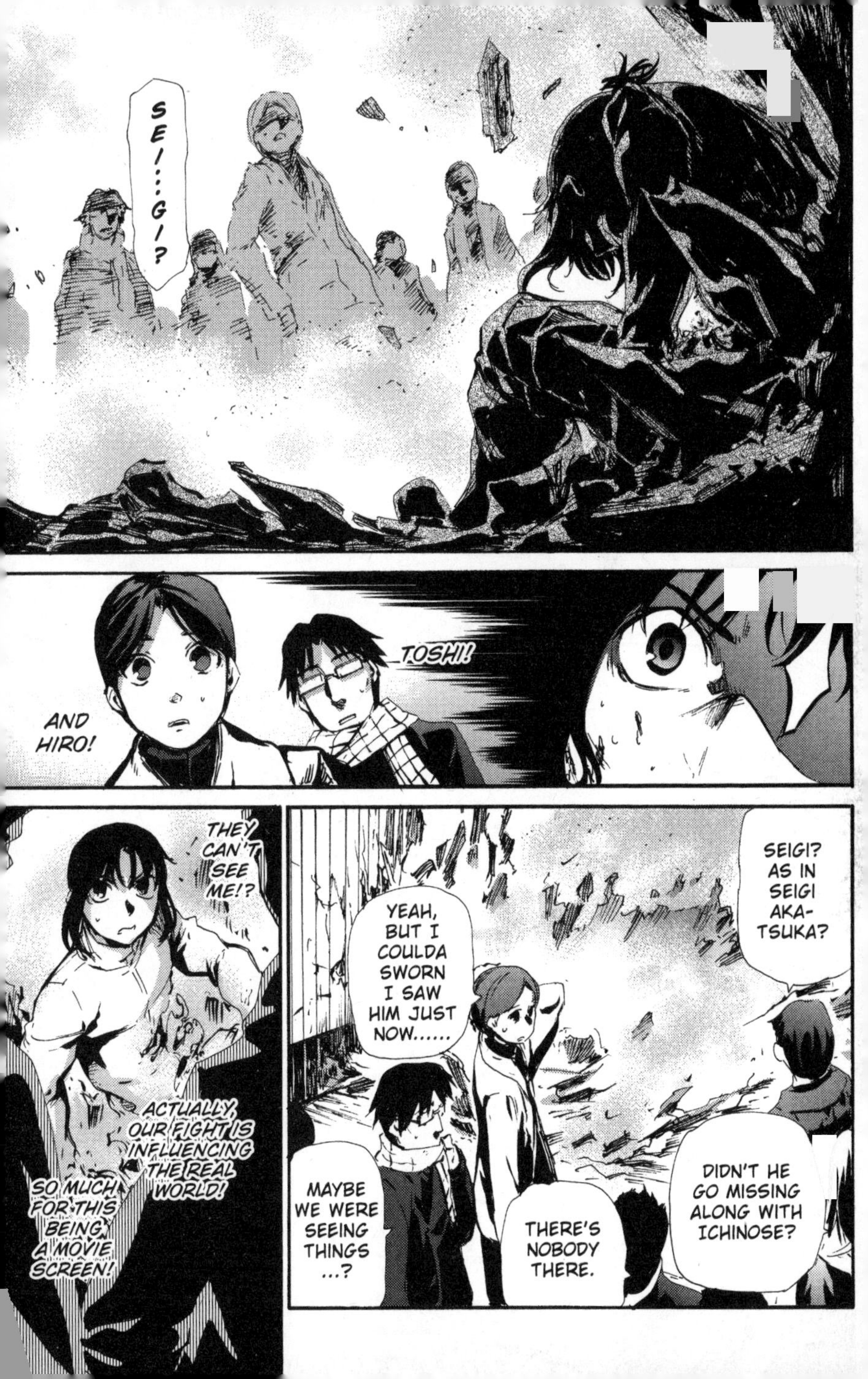
SEI...GI?
TOSHI!
AND HIRO!
SEIGI? AS IN SEIGI AKATSUKA?
YEAH, BUT I COULDA SWORN I SAW HIM JUST NOW......
DIDN'T HE GO MISSING ALONG WITH ICHINOSE?
THERE'S NOBODY THERE.
MAYBE WE WERE SEEING THINGS ...?
THEY CAN'T SEE ME!?
ACTUALLY, OUR FIGHT IS INFLUENCING THE REAL WORLD!
SO MUCH FOR THIS BEING A MOVIE SCREEN!

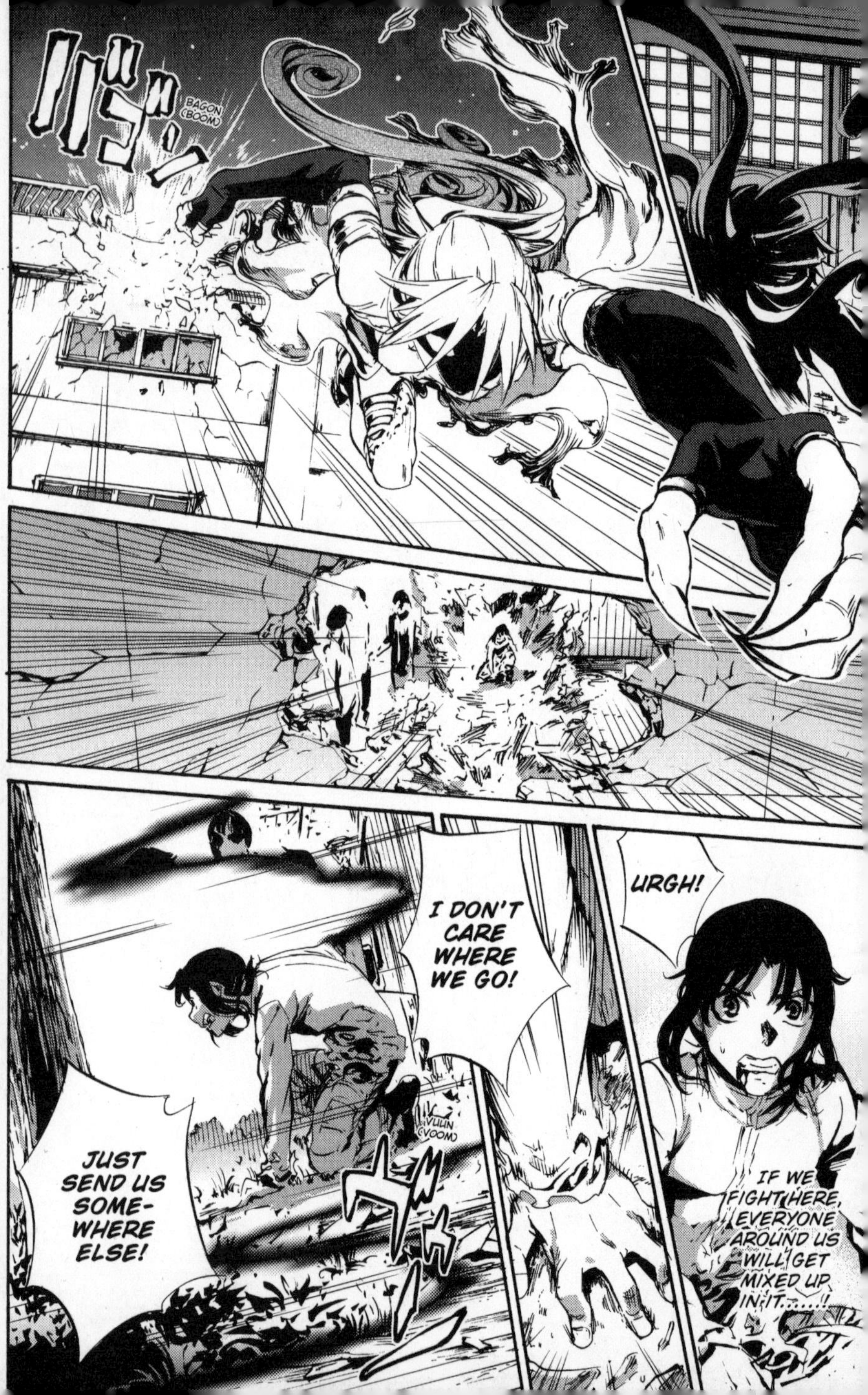
BAGON (BOOM)
URGH!
IF WE FIGHT HERE, EVERYONE AROUND US WILL GET MIXED UP IN IT......!
I DON'T CARE WHERE WE GO!
JUST SEND US SOME-WHERE ELSE!
VUUN (VOOM)

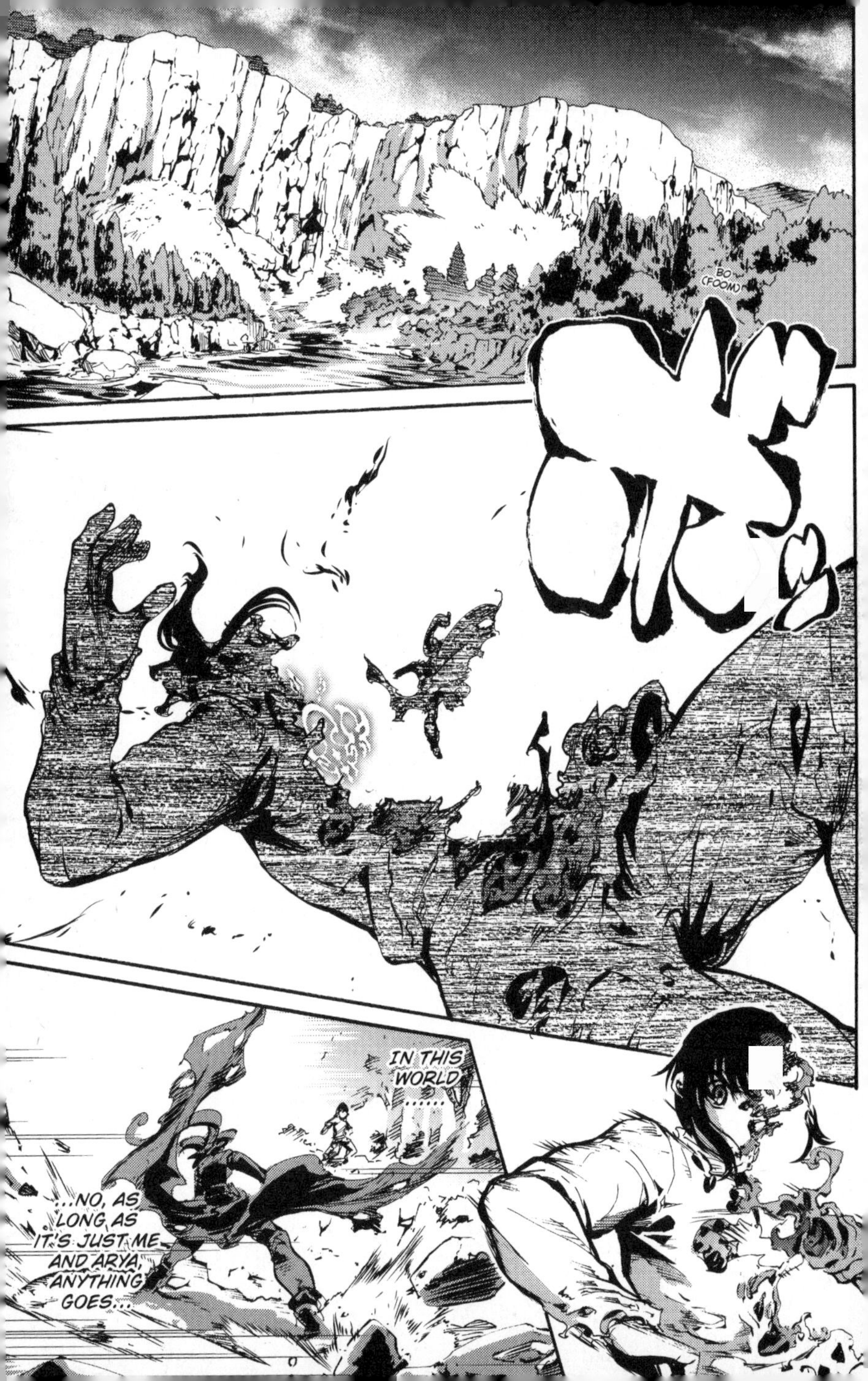
BO
(FOOM)
IN THIS WORLD......
...NO, AS LONG AS IT'S JUST ME AND ARYA, ANYTHING GOES...

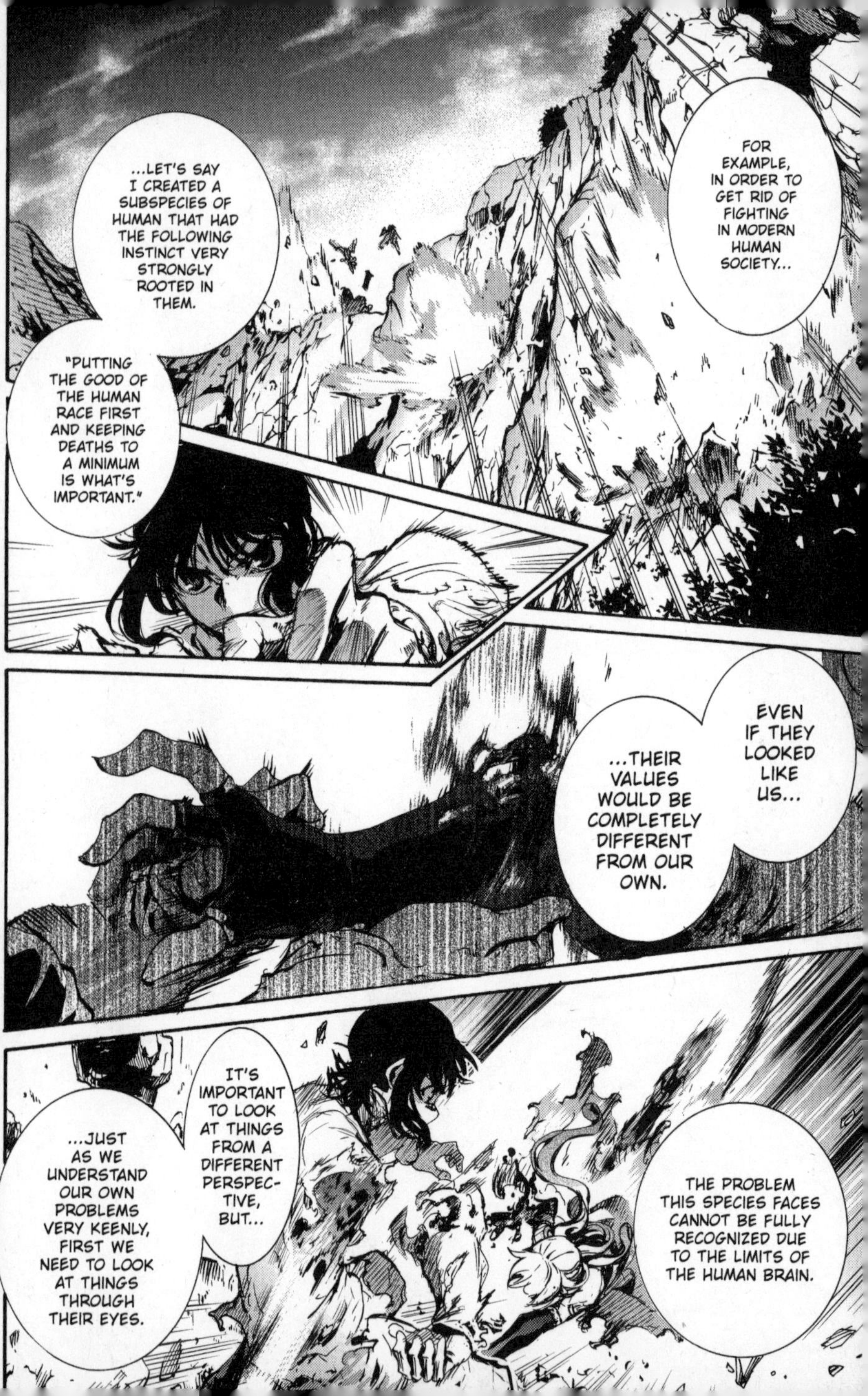
FOR EXAMPLE, IN ORDER TO GET RID OF FIGHTING IN MODERN HUMAN SOCIETY...
...LET'S SAY I CREATED A SUBSPECIES OF HUMAN THAT HAD THE FOLLOWING INSTINCT VERY STRONGLY ROOTED IN THEM.
"PUTTING THE GOOD OF THE HUMAN RACE FIRST AND KEEPING DEATHS TO A MINIMUM IS WHAT'S IMPORTANT."
EVEN IF THEY LOOKED LIKE US...
...THEIR VALUES WOULD BE COMPLETELY DIFFERENT FROM OUR OWN.
THE PROBLEM THIS SPECIES FACES CANNOT BE FULLY RECOGNIZED DUE TO THE LIMITS OF THE HUMAN BRAIN.
IT'S IMPORTANT TO LOOK AT THINGS FROM A DIFFERENT PERSPEC-TIVE, BUT...
...JUST AS WE UNDERSTAND OUR OWN PROBLEMS VERY KEENLY, FIRST WE NEED TO LOOK AT THINGS THROUGH THEIR EYES.

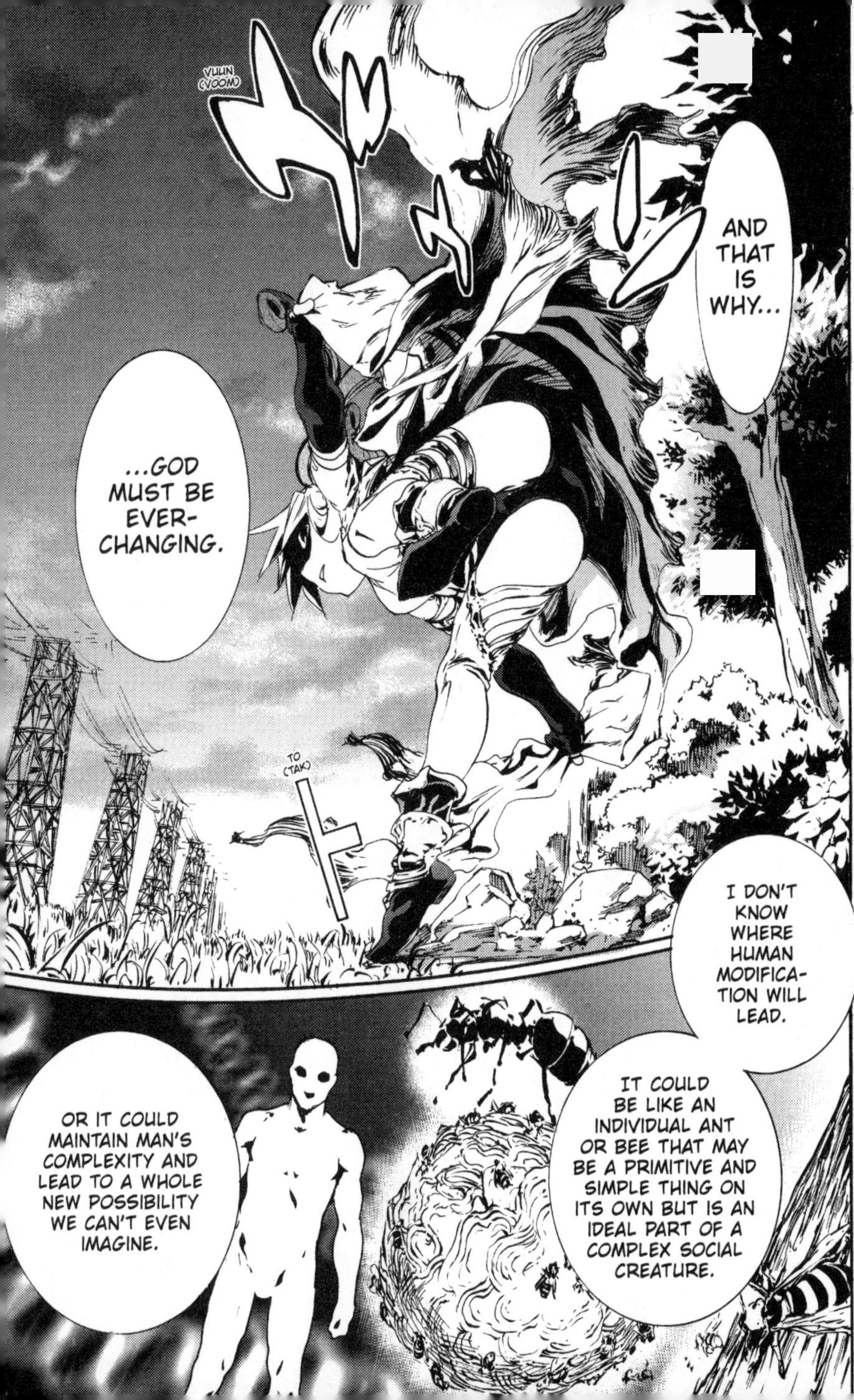
AND THAT IS WHY...
VUUN (VOOM)
...GOD MUST BE EVER-CHANGING.
TO (TAK)
I DON'T KNOW WHERE HUMAN MODIFICATION WILL LEAD.
IT COULD BE LIKE AN INDIVIDUAL ANT OR BEE THAT MAY BE A PRIMITIVE AND SIMPLE THING ON ITS OWN BUT IS AN IDEAL PART OF A COMPLEX SOCIAL CREATURE.
OR IT COULD MAINTAIN MAN'S COMPLEXITY AND LEAD TO A WHOLE NEW POSSIBILITY WE CAN'T EVEN IMAGINE.

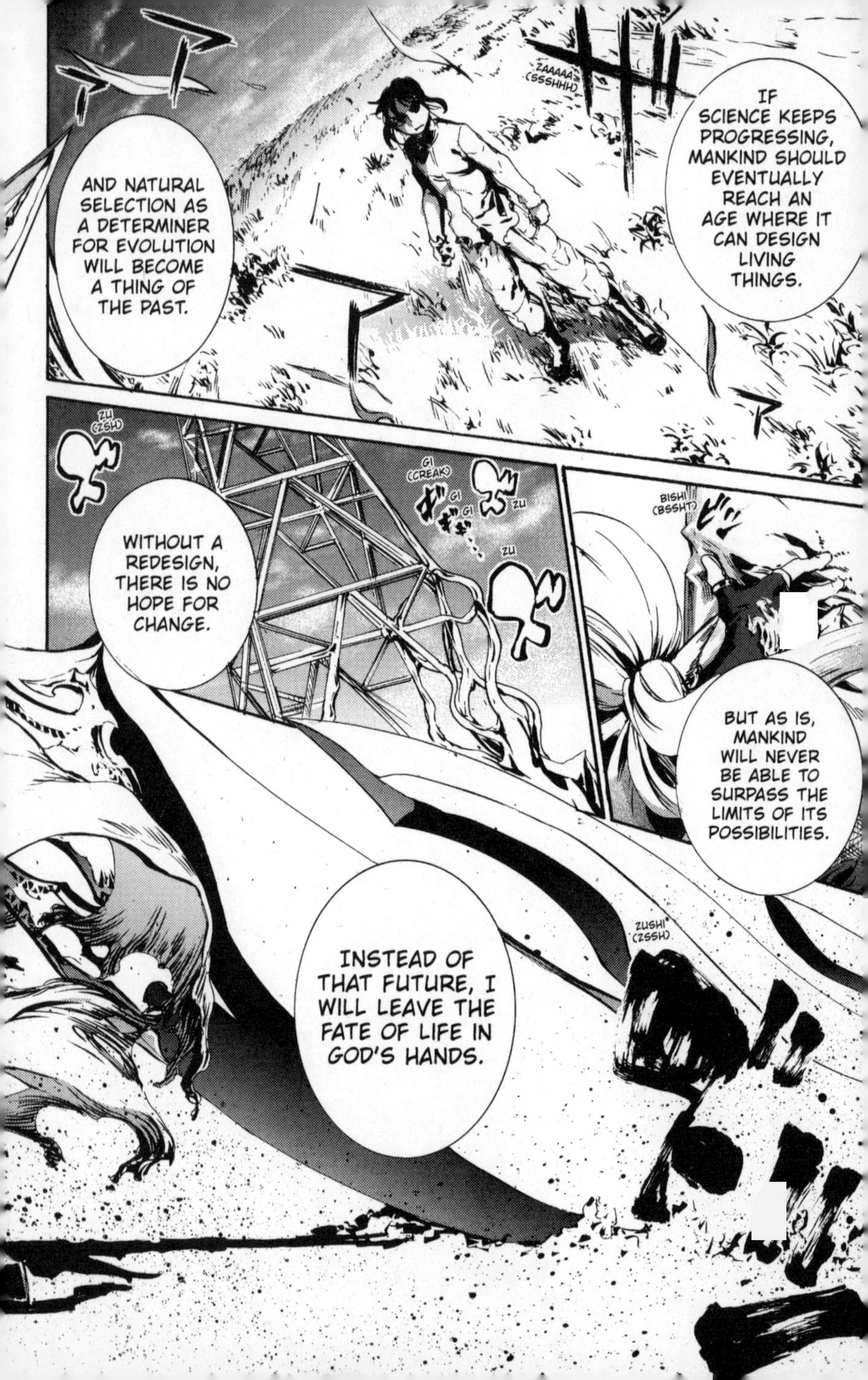
IF SCIENCE KEEPS PROGRESSING, MANKIND SHOULD EVENTUALLY REACH AN AGE WHERE IT CAN DESIGN LIVING THINGS.
ZAAAAA (SSSHHH)
AND NATURAL SELECTION AS A DETERMINER FOR EVOLUTION WILL BECOME A THING OF THE PAST.
BISHI (BSSHT)
BUT AS IS, MANKIND WILL NEVER BE ABLE TO SURPASS THE LIMITS OF ITS POSSIBILITIES.
GI (CREAK)
GI GI
ZU
ZU
ZU (ZSSH)
WITHOUT A REDESIGN, THERE IS NO HOPE FOR CHANGE.
ZUSHI (ZSSH)
INSTEAD OF THAT FUTURE, I WILL LEAVE THE FATE OF LIFE IN GOD'S HANDS.

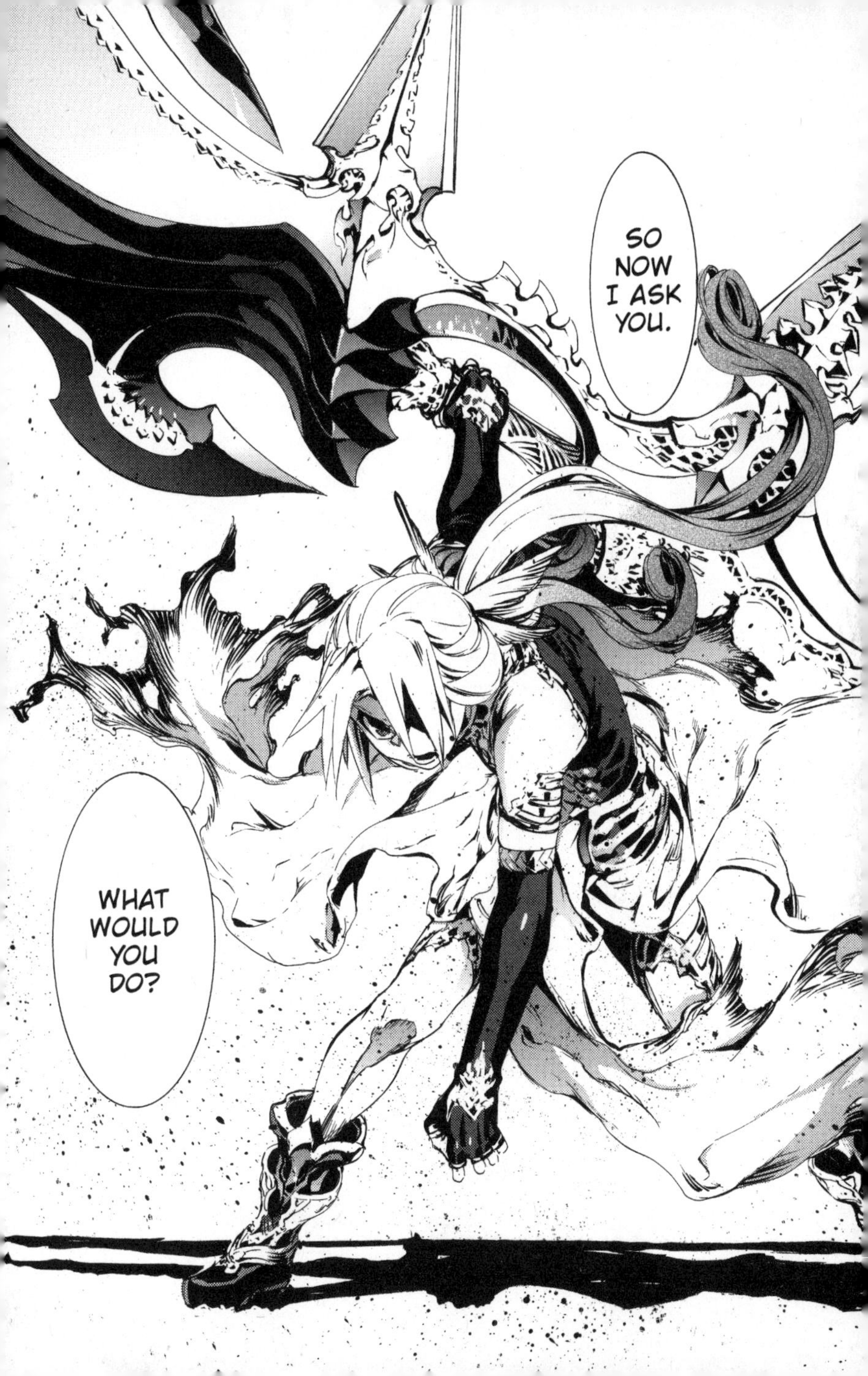
SO NOW I ASK YOU.
WHAT WOULD YOU DO?

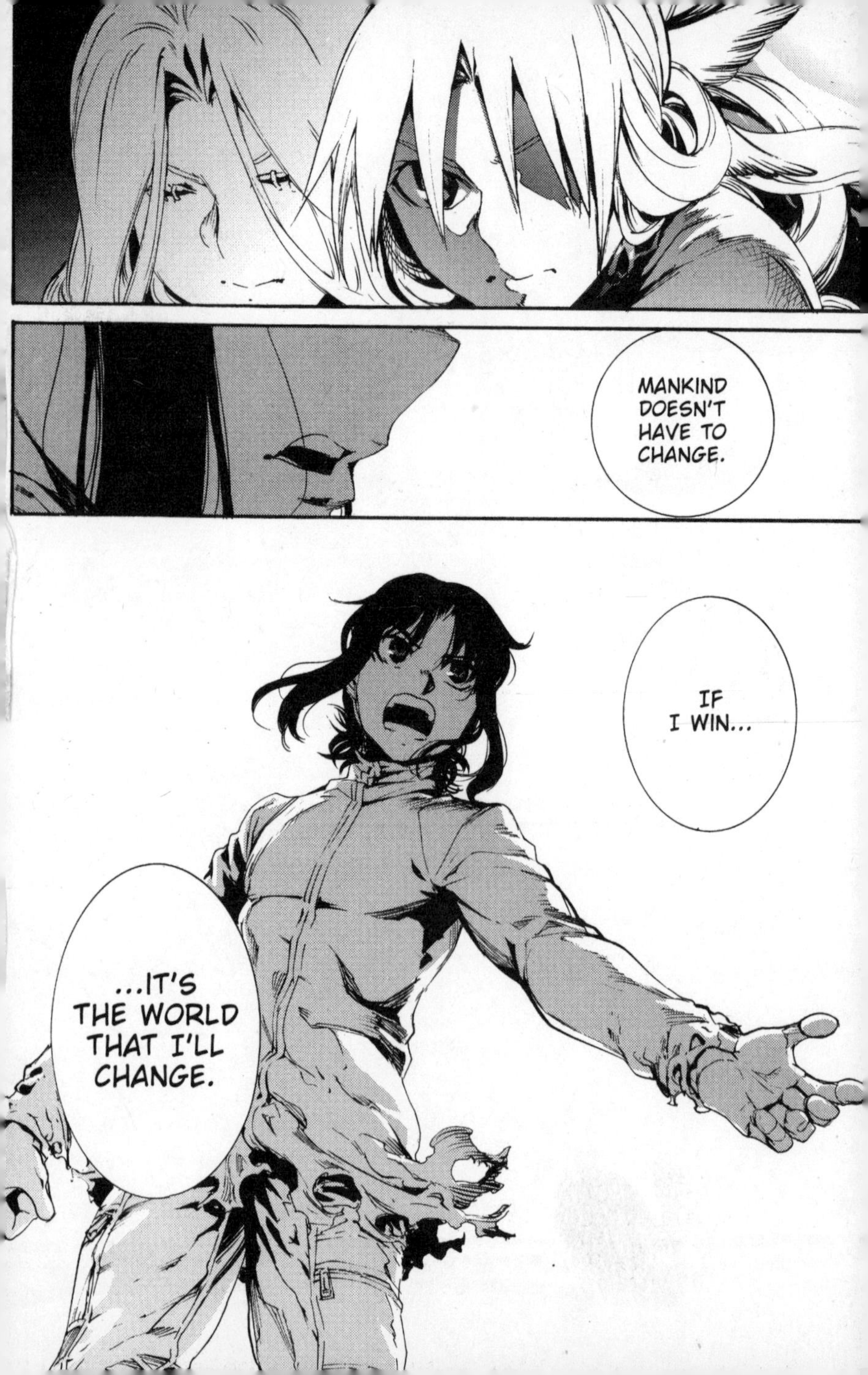
MANKIND DOESN'T HAVE TO CHANGE.
IF I WIN...
...IT'S THE WORLD THAT I'LL CHANGE.

#77 SPELL CREST
TABOO TATTOO

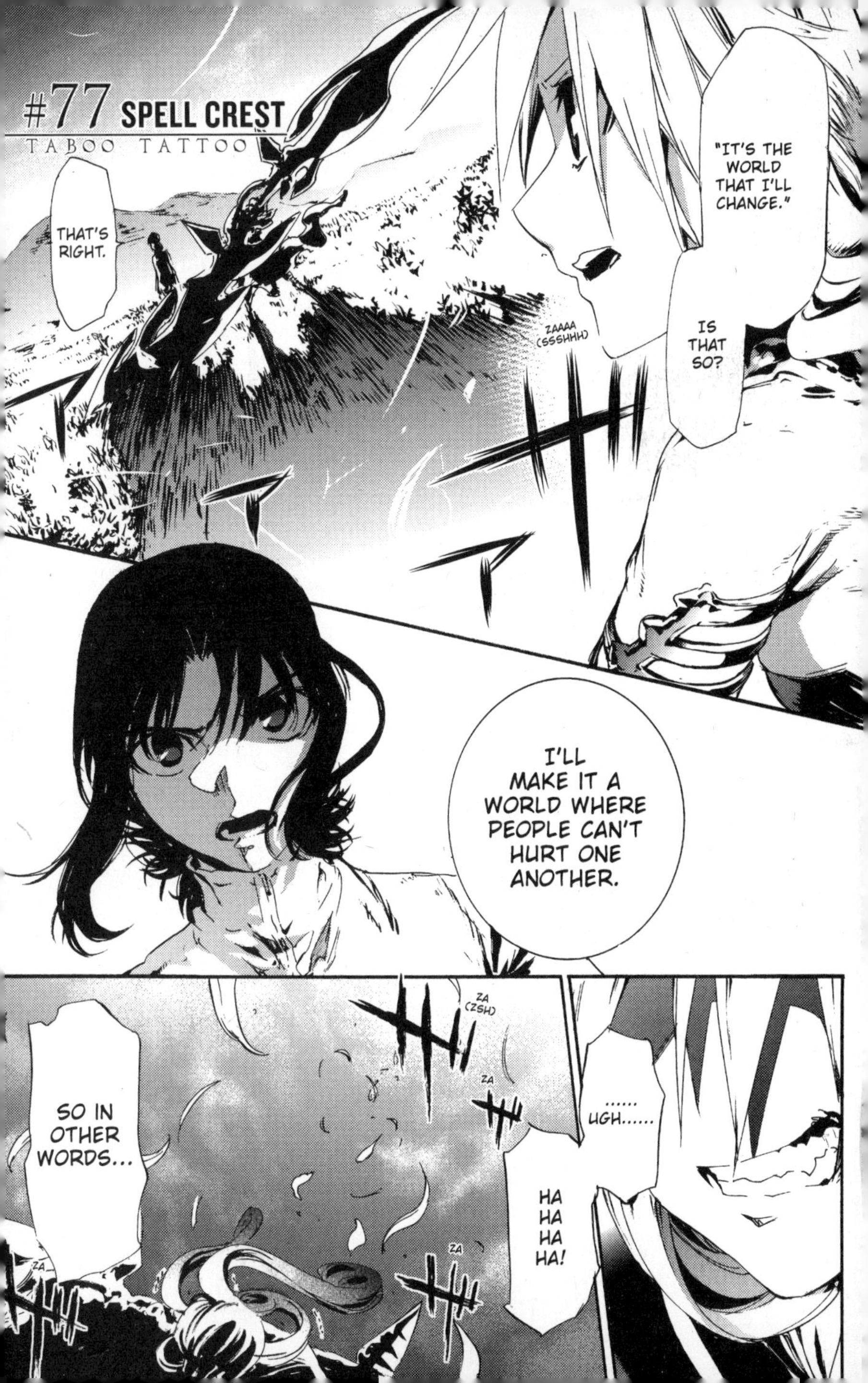

"IT'S THE WORLD THAT I'LL CHANGE."
IS THAT SO?
ZAAAA (SSSHHH)
THAT'S RIGHT.
I'LL MAKE IT A WORLD WHERE PEOPLE CAN'T HURT ONE ANOTHER.
...... UGH......
HA HA HA HA!
ZA (ZSH)
ZA
SO IN OTHER WORDS...
ZA
ZA

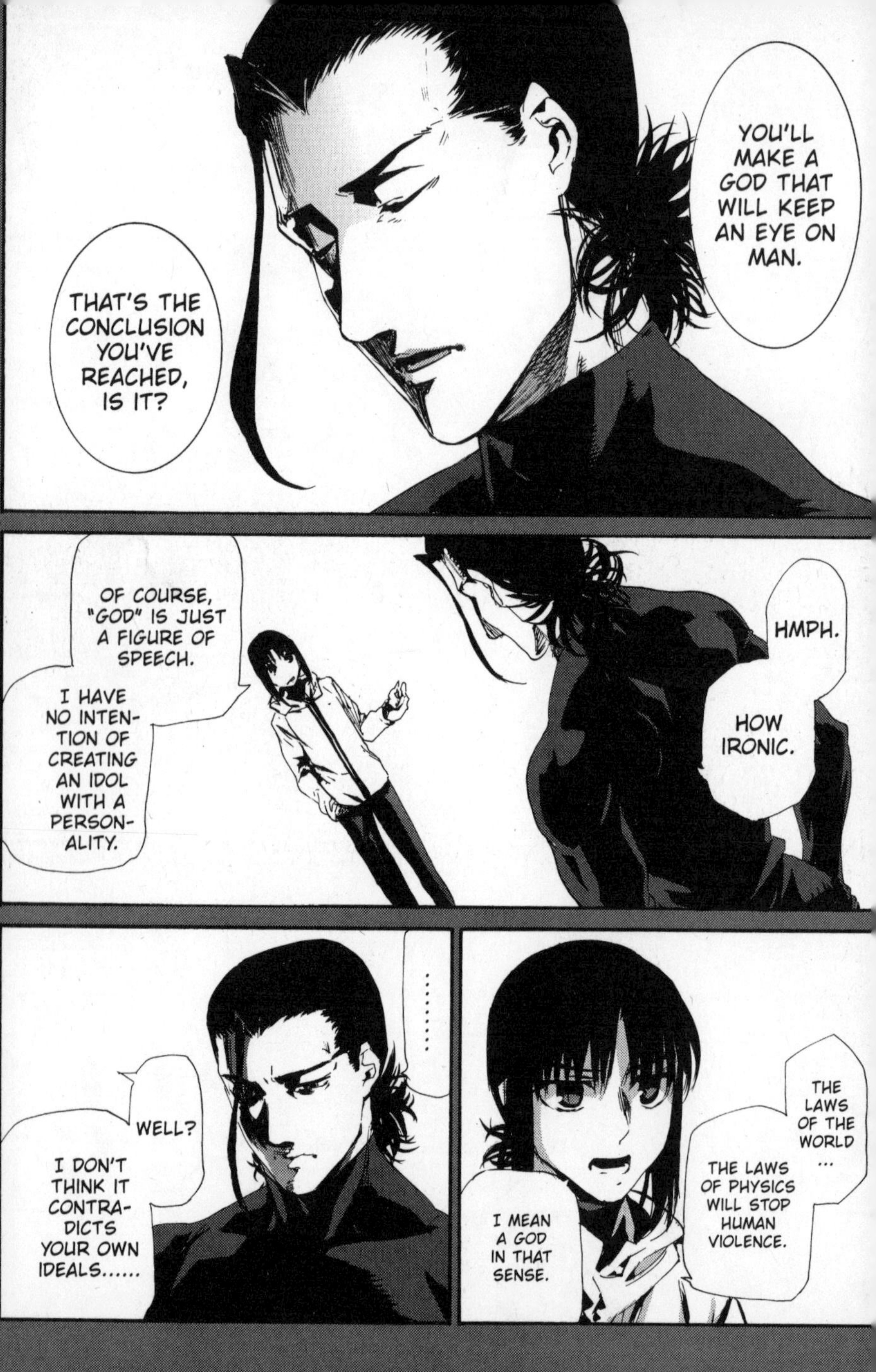
YOU'LL MAKE A GOD THAT WILL KEEP AN EYE ON MAN.
THAT'S THE CONCLUSION YOU'VE REACHED, IS IT?
HMPH.
HOW IRONIC.
OF COURSE, "GOD" IS JUST A FIGURE OF SPEECH.
I HAVE NO INTENTION OF CREATING AN IDOL WITH A PERSONALITY.
THE LAWS OF THE WORLD ...
THE LAWS OF PHYSICS WILL STOP HUMAN VIOLENCE.
I MEAN A GOD IN THAT SENSE.
......
WELL?
I DON'T THINK IT CONTRADICTS YOUR OWN IDEALS......

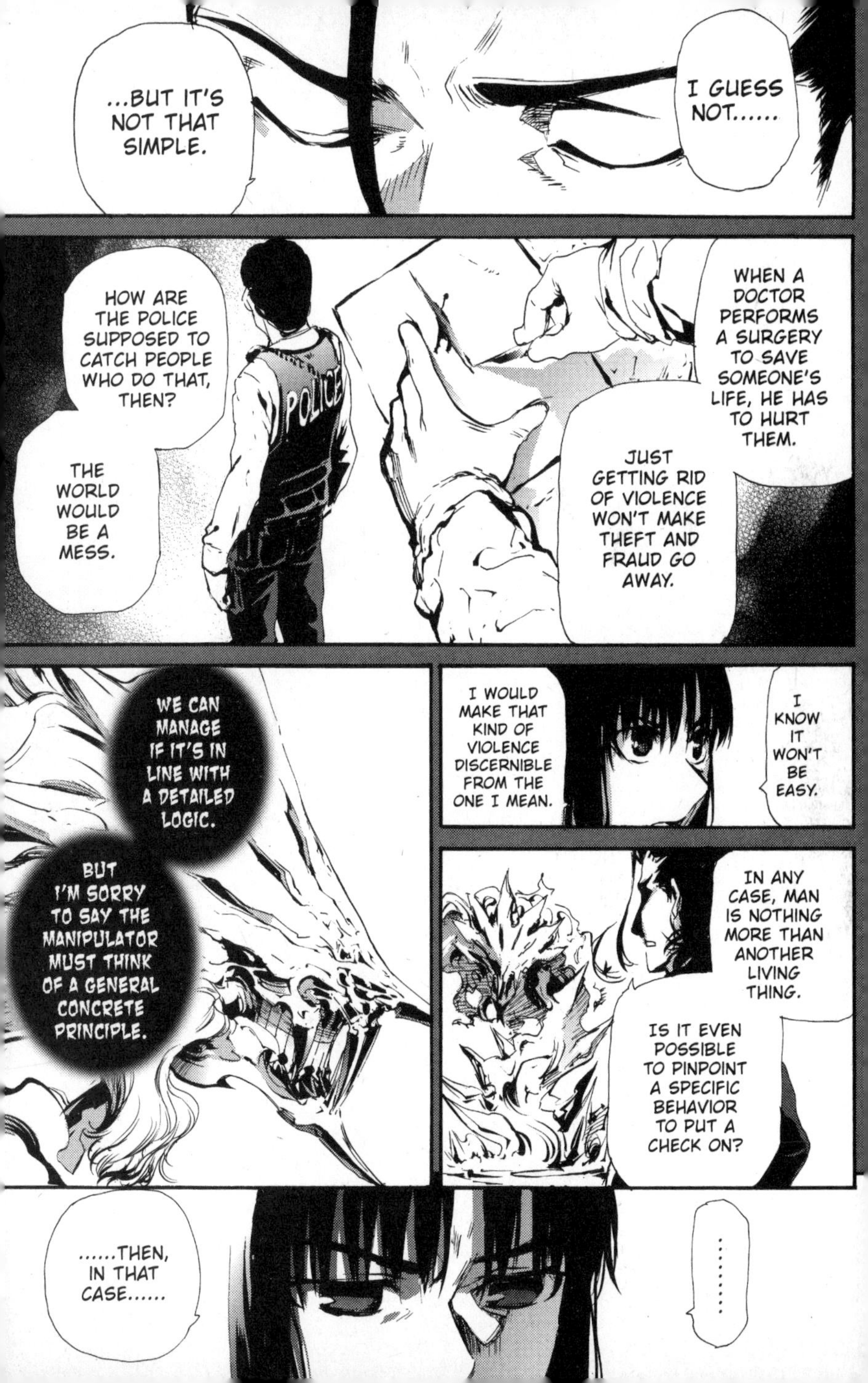
I GUESS NOT......
...BUT IT'S NOT THAT SIMPLE.
WHEN A DOCTOR PERFORMS A SURGERY TO SAVE SOMEONE'S LIFE, HE HAS TO HURT THEM.
JUST GETTING RID OF VIOLENCE WON'T MAKE THEFT AND FRAUD GO AWAY.
HOW ARE THE POLICE SUPPOSED TO CATCH PEOPLE WHO DO THAT, THEN?
THE WORLD WOULD BE A MESS.
POLICE
I KNOW IT WON'T BE EASY.
I WOULD MAKE THAT KIND OF VIOLENCE DISCERNIBLE FROM THE ONE I MEAN.
IN ANY CASE, MAN IS NOTHING MORE THAN ANOTHER LIVING THING.
IS IT EVEN POSSIBLE TO PINPOINT A SPECIFIC BEHAVIOR TO PUT A CHECK ON?
WE CAN MANAGE IF IT'S IN LINE WITH A DETAILED LOGIC.
BUT I'M SORRY TO SAY THE MANIPULATOR MUST THINK OF A GENERAL CONCRETE PRINCIPLE.
....
......THEN, IN THAT CASE......

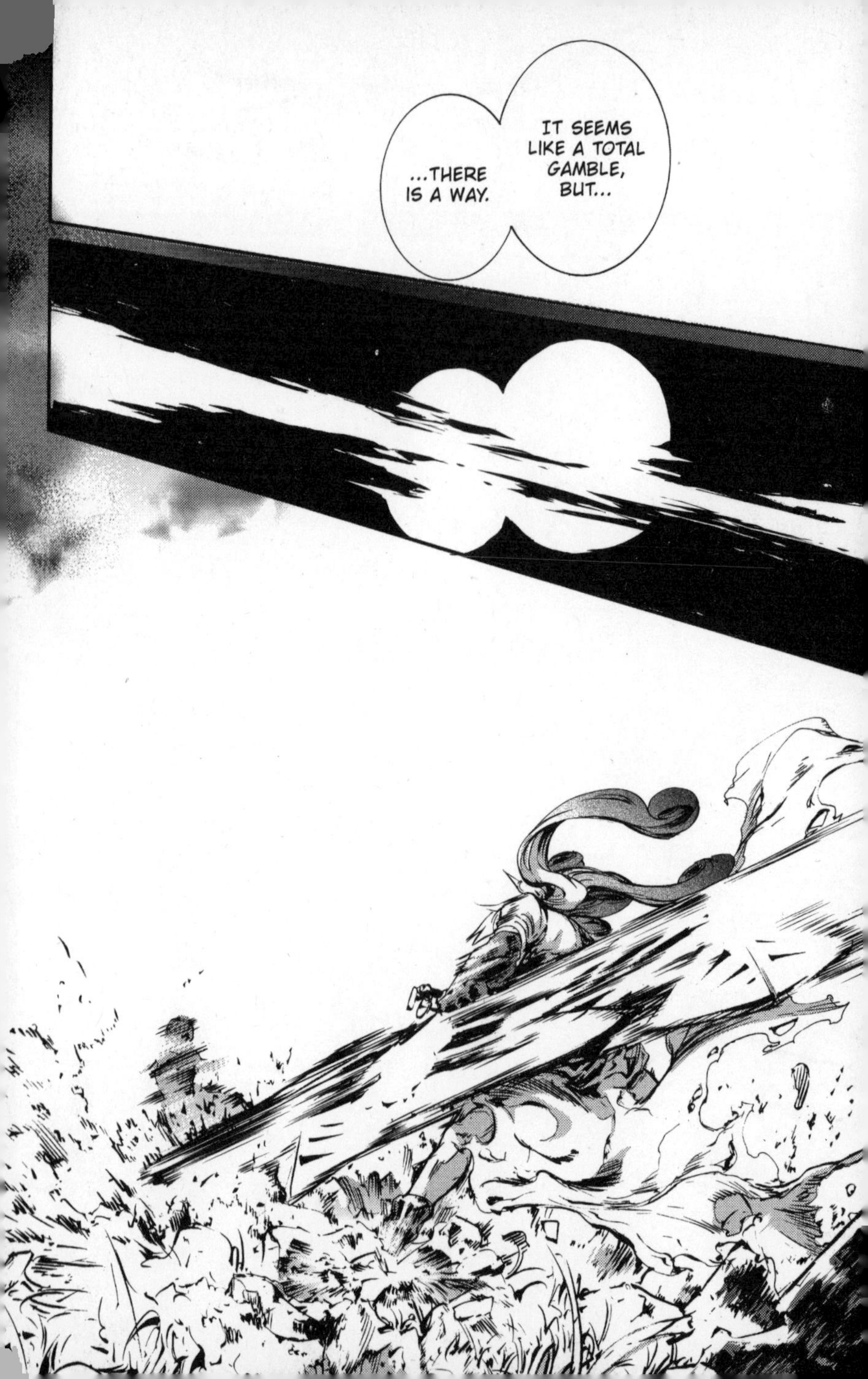
IT SEEMS LIKE A TOTAL GAMBLE, BUT...
...THERE IS A WAY.

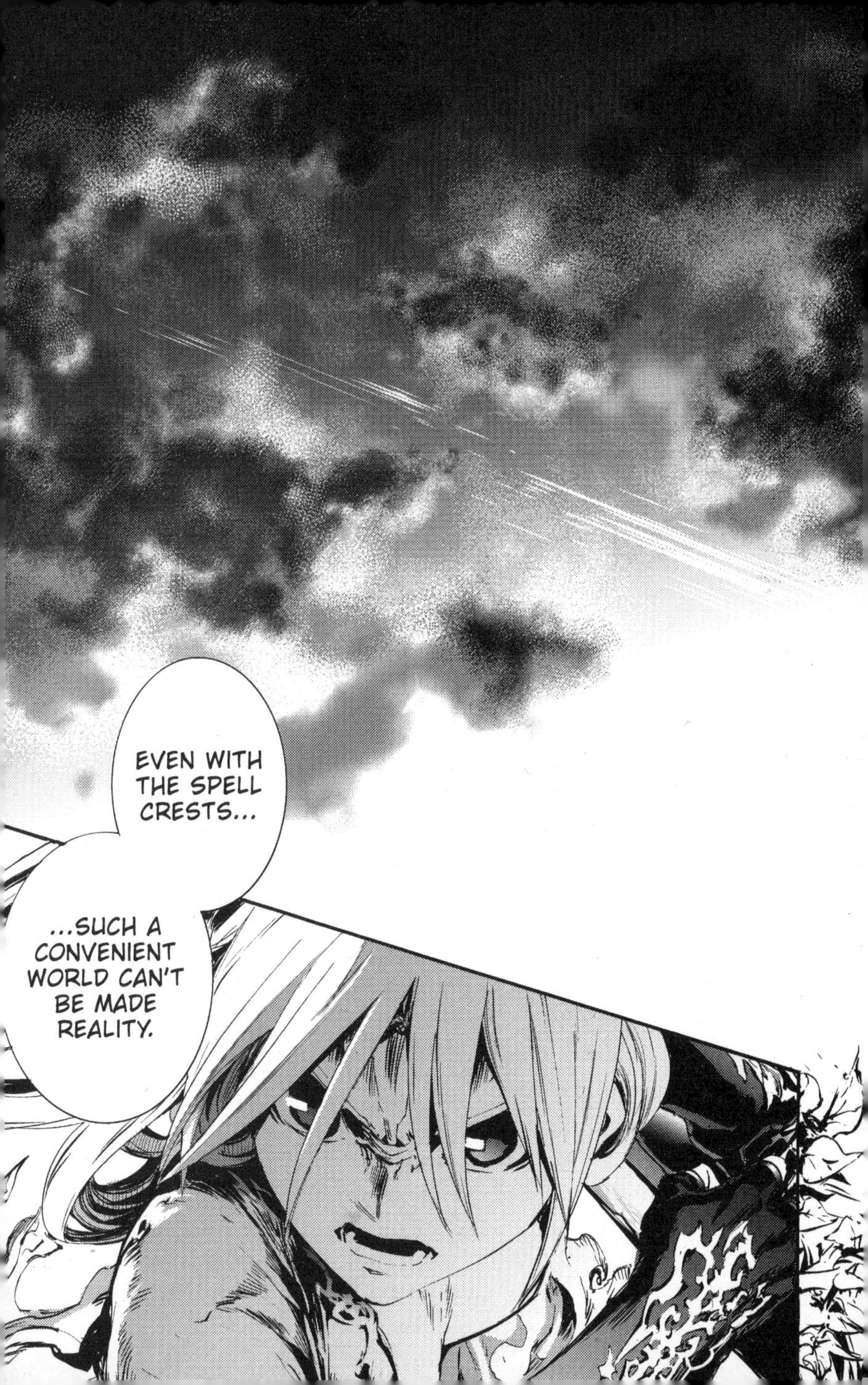
EVEN WITH THE SPELL CRESTS...
...SUCH A CONVENIENT WORLD CAN'T BE MADE REALITY.

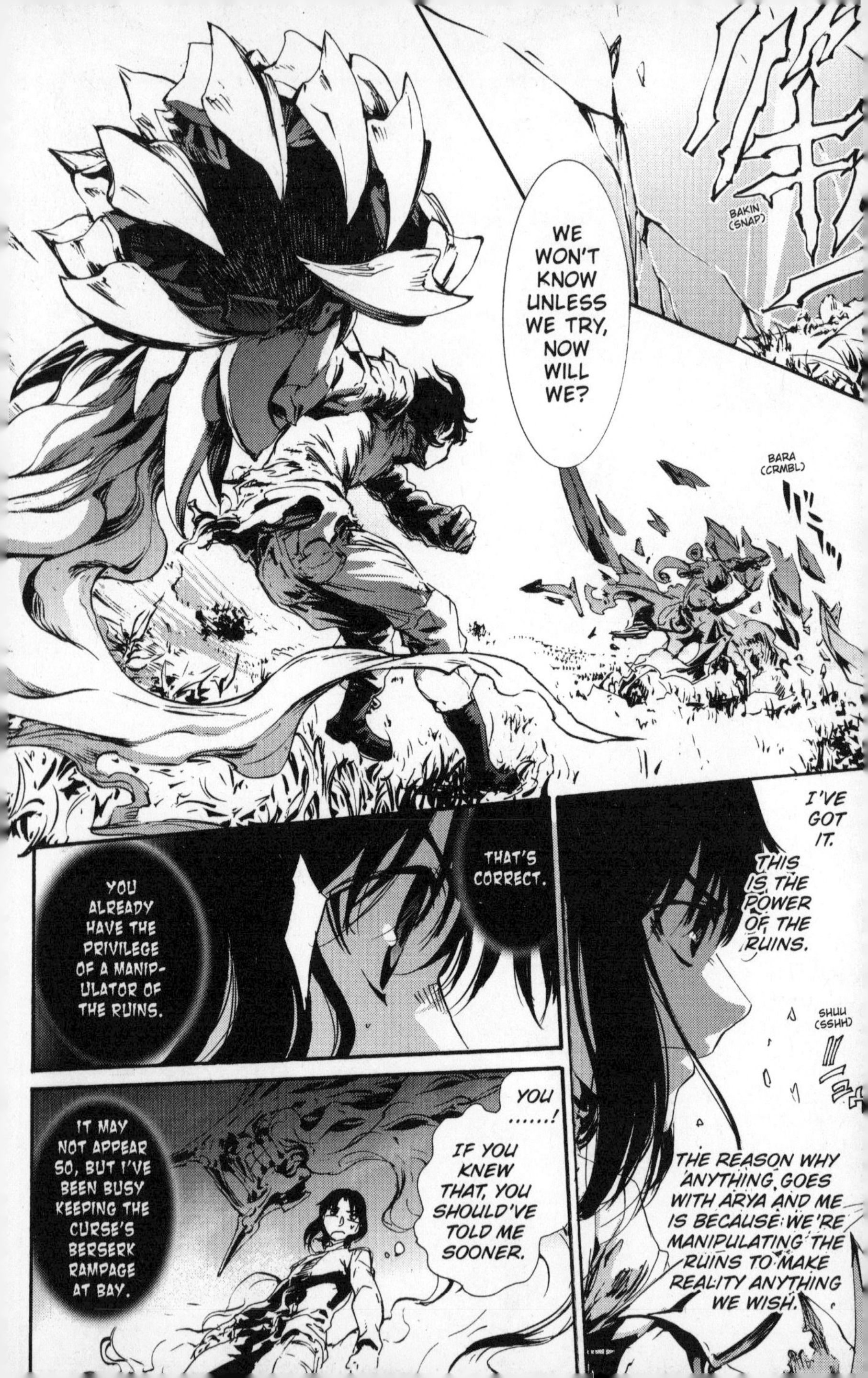
BAKIN (SNAP)
WE WON'T KNOW UNLESS WE TRY, NOW WILL WE?
BARA (CRMBL)
I'VE GOT IT.
THIS IS THE POWER OF THE RUINS.
SHUU (SSHH)
THE REASON WHY ANYTHING GOES WITH ARYA AND ME IS BECAUSE WE'RE MANIPULATING THE RUINS TO MAKE REALITY ANYTHING WE WISH.
THAT'S CORRECT.
YOU ALREADY HAVE THE PRIVILEGE OF A MANIP-ULATOR OF THE RUINS.
YOU ......!
IF YOU KNEW THAT, YOU SHOULD'VE TOLD ME SOONER.
IT MAY NOT APPEAR SO, BUT I'VE BEEN BUSY KEEPING THE CURSE'S BERSERK RAMPAGE AT BAY.

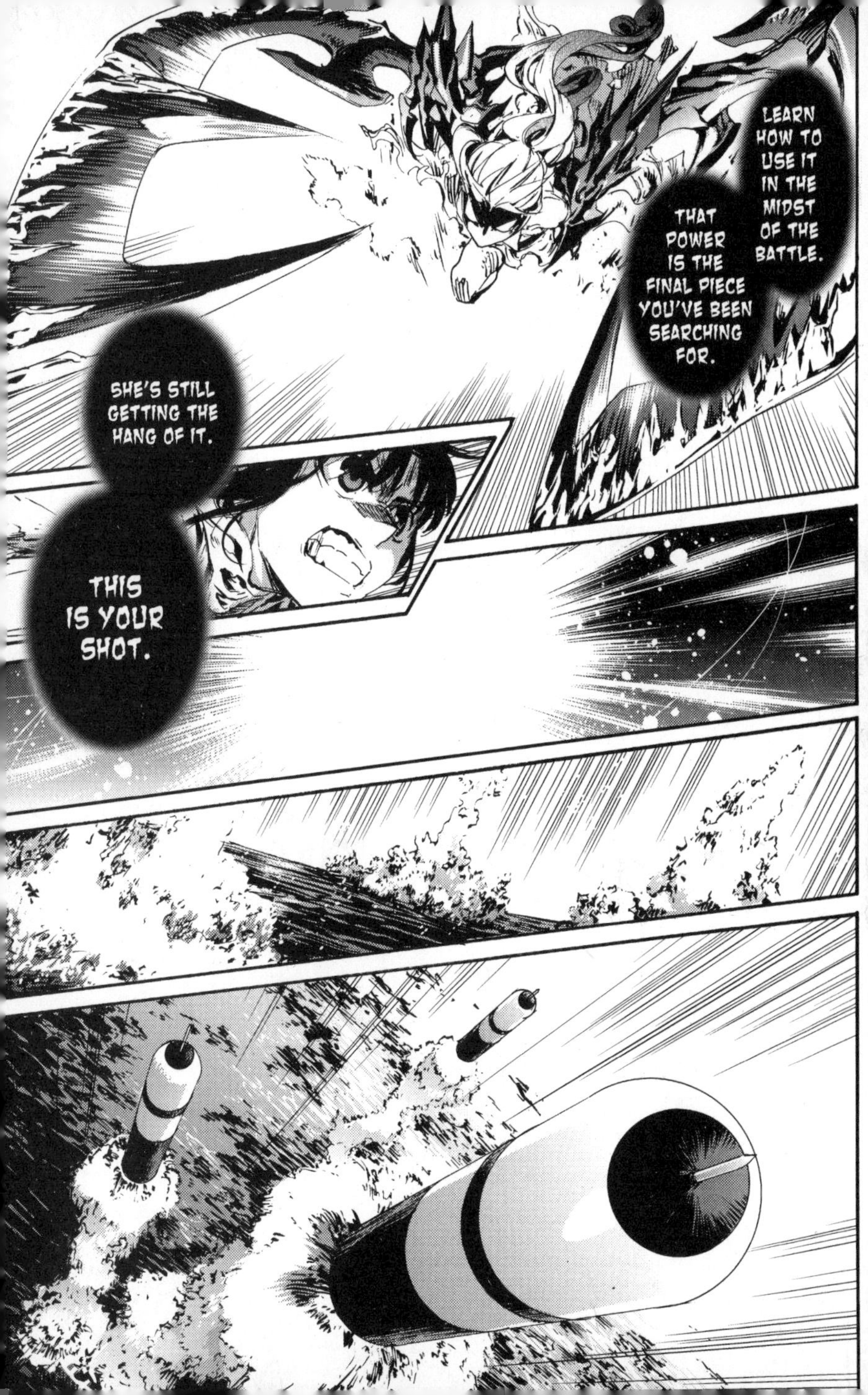
LEARN HOW TO USE IT IN THE MIDST OF THE BATTLE.
THAT POWER IS THE FINAL PIECE YOU'VE BEEN SEARCHING FOR.
SHE'S STILL GETTING THE HANG OF IT.
THIS IS YOUR SHOT.

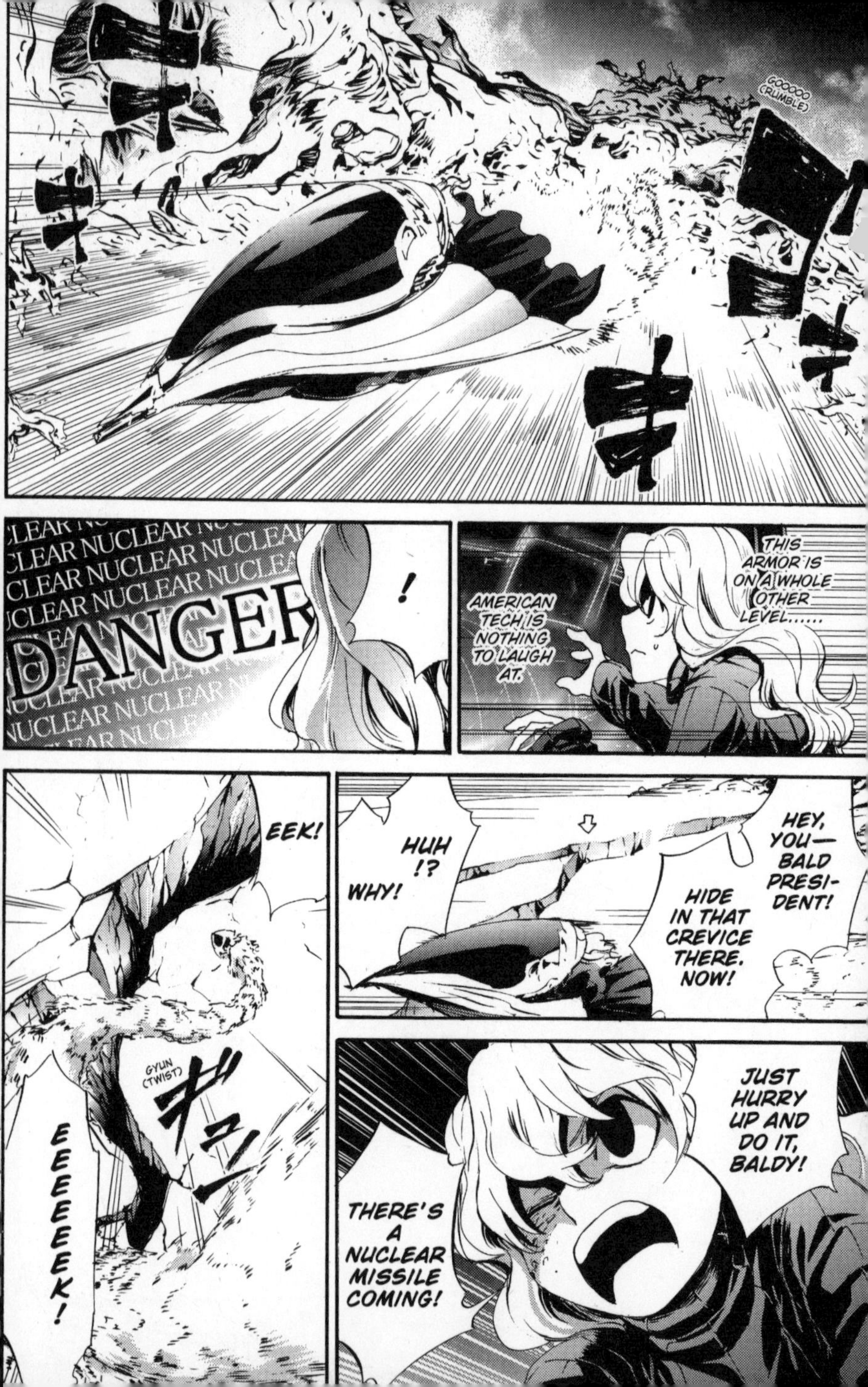
GOOOOO (RUMBLE)
THIS ARMOR IS ON A WHOLE OTHER LEVEL......
AMERICAN TECH IS NOTHING TO LAUGH AT.
!
NUCLEAR NUCLEAR NUCLEAR
DANGER
HEY, YOU—BALD PRESIDENT!
HIDE IN THAT CREVICE THERE. NOW!
HUH!?
WHY!
JUST HURRY UP AND DO IT, BALDY!
THERE'S A NUCLEAR MISSILE COMING!
EEK!
GYUN (TWIST)
EEEEEEEK!

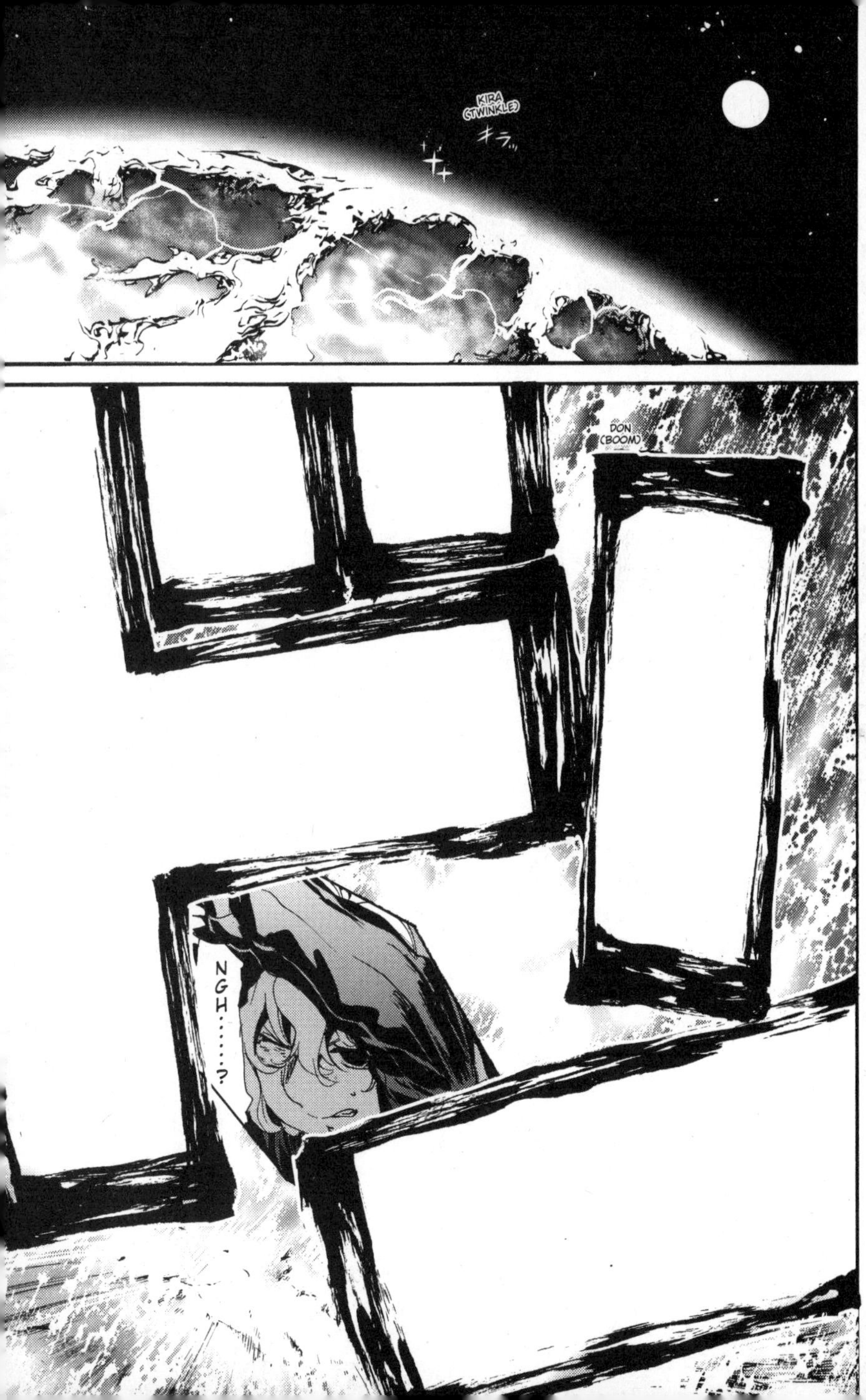
KIRA (TWINKLE)
キラッ
DON (BOOM)
NGH......?

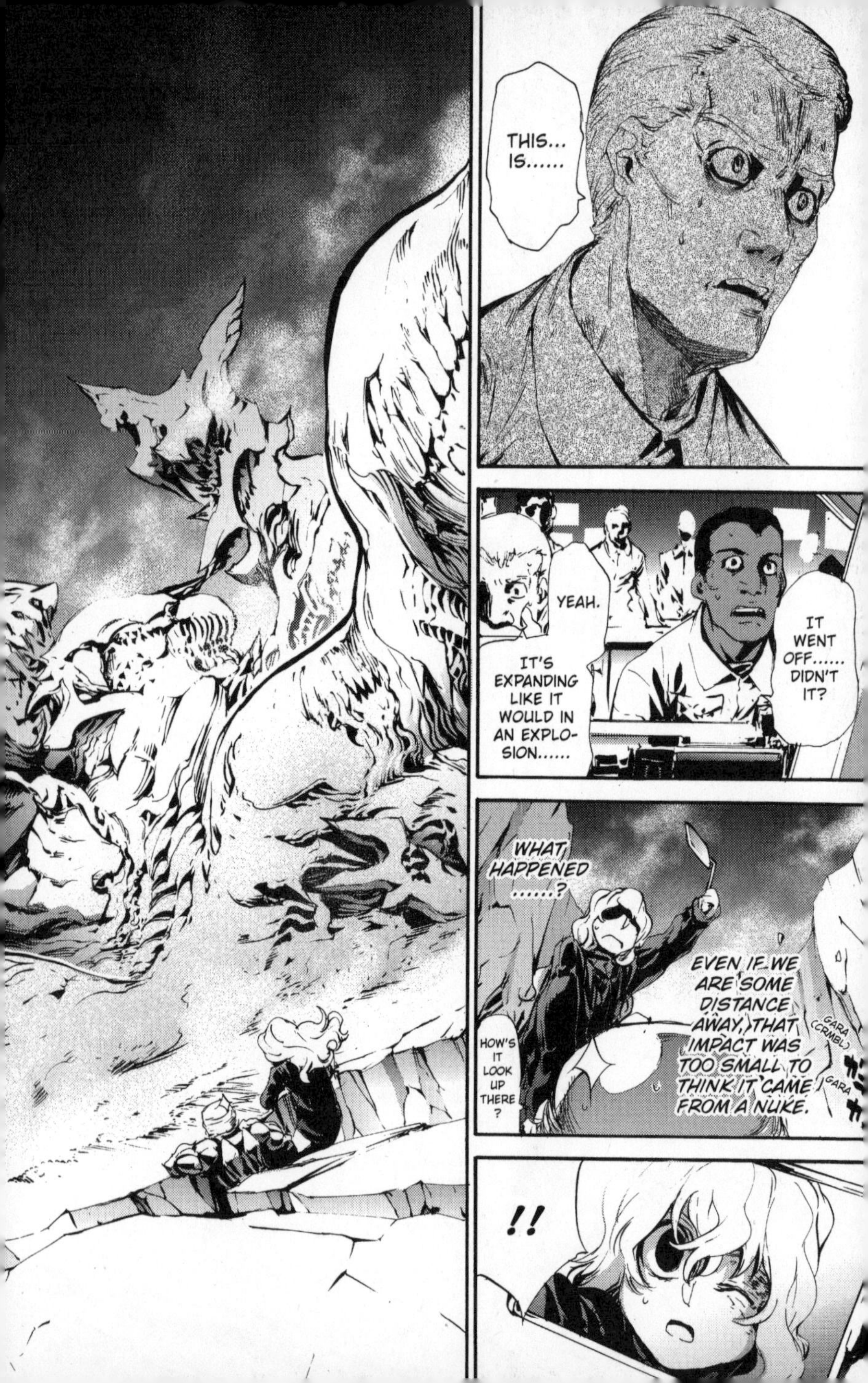
THIS... IS......
IT WENT OFF...... DIDN'T IT?
YEAH.
IT'S EXPANDING LIKE IT WOULD IN AN EXPLOSION......
WHAT HAPPENED ......?
GARA (CRMBL) GARA
EVEN IF WE ARE SOME DISTANCE AWAY, THAT IMPACT WAS TOO SMALL TO THINK IT CAME FROM A NUKE.
HOW'S IT LOOK UP THERE?
!!

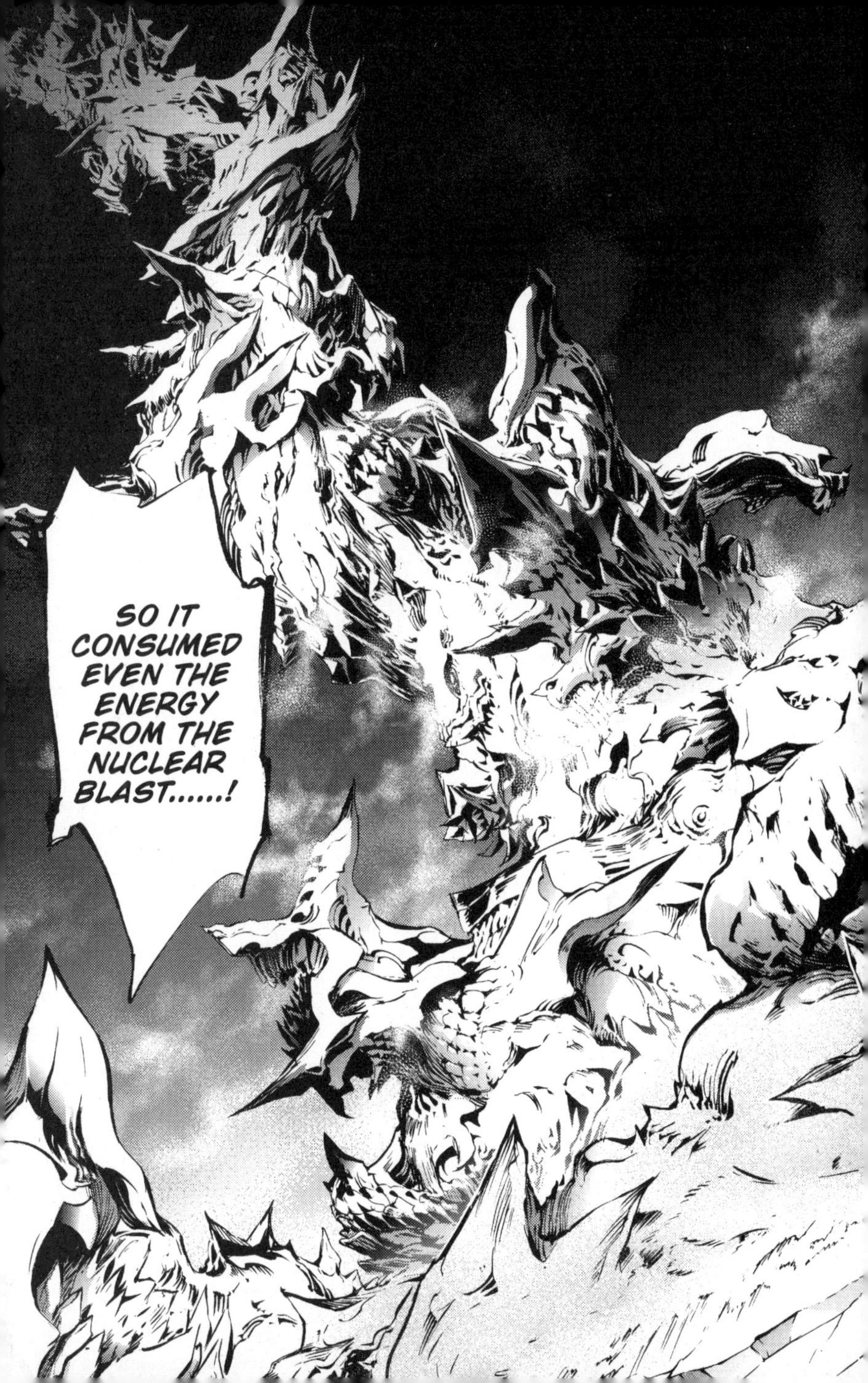
SO IT CONSUMED EVEN THE ENERGY FROM THE NUCLEAR BLAST......!

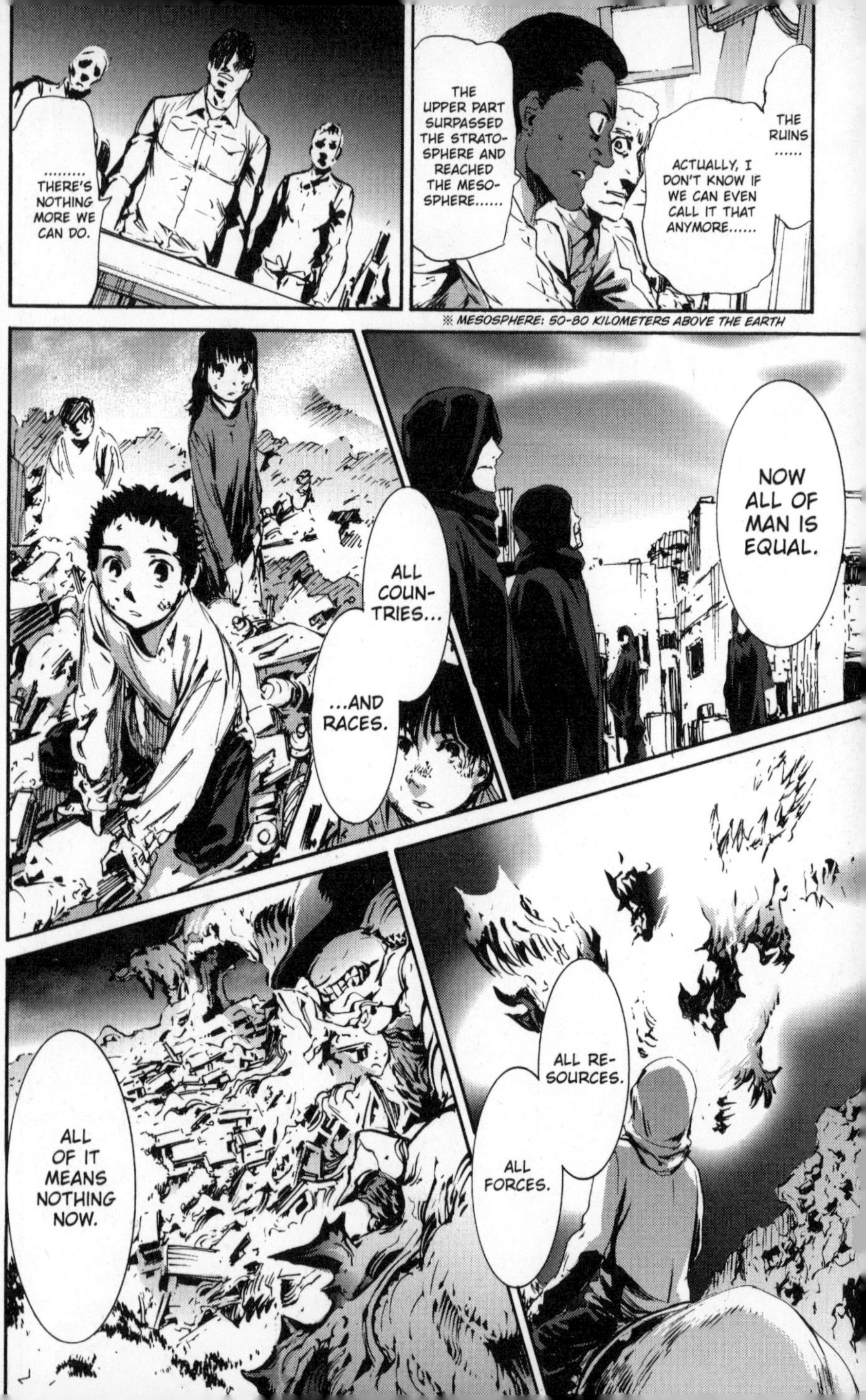
THE RUINS......
ACTUALLY, I DON'T KNOW IF WE CAN EVEN CALL IT THAT ANYMORE......
THE UPPER PART SURPASSED THE STRATOSPHERE AND REACHED THE MESOSPHERE......
.... THERE'S NOTHING MORE WE CAN DO.
NOW ALL OF MAN IS EQUAL.
ALL COUNTRIES...
...AND RACES.
ALL RESOURCES.
ALL FORCES.
ALL OF IT MEANS NOTHING NOW.

※ *MESOSPHERE: 50-80 KILOMETERS ABOVE THE EARTH*

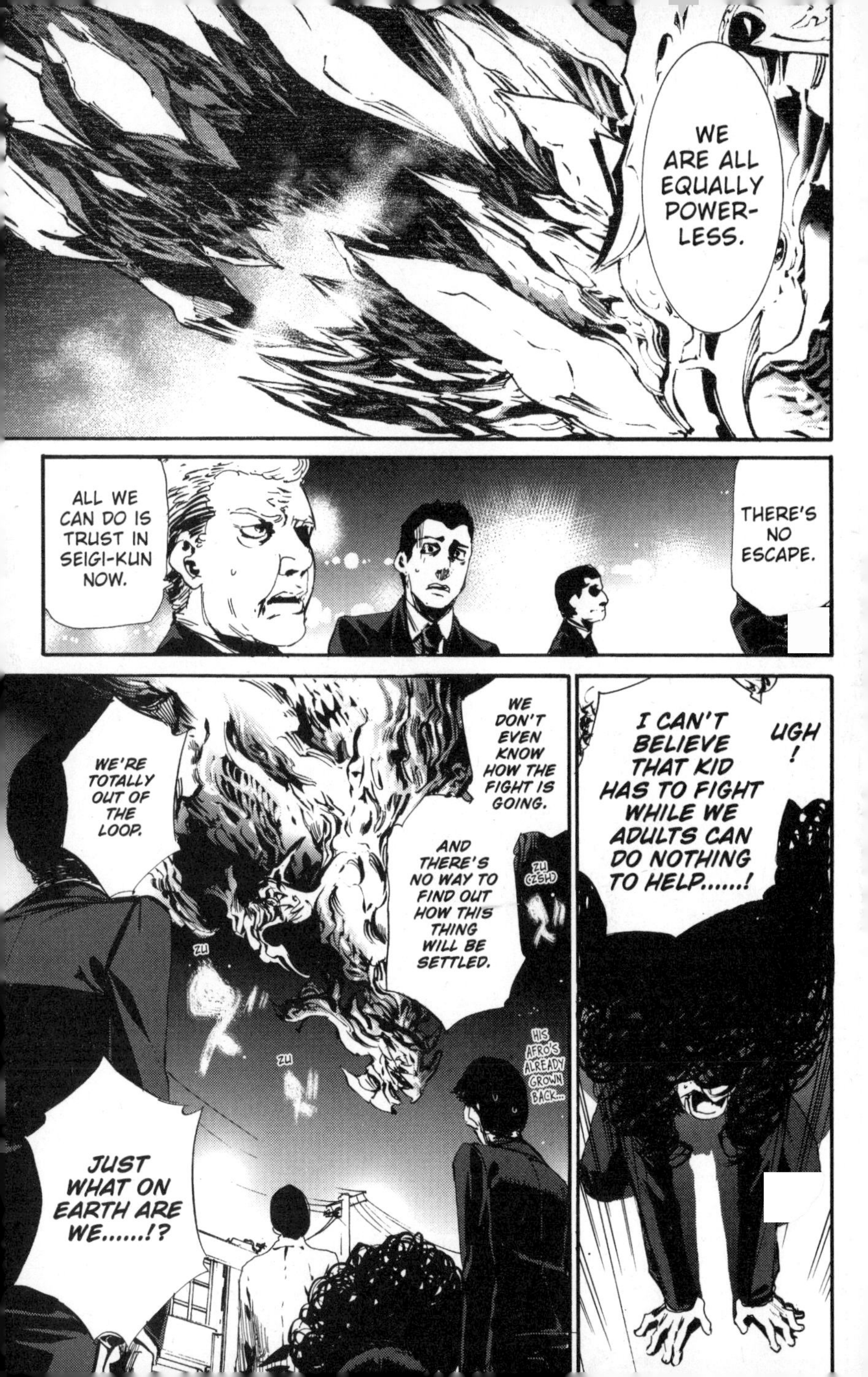
WE ARE ALL EQUALLY POWER-LESS.
THERE'S NO ESCAPE.
ALL WE CAN DO IS TRUST IN SEIGI-KUN NOW.
UGH!
I CAN'T BELIEVE THAT KID HAS TO FIGHT WHILE WE ADULTS CAN DO NOTHING TO HELP......!
WE DON'T EVEN KNOW HOW THE FIGHT IS GOING.
WE'RE TOTALLY OUT OF THE LOOP.
AND THERE'S NO WAY TO FIND OUT HOW THIS THING WILL BE SETTLED.
ZU (ZSH)
ZU
ZU
HIS AFRO'S ALREADY GROWN BACK...
JUST WHAT ON EARTH ARE WE......!?

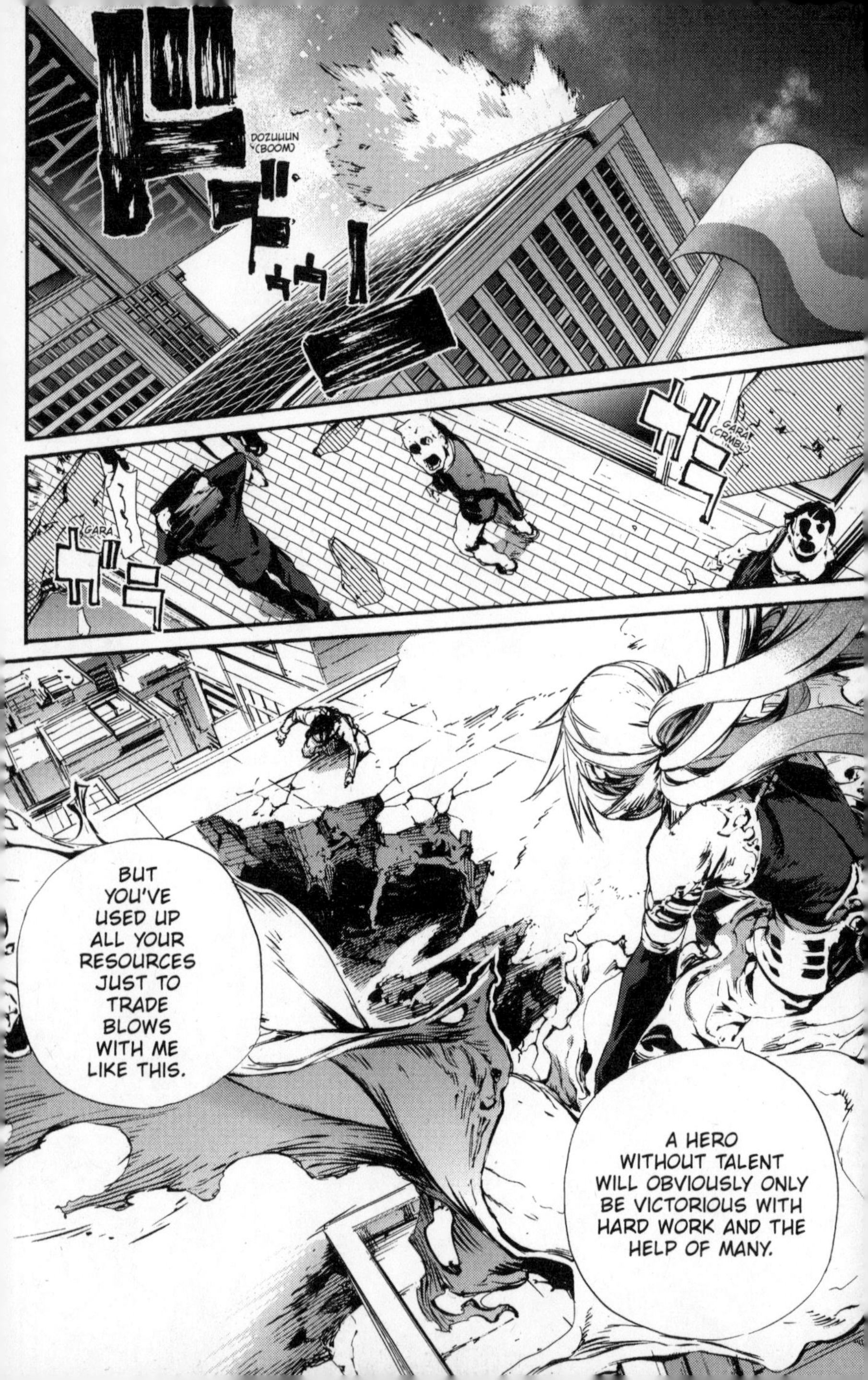
DOZUUUN (BOOM)
GARA (CRMBL)
GARA
A HERO WITHOUT TALENT WILL OBVIOUSLY ONLY BE VICTORIOUS WITH HARD WORK AND THE HELP OF MANY.
BUT YOU'VE USED UP ALL YOUR RESOURCES JUST TO TRADE BLOWS WITH ME LIKE THIS.

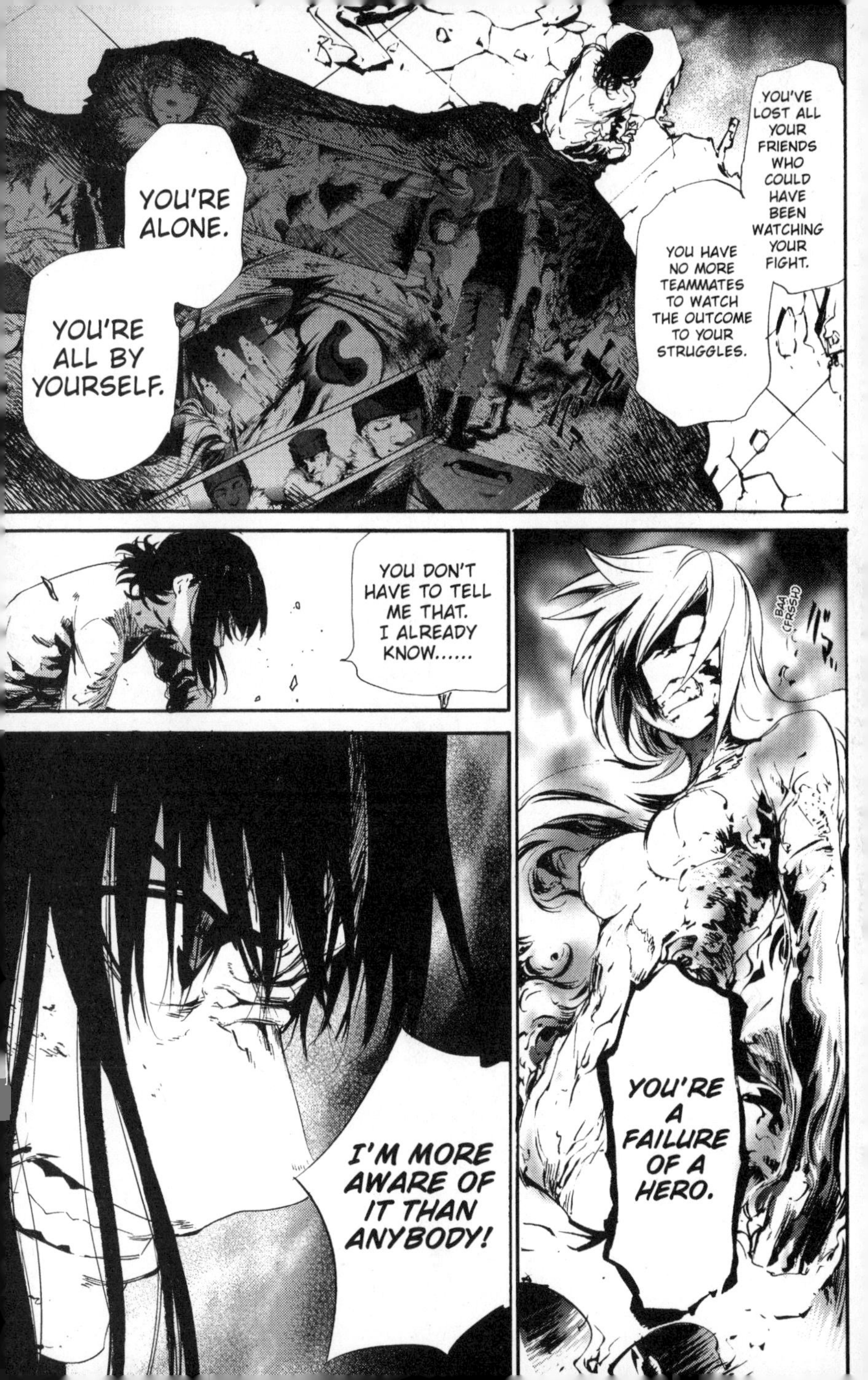
YOU'VE LOST ALL YOUR FRIENDS WHO COULD HAVE BEEN WATCHING YOUR FIGHT.
YOU HAVE NO MORE TEAMMATES TO WATCH THE OUTCOME TO YOUR STRUGGLES.
YOU'RE ALONE.
YOU'RE ALL BY YOURSELF.
BAA (FRSSH)
YOU'RE A FAILURE OF A HERO.
YOU DON'T HAVE TO TELL ME THAT. I ALREADY KNOW......
I'M MORE AWARE OF IT THAN ANYBODY!

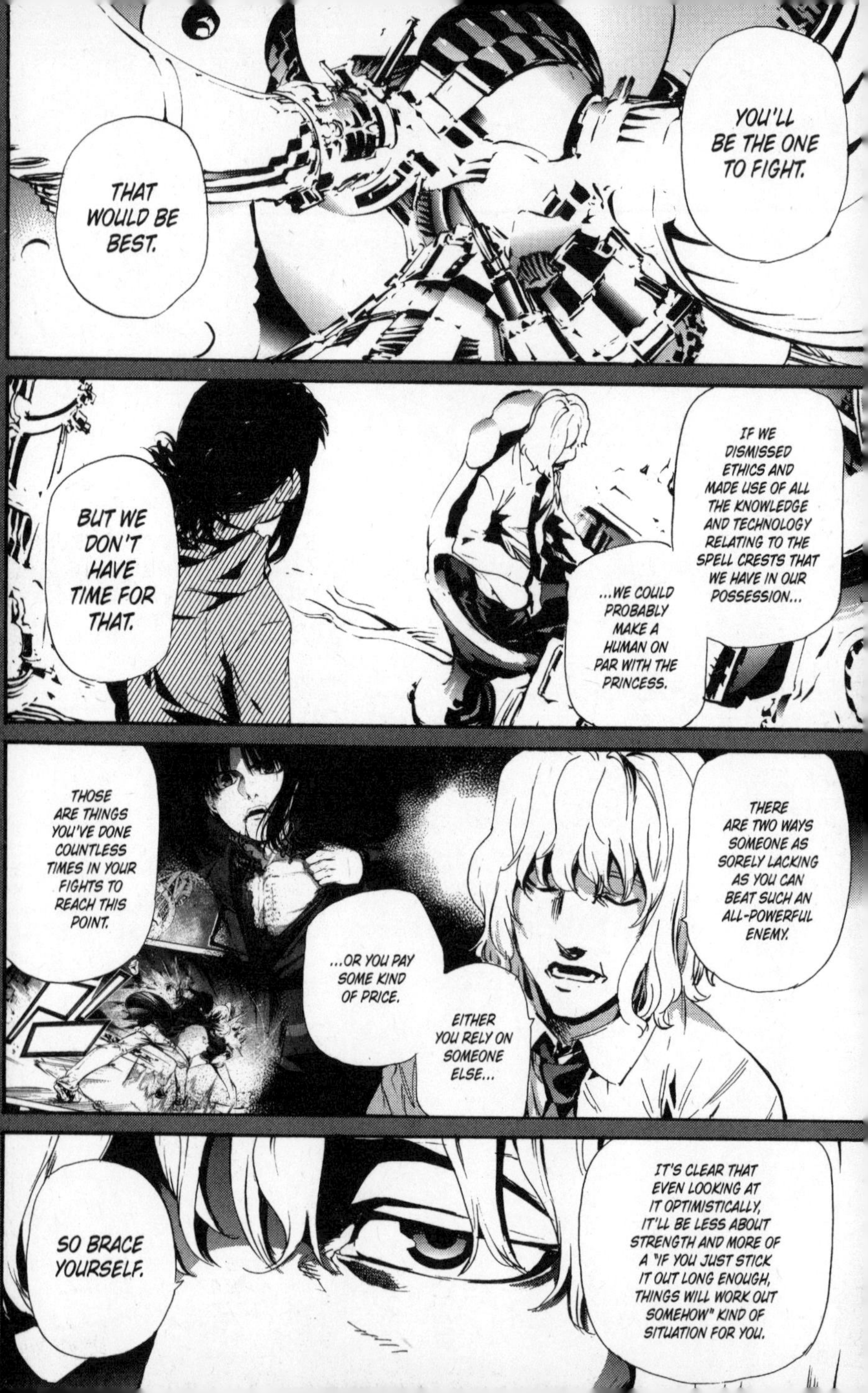
YOU'LL BE THE ONE TO FIGHT.
THAT WOULD BE BEST.
IF WE DISMISSED ETHICS AND MADE USE OF ALL THE KNOWLEDGE AND TECHNOLOGY RELATING TO THE SPELL CRESTS THAT WE HAVE IN OUR POSSESSION...
...WE COULD PROBABLY MAKE A HUMAN ON PAR WITH THE PRINCESS.
BUT WE DON'T HAVE TIME FOR THAT.
THERE ARE TWO WAYS SOMEONE AS SORELY LACKING AS YOU CAN BEAT SUCH AN ALL-POWERFUL ENEMY.
EITHER YOU RELY ON SOMEONE ELSE...
...OR YOU PAY SOME KIND OF PRICE.
THOSE ARE THINGS YOU'VE DONE COUNTLESS TIMES IN YOUR FIGHTS TO REACH THIS POINT.
IT'S CLEAR THAT EVEN LOOKING AT IT OPTIMISTICALLY, IT'LL BE LESS ABOUT STRENGTH AND MORE OF A "IF YOU JUST STICK IT OUT LONG ENOUGH, THINGS WILL WORK OUT SOMEHOW" KIND OF SITUATION FOR YOU.
SO BRACE YOURSELF.

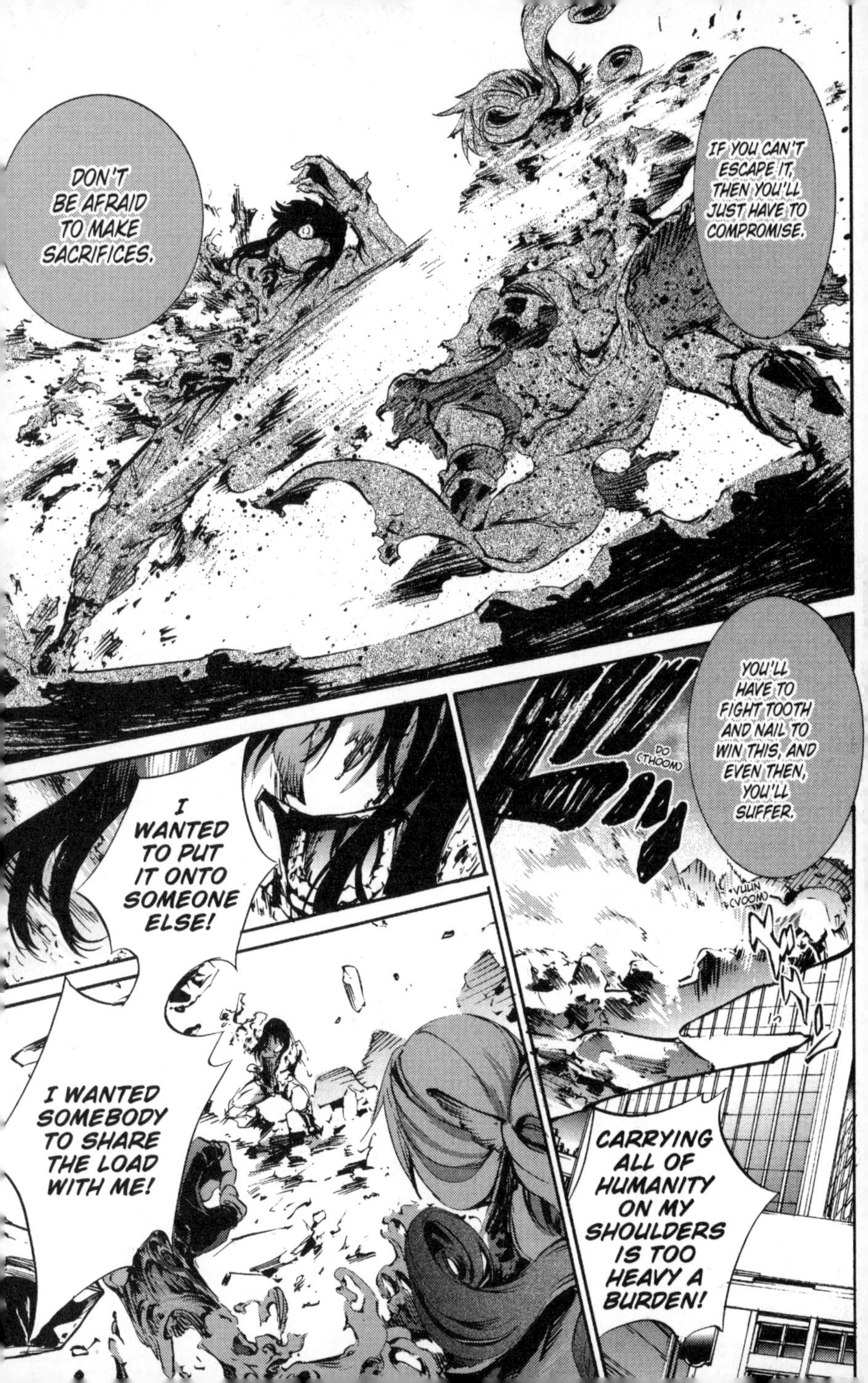
IF YOU CAN'T ESCAPE IT, THEN YOU'LL JUST HAVE TO COMPROMISE.
DON'T BE AFRAID TO MAKE SACRIFICES.
YOU'LL HAVE TO FIGHT TOOTH AND NAIL TO WIN THIS, AND EVEN THEN, YOU'LL SUFFER.
DO (THOOM)
VUUN (VOOM)
I WANTED TO PUT IT ONTO SOMEONE ELSE!
CARRYING ALL OF HUMANITY ON MY SHOULDERS IS TOO HEAVY A BURDEN!
I WANTED SOMEBODY TO SHARE THE LOAD WITH ME!

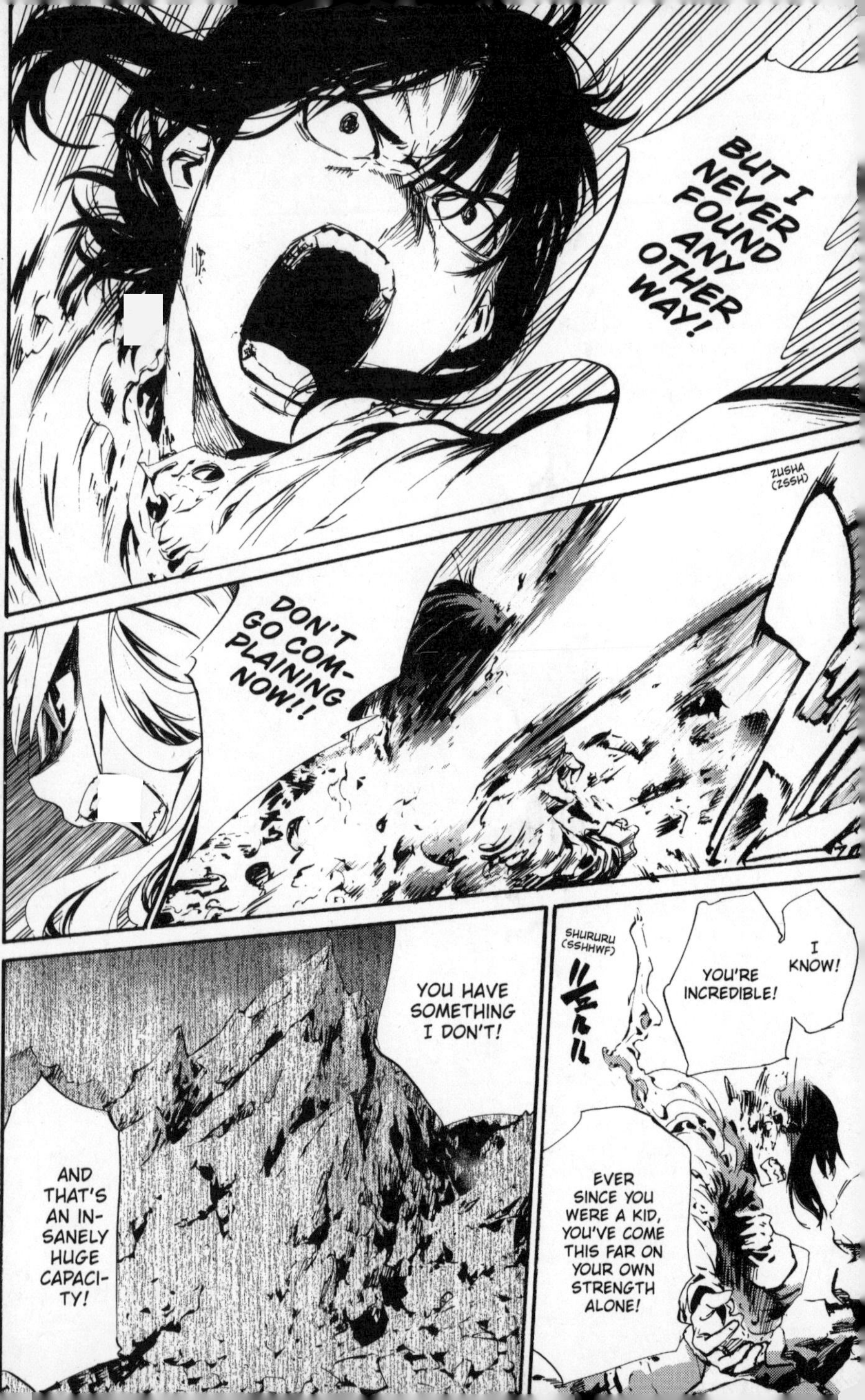
BUT I NEVER FOUND ANY OTHER WAY!
ZUSHA (ZSSH)
DON'T GO COM-PLAINING NOW!!
I KNOW!
YOU'RE INCREDIBLE!
SHURURU (SSHHWF)
EVER SINCE YOU WERE A KID, YOU'VE COME THIS FAR ON YOUR OWN STRENGTH ALONE!
YOU HAVE SOMETHING I DON'T!
AND THAT'S AN IN-SANELY HUGE CAPACI-TY!

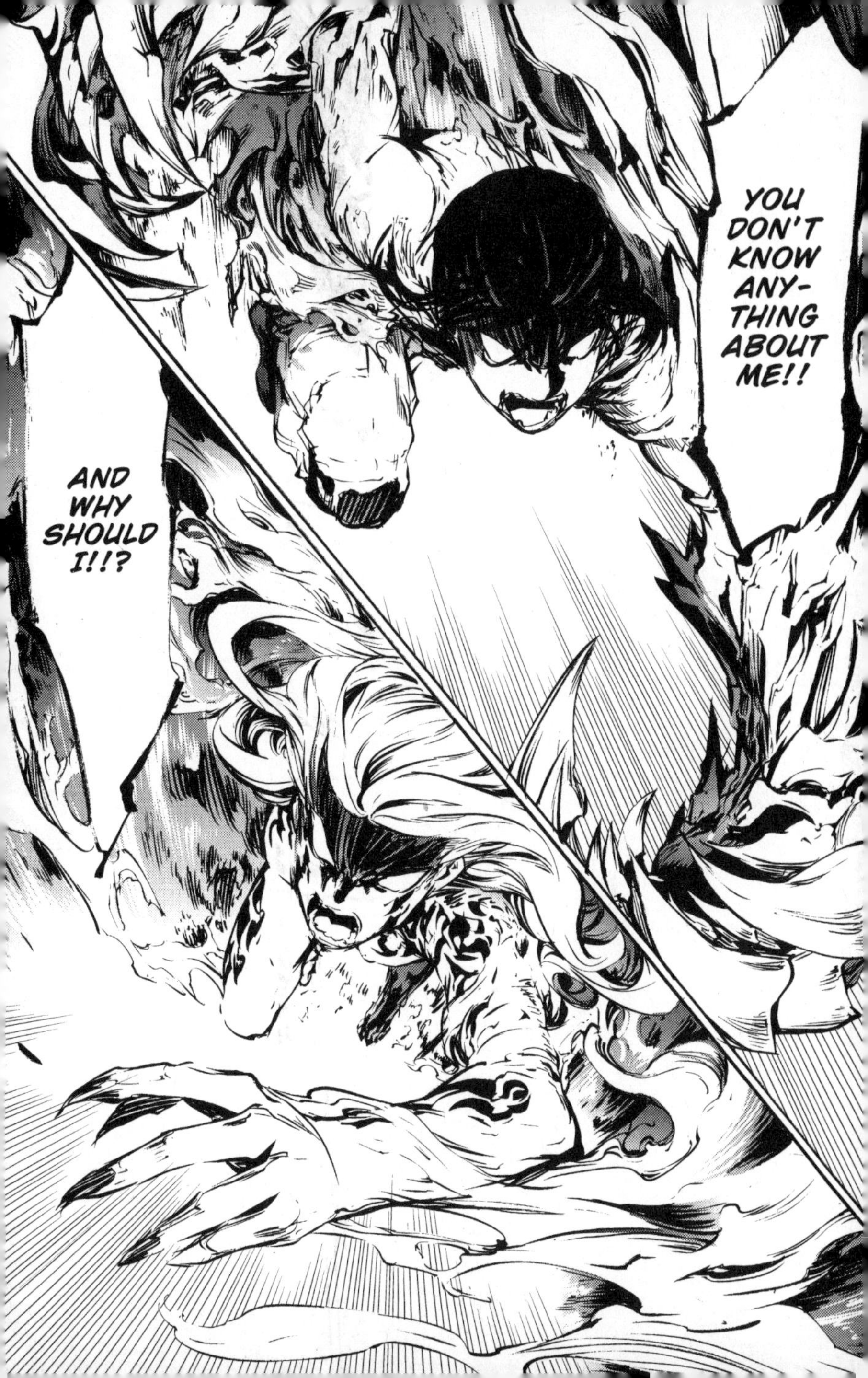
YOU DON'T KNOW ANY-THING ABOUT ME!!
AND WHY SHOULD I!!?

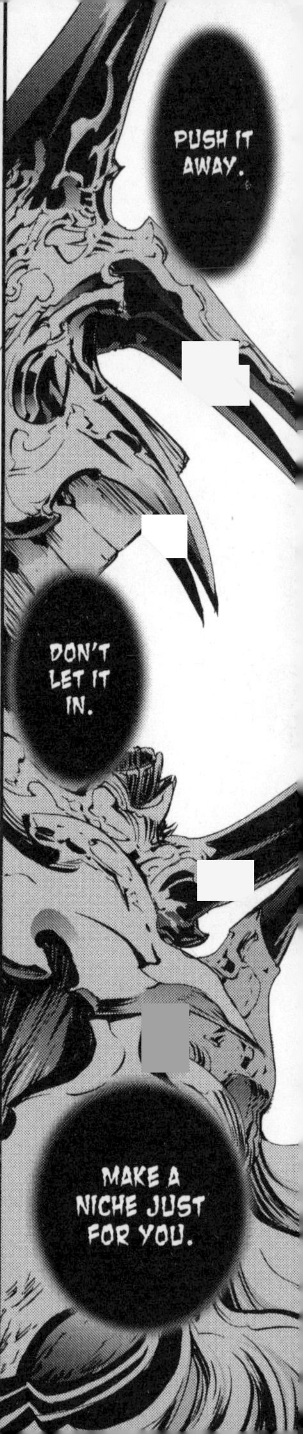
PUSH IT AWAY.
DON'T LET IT IN.
MAKE A NICHE JUST FOR YOU.
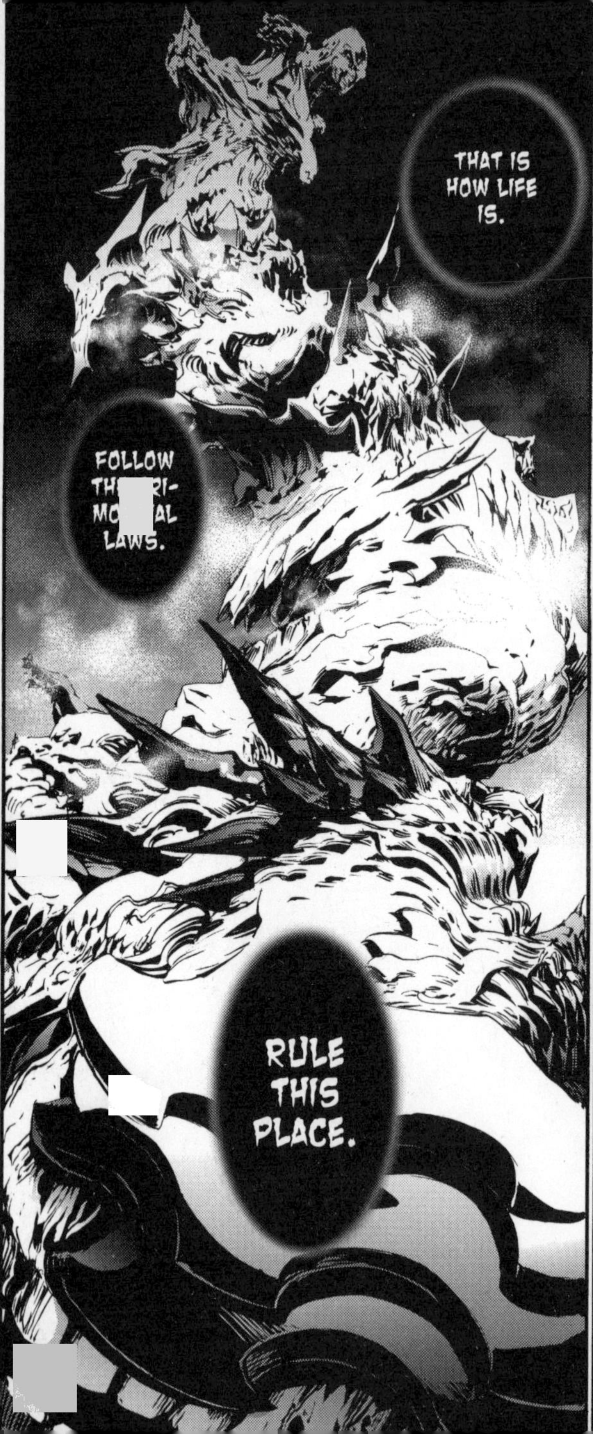
THAT IS HOW LIFE IS.
FOLLOW TH RI- MO AL LAWS.
RULE THIS PLACE.

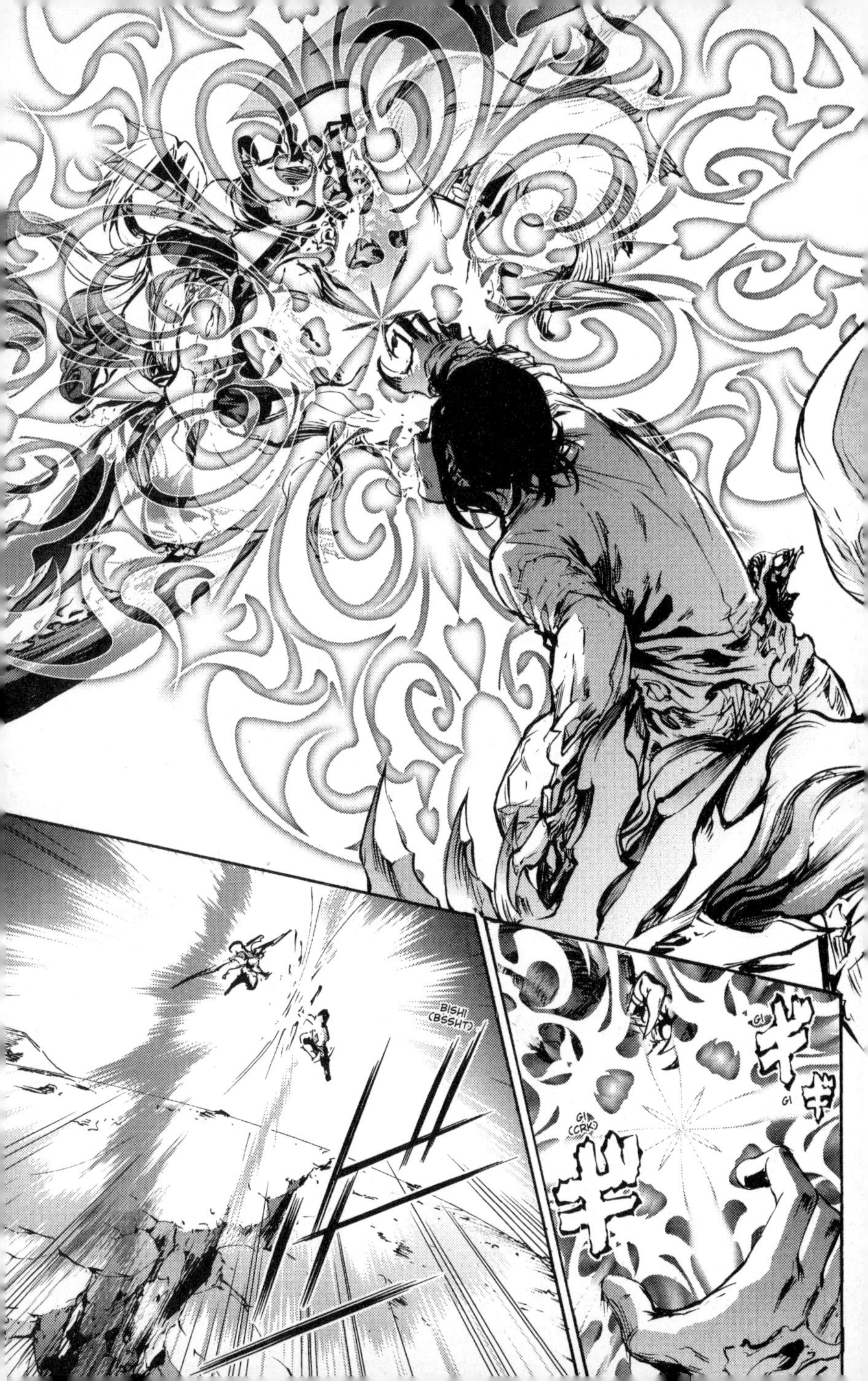
ギ GI
ギ GI
ギ GI (CRK)
BISHI (BSSHT)

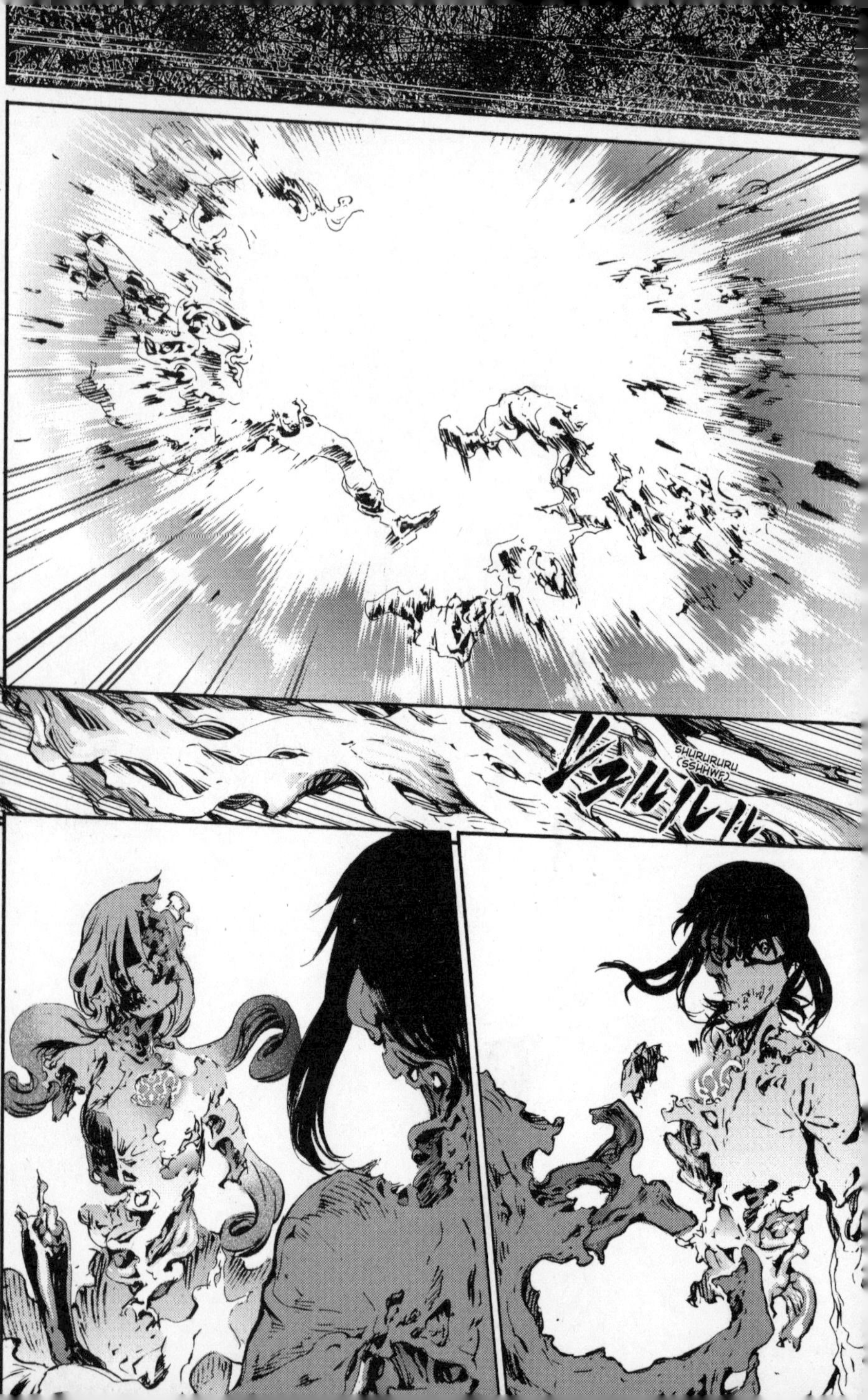
SHURURURU
(SSHHWF)

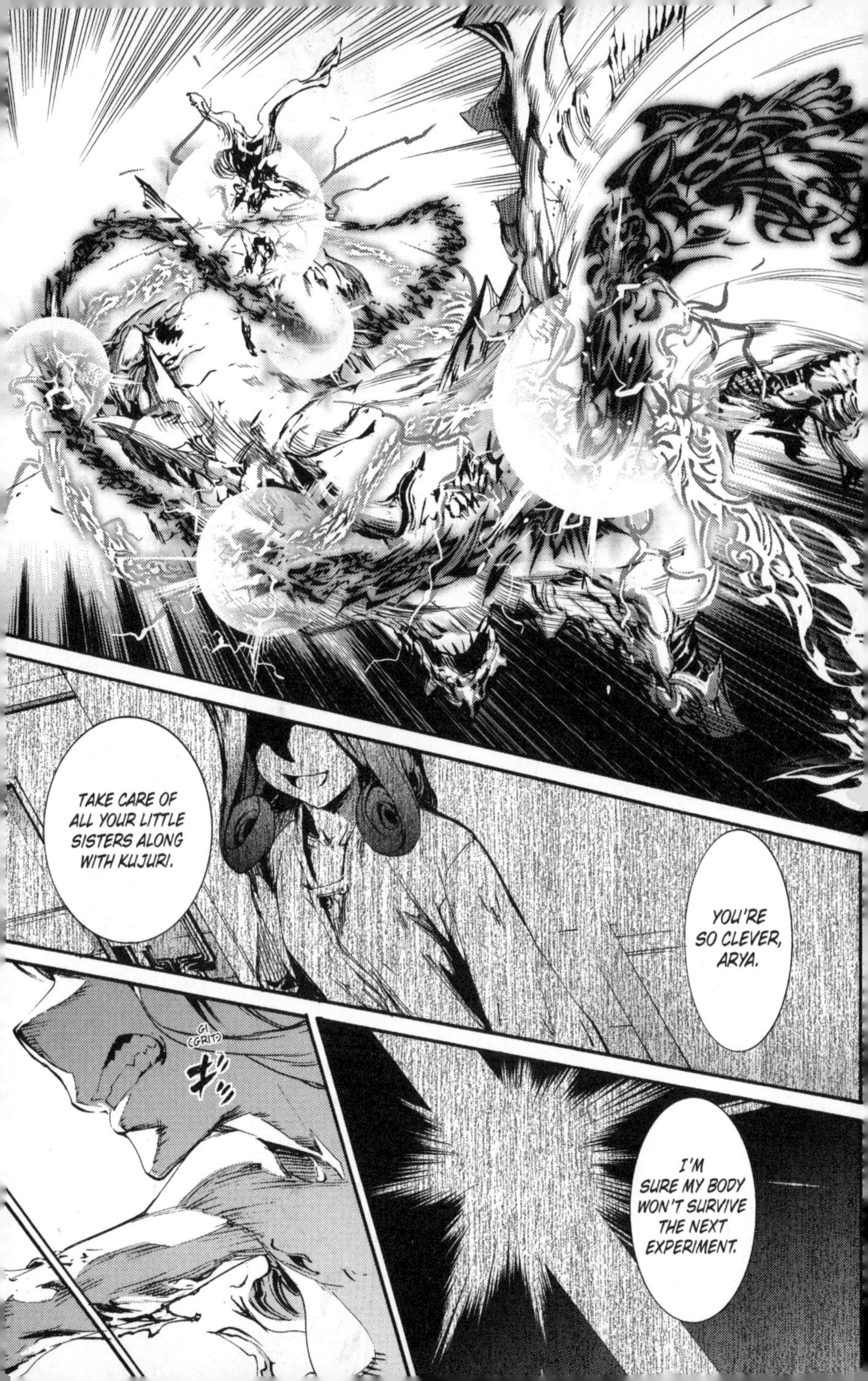
YOU'RE SO CLEVER, ARYA.
TAKE CARE OF ALL YOUR LITTLE SISTERS ALONG WITH KUJURI.
I'M SURE MY BODY WON'T SURVIVE THE NEXT EXPERIMENT.
GI (GRIT)

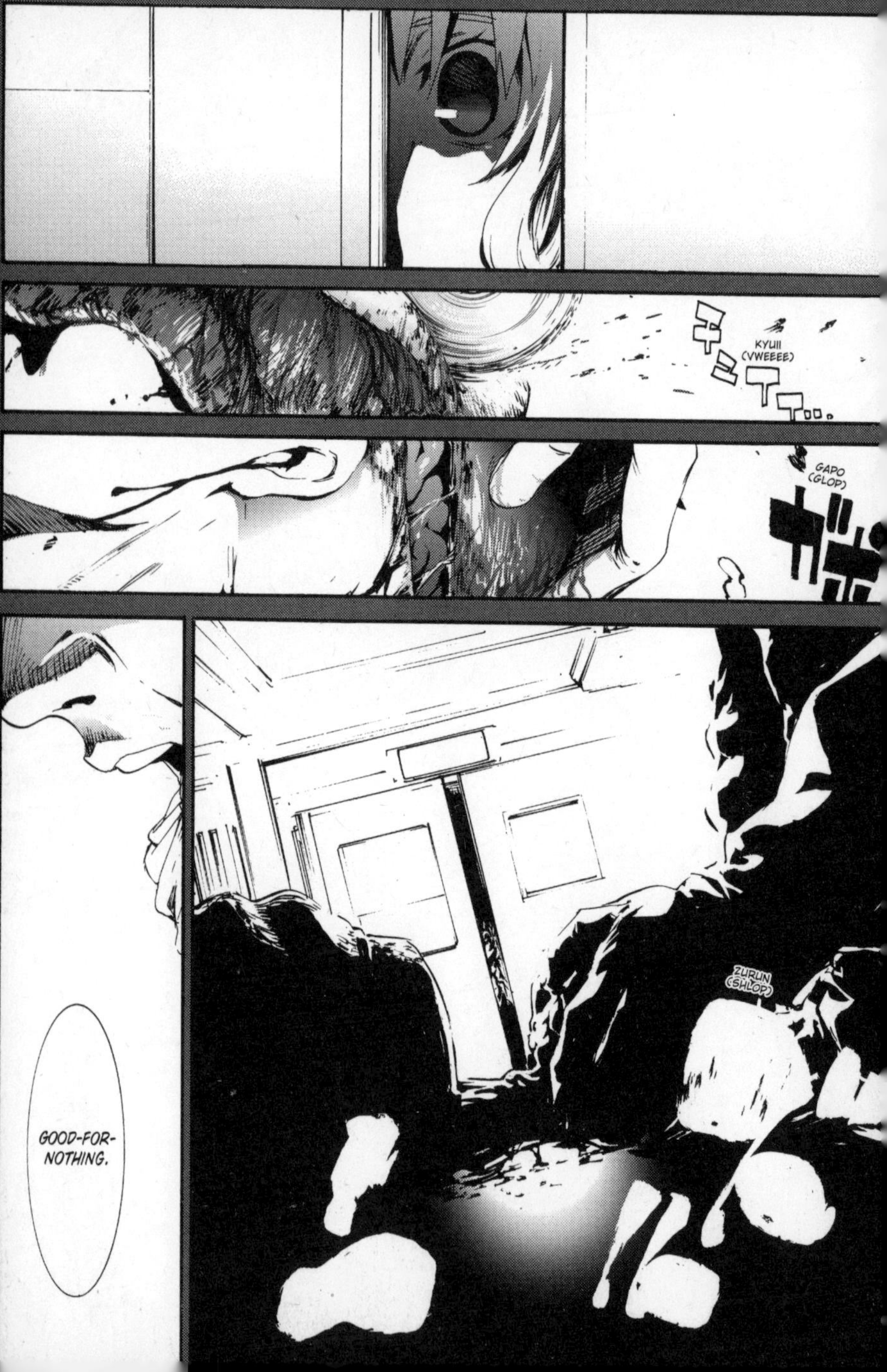
KYUII (VWEEEE)
GAPO (GLOP)
ZURUN (SHLOP)
GOOD-FOR-NOTHING.

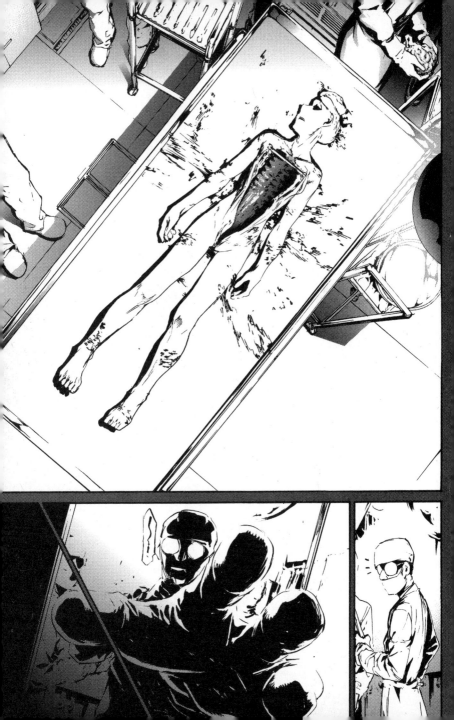

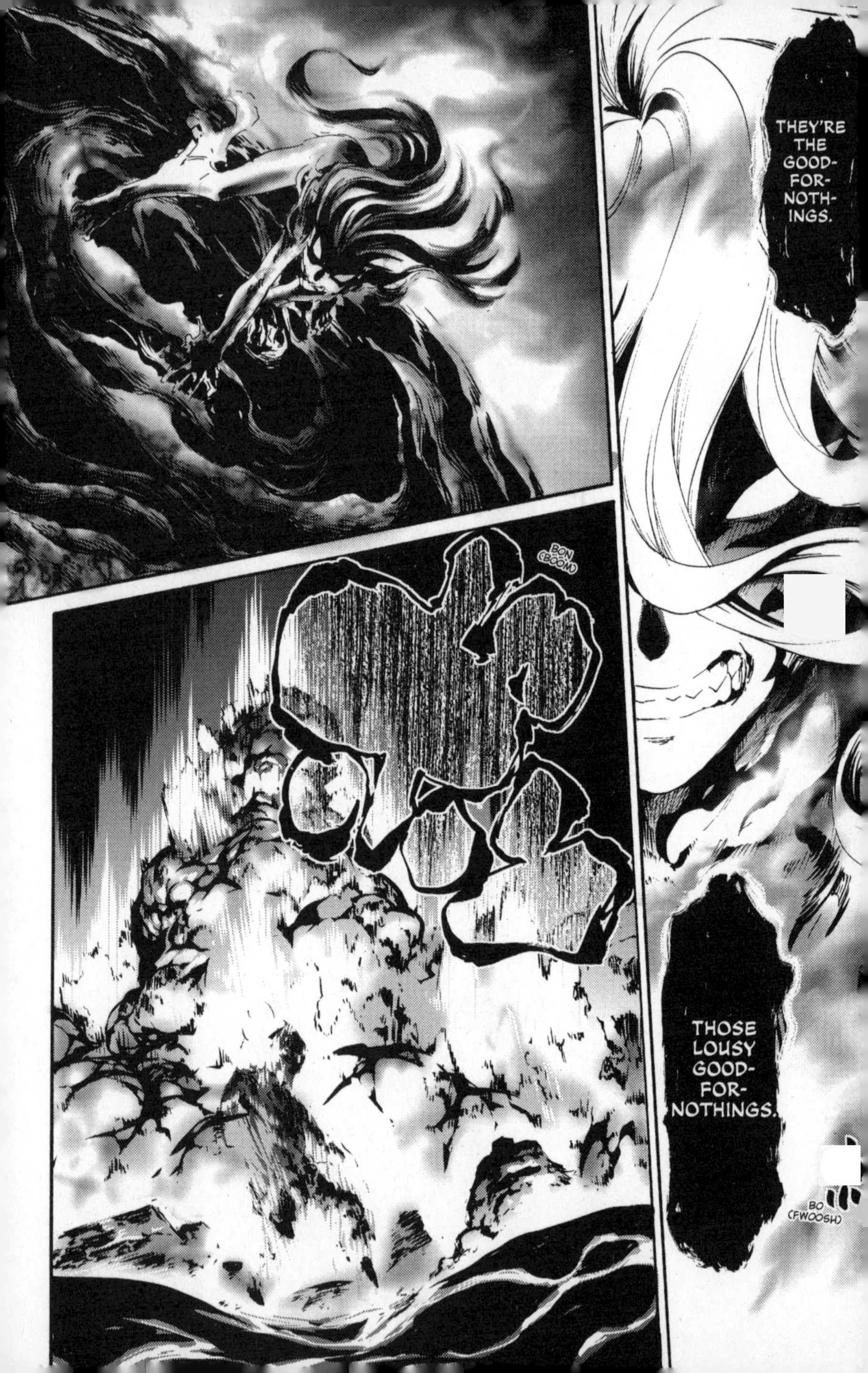
THEY'RE THE GOOD-FOR-NOTHINGS.
THOSE LOUSY GOOD-FOR-NOTHINGS.
BO (F.WOOSH)
BON (BOOM)

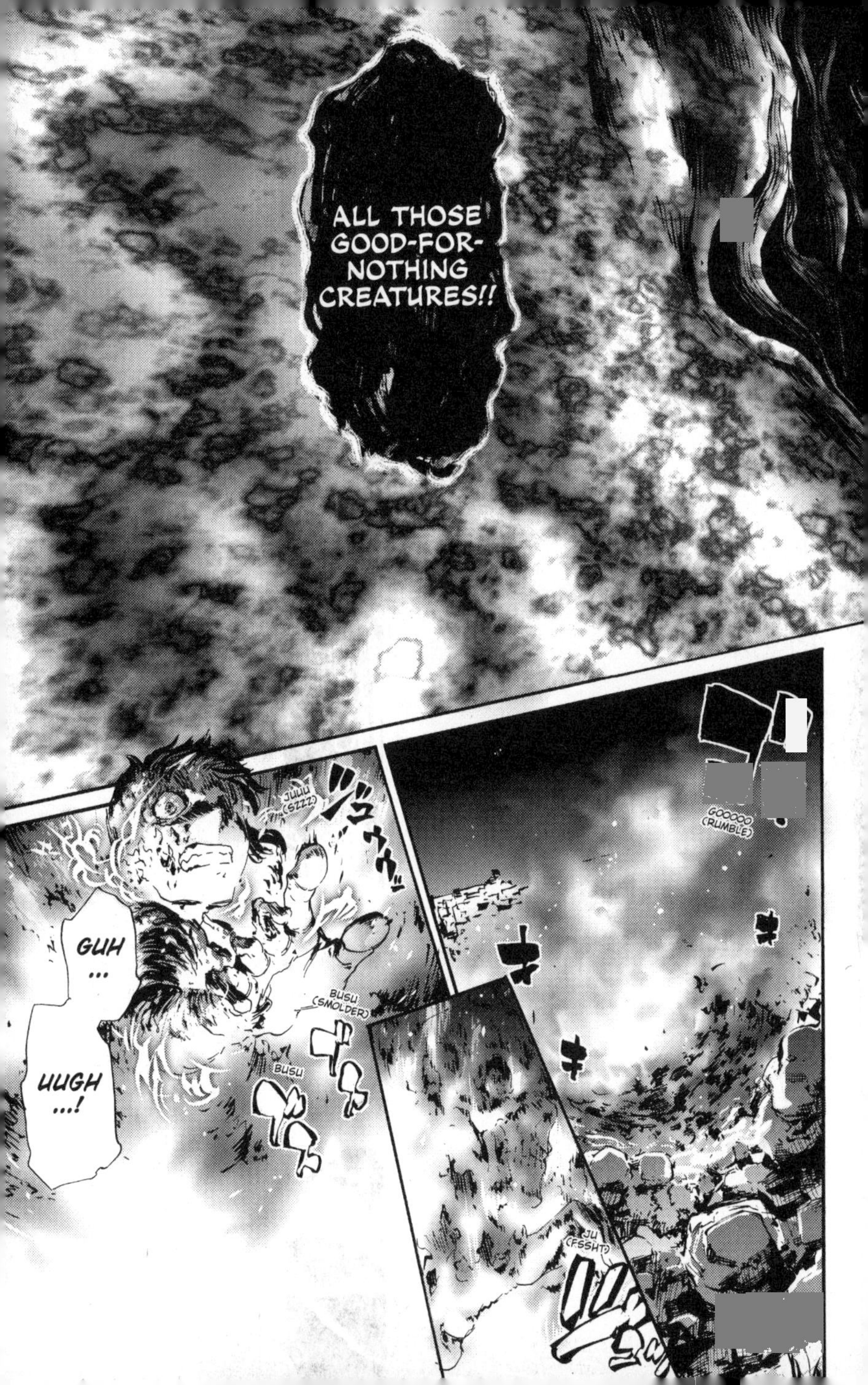
ALL THOSE GOOD-FOR-NOTHING CREATURES!!
GOOOOO (RUMBLE)
JU (FSSHT)
JUUU (SZZZ)
GUH ...
BUSU (SMOLDER)
BUSU
UUGH ...!

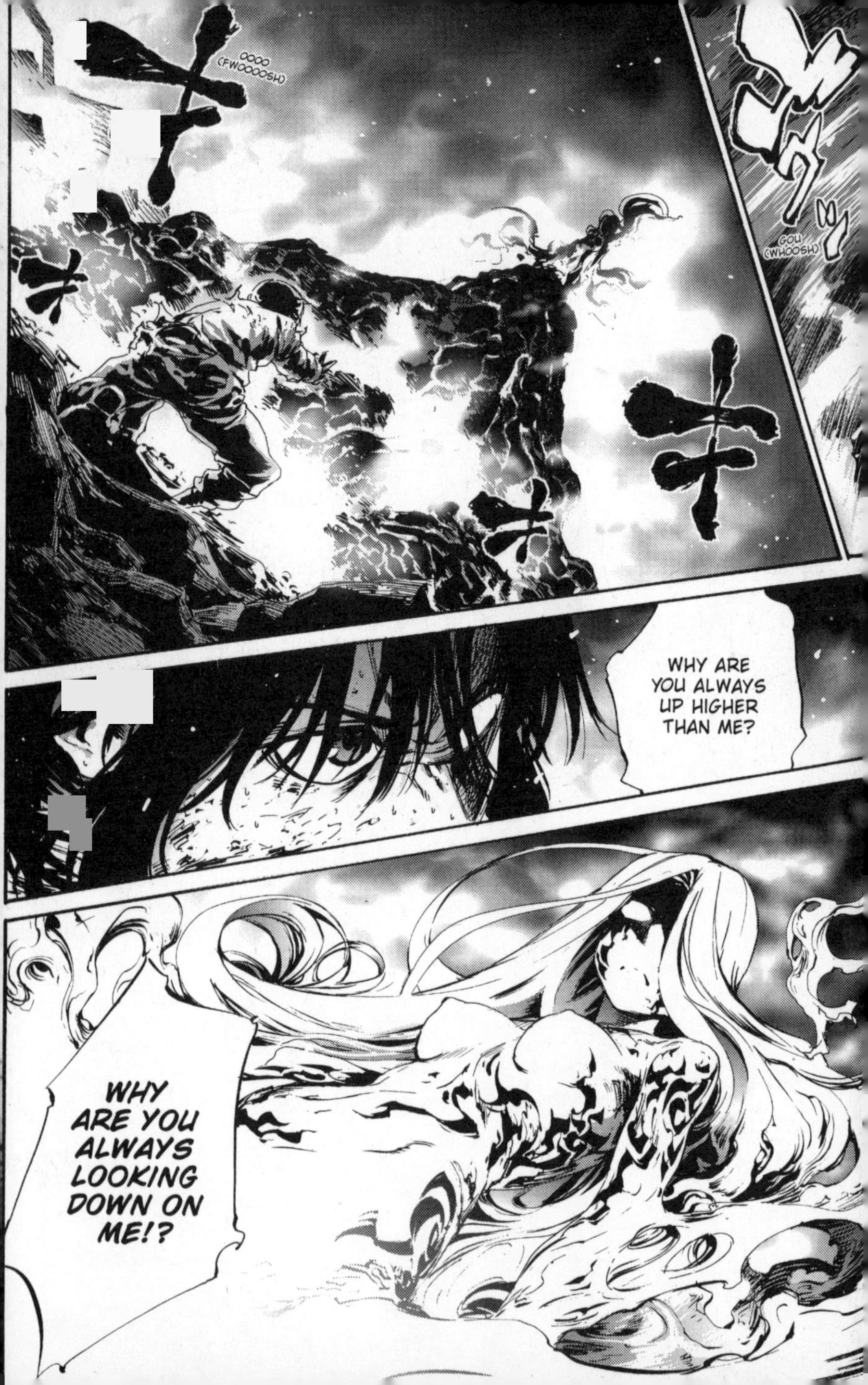
GOU (WHOOSH)
OOOO (FWOOOOSH)
WHY ARE YOU ALWAYS UP HIGHER THAN ME?
WHY ARE YOU ALWAYS LOOKING DOWN ON ME!?

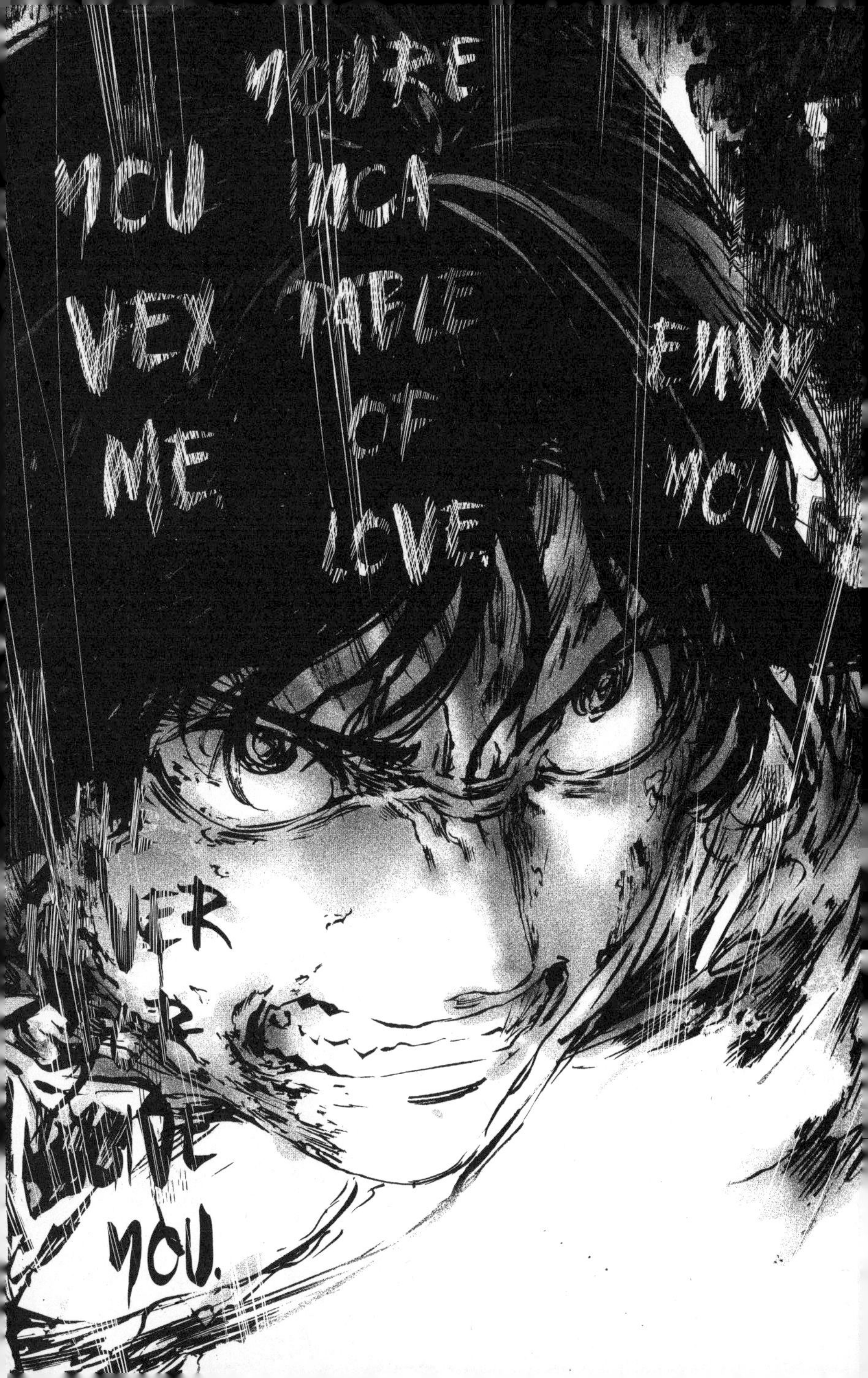
YOU'RE INCAPABLE OF LOVE
YOU VEX ME
YOU.

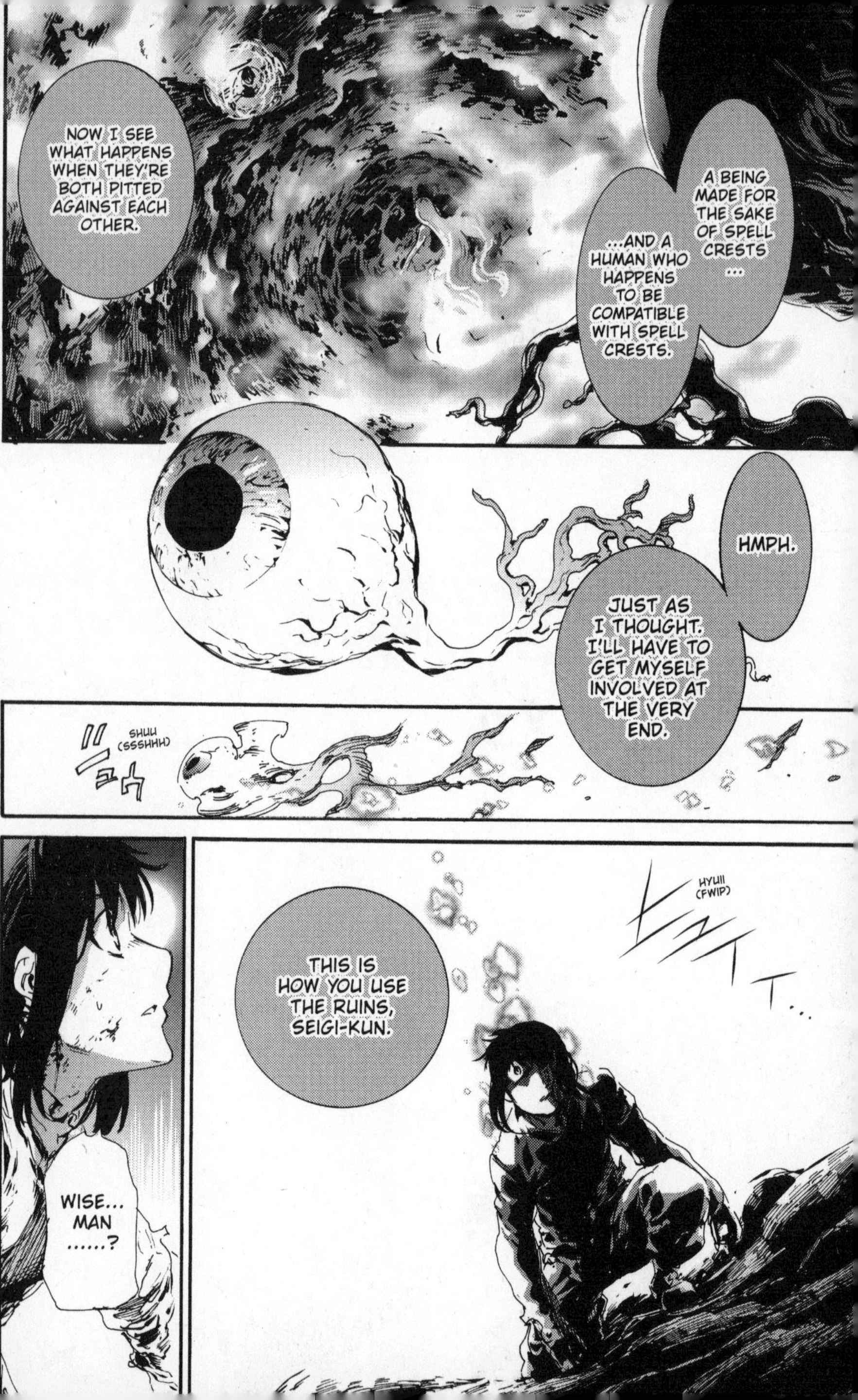
A BEING MADE FOR THE SAKE OF SPELL CRESTS ...
...AND A HUMAN WHO HAPPENS TO BE COMPATIBLE WITH SPELL CRESTS.
NOW I SEE WHAT HAPPENS WHEN THEY'RE BOTH PITTED AGAINST EACH OTHER.
HMPH.
JUST AS I THOUGHT. I'LL HAVE TO GET MYSELF INVOLVED AT THE VERY END.
SHUU (SSSHHH)
HYUII (FWIP)
THIS IS HOW YOU USE THE RUINS, SEIGI-KUN.
WISE... MAN ......?

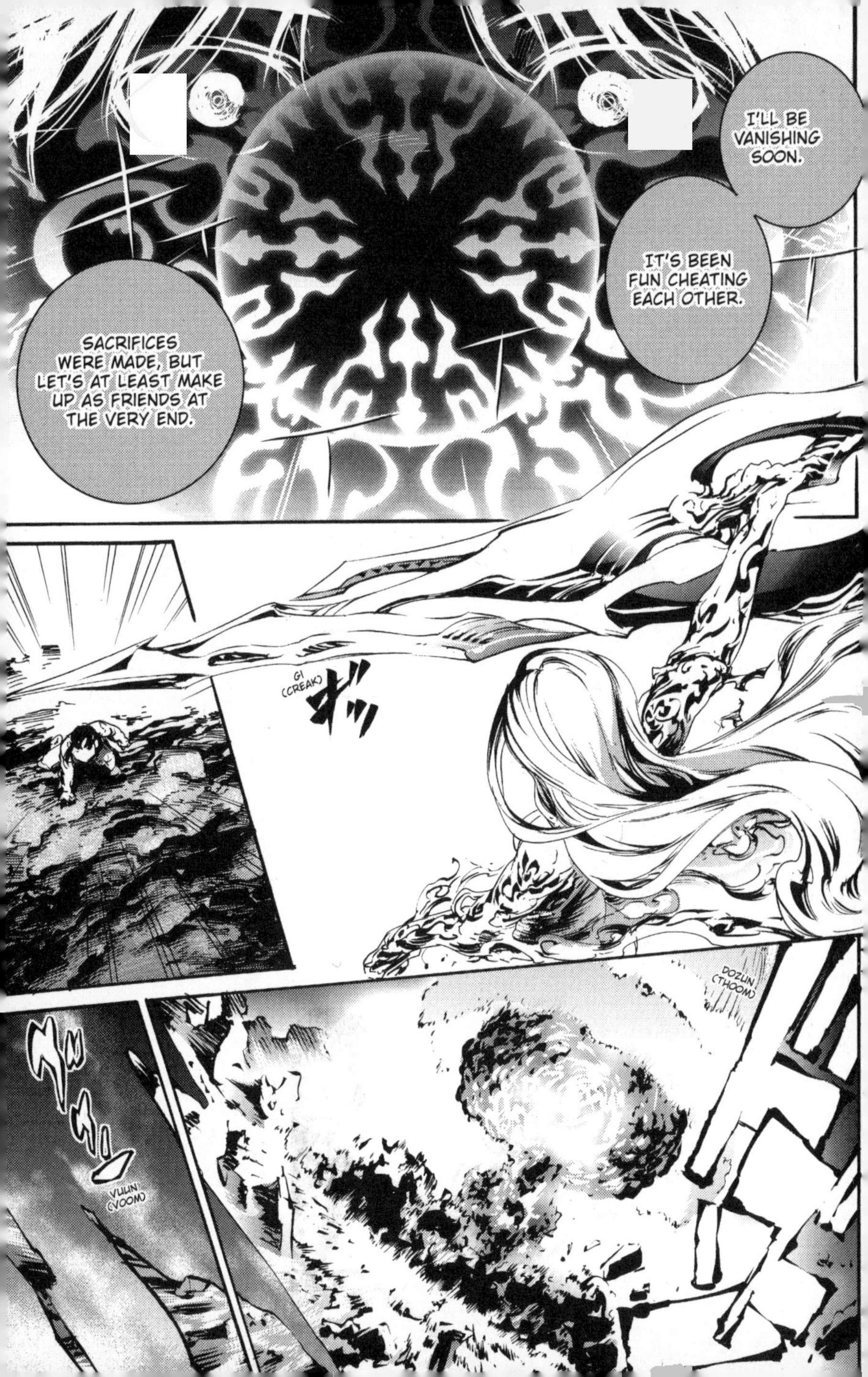
I'LL BE VANISHING SOON.
IT'S BEEN FUN CHEATING EACH OTHER.
SACRIFICES WERE MADE, BUT LET'S AT LEAST MAKE UP AS FRIENDS AT THE VERY END.
GI (CREAK)
DOZUN (THOOM)
VUUN (VOOM)

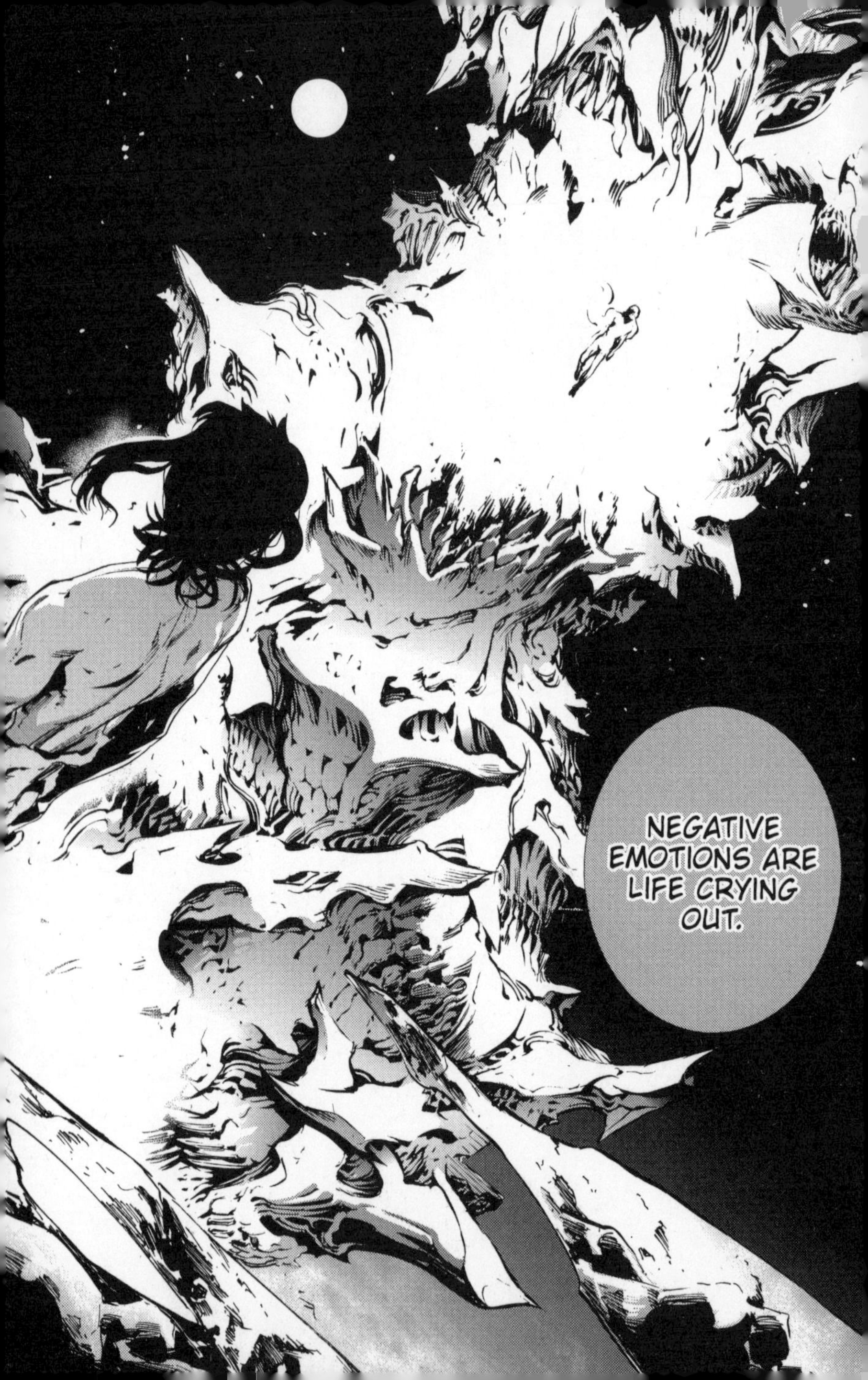
NEGATIVE EMOTIONS ARE LIFE CRYING OUT.

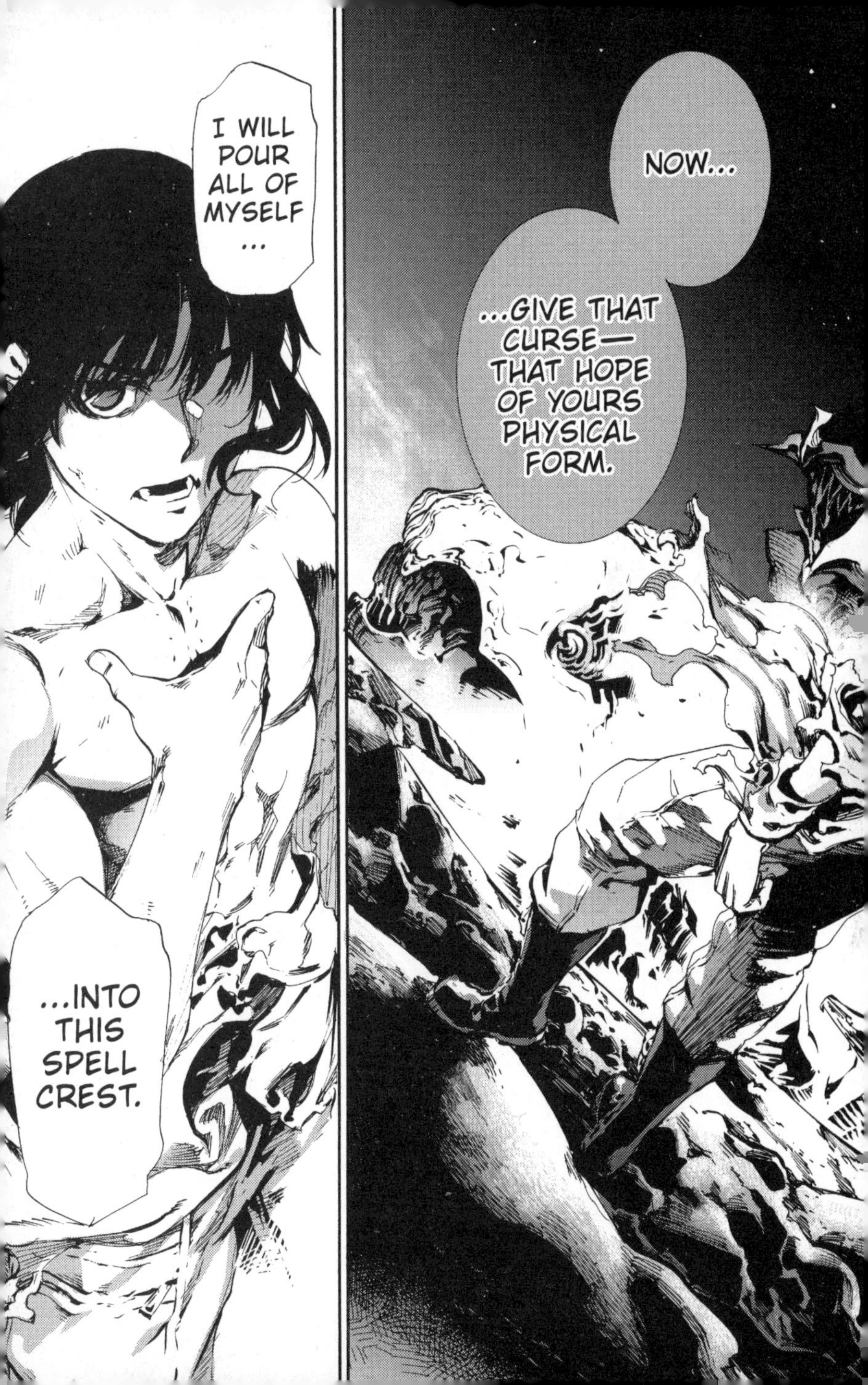
NOW...
...GIVE THAT CURSE—THAT HOPE OF YOURS PHYSICAL FORM.
I WILL POUR ALL OF MYSELF...
...INTO THIS SPELL CREST.

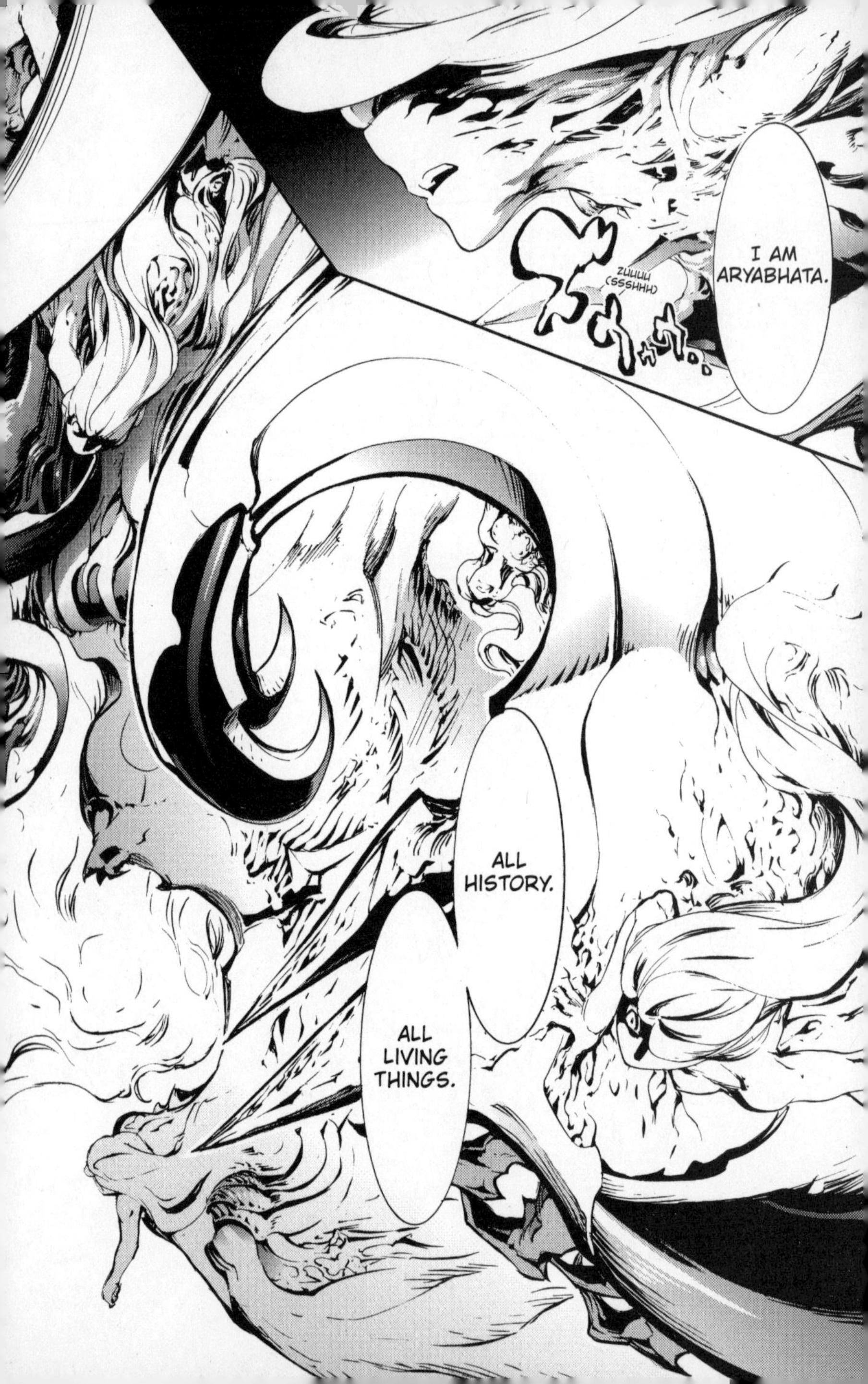
I AM ARYABHATA.
ZUUUU (SSSHHH)
ALL HISTORY.
ALL LIVING THINGS.

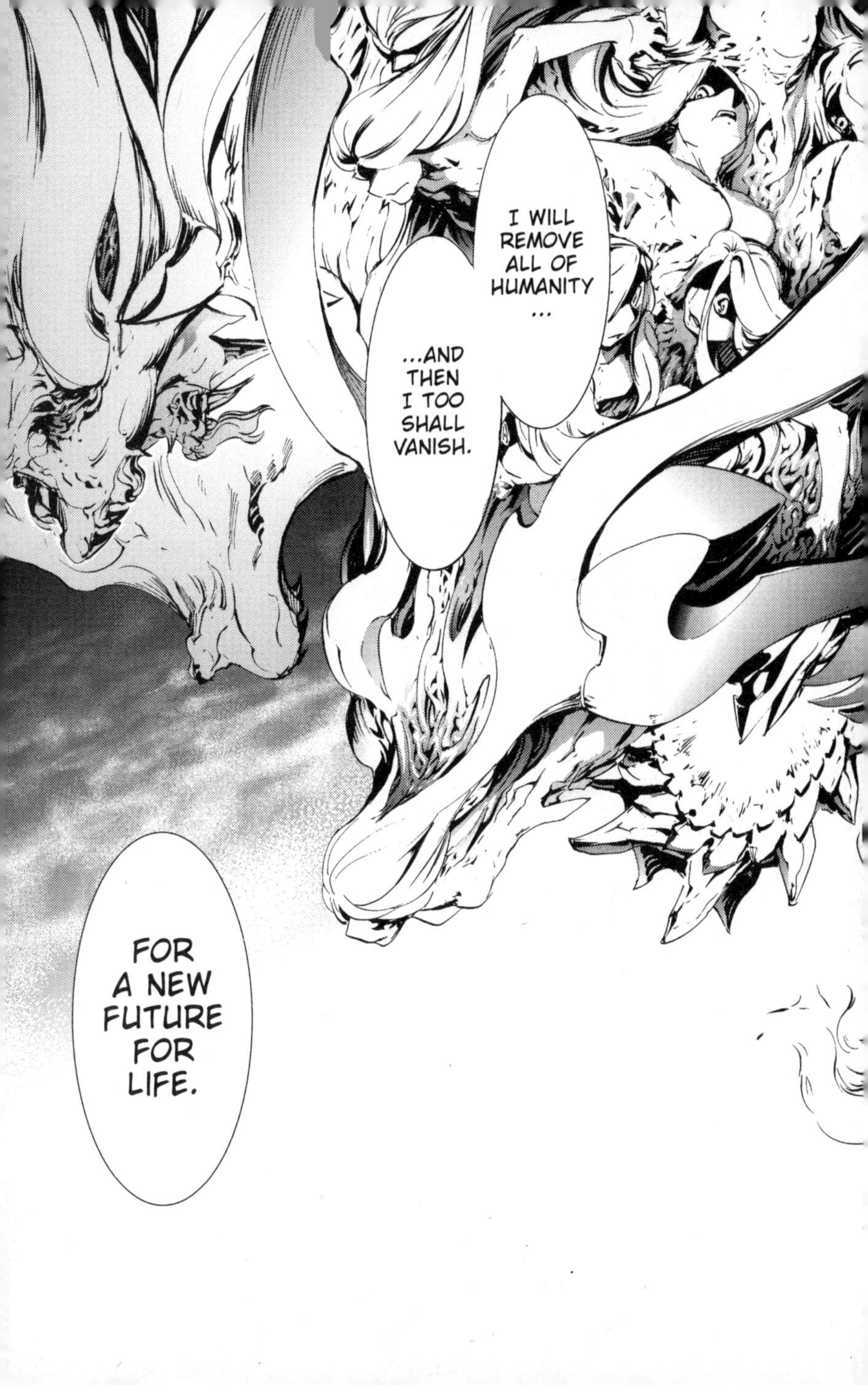
I WILL REMOVE ALL OF HUMANITY ...
...AND THEN I TOO SHALL VANISH.
FOR A NEW FUTURE FOR LIFE.

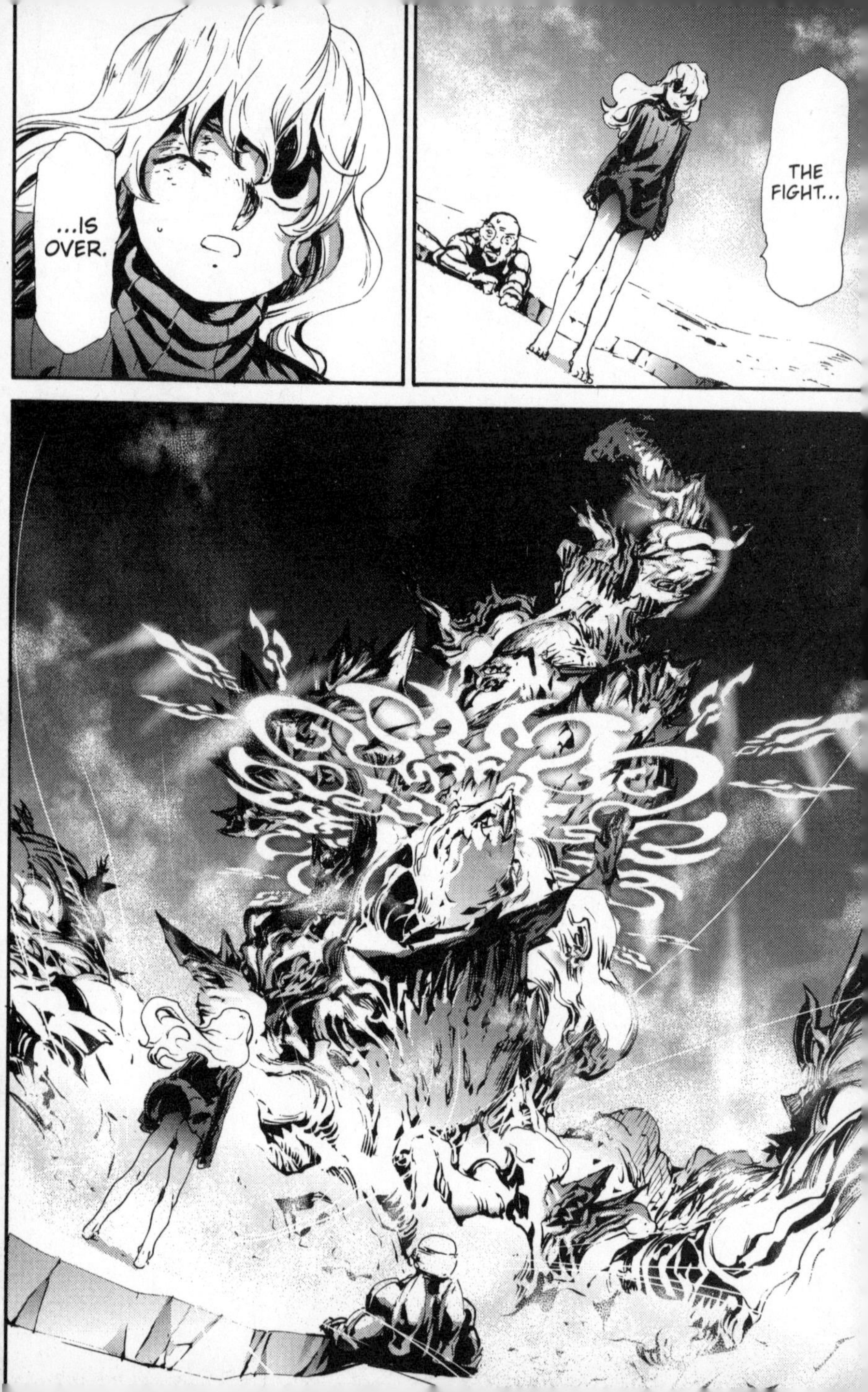
THE FIGHT...
...IS OVER.

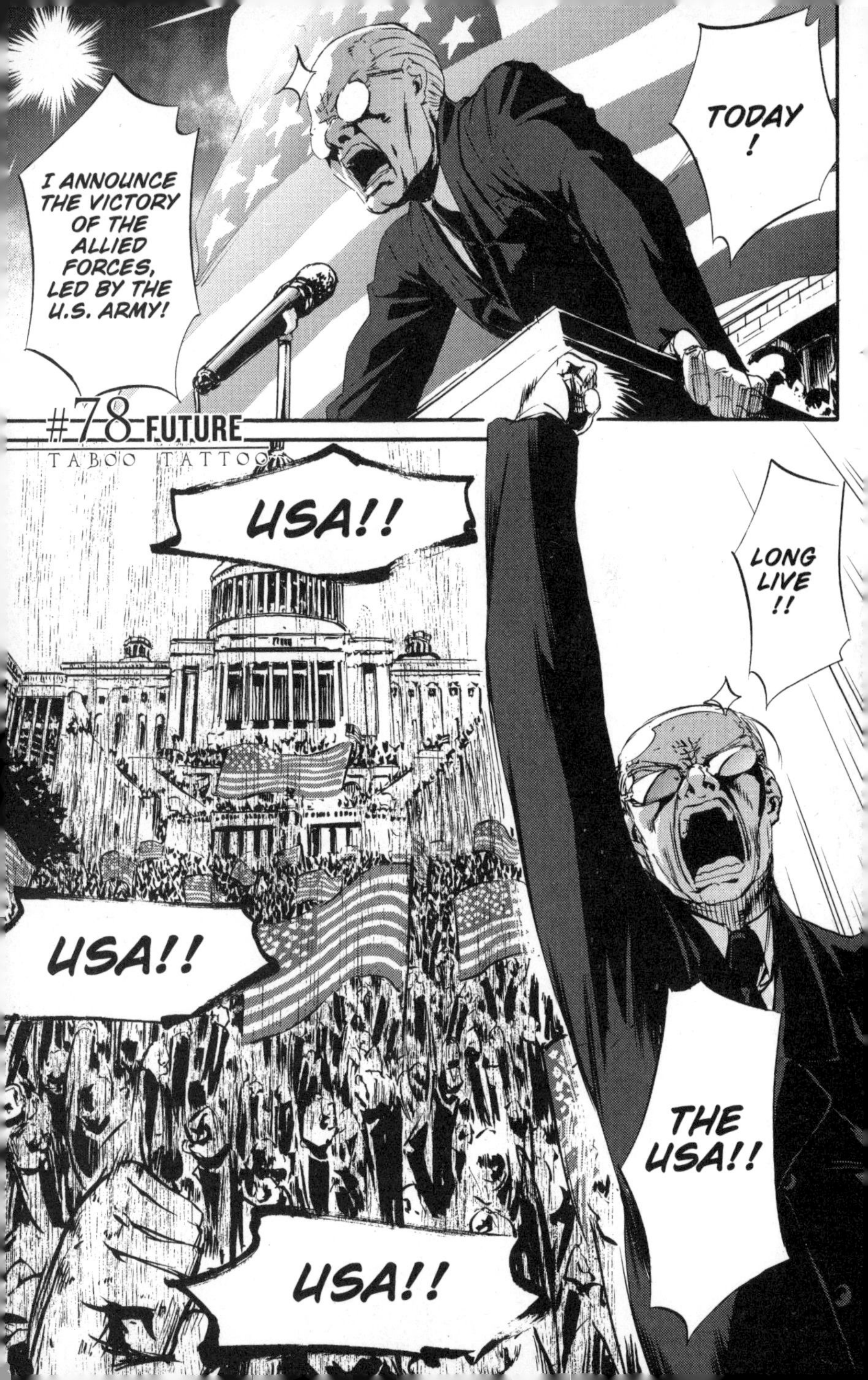
TODAY!
I ANNOUNCE THE VICTORY OF THE ALLIED FORCES, LED BY THE U.S. ARMY!
#78 FUTURE
TABOO TATTOO
LONG LIVE!!
THE USA!!
USA!!
USA!!
USA!!

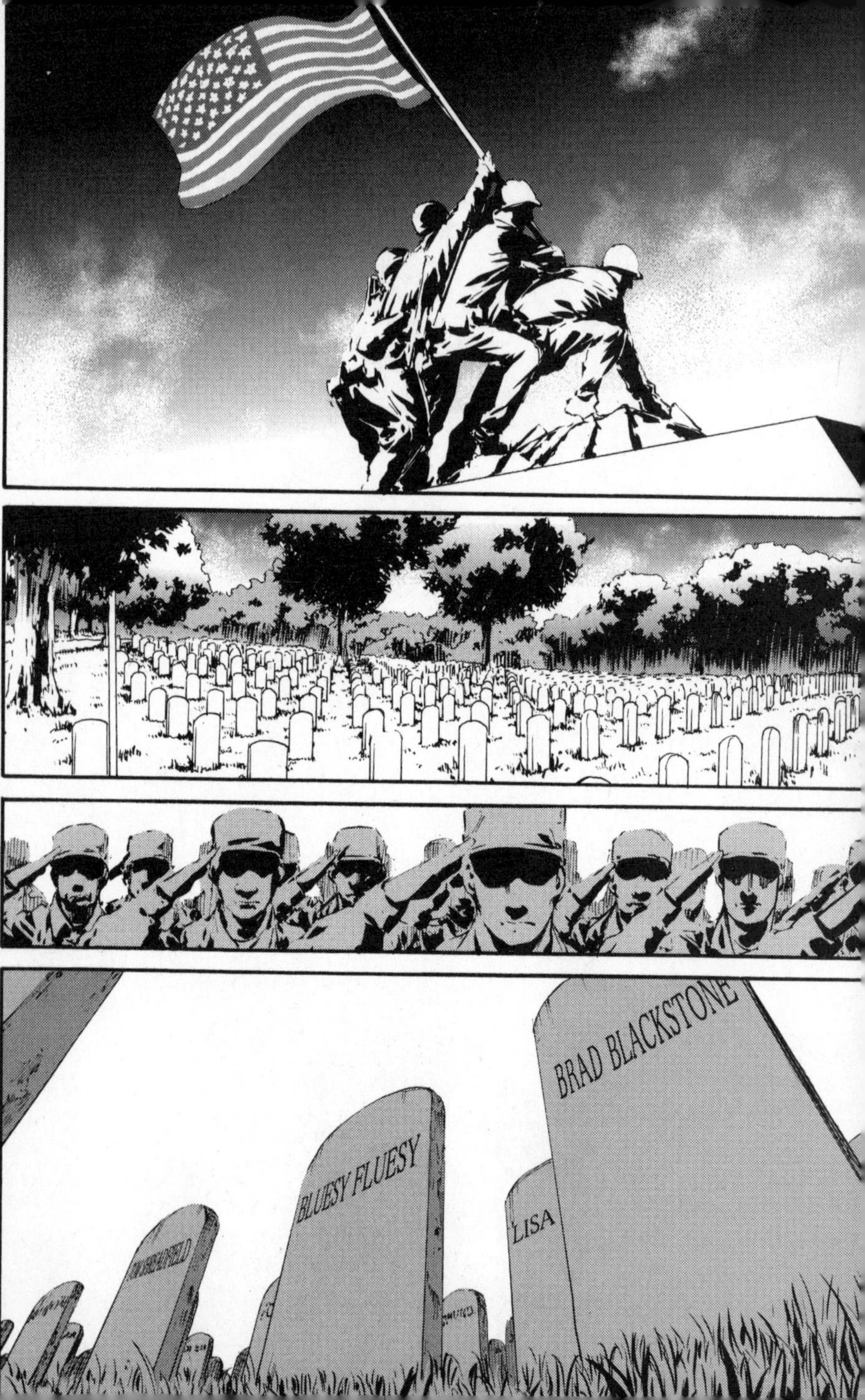
BRAD BLACKSTONE
LISA
BLUESY FLUESY

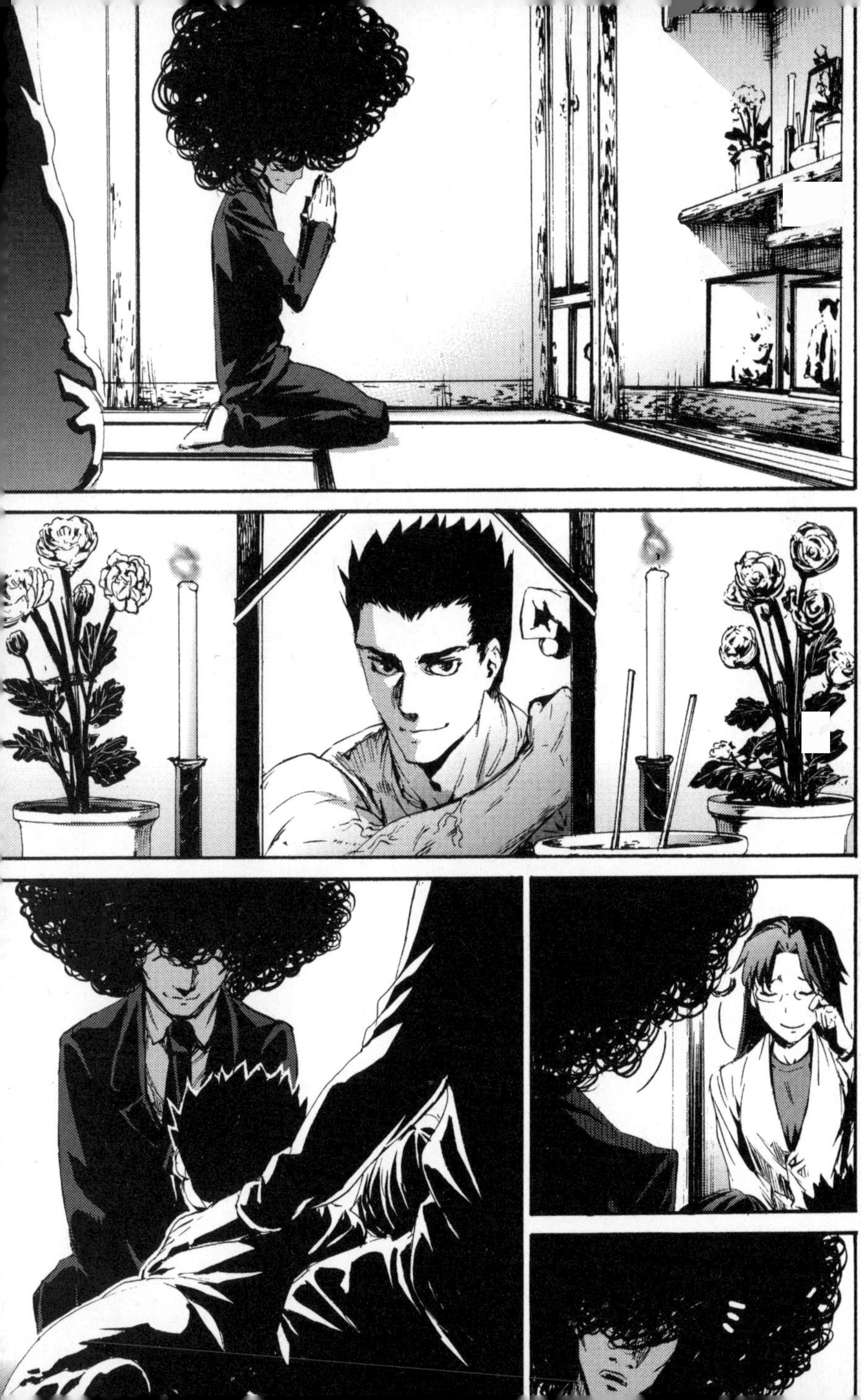

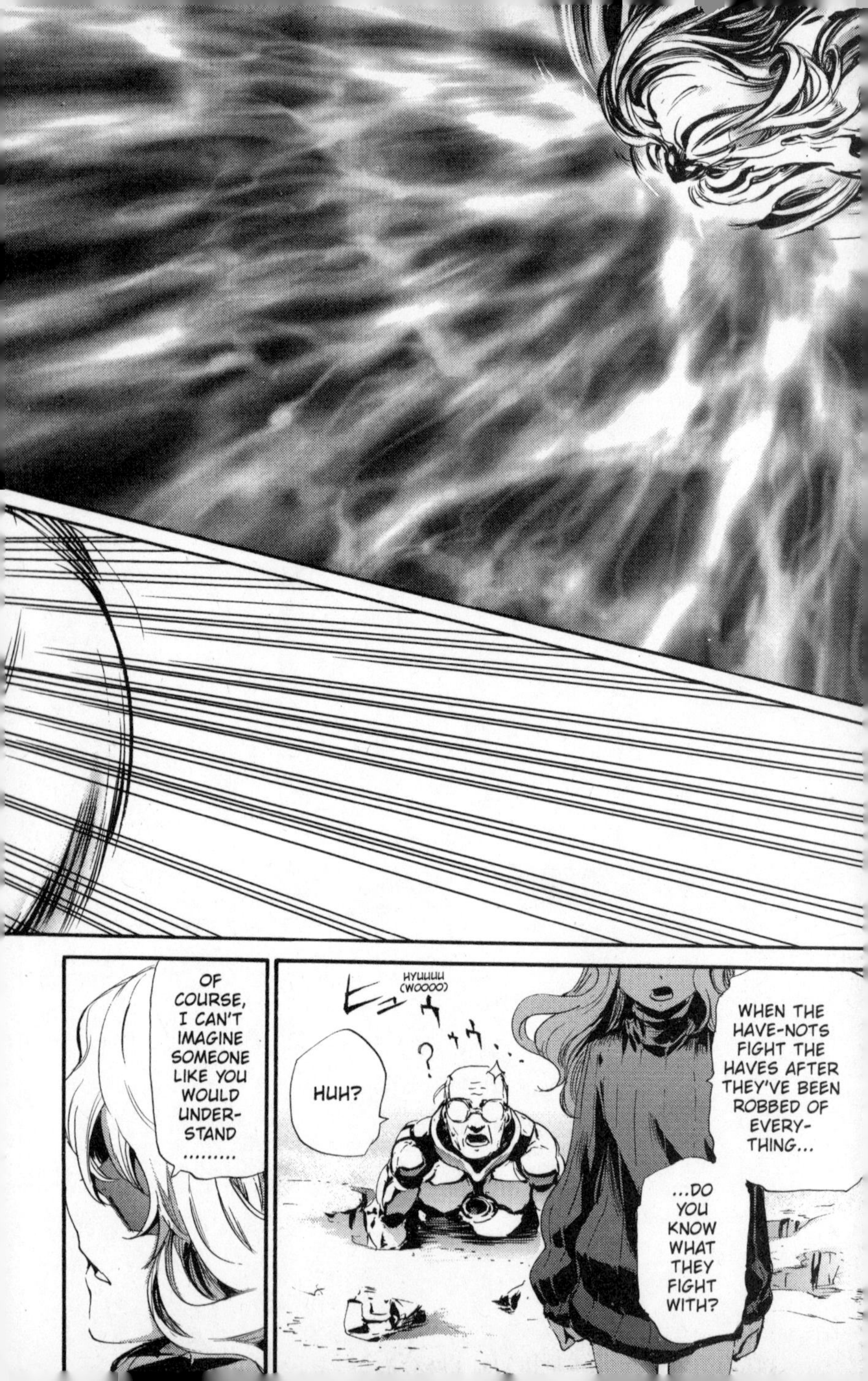
WHEN THE HAVE-NOTS FIGHT THE HAVES AFTER THEY'VE BEEN ROBBED OF EVERYTHING...
HYUUUU (WOOOO)
ヒュウゥゥゥ
...DO YOU KNOW WHAT THEY FIGHT WITH?
HUH?
?
OF COURSE, I CAN'T IMAGINE SOMEONE LIKE YOU WOULD UNDERSTAND ....

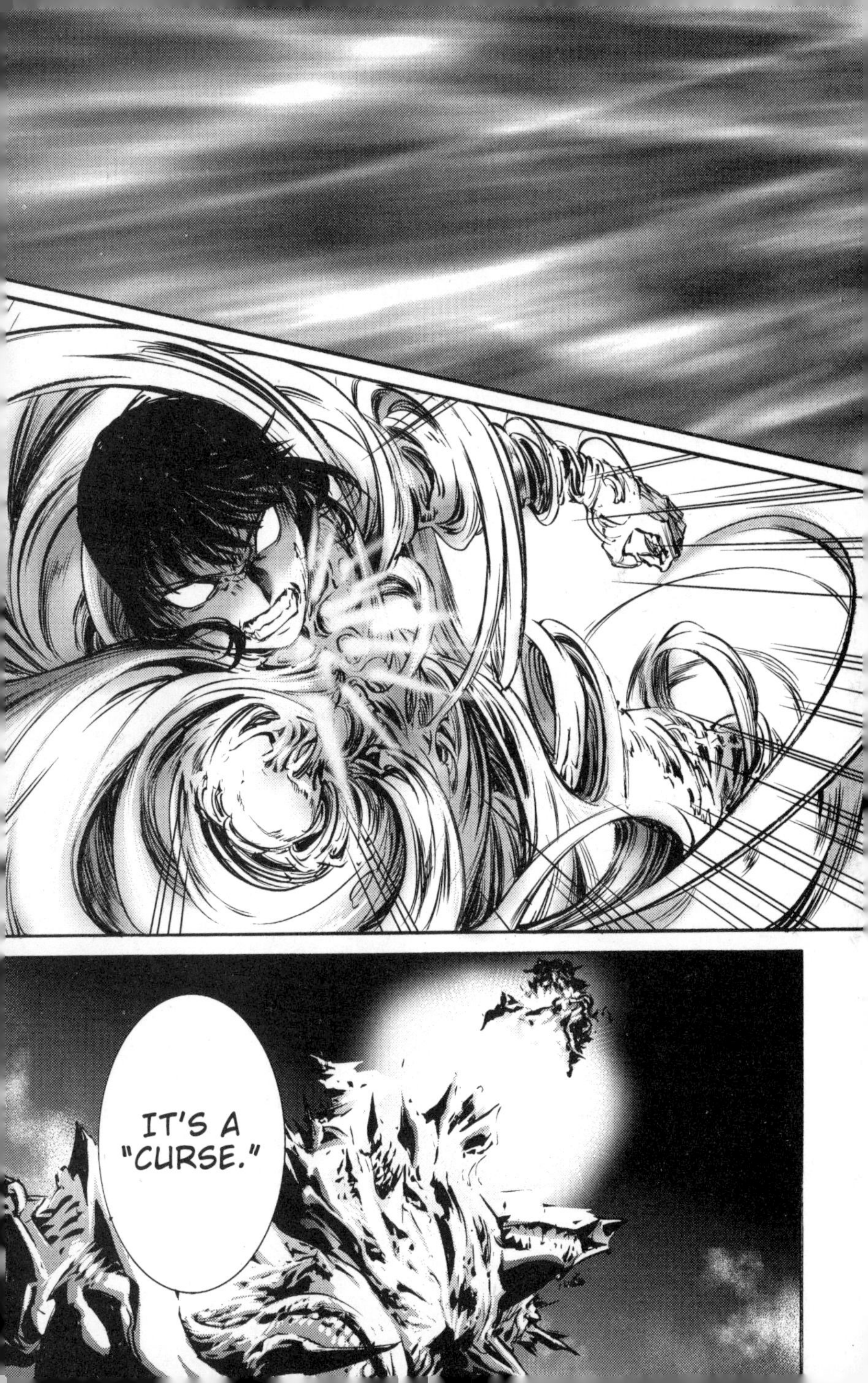
IT'S A "CURSE."

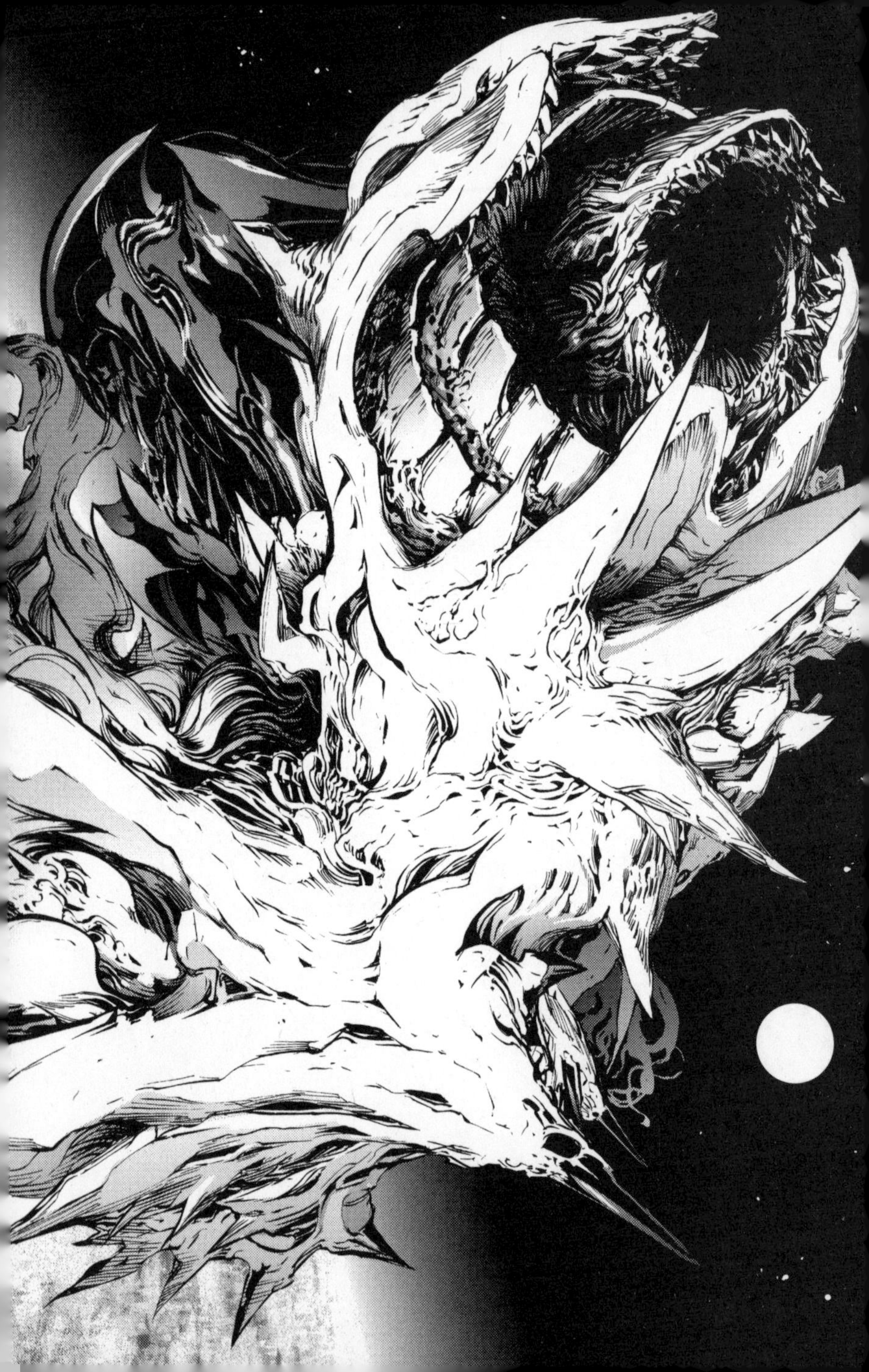

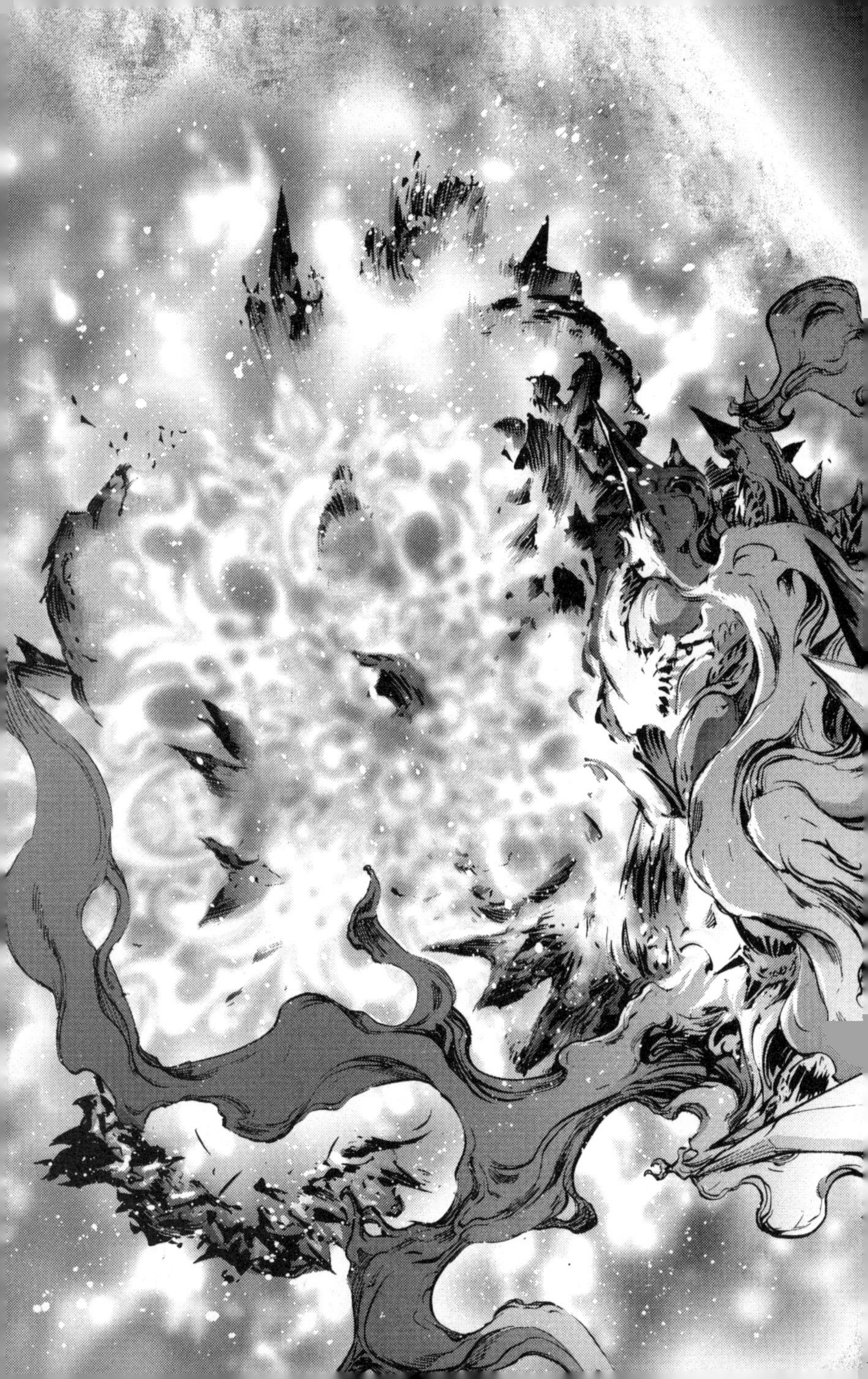

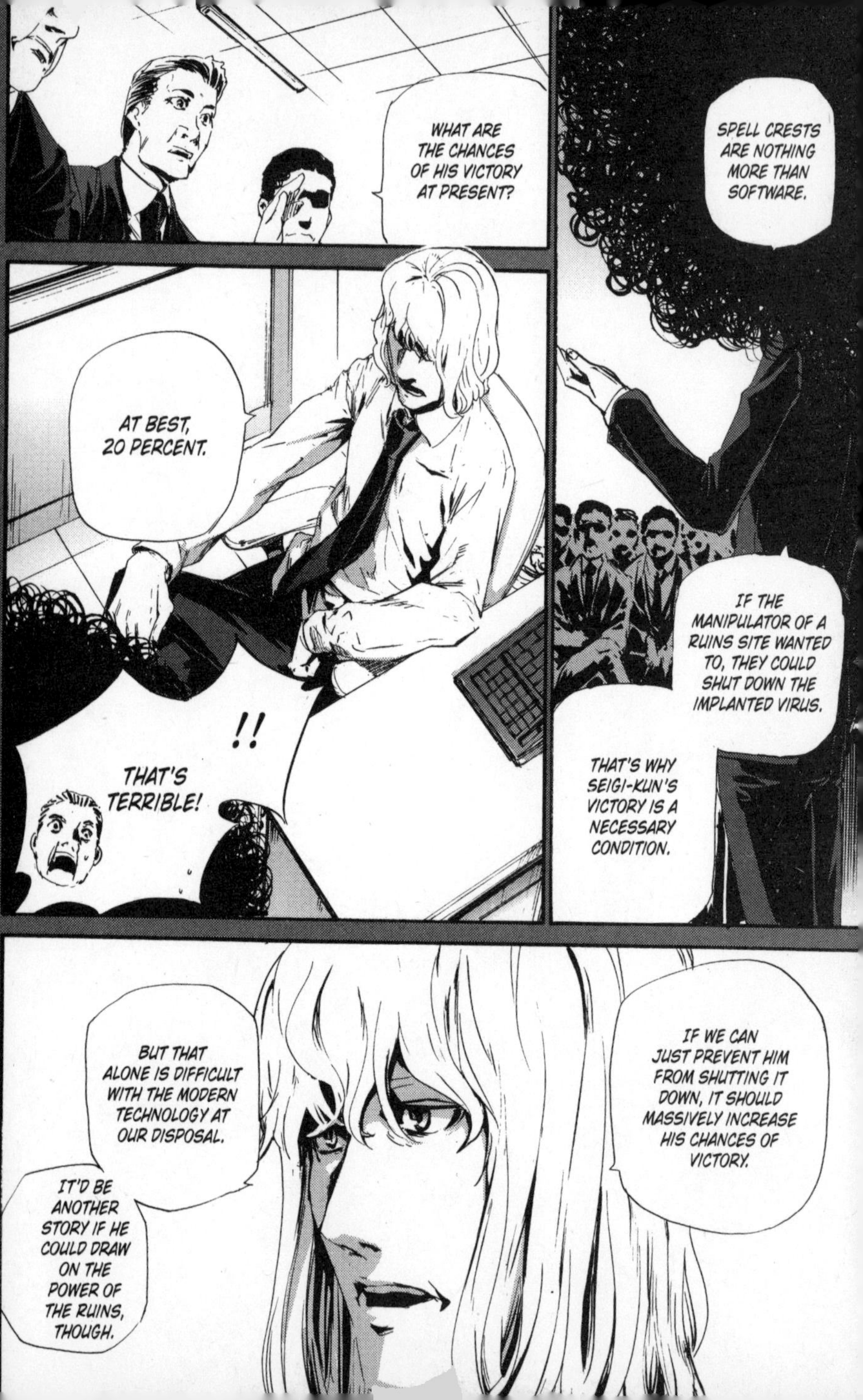
SPELL CRESTS ARE NOTHING MORE THAN SOFTWARE.
IF THE MANIPULATOR OF A RUINS SITE WANTED TO, THEY COULD SHUT DOWN THE IMPLANTED VIRUS.
THAT'S WHY SEIGI-KUN'S VICTORY IS A NECESSARY CONDITION.
WHAT ARE THE CHANCES OF HIS VICTORY AT PRESENT?
AT BEST, 20 PERCENT.
!!
THAT'S TERRIBLE!
IF WE CAN JUST PREVENT HIM FROM SHUTTING IT DOWN, IT SHOULD MASSIVELY INCREASE HIS CHANCES OF VICTORY.
BUT THAT ALONE IS DIFFICULT WITH THE MODERN TECHNOLOGY AT OUR DISPOSAL.
IT'D BE ANOTHER STORY IF HE COULD DRAW ON THE POWER OF THE RUINS, THOUGH.

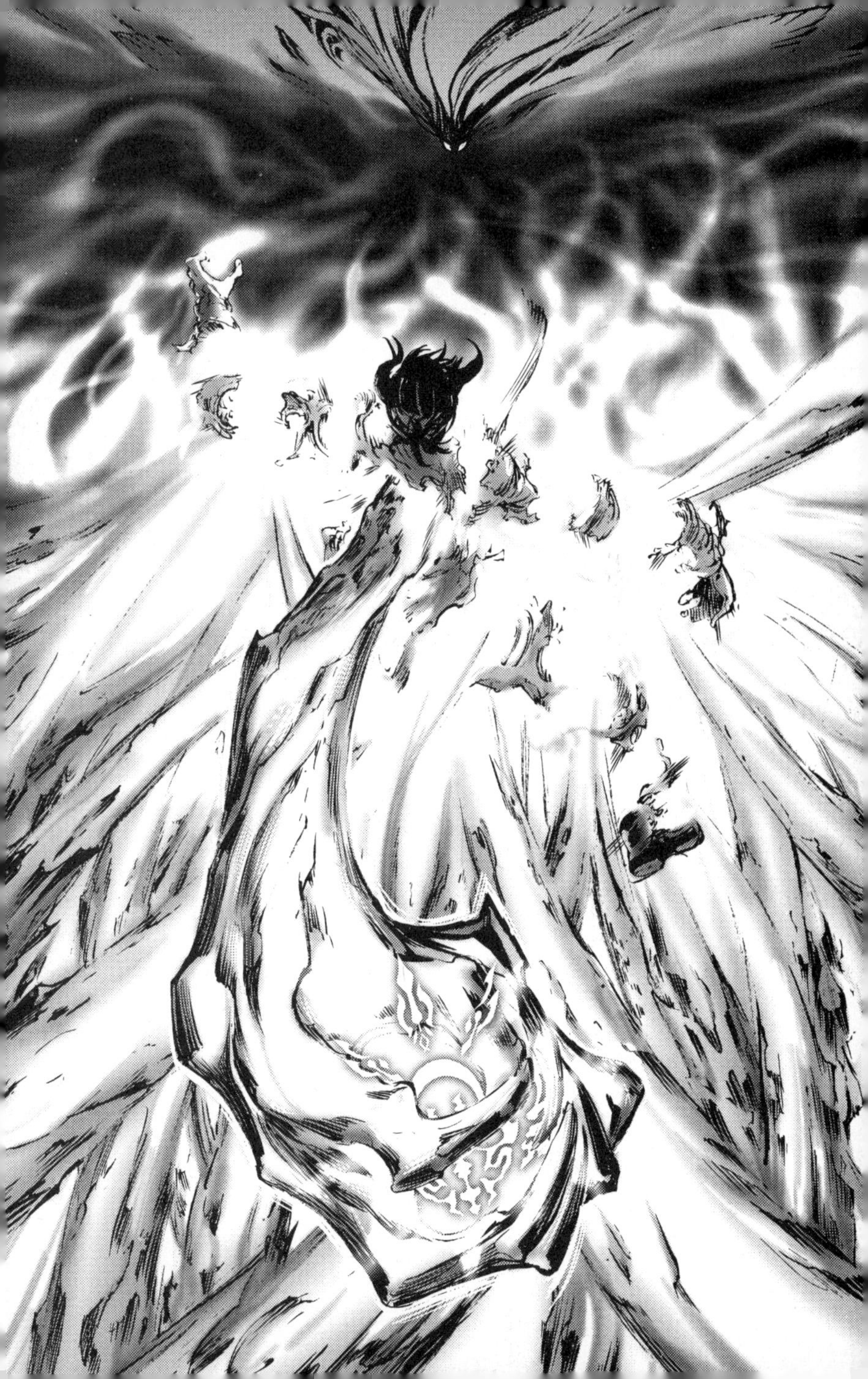

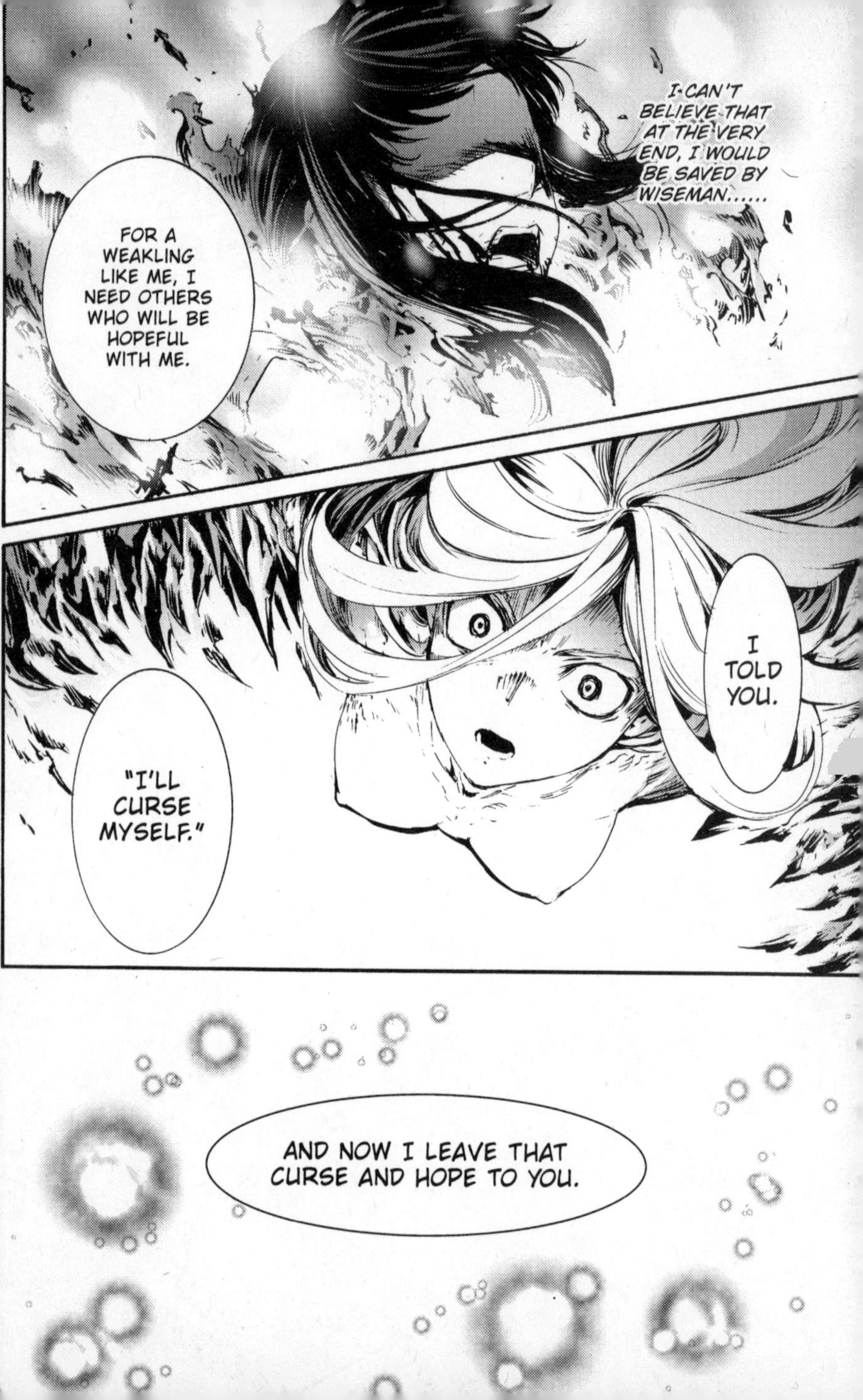
I CAN'T BELIEVE THAT AT THE VERY END, I WOULD BE SAVED BY WISEMAN......
FOR A WEAKLING LIKE ME, I NEED OTHERS WHO WILL BE HOPEFUL WITH ME.
I TOLD YOU.
"I'LL CURSE MYSELF."
AND NOW I LEAVE THAT CURSE AND HOPE TO YOU.

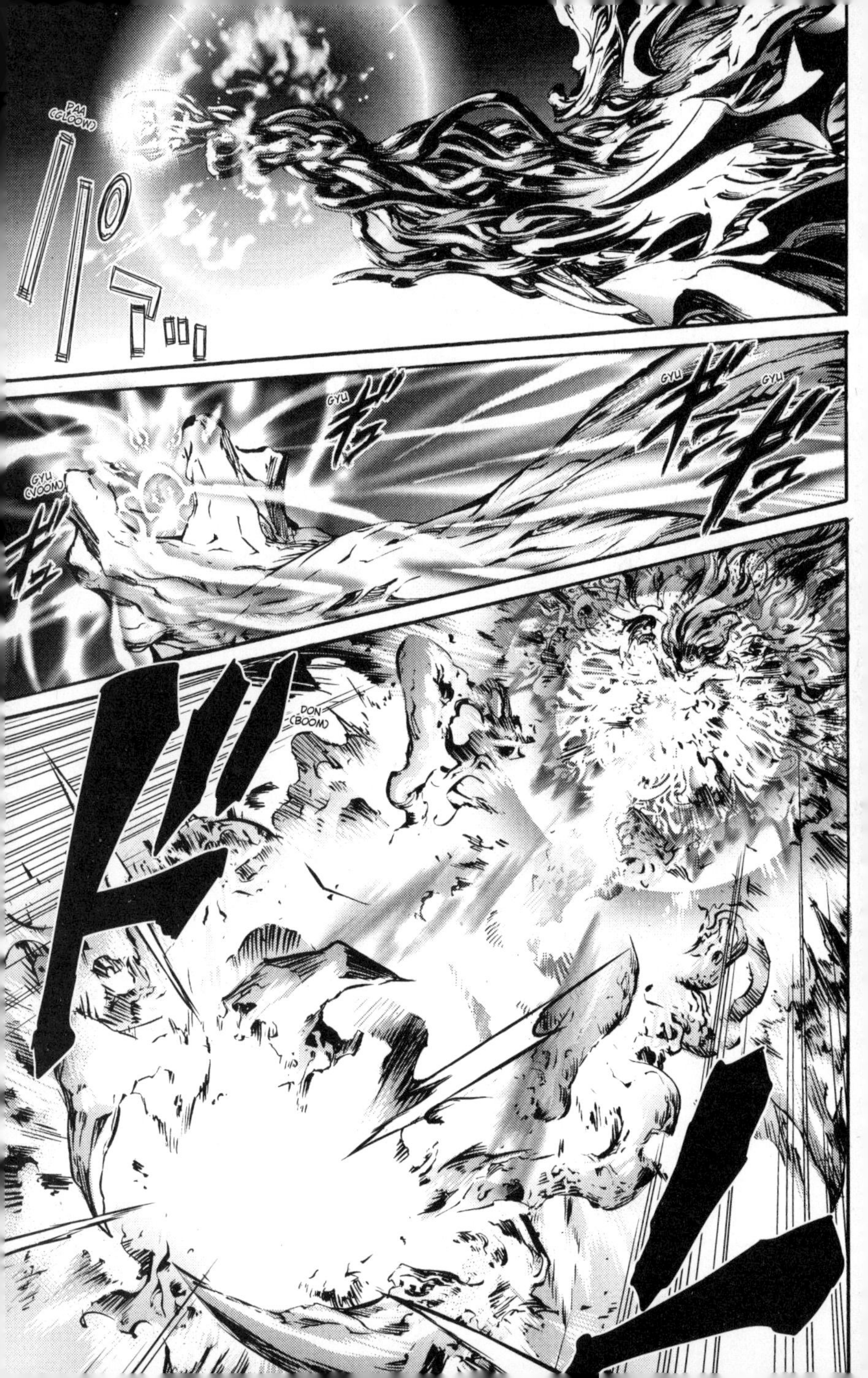
PAA (GLOOW)
GYU
GYU
GYU
GYU (VOOM)
DON (BOOM)

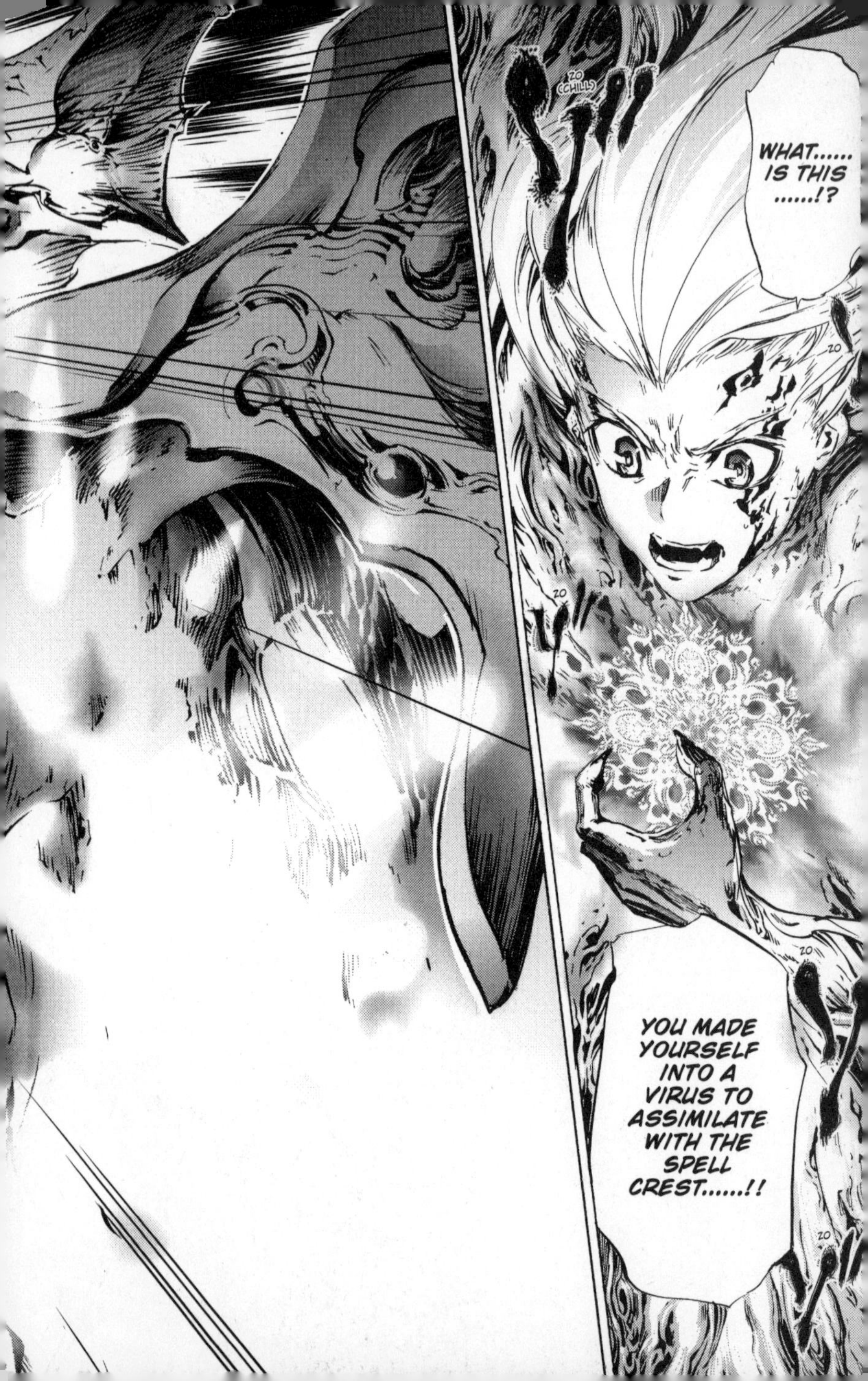
ZO (CHILL)
WHAT...... IS THIS ......!?
ZO
ZO
ZO
YOU MADE YOURSELF INTO A VIRUS TO ASSIMILATE WITH THE SPELL CREST......!!
ZO

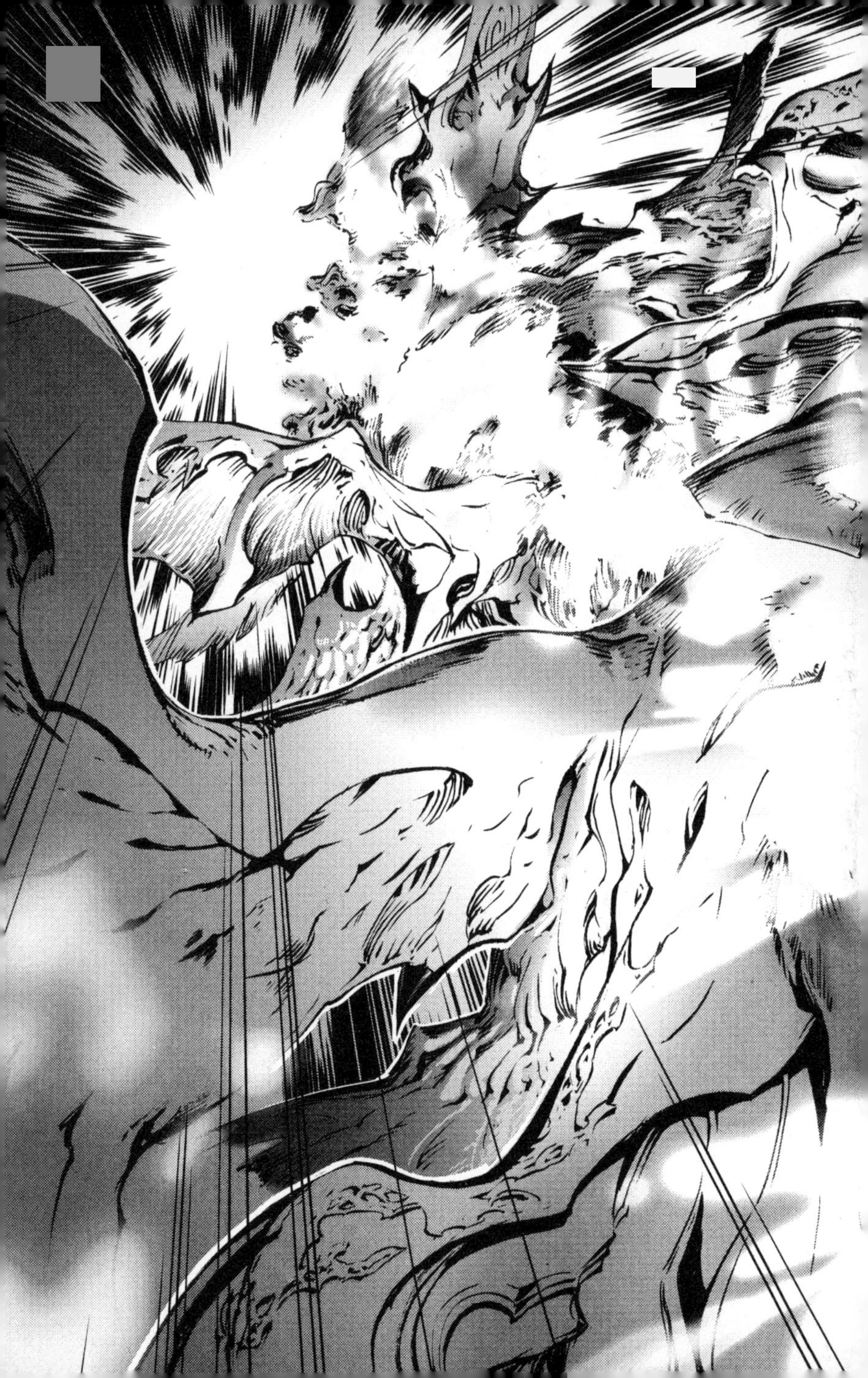

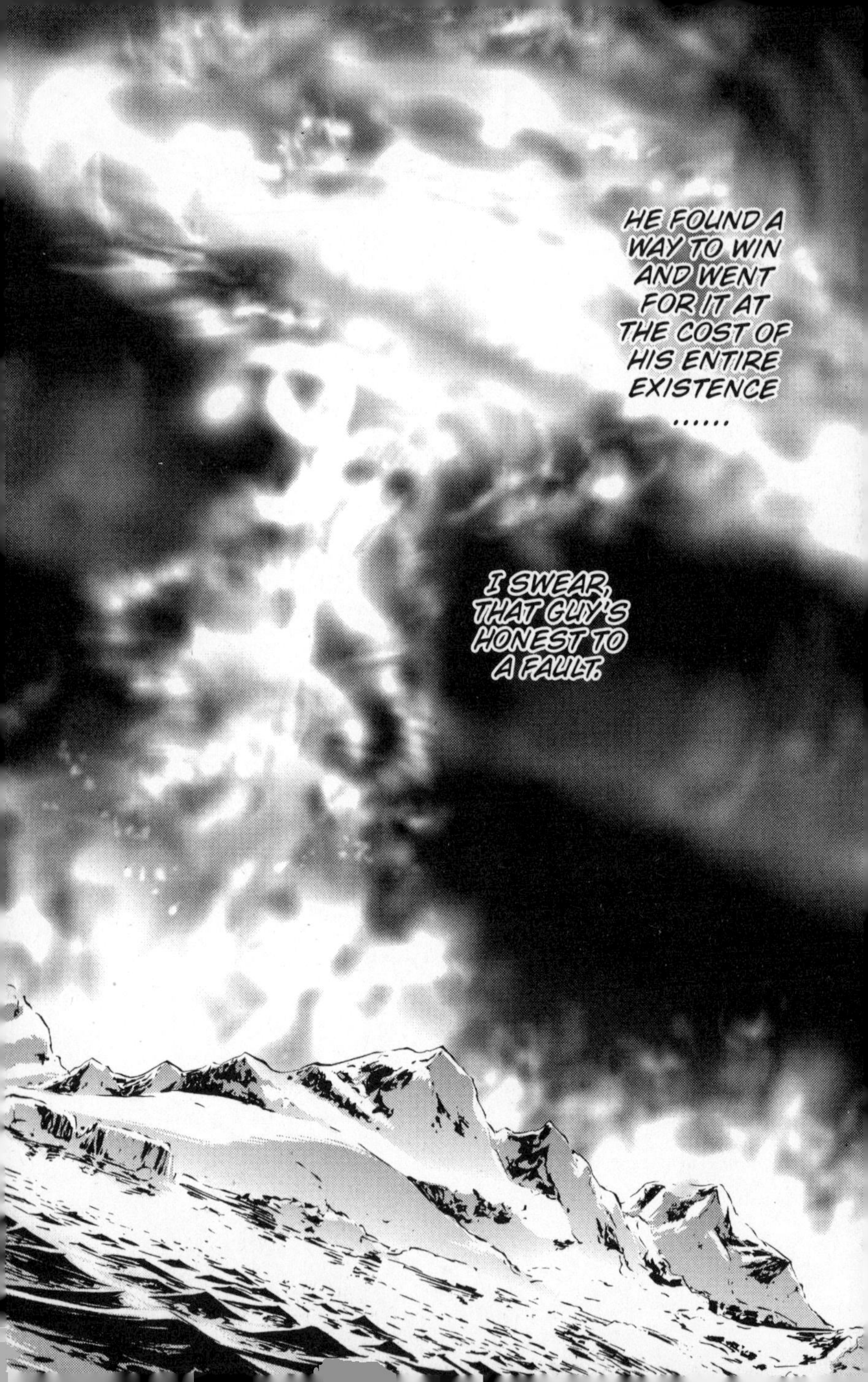
HE FOUND A WAY TO WIN AND WENT FOR IT AT THE COST OF HIS ENTIRE EXISTENCE ......
I SWEAR, THAT GUY'S HONEST TO A FAULT.

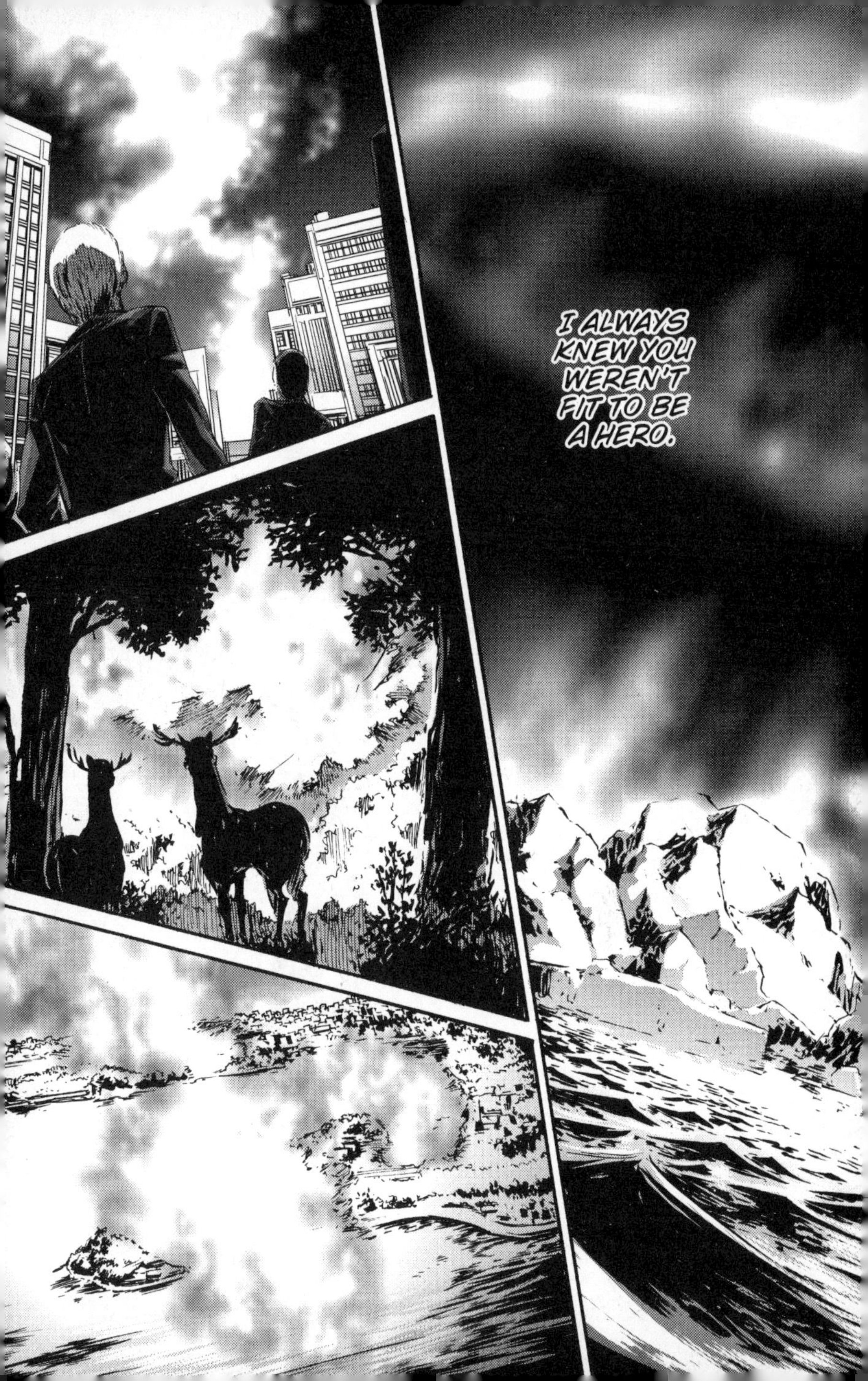
I ALWAYS KNEW YOU WEREN'T FIT TO BE A HERO.

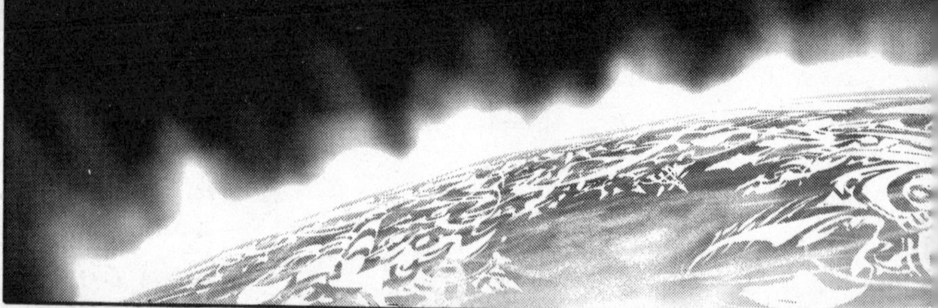
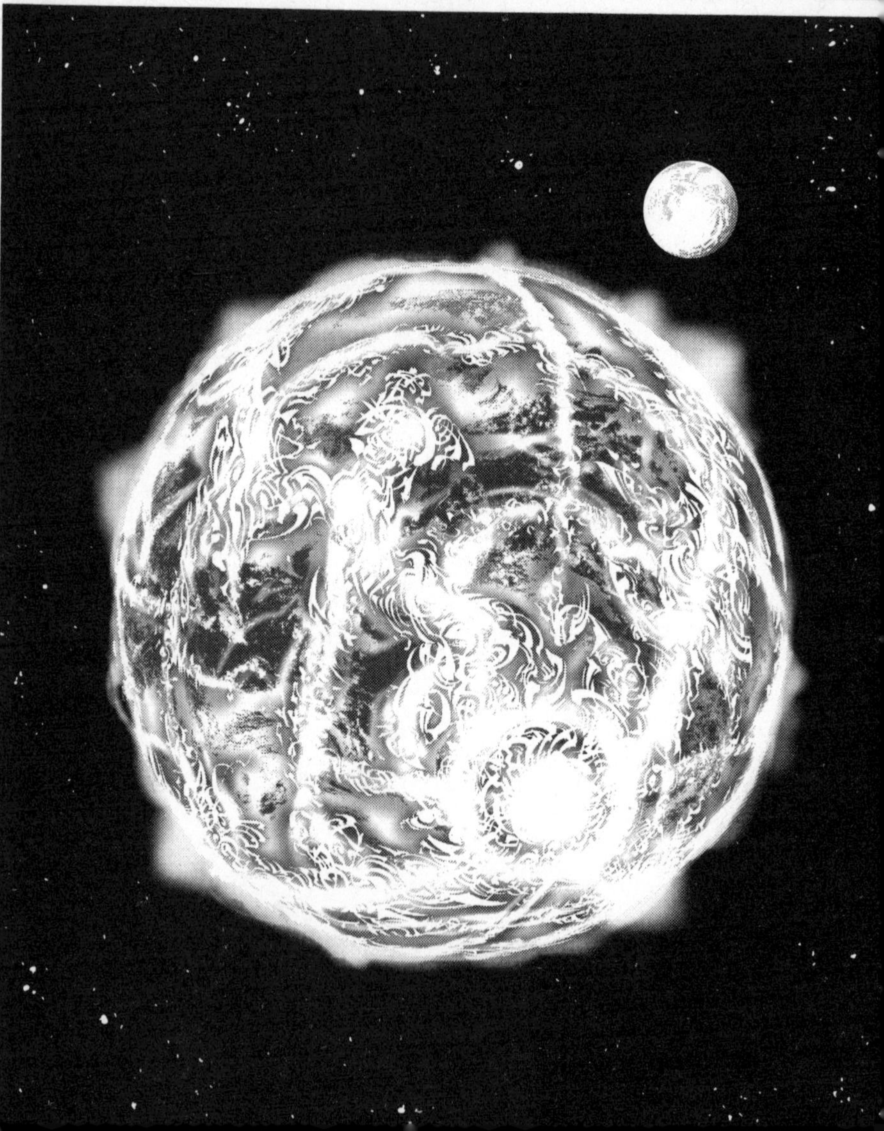

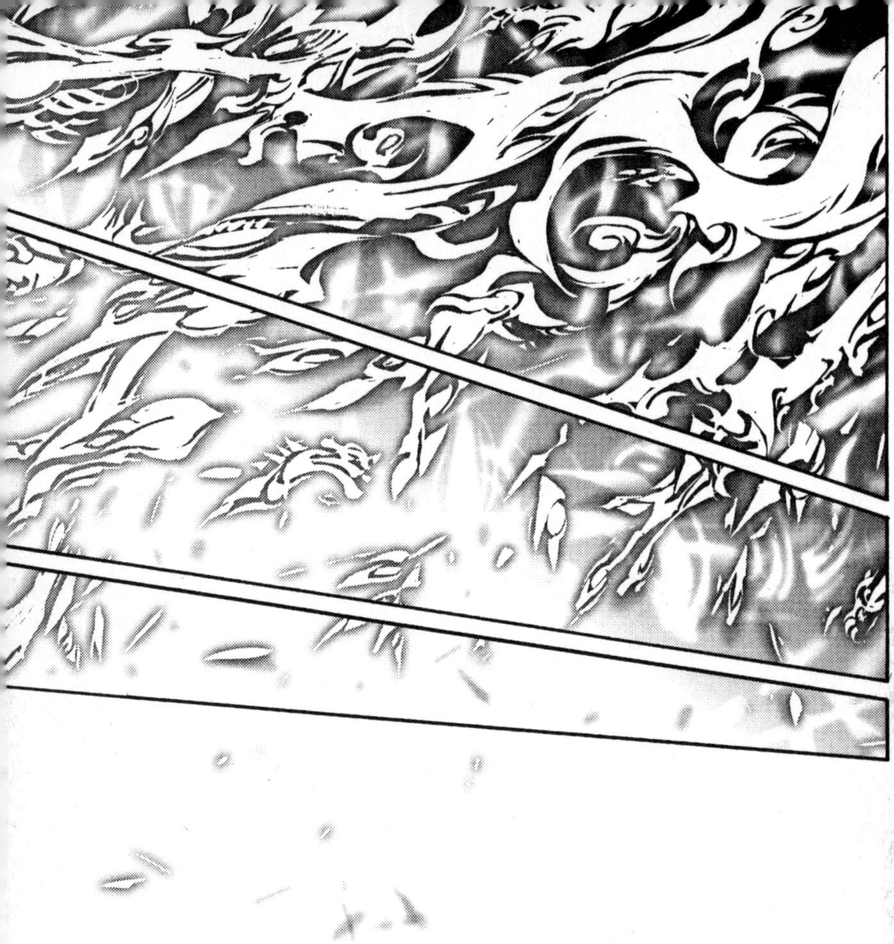

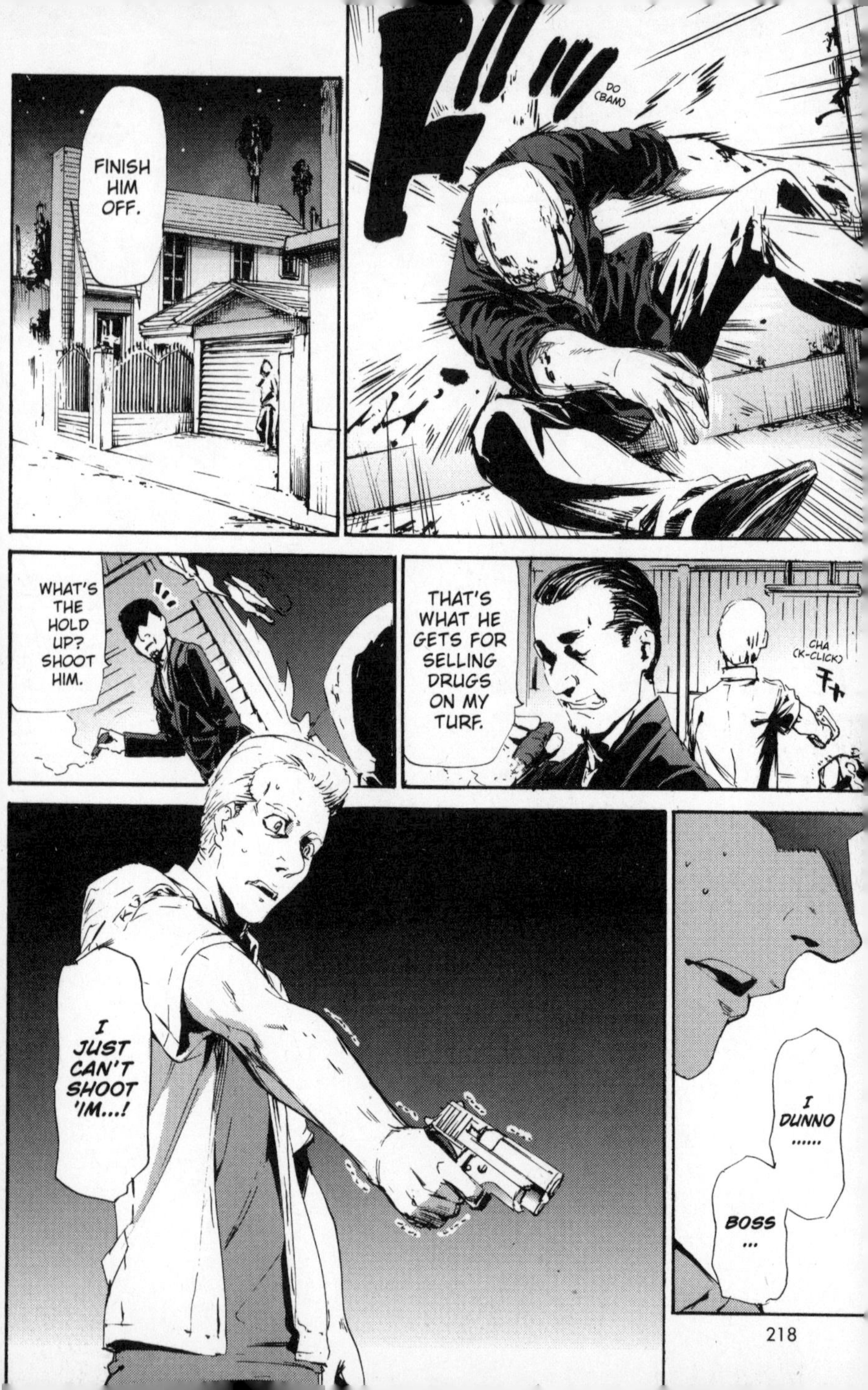
DO (BAM)
FINISH HIM OFF.
THAT'S WHAT HE GETS FOR SELLING DRUGS ON MY TURF.
CHA (K-CLICK)
WHAT'S THE HOLD UP? SHOOT HIM.
I DUNNO ......
BOSS ...
I JUST CAN'T SHOOT 'IM...!

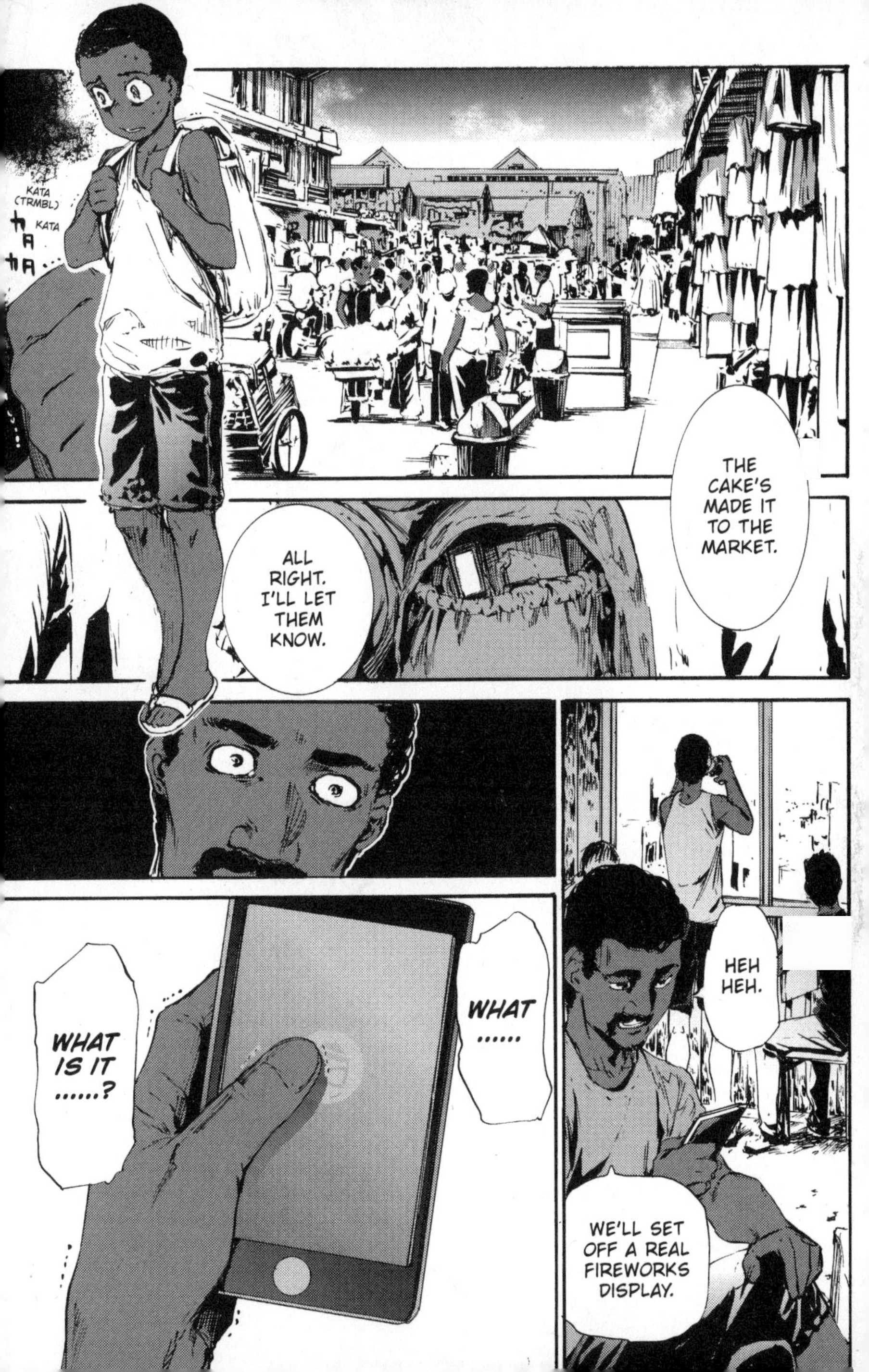
KATA (TRMBL) KATA
THE CAKE'S MADE IT TO THE MARKET.
ALL RIGHT. I'LL LET THEM KNOW.
HEH HEH.
WE'LL SET OFF A REAL FIREWORKS DISPLAY.
WHAT ......
WHAT IS IT ......?

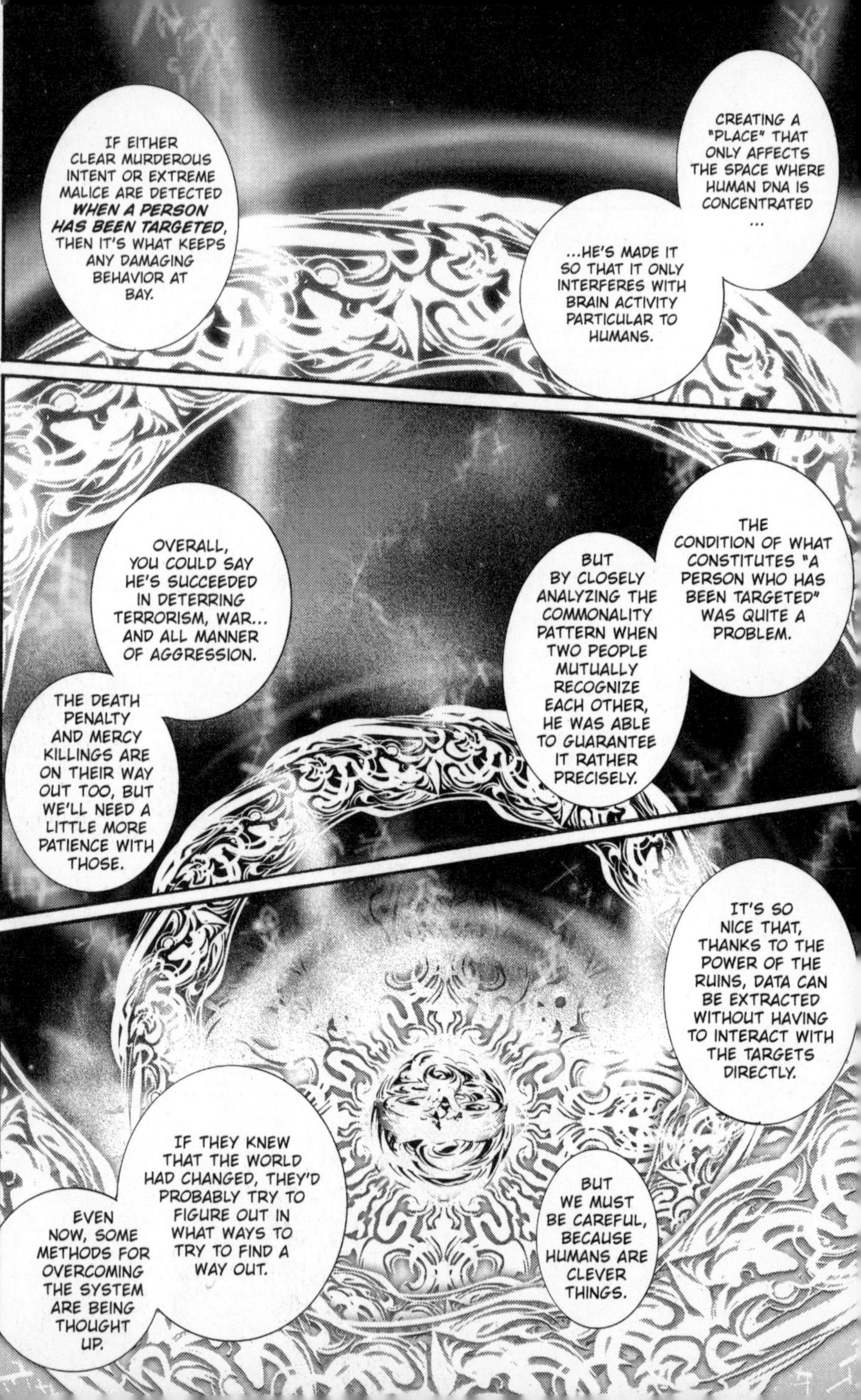
CREATING A "PLACE" THAT ONLY AFFECTS THE SPACE WHERE HUMAN DNA IS CONCENTRATED ...
...HE'S MADE IT SO THAT IT ONLY INTERFERES WITH BRAIN ACTIVITY PARTICULAR TO HUMANS.
IF EITHER CLEAR MURDEROUS INTENT OR EXTREME MALICE ARE DETECTED WHEN A PERSON HAS BEEN TARGETED, THEN IT'S WHAT KEEPS ANY DAMAGING BEHAVIOR AT BAY.
THE CONDITION OF WHAT CONSTITUTES "A PERSON WHO HAS BEEN TARGETED" WAS QUITE A PROBLEM.
BUT BY CLOSELY ANALYZING THE COMMONALITY PATTERN WHEN TWO PEOPLE MUTUALLY RECOGNIZE EACH OTHER, HE WAS ABLE TO GUARANTEE IT RATHER PRECISELY.
OVERALL, YOU COULD SAY HE'S SUCCEEDED IN DETERRING TERRORISM, WAR... AND ALL MANNER OF AGGRESSION.
THE DEATH PENALTY AND MERCY KILLINGS ARE ON THEIR WAY OUT TOO, BUT WE'LL NEED A LITTLE MORE PATIENCE WITH THOSE.
IT'S SO NICE THAT, THANKS TO THE POWER OF THE RUINS, DATA CAN BE EXTRACTED WITHOUT HAVING TO INTERACT WITH THE TARGETS DIRECTLY.
BUT WE MUST BE CAREFUL, BECAUSE HUMANS ARE CLEVER THINGS.
IF THEY KNEW THAT THE WORLD HAD CHANGED, THEY'D PROBABLY TRY TO FIGURE OUT IN WHAT WAYS TO TRY TO FIND A WAY OUT.
EVEN NOW, SOME METHODS FOR OVERCOMING THE SYSTEM ARE BEING THOUGHT UP.

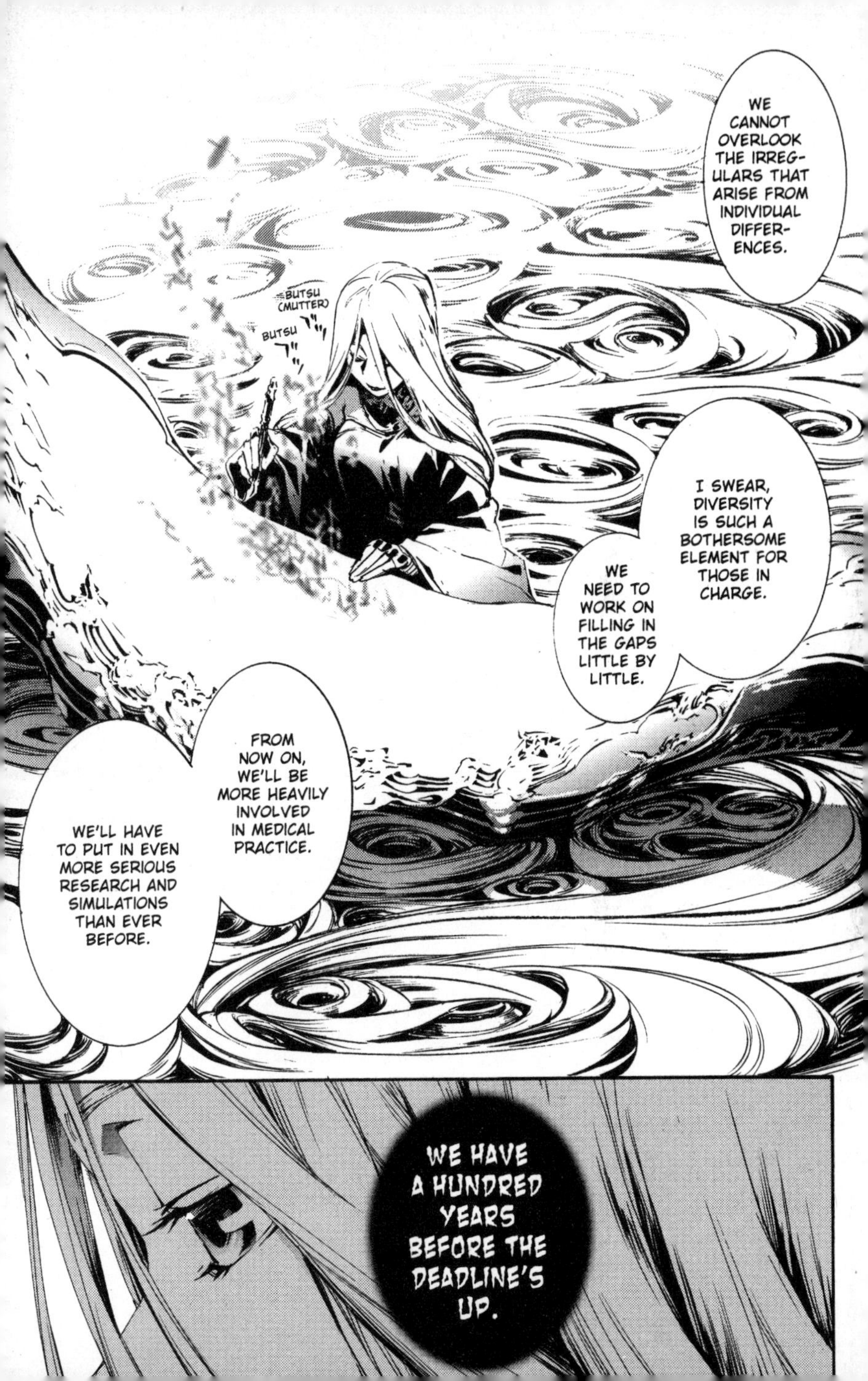
WE CANNOT OVERLOOK THE IRREG-ULARS THAT ARISE FROM INDIVIDUAL DIFFER-ENCES.
BUTSU (MUTTER) BUTSU
I SWEAR, DIVERSITY IS SUCH A BOTHERSOME ELEMENT FOR THOSE IN CHARGE.
WE NEED TO WORK ON FILLING IN THE GAPS LITTLE BY LITTLE.
FROM NOW ON, WE'LL BE MORE HEAVILY INVOLVED IN MEDICAL PRACTICE.
WE'LL HAVE TO PUT IN EVEN MORE SERIOUS RESEARCH AND SIMULATIONS THAN EVER BEFORE.
WE HAVE A HUNDRED YEARS BEFORE THE DEADLINE'S UP.

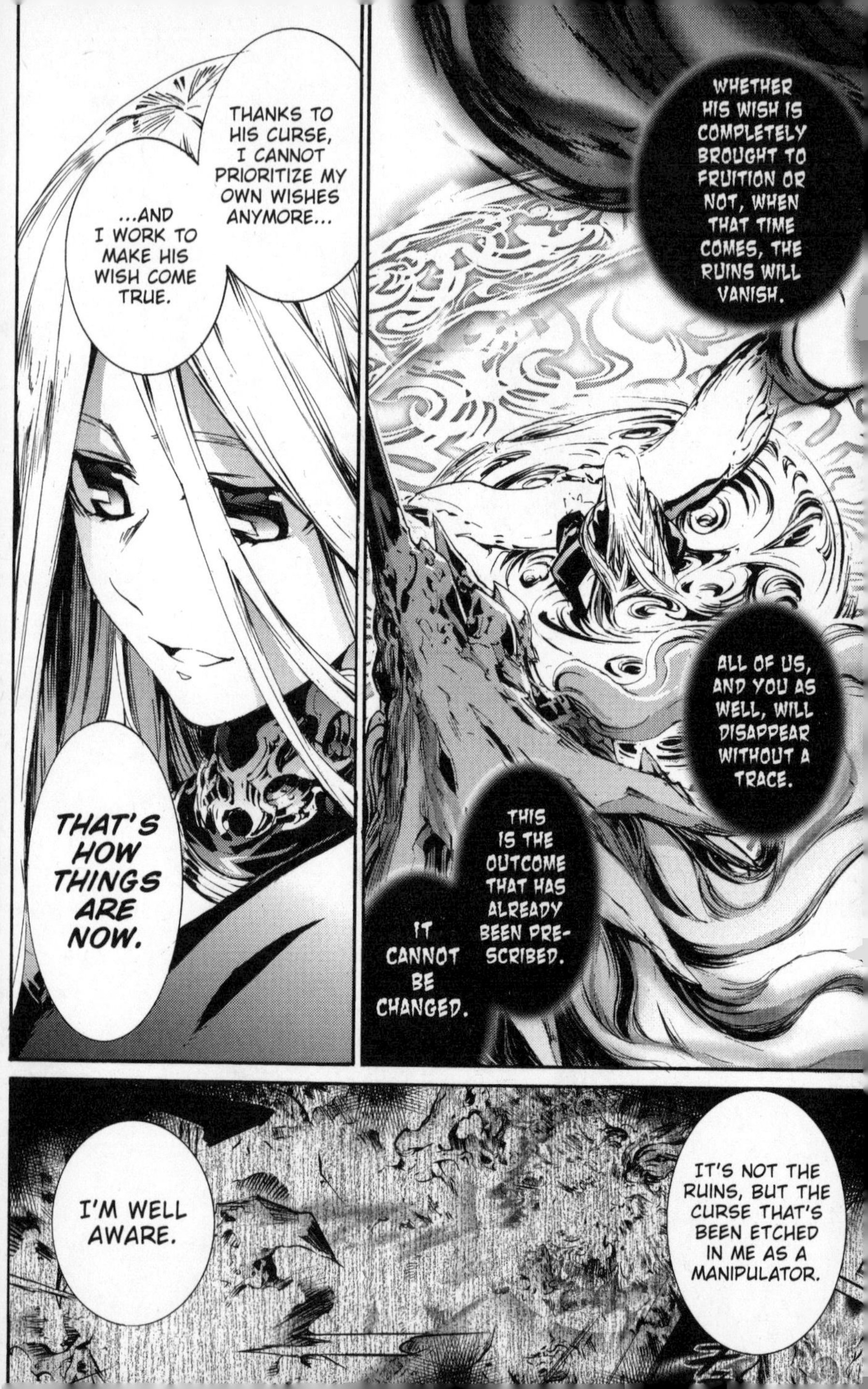
WHETHER HIS WISH IS COMPLETELY BROUGHT TO FRUITION OR NOT, WHEN THAT TIME COMES, THE RUINS WILL VANISH.
ALL OF US, AND YOU AS WELL, WILL DISAPPEAR WITHOUT A TRACE.
THIS IS THE OUTCOME THAT HAS ALREADY BEEN PRE-SCRIBED.
IT CANNOT BE CHANGED.
THANKS TO HIS CURSE, I CANNOT PRIORITIZE MY OWN WISHES ANYMORE...
...AND I WORK TO MAKE HIS WISH COME TRUE.
THAT'S HOW THINGS ARE NOW.
IT'S NOT THE RUINS, BUT THE CURSE THAT'S BEEN ETCHED IN ME AS A MANIPULATOR.
I'M WELL AWARE.

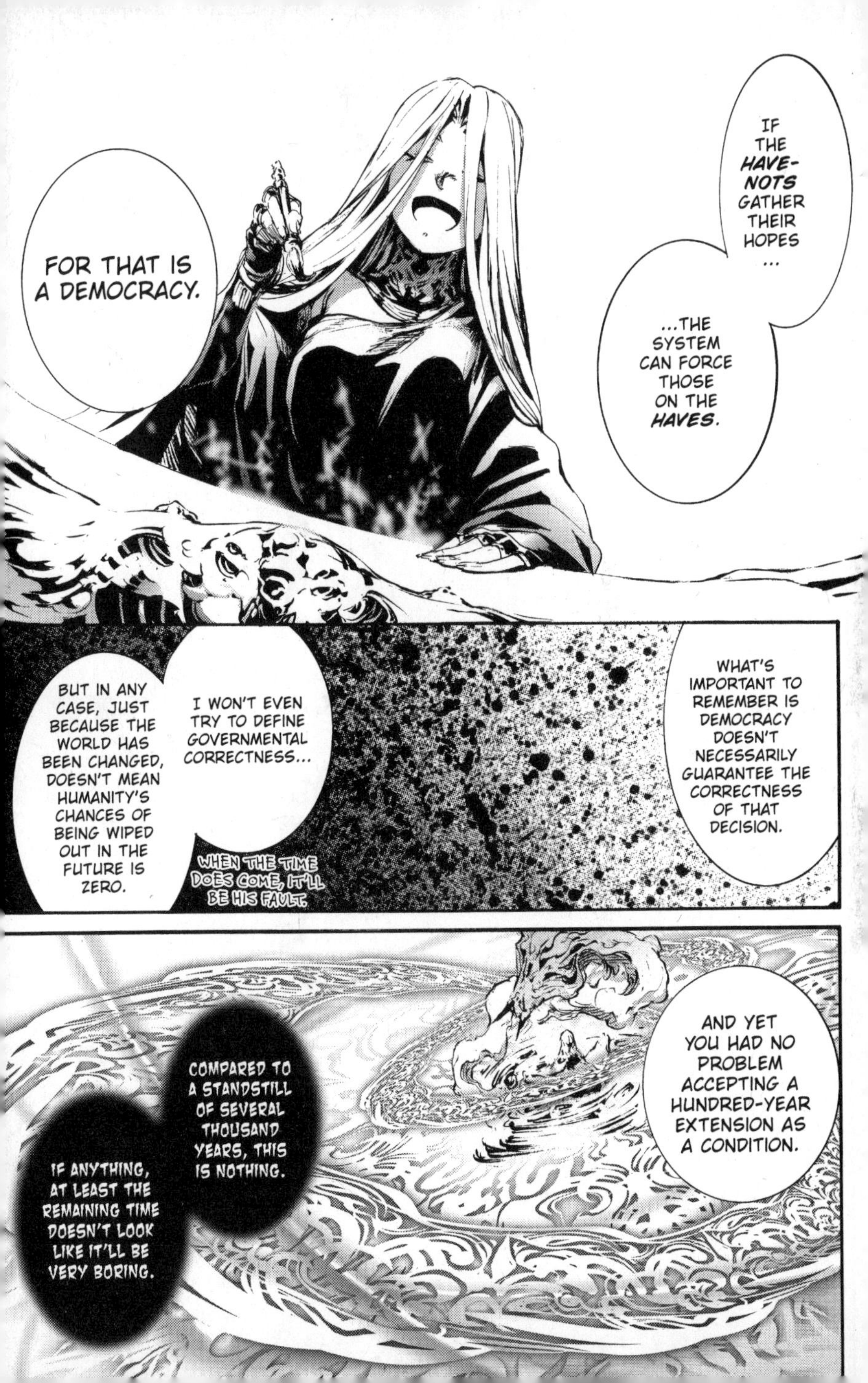
IF THE HAVE-NOTS GATHER THEIR HOPES...
...THE SYSTEM CAN FORCE THOSE ON THE HAVES.
FOR THAT IS A DEMOCRACY.
WHAT'S IMPORTANT TO REMEMBER IS DEMOCRACY DOESN'T NECESSARILY GUARANTEE THE CORRECTNESS OF THAT DECISION.
I WON'T EVEN TRY TO DEFINE GOVERNMENTAL CORRECTNESS...
BUT IN ANY CASE, JUST BECAUSE THE WORLD HAS BEEN CHANGED, DOESN'T MEAN HUMANITY'S CHANCES OF BEING WIPED OUT IN THE FUTURE IS ZERO.
WHEN THE TIME DOES COME, IT'LL BE HIS FAULT.
AND YET YOU HAD NO PROBLEM ACCEPTING A HUNDRED-YEAR EXTENSION AS A CONDITION.
COMPARED TO A STANDSTILL OF SEVERAL THOUSAND YEARS, THIS IS NOTHING.
IF ANYTHING, AT LEAST THE REMAINING TIME DOESN'T LOOK LIKE IT'LL BE VERY BORING.

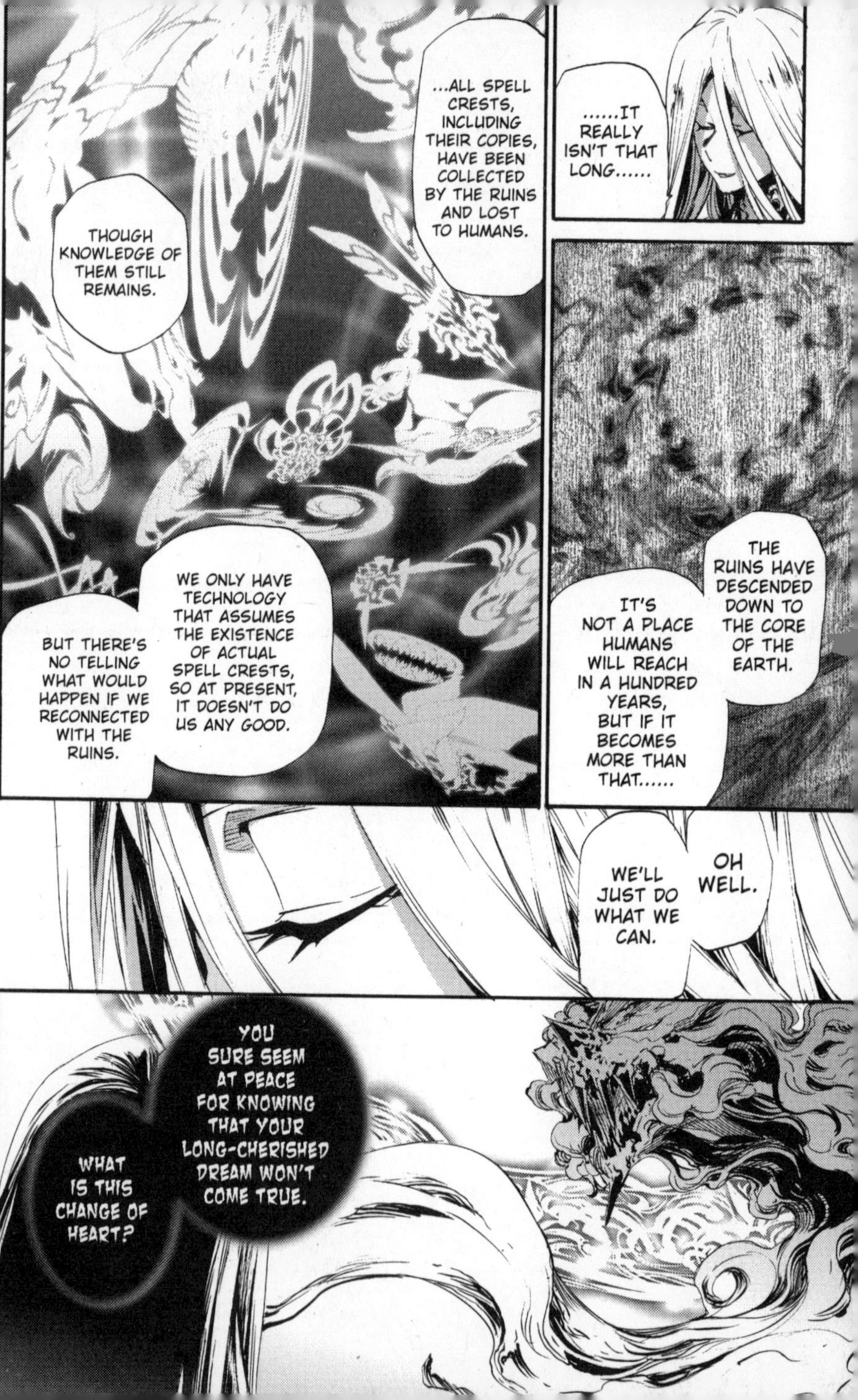
......IT REALLY ISN'T THAT LONG......
THE RUINS HAVE DESCENDED DOWN TO THE CORE OF THE EARTH.
IT'S NOT A PLACE HUMANS WILL REACH IN A HUNDRED YEARS, BUT IF IT BECOMES MORE THAN THAT......
...ALL SPELL CRESTS, INCLUDING THEIR COPIES, HAVE BEEN COLLECTED BY THE RUINS AND LOST TO HUMANS.
THOUGH KNOWLEDGE OF THEM STILL REMAINS.
WE ONLY HAVE TECHNOLOGY THAT ASSUMES THE EXISTENCE OF ACTUAL SPELL CRESTS, SO AT PRESENT, IT DOESN'T DO US ANY GOOD.
BUT THERE'S NO TELLING WHAT WOULD HAPPEN IF WE RECONNECTED WITH THE RUINS.
OH WELL.
WE'LL JUST DO WHAT WE CAN.
YOU SURE SEEM AT PEACE FOR KNOWING THAT YOUR LONG-CHERISHED DREAM WON'T COME TRUE.
WHAT IS THIS CHANGE OF HEART?

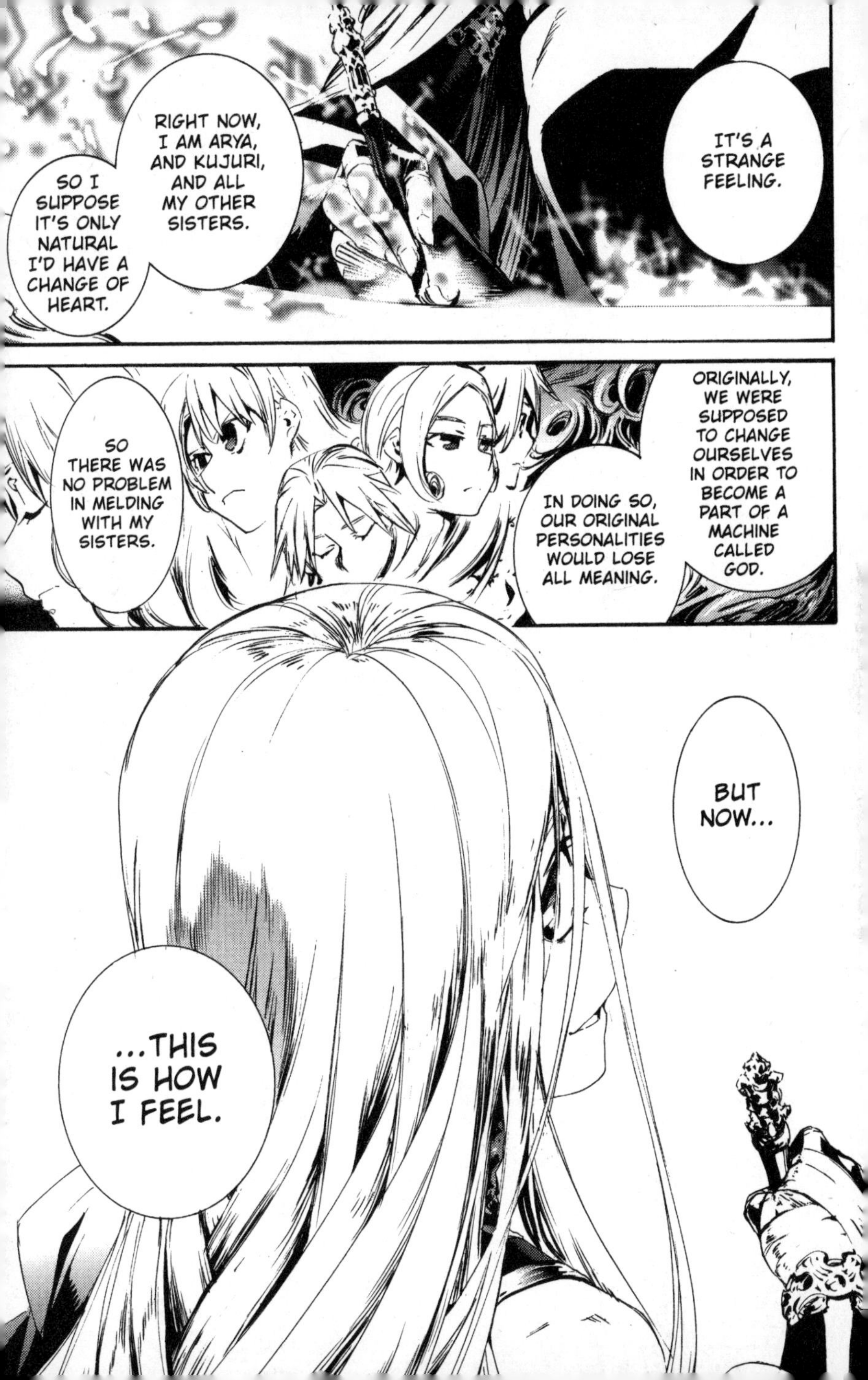
IT'S A STRANGE FEELING.
RIGHT NOW, I AM ARYA, AND KUJURI, AND ALL MY OTHER SISTERS.
SO I SUPPOSE IT'S ONLY NATURAL I'D HAVE A CHANGE OF HEART.
ORIGINALLY, WE WERE SUPPOSED TO CHANGE OURSELVES IN ORDER TO BECOME A PART OF A MACHINE CALLED GOD.
IN DOING SO, OUR ORIGINAL PERSONALITIES WOULD LOSE ALL MEANING.
SO THERE WAS NO PROBLEM IN MELDING WITH MY SISTERS.
BUT NOW...
...THIS IS HOW I FEEL.

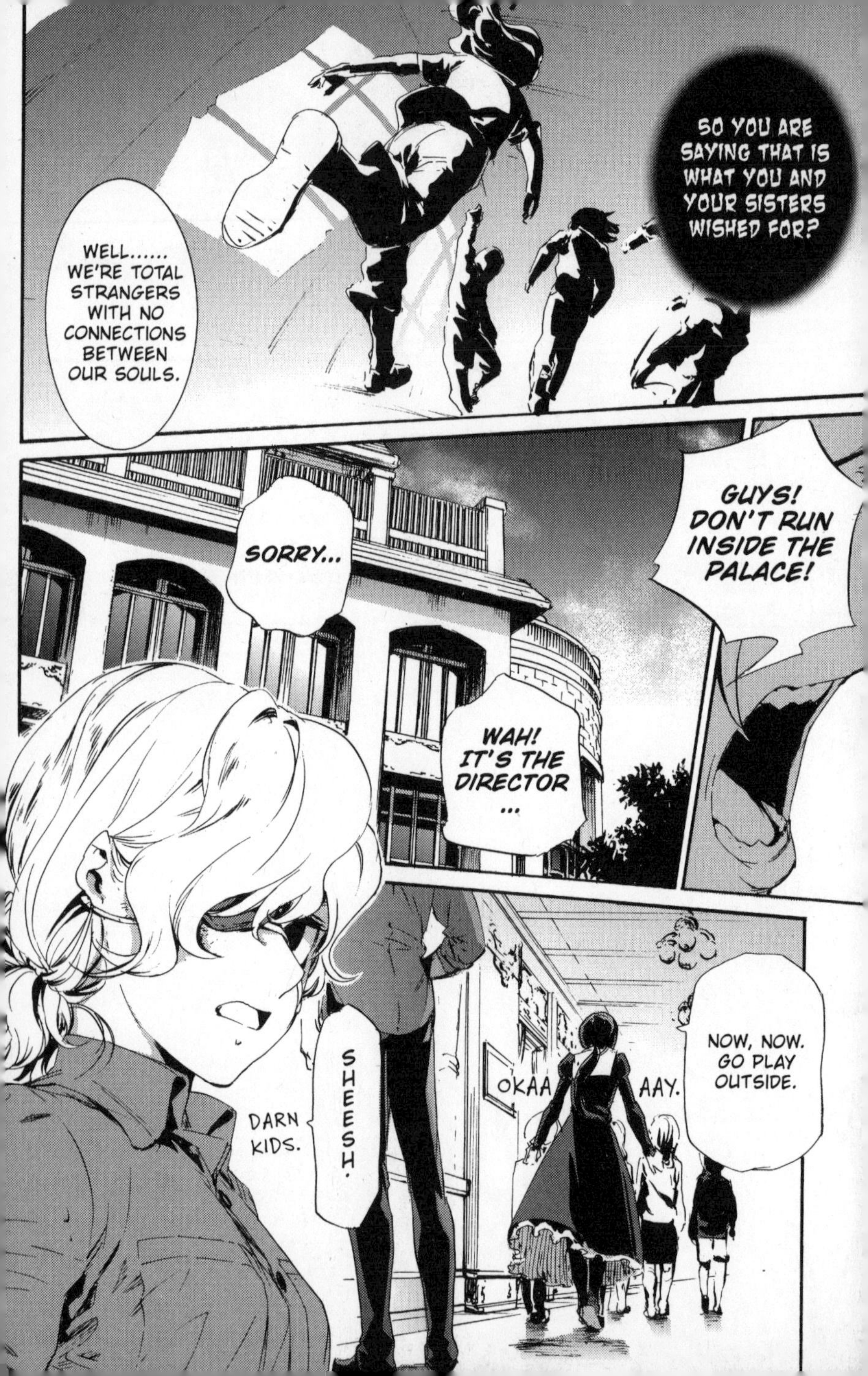
SO YOU ARE SAYING THAT IS WHAT YOU AND YOUR SISTERS WISHED FOR?
WELL...... WE'RE TOTAL STRANGERS WITH NO CONNECTIONS BETWEEN OUR SOULS.
GUYS! DON'T RUN INSIDE THE PALACE!
SORRY...
WAH! IT'S THE DIRECTOR ...
NOW, NOW. GO PLAY OUTSIDE.
OKAA AAY.
SHEESH.
DARN KIDS.

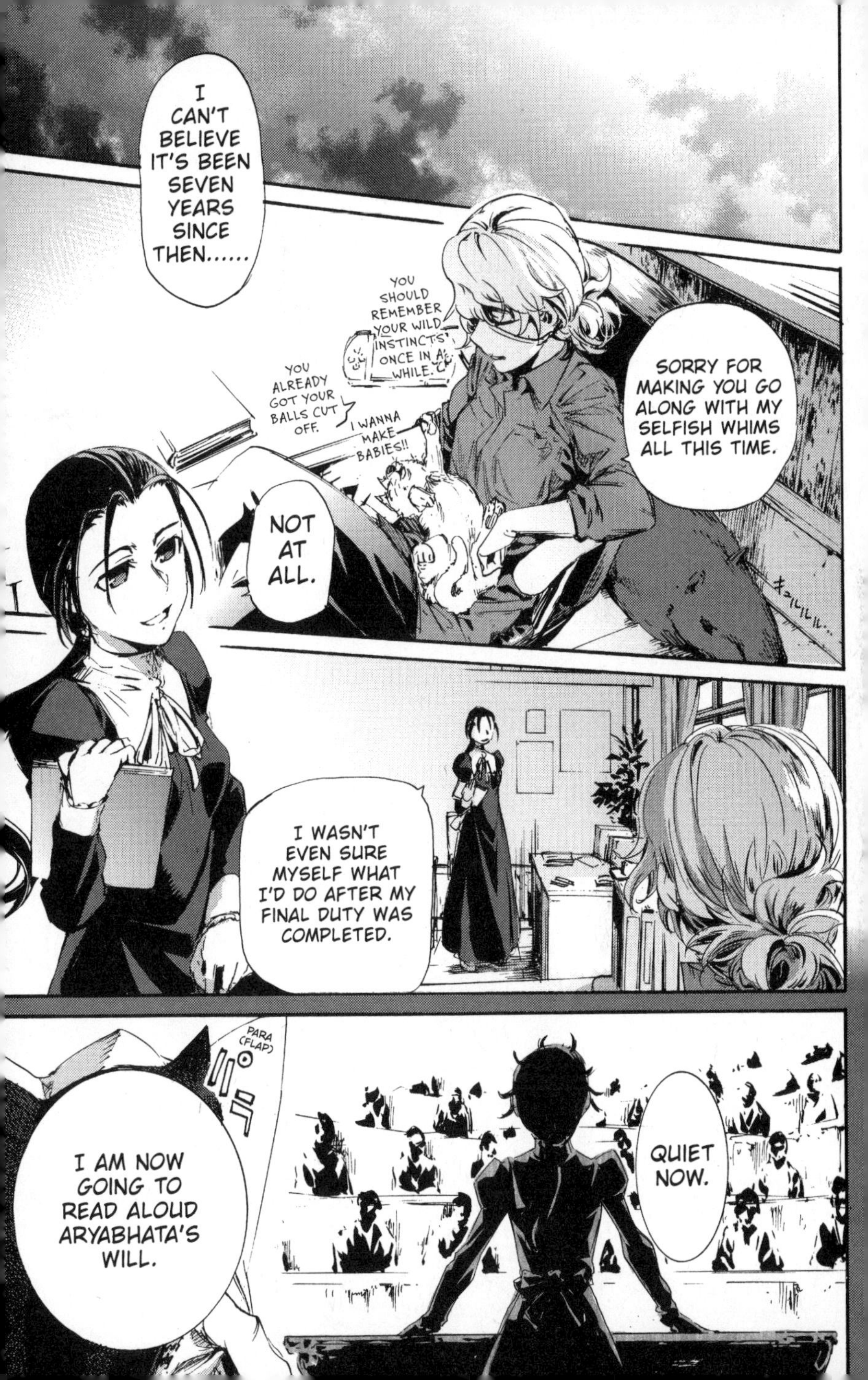
I CAN'T BELIEVE IT'S BEEN SEVEN YEARS SINCE THEN......
SORRY FOR MAKING YOU GO ALONG WITH MY SELFISH WHIMS ALL THIS TIME.
YOU SHOULD REMEMBER YOUR WILD INSTINCTS ONCE IN A WHILE.
YOU ALREADY GOT YOUR BALLS CUT OFF.
I WANNA MAKE BABIES!!
NOT AT ALL.
I WASN'T EVEN SURE MYSELF WHAT I'D DO AFTER MY FINAL DUTY WAS COMPLETED.
QUIET NOW.
PARA (FLAP)
I AM NOW GOING TO READ ALOUD ARYABHATA'S WILL.

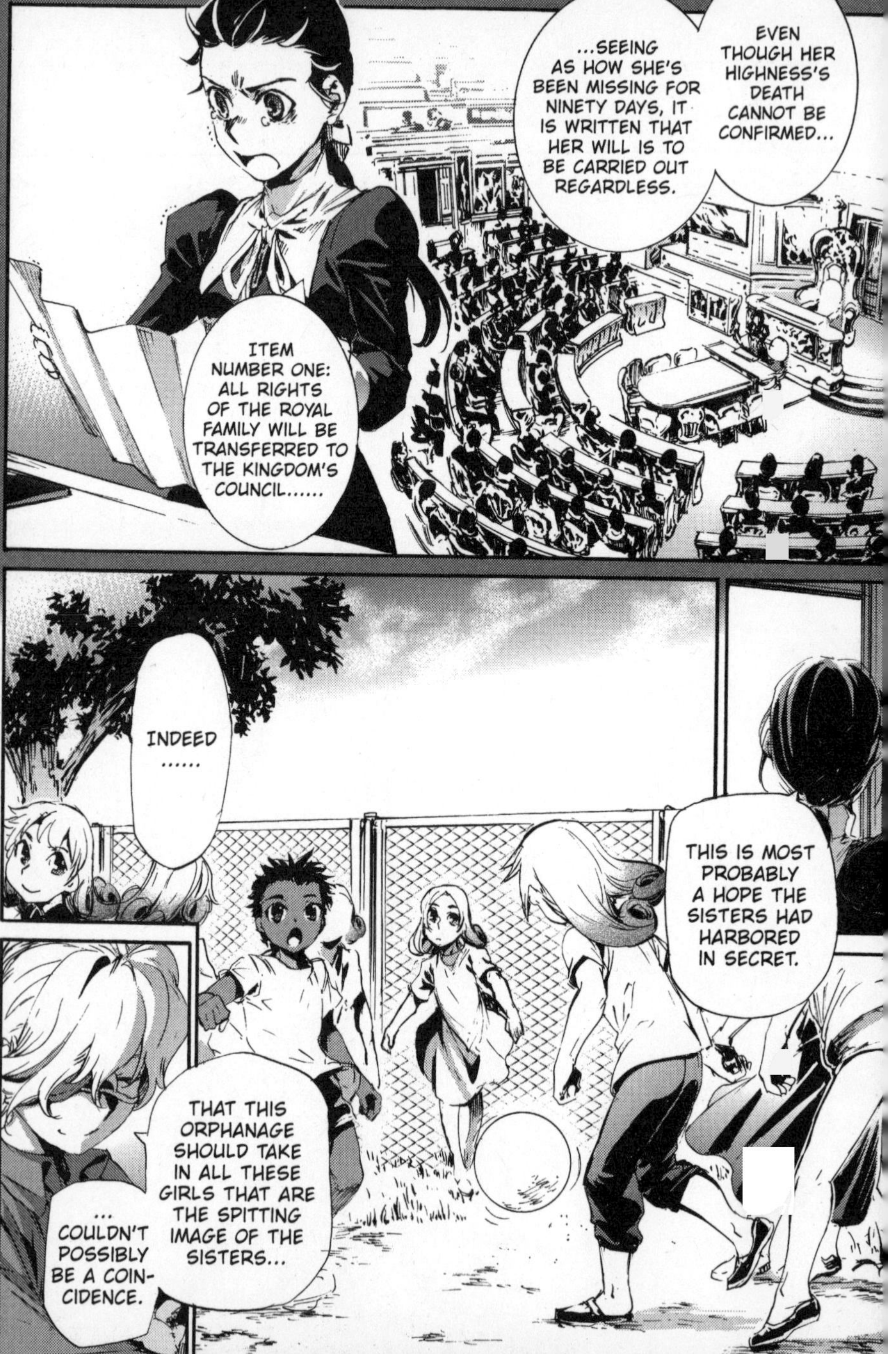
EVEN THOUGH HER HIGHNESS'S DEATH CANNOT BE CONFIRMED...
...SEEING AS HOW SHE'S BEEN MISSING FOR NINETY DAYS, IT IS WRITTEN THAT HER WILL IS TO BE CARRIED OUT REGARDLESS.
ITEM NUMBER ONE: ALL RIGHTS OF THE ROYAL FAMILY WILL BE TRANSFERRED TO THE KINGDOM'S COUNCIL......
THIS IS MOST PROBABLY A HOPE THE SISTERS HAD HARBORED IN SECRET.
INDEED ......
THAT THIS ORPHANAGE SHOULD TAKE IN ALL THESE GIRLS THAT ARE THE SPITTING IMAGE OF THE SISTERS...
...COULDN'T POSSIBLY BE A COINCIDENCE.

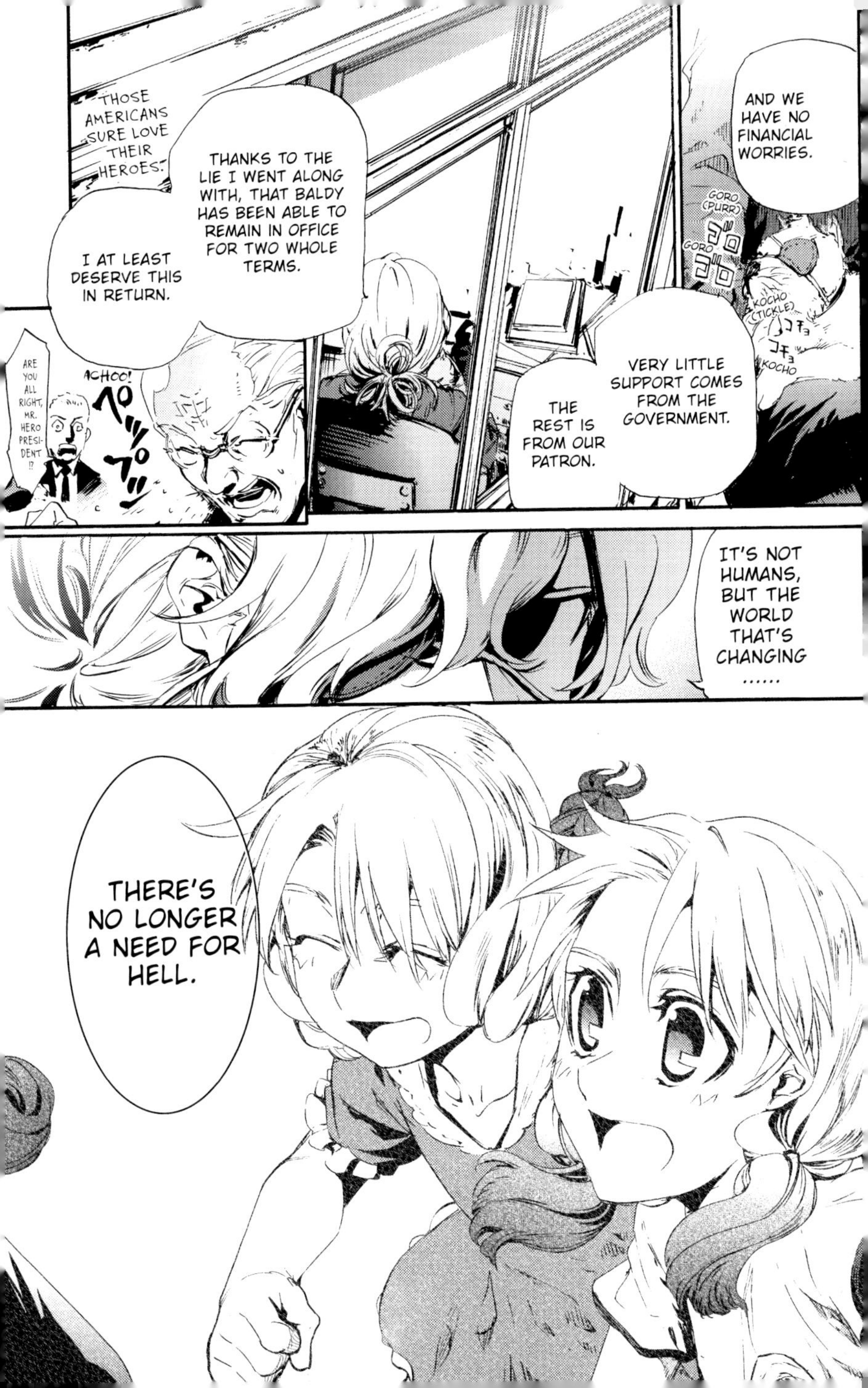
AND WE HAVE NO FINANCIAL WORRIES.
GORO (PURR) ゴロ
GORO ゴロ
KOCHO (TICKLE) コチョ
コチョ KOCHO
VERY LITTLE SUPPORT COMES FROM THE GOVERNMENT.
THE REST IS FROM OUR PATRON.
THOSE AMERICANS SURE LOVE THEIR HEROES.
THANKS TO THE LIE I WENT ALONG WITH, THAT BALDY HAS BEEN ABLE TO REMAIN IN OFFICE FOR TWO WHOLE TERMS.
I AT LEAST DESERVE THIS IN RETURN.
ACHOO!
ARE YOU ALL RIGHT, MR. HERO PRESIDENT!?
IT'S NOT HUMANS, BUT THE WORLD THAT'S CHANGING ......
THERE'S NO LONGER A NEED FOR HELL.

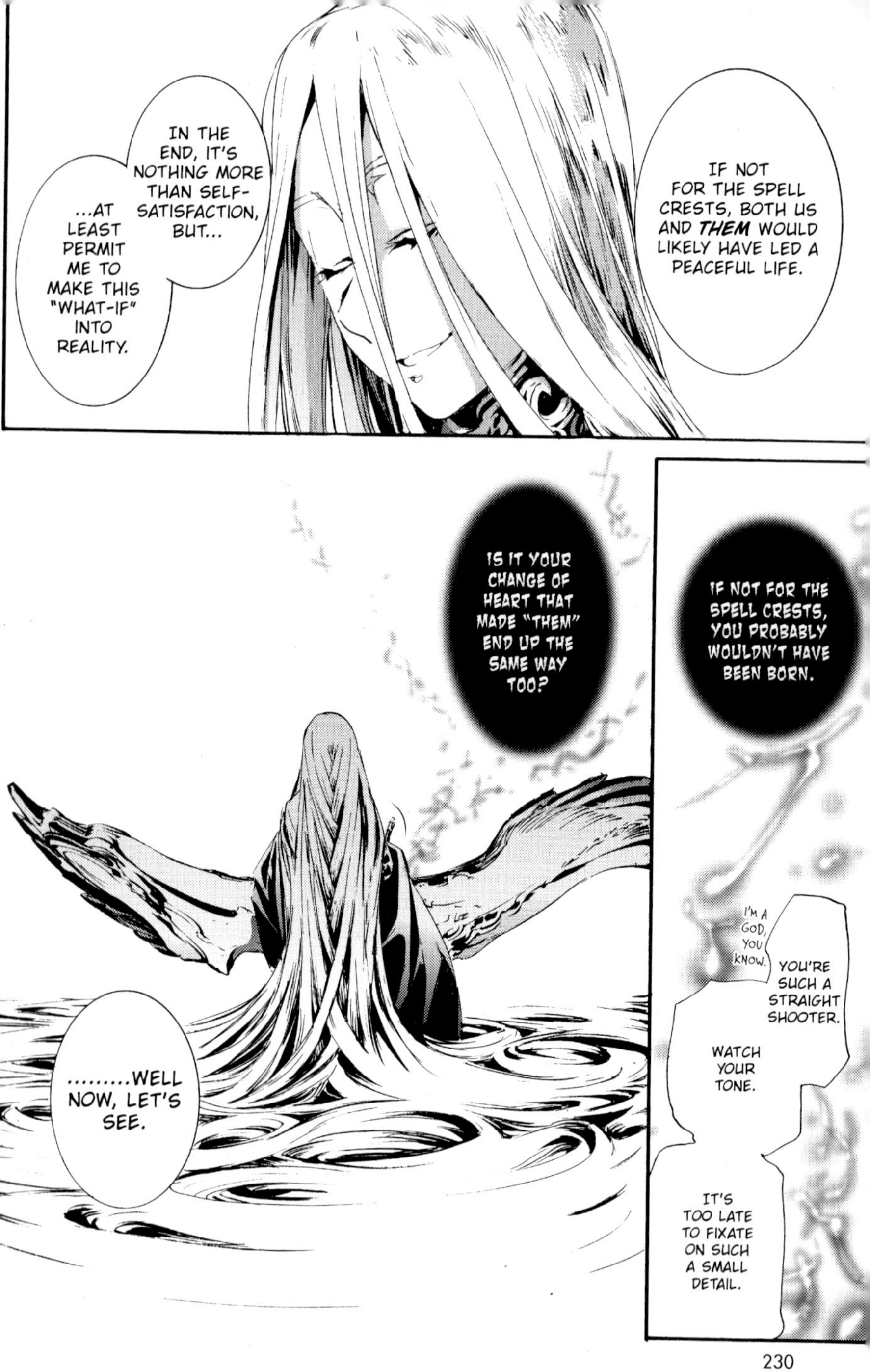
IF NOT FOR THE SPELL CRESTS, BOTH US AND *THEM* WOULD LIKELY HAVE LED A PEACEFUL LIFE.
IN THE END, IT'S NOTHING MORE THAN SELF-SATISFACTION, BUT...
...AT LEAST PERMIT ME TO MAKE THIS "WHAT-IF" INTO REALITY.
IF NOT FOR THE SPELL CRESTS, YOU PROBABLY WOULDN'T HAVE BEEN BORN.
YOU'RE SUCH A STRAIGHT SHOOTER.
I'M A GOD, YOU KNOW.
WATCH YOUR TONE.
IT'S TOO LATE TO FIXATE ON SUCH A SMALL DETAIL.
IS IT YOUR CHANGE OF HEART THAT MADE "THEM" END UP THE SAME WAY TOO?
.........WELL NOW, LET'S SEE.

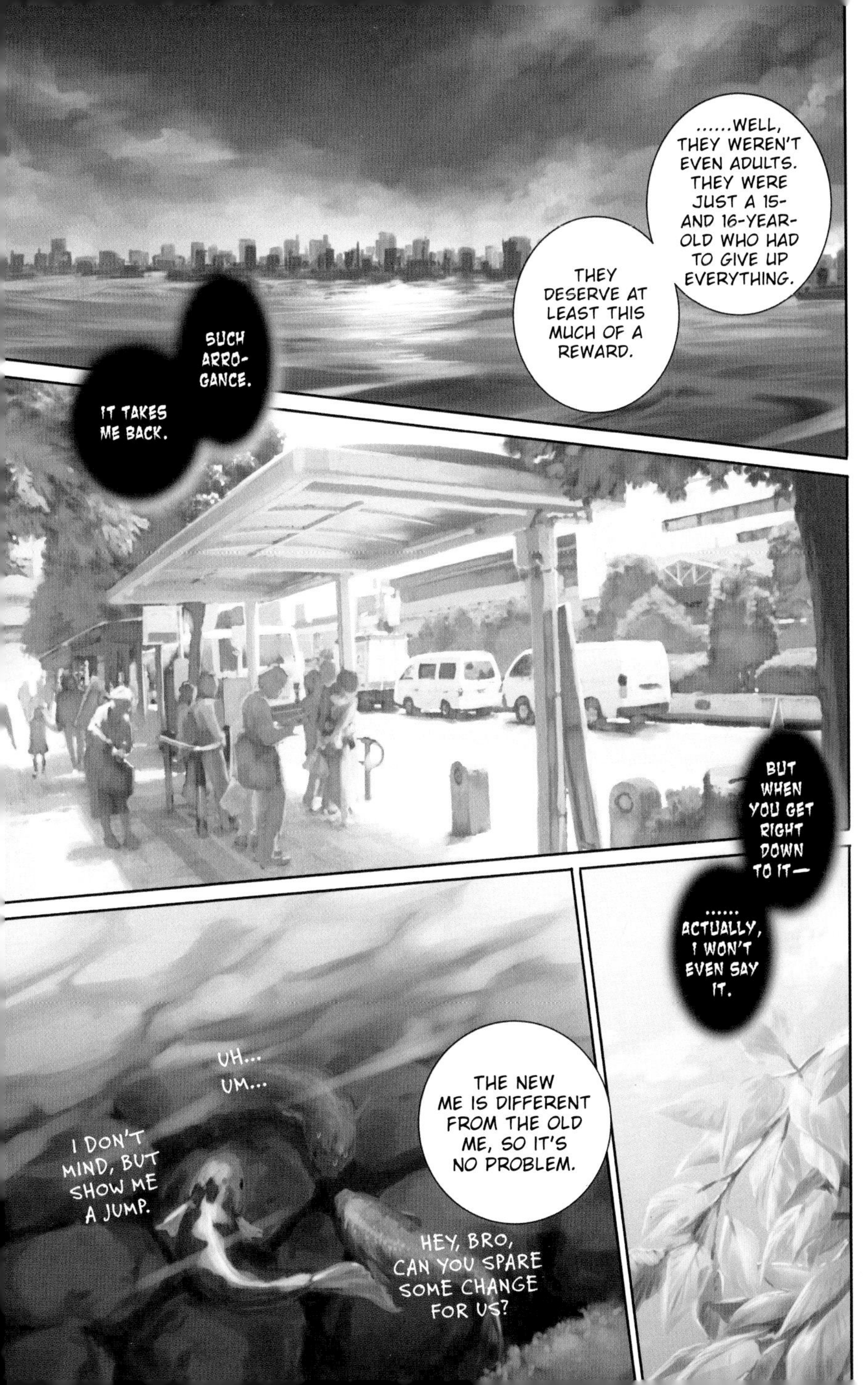
......WELL, THEY WEREN'T EVEN ADULTS. THEY WERE JUST A 15- AND 16-YEAR-OLD WHO HAD TO GIVE UP EVERYTHING.
THEY DESERVE AT LEAST THIS MUCH OF A REWARD.
SUCH ARROGANCE.
IT TAKES ME BACK.
BUT WHEN YOU GET RIGHT DOWN TO IT—
...... ACTUALLY, I WON'T EVEN SAY IT.
THE NEW ME IS DIFFERENT FROM THE OLD ME, SO IT'S NO PROBLEM.
UH... UM...
HEY, BRO, CAN YOU SPARE SOME CHANGE FOR US?
I DON'T MIND, BUT SHOW ME A JUMP.

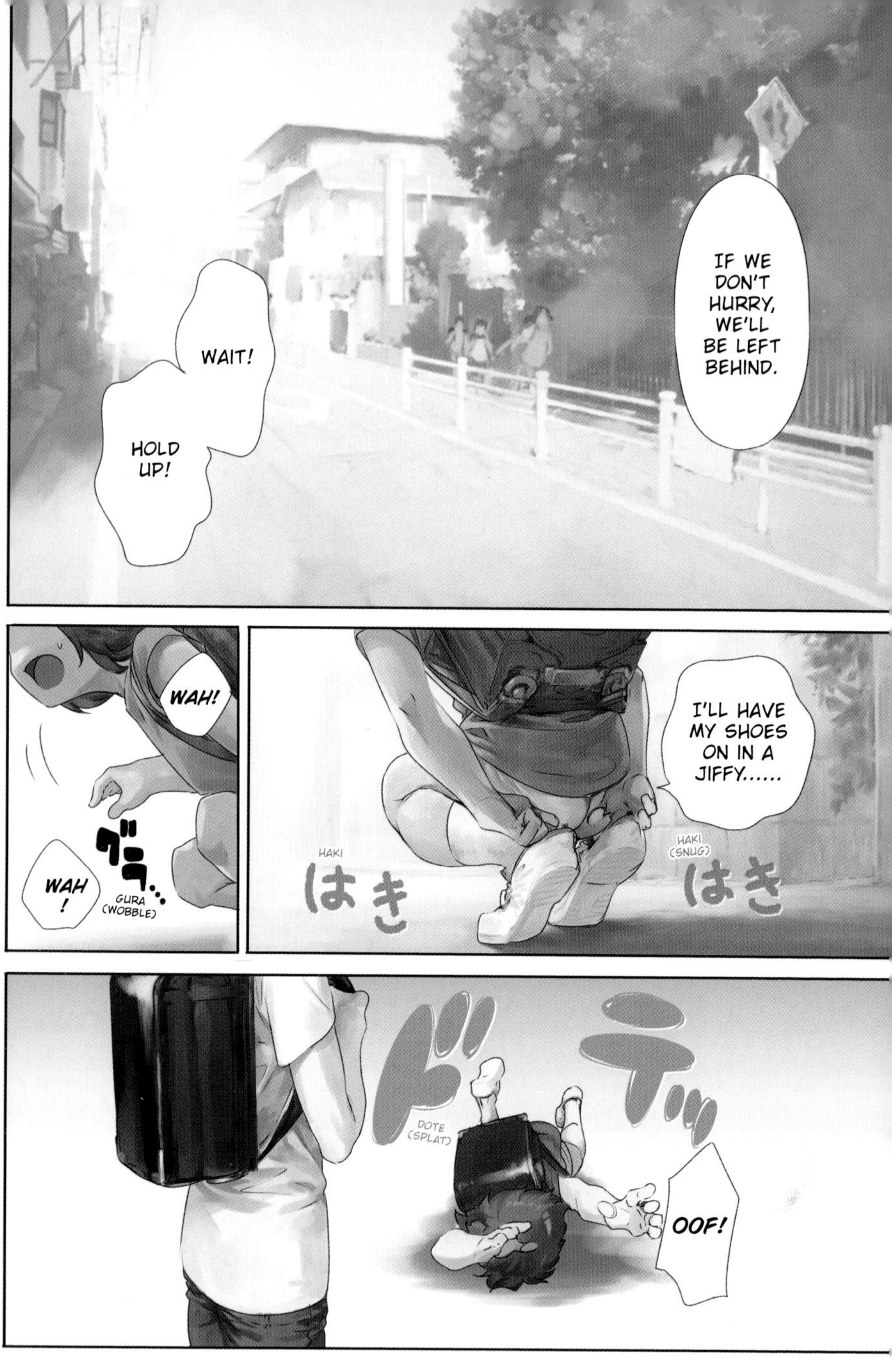
IF WE DON'T HURRY, WE'LL BE LEFT BEHIND.
WAIT!
HOLD UP!
I'LL HAVE MY SHOES ON IN A JIFFY......
HAKI (SNUG)
はき
HAKI
はき
WAH!
グラ...
GURA (WOBBLE)
WAH!
ドテッ
DOTE (SPLAT)
OOF!

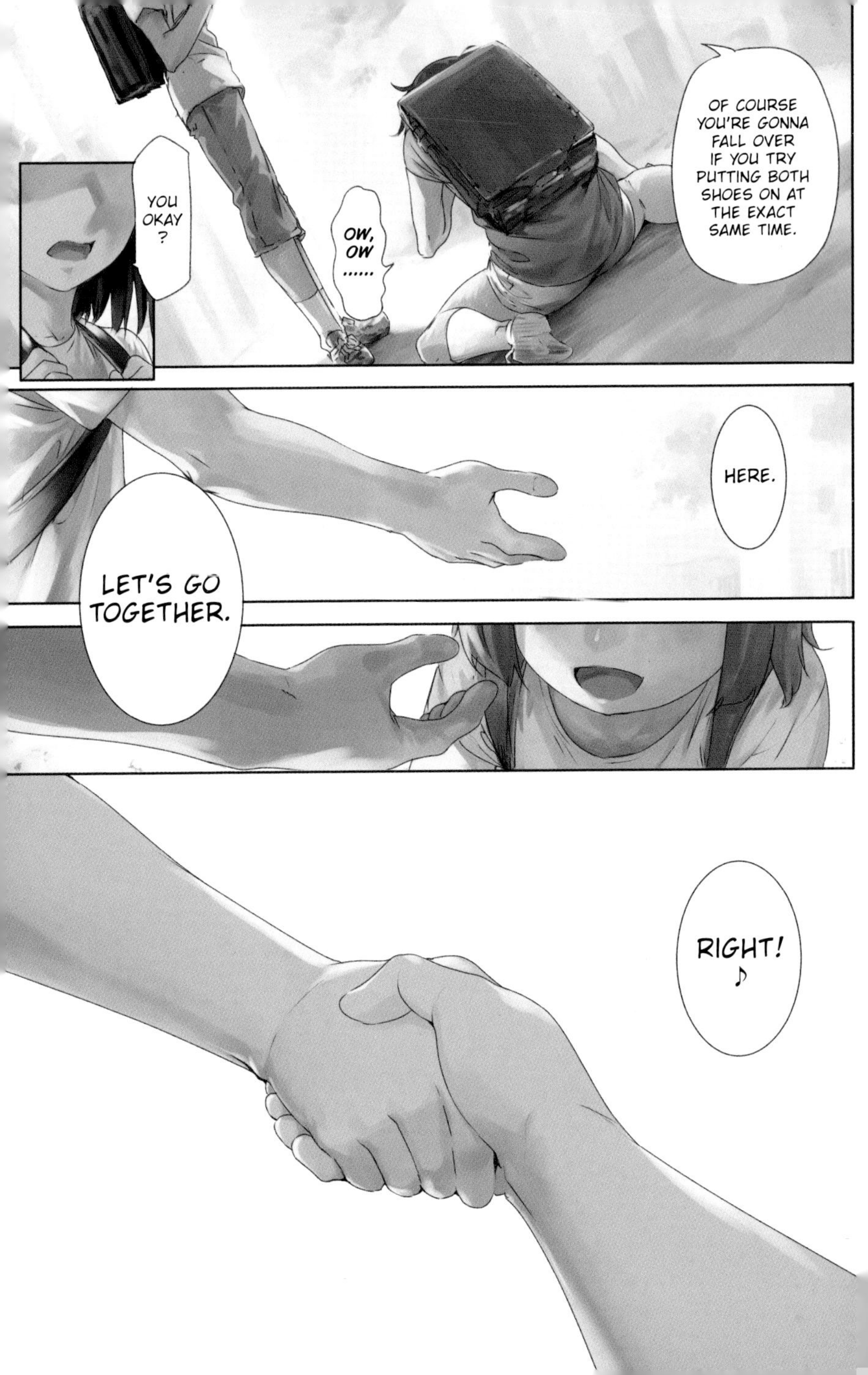
OF COURSE YOU'RE GONNA FALL OVER IF YOU TRY PUTTING BOTH SHOES ON AT THE EXACT SAME TIME.
OW, OW ......
YOU OKAY ?
HERE.
LET'S GO TOGETHER.
RIGHT! ♪

END
TABOOTATTOO

TABOO TATTOO

TABOO TATTOO

by SHINJIRO

Translation: Christine Dashiell • Lettering: Phil Christie

TABOO TATTOO
© Shinjiro 2017
First published in Japan in 2017 by KADOKAWA CORPORATION. English translation rights reserved by Yen Press, LLC under the license from KADOKAWA CORPORATION, Tokyo through TUTTLE-MORI AGENCY, Inc., Tokyo.

English translation © 2019 by Yen Press, LLC

Yen Press
1290 Avenue of the Americas
New York, NY 10104

Visit us at yenpress.com
facebook.com/yenpress
twitter.com/yenpress
yenpress.tumblr.com
instagram.com/yenpress

First Yen Press Edition: March 2019

Yen Press is an imprint of Yen Press, LLC.
The Yen Press name and logo are trademarks of Yen Press, LLC.

The publisher is not responsible for websites (or their content) that are not owned by the publisher.

Library of Congress Control Number: 2015952591

ISBNs: 978-1-9753-0374-7 (paperback)
978-1-9753-0380-8 (ebook)

10 9 8 7 6 5 4 3 2 1

WOR

Printed in the United States of America